Outer Hebrides

Published by
Imray, Laurie, Norie & Wilson Ltd
Wych House St Ives Cambridgeshire PE27 5BT England
☎+44 (0)1480 462114
www.imray.com
2017

All rights reserved. No part of this publication may be reproduced, transmitted or used in any form by any means – graphic, electronic or mechanical, including photocopying, recording, taping or information storage and retrieval systems or otherwise – without the prior permission of the Publishers.

© Clyde Cruising Club Publications Ltd 2017
First edition 2012
Second edition 2017

ISBN 978 184623 903 8 Printed book
ISBN 978 178679 143 6 PDF book

Clyde Cruising Club Publications Ltd has asserted its right under the Copyright, Designs and Patents Act 1988 to be identified as the author of this work.

British Library Cataloguing in Publication Data.
A catalogue record for this title is available from the British Library.

CAUTION

Whilst the Publishers and Author have used reasonable endeavours to ensure the accuracy of the contents of these Sailing Directions they contain selected information and thus are not definitive and do not include all known information for each and every location described, nor for all conditions of weather and tide. They are written for yachts of moderate draft and should not be used by larger craft. They should be used only as an aid to navigation in conjunction with official charts, pilots, hydrographic data and all other information, published or unpublished, available to the navigator. Skippers should not place reliance on these Sailing Directions in preference to exercising their own judgement.

To the extent permitted by law, the Publishers and Author do not accept liability for any loss and/or damage howsoever caused that may arise from reliance on these Sailing Directions nor for any error, omission or failure to update the information that they contain.

The UK Hydrographic Office (UKHO) and its licensors make no warranties or representations, express or implied, with respect to this product. The UKHO and its licensors have not verified the information within this product or quality assured it.

PLANS

The plans in these Sailing Directions are not to be used for navigation.
They are designed to support the text and should at all times be used with navigational charts.

This product has been derived in part from material obtained from the UK Hydrographic Office with the permission of the UK Hydrographic Office, Her Majesty's Stationery Office, Licence No. GB AA - 005 - Imray
© British Crown Copyright, Outer Hebrides 2017
All rights reserved.

The copyright in a number of plans reproduced in this publication is owned by Bob Bradfield and Antares Charts, who have kindly given permission for their reproduction in this publication.

The last input of technical information was September 2017.

CORRECTIONAL SUPPLEMENTS

These Sailing Directions may be amended at intervals by the issue of correctional supplements. These are published on the internet at the web sites www.clyde.org and www.imray.com and may be downloaded free of charge. Printed copies are also available on request from the publishers at the above address.

The Publishers and Author will at all times be grateful to receive information which tends to the improvement of the work.

Reprinted in Croatia in 2022 by Denona

CCC Sailing Directions and Anchorages

Outer Hebrides

Incorporating The Yachtsman's Pilots by Martin Lawrence

Edited by **Edward Mason**

Imray Laurie Norie & Wilson Ltd

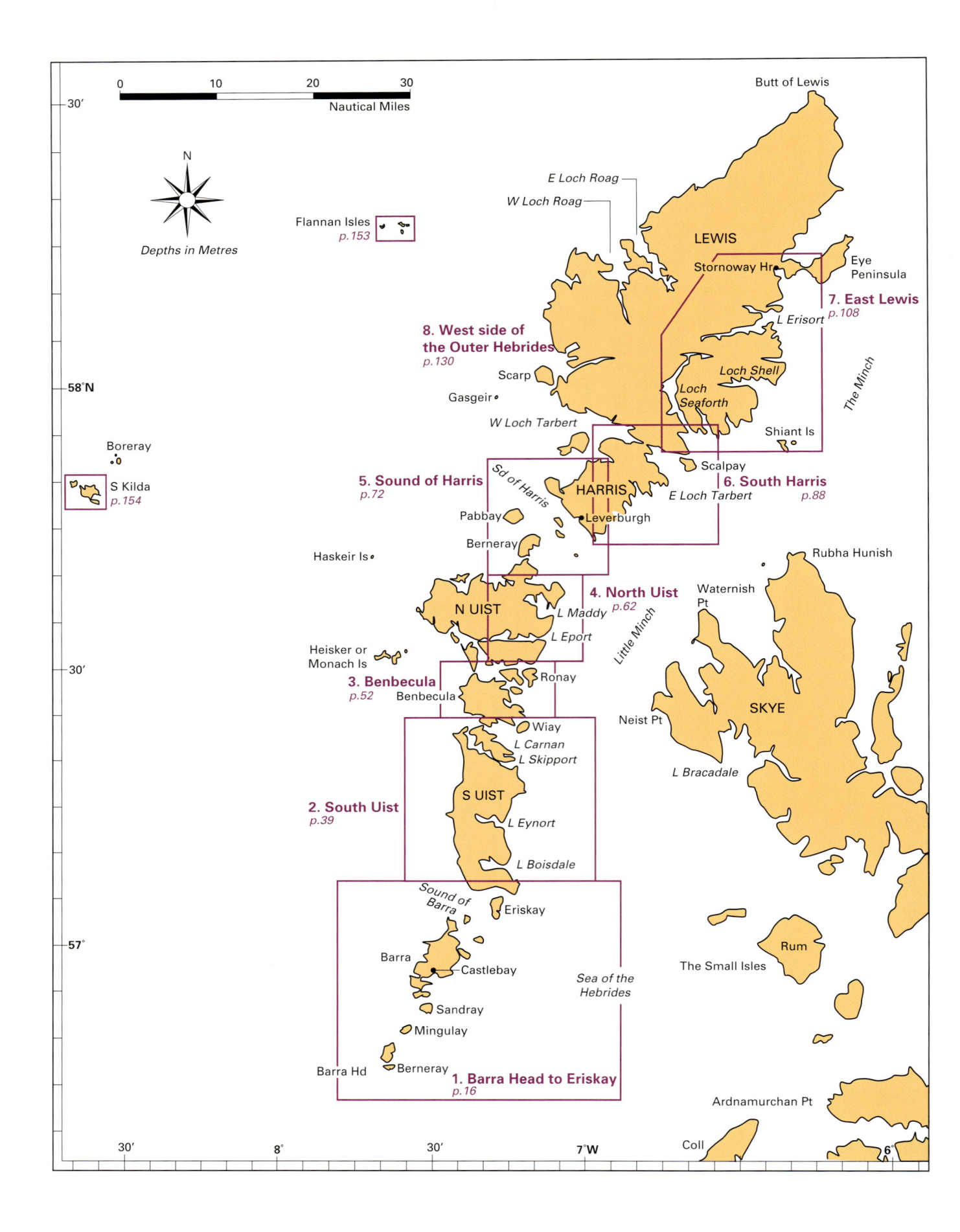

Map of the Outer Hebrides

Scale: 0 – 10 – 20 – 30 Nautical Miles

Depths in Metres

Chart Index

- **1. Barra Head to Eriskay** *p.16*
- **2. South Uist** *p.39*
- **3. Benbecula** *p.52*
- **4. North Uist** *p.62*
- **5. Sound of Harris** *p.72*
- **6. South Harris** *p.88*
- **7. East Lewis** *p.108*
- **8. West side of the Outer Hebrides** *p.130*
- **Flannan Isles** *p.153*
- **S Kilda** *p.154*

Labelled Features

Islands / Land: LEWIS, HARRIS, N UIST, Benbecula, S UIST, Barra, Sandray, Mingulay, Berneray, Eriskay, Pabbay, Berneray, Scalpay, Ronay, Wiay, Scarp, Gasgeir, Haskeir Is, Heisker or Monach Is, Boreray, S Kilda, Flannan Isles, Shiant Is, SKYE, Rum, The Small Isles, Coll

Points / Headlands: Butt of Lewis, Eye Peninsula, Rubha Hunish, Waternish Pt, Neist Pt, Barra Hd, Ardnamurchan Pt

Lochs / Sounds: E Loch Roag, W Loch Roag, L Erisort, Loch Shell, Loch Seaforth, W Loch Tarbert, E Loch Tarbert, Sd of Harris, L Maddy, L Eport, L Carnan, L Skipport, L Eynort, L Boisdale, Sound of Barra, L Bracadale

Seas: The Minch, Little Minch, Sea of the Hebrides

Settlements: Stornoway Hr, Leverburgh, Castlebay

Contents

Preface *2*
Introduction *4*
   General introduction to sailing in the Outer Hebrides 4
   Charts and maps 5
   Tides 6
   Weather and forecasting 6
   Anchorages, moorings & berthing 8
   Equipment 10
   Chartering & instruction 11
   Communications 12
   Travel 13
   Emergencies 14
   Notes on sailing directions & plans 14

1 **Barra Head to Eriskay** *16*

2 **South Uist** *39*

3 **Benbecula** *52*

4 **North Uist** *62*

5 **Sound of Harris** *72*

6 **South Harris** *88*

7 **East Lewis** *108*

8 **West of the Outer Hebrides** *130*

Appendix *156*
   Charts and other publications 156
   Services and supplies 159
   Distance tables 160
   Submarine exercise areas 163
   Gaelic glossary 164
   Western Isles Council mooring fees 166
   Western Isles Council fuel registration form 167
Index *169*

Preface

This book is the second in the new series of Pilots for Scottish waters in which the *Sailing Directions* of the Clyde Cruising Club have been merged with the *Yachtsman's Pilots* of Martin Lawrence. As such, it is one of a long line of west coast Sailing Directions for yachtsmen, the first being the fifth and final volume of Frank Cowper's *Sailing Tours* written just over a hundred years ago.

Cowper had little enthusiasm for the Outer Hebrides. Perhaps he was jaded after the effort of producing the first four volumes, which covered all the British Isles, or maybe he encountered one of the less than perfect spells of weather with which the islands are occasionally afflicted but, whatever the reason, his view was certainly jaundiced: 'as regards a cruise among the Outer Hebrides ... I do not think that unless one has unlimited time the scenery is worth the trouble. Rocks, endless rocks; land barren, bleak, mountainous here and there, but with mountains of no great height ... Of all the shelters none is better than Stornoway and everything worth seeing can be visited from there.' Whilst few could argue with his assessment of the shelter offered by Stornoway Harbour, I believe that many present day yachtsmen would place a much higher value on the countless remote anchorages, abundant wildlife and even the 'Rocks, endless rocks' than did Cowper. Those who don't will be in for a disappointment.

Hard on the heels of *Sailing Tours* came the formation of the Clyde Cruising Club. One of the principal objectives of the Club was 'to help the cruiser to a greater knowledge concerning the vital things of the cruising ground' which they did through the publication of sailing directions and eventually, in the late 1920s, these were extended to include the Outer Hebrides. Written in the terse style of the Admiralty *Directions* they were full of hard facts and were the standard reference for yachtsmen over the next fifty years. The handy-sized, hard-backed volumes covering the whole west coast became a constant companion to the harassed skipper and 'the blue Bible', as it was known, is fondly remembered by many and, much to the chagrin of the present editorial team, still used by a few.

It was when he was editor of the CCC Sailing Directions that Martin Lawrence sought out a number of unpublished Admiralty surveys in the archives of the Hydrographer and used these as the basis for some of his plans, including many of the anchorages in South Harris - an otherwise poorly charted area of the islands. These were incorporated into the new A4 editions which he was preparing for the Club at the time and later used in his *Yachtsman's Pilots*. The latter also introduced several passages or anchorages of a more challenging nature than those included in the CCC book, suitable for those he described as 'experienced rock-dodgers'. In the interests of taking the best from both books these are included in this new edition; the Hidden Harbour and Griminish are examples. However, I have drawn the line at the Gunwale, or Rangas, Channel, on the south side of the Sound of Harris, which even Martin suggests is suitable only for boats 'without any underwater appendages'. On the assumption that most readers' boats will have an underwater appendage of some description, if only a propellor, I am happy to leave this one to the sea-kayakers.

During the research for this edition it was a pleasant surprise to find that many smaller anchorages which are shown on the chart as containing fish farms were now clear. This is principally because the increasing scale of fish farming now demands much larger installations which have to be moored in deeper water, generally in places where no yacht would ever consider anchoring. Additionally, in the early days of fish farming, many licenses were granted but never taken up, although the locations were marked on the chart. It is now unlikely that they ever will be established but developments in the fish farming industry continue to move rapidly and I would urge readers to let me know, through the Club office, if they find any places where they exist and are not shown in these *Directions,* or vice versa.

A welcome development, which was just getting underway as this book was in its final stages, is the re-surveying by the UKHO of the east coast of Barra, the islands to the south and

Preface

'Rocks, endless rocks ...' Loch Erisort, Lewis, has its fair share although the anchorage at Camus Orasaidh (above) is quite clean - until you get ashore.

the Sound of Barra. This will eventually lead to the publication of a new chart or charts which will go a long way towards rectifying the drawbacks mentioned in the Introduction and p.26. Even so, the new survey will not cover many of the areas very close inshore which are of interest to yachts so caution and a good lookout will still be required in many places. However, it is hoped that Curachan, the key to navigation in much of this area and which is, frustratingly, excluded from Chart 2769, Barra Head to Greian Head, will be shown on the new chart of the east coast of Barra.

Acknowledgements

Once again I must thank Martin Lawrence for the use of all his material, this time from his Yachtsman's Pilot series volume, *The Western Isles*. In this book his aerial photographs are even more comprehensive and there are not many anchorages that do not have an aerial view to supplement the text and plans. Roddy Jardine, the harbourmaster of Comhairle nan Eilean Siar (Western Isles Council) has been most helpful to me, as have Paul McNeil, a CCC member who runs Westbound Adventures sailing school from Barra and Donald MacLean of Berneray, who used to run the Berneray to Leverburgh ferry. I thank them all.

Arthur Houston has checked the text thoroughly and I am grateful to him for his many suggestions and sound advice, as I am to Jimmy Dinsmore who has scoured the final proofs for any remaining errors.

The majority of photographs are Martin Lawrence's but I would like to thank all those who provided supplementary photographs, whether taken from previous CCC books or selected for this new edition.

This book is the first in which we have been able to incorporate the work of CCC member Bob Bradfield, of *Antares Charts*, who has kindly agreed that we can use some of the detailed survey information which he has painstakingly gathered. Whilst *Antares* charts are primarily intended to be used in conjunction with GPS, I am very grateful to Bob for allowing our plans to benefit from his work.

Edward Mason, Editor
CCC Sailing Directions, October 2012

Preface to the second edition

Not much has changed in the Outer Hebrides since the publication of the first edition but, for the cruising yachtsman, the establishment of a new marina at Loch Boisdale and the significant enlargement of Stornoway marina will greatly extend the options available for leaving a yacht unattended. New pontoons in Loch Maddy, Castle Bay, East Loch Tarbert and Scalpay are also very welcome.

The UKHO survey in the Barra area has been completed and new editions of Chart 2769 *Barra Head to Greian Head* (Sept 2013) and Chart 2770 *Sound of Barra* (Aug 2013) have been published. The amendments to a great many depths are too numerous to describe in the Sailing Directions but, as they frequently report less water, they are of significance and the new editions should be carried by all yachts.

I am greatly indebted to CCC member Ian Buchanan who has compiled a comprehensive list of suggested amendments and additions to the previous edition which has been an invaluable help in the updating process.

Edward Mason, Editor
CCC Sailing Directions, July 2017

Introduction

The Outer Hebrides, or Western Isles, extend about 120 miles from Barra Head at the south-southwest to the Butt of Lewis at the north-northeast end, with a few distant outliers such as St Kilda and the Flannan Islands.

The east side of the Outer Hebrides, which is sheltered from the prevailing westerly winds and the Atlantic Ocean, has many islands, lochs and inlets which provide innumerable well sheltered anchorages. These anchorages, some large and some small, are often within a short distance of each other and many are remote from habitation. Some are easily approached while others require great care and very skilful pilotage.

For obvious reasons, the west side of the Outer Hebrides is much less frequented by cruising yachts though the west coasts of Harris and Lewis, given suitable conditions, offer what is possibly the finest cruising to be found anywhere in the British Isles, with the remote islands of the St Kilda group being the ultimate challenge.

There are few commercial harbours and supplies can involve a long walk, but the local people are friendly and helpful and a lift will frequently be offered. Pontoon berthing for yachts is becoming more common; Stornoway marina has recently been enlarged and there is a new marina at Lochboisdale. Serviced pontoons with finger berths have also been established at Lochmaddy, Castlebay, East Loch Tarbert and Scalpay and smaller pontoons are available in other locations listed on p.10.

Daylight in summer is longer than in the English Channel owing to being 400-500 miles further north and the weather is, on the whole, less settled. But if you are prepared for the conditions at which this paragraph merely hints, you may experience some unique and memorable cruising.

These *Directions* set out to provide, clearly and concisely, as much information as may be useful to small-boat visitors to the Outer Hebrides. The upper limit of size for which they cater is a draught of 2 metres, and they include information specifically applicable to shoal-draught boats, centreboarders, trailer-sailers, twin-keel boats, multihulls and motor cruisers. In many anchorages there are parts which are only accessible to shoal-draught boats, particularly those which can dry out fairly upright. Some passages are only suitable for shoal-draught boats, and for the benefit of 'trailer-sailers' there is an appendix of launching and recovery places at the end of the book.

However, the majority of those cruising the Outer Hebrides will approach the islands from the Scottish west coast or the Inner Hebrides. At their closest, the islands lie 15 miles from Skye; the shortest crossing from the mainland south of Skye is about 45 miles, with anchorages at the Small Isles and on Skye to break the passage; from the mainland north of Skye the shortest crossing is 30 miles.

Approaching from the east it is better to make initially for one of the centres of population e.g. Castlebay (Barra), Lochboisdale (South Uist), East Loch Tarbert (Harris), or Stornoway (Lewis), all of which are comparatively well marked and lit. Whilst Loch Skipport, South Uist in the south and Loch Shell, Lewis in the north are relatively easy to identify and enter and provide well sheltered anchorages, neither has any facilities. Initially it is better to explore the more isolated lochs and difficult entrances from one of the foregoing locations.

From the south, the west side of the Outer Hebrides has little shelter until the Monach Islands are reached. However from here northwards, well sheltered summer anchorages can be found in the areas of West Loch Tarbert, Loch Resort and Loch Roag. Being exposed to the open Atlantic these lochs are best visited in settled weather with an experienced crew.

Whilst the smallest boats, even cruising dinghies, may be at home in much of the area described in these *Directions*, they must be soundly equipped and competently handled by experienced crews. The Outer Hebrides is no place for anyone who is unable to deal with adverse conditions which may arise unexpectedly. However, anyone who is capable of managing a yacht at a comparable distance from the shore whether in the North Sea, the Baltic, the English Channel, the Atlantic coast of France or the Irish Sea should have little problem on the west coast of Scotland and the Outer Hebrides.

Introduction

Charts

For one of the more remote parts of the British Isles, the Outer Hebrides are surprisingly well charted. They were, in fact, one of the first areas to be comprehensively surveyed when, in 1748, Murdoch Mackenzie was commissioned to do this by the Admiralty in the wake of the Royal Navy's fruitless search for Bonnie Prince Charlie after the 1745 uprising. More recently the Sound of Harris was selected by the UKHO to pioneer their use of LIDAR aerial surveying, resulting in the awe-inspiring depiction of rocks and shallows that is now Chart 2802.

These *Directions* contain many plans but they are not intended as a substitute for Admiralty charts. Although many of the plans in the book are of a larger scale than the charts and include more detail, they cover only small areas and it is essential to have a comprehensive set of charts at both small and large scales. A complete list of current charts is given in the Appendix. For passage-making, Imray's charts C65, C66 and C67 at around 1:150,000 give better coverage than any current Admiralty charts and are more convenient to use. Admiralty Leisure Folio 5616 covers the Sea of the Hebrides, the Little Minch and the east coast of the Outer Hebrides from Barra to South Harris.

Corrections for both Imray: *www.imray.com* and Admiralty: *www.ukho.gov.uk/weekly_nms* charts are published on the internet.

When plotting a position it is important to be aware that the conversion of Admiralty charts to WGS84 datum was only completed for the west coast of Scotland in August 2016. Therefore even fairly recent charts may be referred to the horizontal datum OSGB36, on which a position given by geographical co-ordinates may differ by as much as 100 metres from the position on current charts.

The increasing use of chart plotters has greatly reduced the practice of plotting on paper charts and, accordingly, the need to be aware of the discrepancies discussed above. However, the limitations of the charts used as the basis of the plotter display must be recognised and allowed for. This is particularly the case in the Outer Hebrides where much inshore pilotage is conducted in relatively deep water but in close proximity to sunken rocks.

This is acknowledged by the UKHO which over the past few years has added the following cautionary note to many of their charts:

'*Mariners are warned that positions obtained from Global Navigation Satellite Systems such as GPS, may be more accurate than the charted detail, due to the age and quality of some of the source information. Mariners are therefore advised to exercise particular caution when navigating close to the shore or in the vicinity of dangers.*'

The ability to enlarge the area of interest on a plotter display to a size much bigger than the original chart can easily lead to a false sense of security and must be guarded against. Even the latest editions of UKHO charts using information from recent surveys are unlikely to incorporate more accurate detail in the many intricate anchorages into which a yacht may sometimes enter. If traditional bearings, transits and leading lines are available they should be used in preference to blind reliance on a plotter.

In an attempt to overcome some of the above problems a group of enthusiasts has been conducting surveys in many west coast anchorages and publishing the results, under the name of *Antares Charts*, as a series of very large scale electronic charts, accurate enough to be used in conjunction with a GPS derived position. Using information gathered by sophisticated sounding and sidescanning equipment linked to marine surveying software the resulting charts can be run with suitable plotting software on PCs or Macs, certain Garmin handheld plotters, iPads and other tablets and even mobile phones.

To date, well over 400 locations have been surveyed. The majority are on the mainland and inner islands but there are now many of anchorages in the Outer Hebrides; one of them being the notoriously rock-strewn lagoon between Hellisay and Gighay (p.30). The possession of an accurate GPS-compatible chart of this anchorage would alone justify the modest charge that Antares make for the use of them.

A list of the charts and map of their location is given in the Appendix and further details can be found on the Antares Charts website: *www.antarescharts.co.uk*

An example of an Antares chart of the Hellisay anchorage displayed on an iPad with the GPS derived position indicated by the red circle

Outer Hebrides

The anchorage behind Eilean Thinngarstaigh, Loch Claidh

Maps

Ordnance Survey maps at 1:50,000 are well worth having on board to make up for the lack of topographical detail on current charts. In places where the charts are at a small scale the Ordnance Survey maps actually provide useful navigational detail. In some cases the OS Explorer series of maps at 1:25,000 supply essential detail where there is no Admiralty chart at an adequate scale.

Note that OS maps use a different grid of coordinates which do not even align with those of an Admiralty chart. Some GPS receivers can display OS coordinates.

Tides

The general direction of tidal streams around the Outer Hebrides is north-going (in-coming) flood tide and south-going (out-going) ebb tide. However the in-coming tide runs east at the Butt of Lewis and south to meet the north-going stream off the entrance to Stornoway. The in-coming tide runs east in the sounds south of Barra but enters the Sound of Barra from both ends. In the Sound of Harris the tides are complex but can usually be predicted at the various parts of the sound.

On the whole, streams to the west of the Outer Hebrides are weaker than those on the east side but even these rarely exceed 1 knot, except off salient headlands where 2 knots can be the norm. This can cause overfalls to occur though these are generally not of a dangerous nature. Streams are strong wherever the movement of a large body of water is constricted by narrows, and there are often overfalls at the seaward end of narrow passages, particularly with wind against tide.

The main area where care must be taken to time a passage correctly is that between the Shiant Islands and Harris where even a moderate stream is disturbed by the very uneven bottom and, with wind against tide, can produce very bad seas that could be dangerous to small craft. The spring range varies from 3·6 metres at Barra to 4·8 metres at Stornoway.

Weather

On the West Coast of Scotland the weather is very variable at any time, being influenced by the passage of depressions from the Atlantic, and rapid changes can frequently be experienced; an effect which is even more noticeable in the Outer Hebrides. The prevailing wind is between south and west, with a higher proportion of northerly and easterly winds in May and June, when an anticyclone is more likely to become established to the north of Scotland.

Visibility is usually good and fog, as such, is rare though heavy rain or drizzle can reduce visibility markedly, though generally only for a short time. The *Admiralty Pilot* says that 'visibility of less than ½ mile may reach 3 days per month in midsummer' and visibility of less than 2 miles 'does not average more than 3 days per month during the worst summer weather at Stornoway and Tiree'.

Gales occur on average on less than half a day per month at Castlebay during April-September and one day per month at Stornoway during May-August although, it must be said, there are times when these statistics can readily be doubted.

Rainfall is greatly affected by the proximity to high ground, and annual figures vary from less than 1000mm at the south end of the Outer Hebrides to between 1250 and 1800mm in the sea lochs on the east side of Harris.

6 CCC Sailing Directions and Anchorages

Introduction

Weather forecasts

The majority of yachtsmen rely on the Marine Safety Information (MSI) forecasts broadcast by the Marine and Coastguard Agency (MCA). These forecasts were re-structured in 2007 and although the recent modernisation of HM Coastguard has affected many parts of the UK coast, the Stornoway CG station is still responsible for the whole area covered by these *Directions* and the format and timing remain unchanged.

HMCG Broadcasts

- These are issued at three-hour intervals, that is eight times a day, and the HMCG complete most transmissions around the coast within one hour. Four broadcasts provide new forecasts and four are repeats.
- Two of the new forecasts include gale warnings, the shipping forecast and inshore waters forecast and outlook, as well as navigation warnings and the three-day fisherman's forecast when applicable (in winter time only).
- The other two new forecasts include inshore waters forecasts, a repeat of the previous 24-hour outlook and any gale warnings or strong wind warnings. Mariners thus have new inshore waters forecasts every six hours.
- The repeats are for the benefit of mariners who missed the new forecast made three hours previously and consist of the inshore waters forecasts and gale warnings and any new strong wind warnings.
- The full broadcasts are based on 0710 and 1910 start times so as to catch navigators at the beginning of the sailing day or night passage. All broadcasts are in local time to avoid confusion between UTC and BST.
- Forecasts for UK inshore waters are issued by the Met Office four times a day at 0500, 1100, 1700 and 2300 local time and cover the next 24 hours. Outlooks for the following 24 hours are only issued at 0500 and 1700.
- Warnings for all forecasts are transmitted on VHF Ch 16, indicating the forecast on VHF Ch 62, 63, 64 and 10. Aerials will be combined for the warnings to avoid apparent repetition.
- Warnings are brief: 'All stations – this is Stornoway Coastguard – for a weather information broadcast listen channel 63', but made slowly. The forecast broadcasts are made clearly and at dictation speed.

Stornoway Coastguard forecast areas

The sea area is divided into two:
- Ardnamurchan Point to Cape Wrath, excluding the Minch, and extending up to 12 miles west of the Outer Hebrides.
- The Minch, bounded by lines from South Uist to Rum in the South, and the Butt of Lewis to Lochinver in the North.

Initial announcements are made on Ch 16 and thereafter the forecasts are made from the following aerials (see p.13 for location plan);
Ch 10
  Barra, Butt of Lewis, Skriag, Torosay
Ch 62
  Clettravel, Drumfearn, Portnaguran, Tiree
Ch 63
  Forsnaval, Rodel, Glengorm
Ch 64
  Arisaig, Melvaig

Listen for the strongest signal on these channels for optimum reception. The forecasts by Stornoway Coastguard are made every three hours commencing at 0110 and thereafter at 0410, 0710, 1010, 1310, 1610, 1910, and 2210. The times given are not precise as forecasts may be delayed or omitted during casualty working. **All times are Local Time.**

BBC Radio Forecasts

Shipping Forecast
BBC Radio 4 198 kHz (1500m). Sea area Hebrides. Broadcast at: 0048, 0520, 1201 and 1754.

Inshore Waters Forecast
BBC Radio 4 198 kHz (1500m) and VHF frequencies. Sea areas The Minch and Ardnamurchan Point to Cape Wrath. Broadcast at: 0053 and 0525.

Landward forecasts
BBC Radio Scotland 810 kHz (370m) and VHF frequencies.

Navtex

Navtex reception on the west coast of Scotland and in the Outer Hebrides has now been much improved by the establishment of a transmitter at Malin Head. This broadcasts Inshore Waters forecasts for sea areas The Minch and Ardnamurchan to Cape Wrath on 490kHz (A) at the following times: 0000, 0400, 0800, 1200, 1600 and 2000.

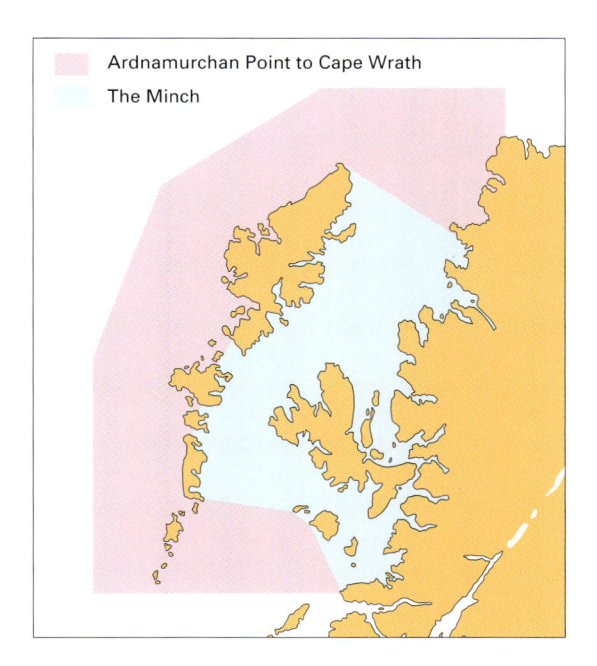

Diagram showing the division of the Stornoway coastguard forecast area

Outer Hebrides

The west anchorage in the Shiant Islands; a temporary anchorage only tenable on a handful of days in the year

Anchorages, moorings & berthing

The east coast of the Outer Hebrides, with its fragmented coast line, offers a rich source of intriguingly different anchorages. If this unique area is to be properly explored it is essential for the yacht to be well equipped with ground tackle and the crew thoroughly familiar with anchor handling. Visitors' moorings are few and, where they do exist, they are quite likely to be already occupied.

In many anchorages the bottom is mud, sometimes too soft to provide good holding, but in general it is mostly satisfactory. Weed is frequently found, and choice of ground tackle must take this into account. It is worth taking care to avoid putting the anchor down on weed. Rock is usually confined to odd patches, and many anchorages, generally within the sounds between the main islands, have clean white sand. Some of the most apparently sheltered anchorages are subject to severe squalls off surrounding hills, especially in steep-sided lochs.

These *Sailing Directions* aim to provide details of less familiar anchorages as well as the more popular ones, although they make no claim to be comprehensive and, under suitable conditions, independently minded yachtsmen will find, with the help of charts, sketch plans and experience, anchorages other than those described in this book.

Choosing an anchorage

Many places are only suitable for a short daytime visit in settled conditions and the inclusion of an anchorage in these *Directions* is no indication that it is suitable for all conditions. It is the skipper's responsibility to decide whether to use an anchorage at all, and for how long, in light of conditions (both current and predicted) and all the information available. Even the most apparently sheltered place will sometimes have the crew standing anchor watches throughout the night.

The description 'occasional anchorage' is intended to convey that the place described is only suitable for use under certain conditions; perhaps for a brief visit ashore during daylight, or in winds from certain directions to await a change of wind or tide. In ideal conditions it might be possible for it to be used overnight.

The description 'temporary anchorage' is used to describe an anchorage which must be used with caution even in good conditions and which would rarely ever be suitable for leaving a boat unattended or anchoring overnight.

Conversely, the absence of the description 'occasional' or 'temporary' should not be taken as a recommendation that an anchorage may be used in any weather.

Some anchorages, and particularly piers and boat harbours, are only suitable for shoal-draught boats, and this should be obvious from the description; the inclusion of an anchorage does not imply that it is suitable for all yachts.

Within some anchorages there are often several suitable places to lie depending on weather conditions and the type of boat. It is not always practicable to describe them all, or to mark each one on the plans.

Steep high ground to windward is unlikely to provide good shelter; in fresh winds there may be turbulent gusts on its lee side, or the wind may be deflected to blow from a completely different direction. Conversely, trees to windward will absorb a lot of wind and provide good shelter.

Rivers, burns and streams generally carry down debris, often leaving a shallow or drying bank of stones, sand or silt, over which the unwary may swing, invariably in the middle of the night.

Fish farms

Fish farming is a major industry in the Outer Hebrides and their cages, ropes, feeding pipes and buoys can be found almost anywhere with suitable mooring depths in sheltered waters. They are usually outwith the most popular places and their ever-increasing scale often means that they are located in areas that are not suitable for anchoring a yacht. However, some of the smaller ones can obstruct what appears to be a suitable anchorage and the temptation to anchor too close to them must be resisted.

There are two main forms: cages for 'fin fish' (usually salmon), and rows of buoys from which ropes are suspended, on which shellfish are 'grown'. These buoys may have ropes between them on, or close to, the surface. Fish cages may be moved around within a bay or their designated area and the symbols on charts or the plans in this book should be taken as an indication that a fish farm may be present, rather than its precise location.

The boundary of an area licensed for fish farming is sometimes marked by buoys, usually yellow and sometimes lit. These are often a long way from the cages, and there may or may not be moorings or other obstructions within the area marked out by the buoys. Anchor well clear of all fish farming equipment and, if in doubt, use a tripping line.

Moorings

Some bays and inlets offering conditions suitable for anchoring often appear to be taken up by moorings for fishing boats and other small local craft although, with care, space may well be found to anchor. Vacant moorings should not be used without first checking their ownership, availability and suitability.

The allocation of licences for moorings is the responsibility of the Crown Estates and new applications are rarely approved unless they have satisfied themselves that some anchoring space for visiting yachts is set aside. This is done through consultation with RYA Scotland and the West Highlands Anchorage and Mooring Association (WHAM). The latter would be interested to learn from cruising yachtsmen of any apparently unauthorised obstruction or over-proliferation of moorings and can be contacted through their website: *www.whamassoc.org.uk*

Visitors' moorings

A small number of visitors' moorings in the Outer Hebrides are maintained, insured and operated by Comhairle nan Eilean Siar, the Western Isles Council. They are of the usual type, cylindrical blue buoys with a maximum allowable boat size of 15 tonnes. Because they are situated in remote locations with no nearby population, let alone a harbourmaster, payment for their use is entirely the responsibility of the user. If the Council are to continue offering this valuable service it is vital that all yachtsmen make every effort to pay their dues.

In some places an Honesty box is provided at the dinghy landing but the simplest way is to pay online after a cruise at *www.cne-siar.gov.uk* or send payment to them using the form reproduced on p.166.

Alternatively cruising yachts aiming to spend a week or more in the Outer Hebrides may opt to obtain a visitor pass in advance at a cost of £80.00 (2017 - for craft up to 10m) plus VAT. This allows use of all the Council's piers, harbours, pontoons and visitors' moorings for four weeks, with the exception of Stornoway, Lochmaddy, Lochboisdale and Castlebay, where there are locally run marinas, pontoons and moorings.

Visitors' moorings are provided by the Council at the following places:
  Berneray, North Uist; 2 moorings
  Rodel, Harris; 3 moorings
  Acairsaid Mhor, Eriskay; 2 moorings
And by local enterprise organisations at:
  Castlebay, Barra; 8 moorings
  Loch Maddy, North Uist; 4 moorings

An anchorage in Loch Mariveg, Lewis which is typical of many Outer Hebridean anchorages that do not have, and do not need, any visitors' moorings

Outer Hebrides

Pontoons

The Council has provided loading pontoons, principally for the use of fishing vessels, at the following places:

Acairseid Mhor, Eriskay
Pol Scrot, Loch Stockinish, Harris
Miavaig, West Loch Roag
Leverburgh, Harris

Yachts are welcome to use the pontoons for taking on stores, diesel and water but they must not be left unattended or impede fishing boats.

Pontoons for visiting yachts are also provided at the marina in the inner harbour at Stornoway, Loch Boisdale marina, Lochmaddy, Castlebay, East Loch Tarbert and Scalpay.

Quays, piers, jetties, slips, linkspans

Yachts may well find that they will have to share harbour berths with commercial craft; a practice that used to be the norm around all our coasts but is now becoming increasingly rare.

These, and related structures, need some definition and description. The categories overlap somewhat and a structure identified on the chart may have fallen into disuse, or been replaced by one of a different type, or have a description well above its status. The definitions used in this book are as follows, and give some indication of what you might expect to find.

A quay, wharf or pier is used by fishing boats and occasional coasters, and usually has at least 2 metres of water at its head at chart datum. It is often constructed of piles or open framing, or stone or concrete with vertical timber fendering, alongside which it is difficult for a small yacht to lie without a robust fender board. A pier projects from the shore, but a quay or wharf is either part of a harbour or parallel to the shore.

Pontoon at Miavaig, West Loch Roag

Ferry terminals serving the Outer Hebrides all have a linkspan for a bow-loading car ferry. The inner end is hinged and the outer end, supported between concrete towers, is raised or lowered to match the height of the ramp on the ferry, according to the state of the tide. The linkspan is usually at one end of a quay alongside which the ferry lies.

A jetty is smaller and, for yachts, more user-friendly but often dries alongside. Newer jetties are constructed of more or less smooth concrete, older ones of stone, often with a very uneven surface; a few are of timber.

A slip, or slipway, runs down at an angle into the water, although its outer end may be above water at low tide and it may be used by a ferry to an inshore island. There is sometimes sufficient depth for a yacht to go alongside a slip for a brief visit ashore for stores.

With the enormous growth in inshore fishing and fish-farming, many of these structures are in regular use by fishermen whose livelihood depends on being able to land their produce quickly, and yachts should take care not to obstruct them.

Dues are charged at some piers and harbours, even for a brief visit to take on water. Comhairle nan Eilean Siar offers a 'season ticket' for a yacht to use two or several of its piers or harbours over a period of time. (see *Visitors' moorings p.9*)

Equipment

This should be as robust and reliable as for a yacht going a similar distance offshore anywhere in the English Channel or the North Sea.

Anchors

A boat needs at least two anchors, of the sizes recommended by anchor manufacturers or independent reference books, rather than those supplied as standard by boat manufacturers which are often on the light side.

Chain rather than rope will prevent a yacht roving around in gusts and at least 60 metres of chain is recommended. If you do use rope it will help to have a weight ('angel', 'chum') which can be let down to the seabed on a traveller.

In view of the variety of conditions two different types of anchor should be carried. The choice is very much a matter of individual preference but about half the yachts moored in marinas carry a CQR pattern anchor. However, the adoption of 'second generation' anchors such as the Delta, Spade and Rocna seems to be gathering momentum and they certainly get good reports from those who have used them in Scottish waters.

Introduction

Pat and Jill Barron

Kearstay anchorage, Scarp

Chartering & instruction

There is one bareboat charter company in the Outer Hebrides but a good number of mainland and Skye-based charter yachts make the Outer Hebrides and beyond their objective. Those starting from Skye should easily manage to fit the cruise into a week or so but if coming from Argyll, where the majority are based, a two week charter should allow much more of the Outer Hebrides to be explored.

However, if wanting tuition or skippered charter, the most westerly sailing school in Britain operates out of Barra during the months of June, July and August and for those who would like a taste of the Outer Hebrides, but are unable to spend much time getting there, they offer a valuable alternative. They can be contacted at *www.westboundadventures.co.uk*

All these activities, and much more, are covered in great detail in the excellent full colour brochure published by Sail Scotland which is freely available direct from them or many marinas. It can also be read and downloaded from *www.sailscotland.co.uk*

Services and supplies

In planning a cruise to the Outer Hebrides it must be recognised that obtaining provisions, fuel, repairs and even water is not as easy as it is on the mainland This is partly because the majority of the population live on the fertile west side of the islands and on the east side, the most frequented cruising area, major settlements are only to be found clustering round the principal ferry terminals of Castlebay, Lochboisdale, Lochmaddy, Tarbert and Stornoway.

All this is of little consequence to boats with capacious lockers and tanks who can stock up well at the start of a cruise but for the others, or those who like fresh produce, a certain amount of pre-planning is required. However distances are small and with the willing help of the locals, who always seem ready to offer a lift or deliver an item, few problems will arise.

Diesel

Marine diesel is available by hose at the following locations:
Brevig (Broad Bay), Stornoway, Carloway, Kirkibost, Miavaig, Scalpay, Stockinish, Leverburgh, Berneray (North Uist), Griminish, Kallin, Ludag (Sound of Eriskay - West), Eriskay (Acairseid Mhor), Vatersay (causeway slipway) and North Bay, Barra. All installations apart from Stornoway, Scalpay and North Bay (which is suitable for large quantities only) are operated by Comhairle nan Eilean Siar, the Western Isles Council. The system is unmanned and requires users to have a key fob. These can be obtained on prior application to the Council (a copy of the application form is included in the Appendix) and a few weeks must be allowed for the issue of the fob. Application should be made to: The Harbour Master, Comhairle nan Eilean Siar, Balivanich, Isle of Benbecula. HS7 5LA. ☏ 0845 6007090 or 01870 604991. Fob holders are required to register as leisure or commercial users and will be direct debited monthly at the appropriate duty and VAT inclusive rate.

However, in Stornoway and Scalpay diesel is available through agents without the use of a key fob. In Stornoway it can be obtained through the Stornoway Port Authority. In Scalpay, following the closure of the community shop in 2017, a new agent is yet to be appointed.

In other locations it may be possible to obtain diesel with the assistance of a helpful local who has an account with the Council but it is unwise to rely on this and the best plan is to arrive at the Outer Hebrides with tanks as full as possible and also carry a generous reserve.

CCC Sailing Directions and Anchorages 11

Outer Hebrides

Water supplies
These are fairly rare at the quayside, and a yacht with built-in tanks should have a portable container or two, together with a straight-sided funnel, with which to fill the tank. A 20-metre hose of the flat variety on a reel, with a universal coupling to fit on any sort of tap, is also well worth carrying, as several small jetties have taps but no hoses. These small jetties, although they may only be approachable above half tide, are usually more convenient than the massive piled ferry piers, where the only hose may be too large to serve a yacht. The most convenient supplies of water by hose can be found at the pontoons listed previously (p.10) though these are few and far between.

Provisions
All the ferry ports mentioned above have shops catering for most basic needs although some, eg. Lochboisdale, will involve a fair walk. In between these centres very little will be found and wherever small shops might once have existed it is highly likely that they may now be closed. The quick reference table in the Appendix gives an overall picture at the time of writing but it must be used with reservations as businesses can come and go quite rapidly.

Repairs
There are no yacht yards as such and only Stornoway offers comprehensive facilities for hull, engine and electronic repairs. Elsewhere it will be necessary to visit a fishing harbour such as Kallin or North Bay, Barra where it might be possible to obtain the services of an engineer who will probably have to travel some distance.

The anchorage off the beach at Ensay, Sound of Harris

Eating ashore
All the ferry ports contain at least one hotel or restaurant where a good meal can be had but otherwise most of the tourist hotels are quite some distance from anywhere a yacht might anchor. Wherever hotels and restaurant do occur they are mentioned in the text but no recommendations can be given as standards can vary so quickly from year to year.

For further details of facilities for visiting yachts, see the publication *Welcome Anchorages* which is published annually and is available free from marinas and marine companies all over Scotland, or on the internet by downloading from: *www.welcomeanchoragesscotland.com*

Communications

Public phone boxes
These used to be found close by most small groups of houses but, like small Post Offices, they are fast disappearing. Because of the difficulty in maintaining accurate information all references to them have been omitted.

Mobile phones
Coverage by mobile phone companies continues to improve and now most populated parts of the Outer Hebrides can receive a 2G service, though reception along the east coast of the islands can be very patchy, especially in any of the anchorages near high ground. At sea, away from the hills, coverage is generally good in the Minches but in the Sea of the Hebrides, from South Uist down to Barra Head, it is poor.

To the west reception is good on the whole, both on land and up to a few miles out to sea, apart from a large area between Scarp and

Edward Mason

Introduction

Loch Roag where reception is very limited or non-existent.

The Vodafone network is usually acknowledged by most yachtsmen as providing the best coverage of Scottish west coast waters but EE(BT) is now fast catching up and in some locations can offer a 4G signal.

VHF radiotelephones

VHF reception is generally good but there are a few areas of poor or no VHF communications of which yachtsmen should be aware. Three are on the west coasts of Lewis and Harris but the one which is likely to affect the majority of boats is a large area to the southeast of Barra.

The adjacent map shows all the VHF aerial sites with, shaded, the areas of doubtful VHF reception. They are based on experience and are from a variety of sources and are in no way definitive. They simply indicate areas where VHF reception/transmission from and to emergency services can be difficult. It is important to state the obvious i.e. in making use of these maps account has to be taken of height of aerial, age of set, topography, atmospheric conditions etc. For these reasons some craft may be able to make contact while others close by may not.

The map also shows the names of the stations used for VHF transmissions and in conjunction with the transmitting channel information it may help users to tune into the best channel for reception of the Coastguard weather forecasts.

Travel

Travel to, from and within the Outer Hebrides is in many ways better than it is to some parts of the Scottish mainland. Because of the excellent air and ferry services it is often easier and quicker to change crews at, say, Barra or Stornoway or even Loch Roag, than at many places on the mainland north of Skye.

For planning journeys by all forms of public transport within and to Scotland the excellent website *www.travelinescotland.com* will be found to be most helpful. They also produce an iPhone app.

Sea

Regular ferry services run to the Outer Hebrides as follows:
- Oban to Castlebay, Barra
- Mallaig to Lochboisdale, South Uist
- Uig, Skye to Lochmaddy, North Uist and East Loch Tarbert, Harris
- Ullapool to Stornoway

Between the islands vehicle ferries run as follows:
- Leverburgh, Harris to Berneray and North Uist across the Sound of Harris
- Eriskay to Barra across the Sound of Barra

All the above are operated by Caledonian MacBrayne.

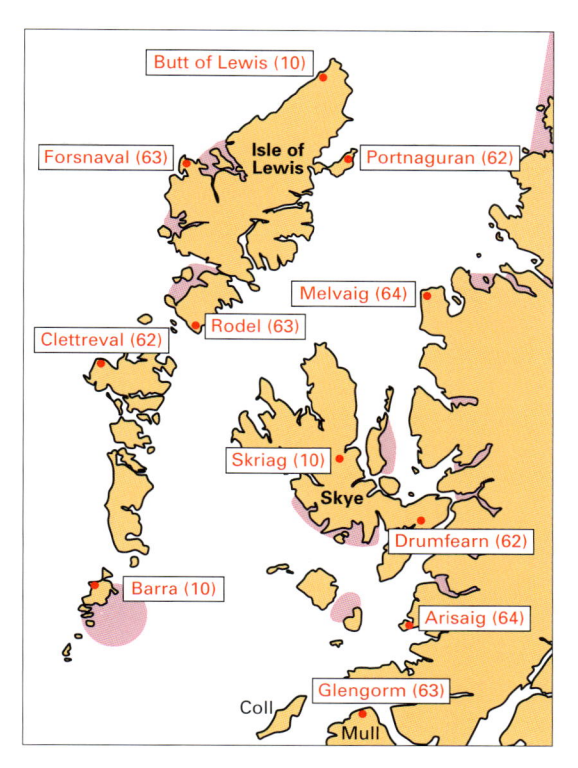

Aerial sites used by Stornoway Coastguard for broadcasting Maritime Safety Information (MSI). VHF channels shown in brackets. Shading indicates areas of poor or no VHF reception

Air

Flights from the mainland are as follows:
- Glasgow, Edinburgh, Inverness to Stornoway
- Glasgow to Barra and Benbecula
- Aberdeen to Stornoway

Flights are operated by either Loganair or FlyBe/Eastern Airways.

Road

There is a good bus service in the Outer Hebrides which links all the major ferry ports. and in conjunction with the Sound of Barra and Sound of Harris ferries it is possible to travel from Castlebay to Stornoway in approximately eight hours.

The CCC Centenary Cruise fleet at anchor in Vatersay Bay

David Gillibrand

CCC Sailing Directions and Anchorages

Outer Hebrides

Emergencies

Serious and immediate emergencies (including medical emergencies) are usually best referred to the coastguard.

Coastguard

Under the the reorganisation of the MCA, the Stornoway coastguard station has been retained as the principal 24 hour Maritime Rescue Coordination Centre between Belfast MRCC and Shetland MRCC.

The Service maintains a continuous listening watch on VHF Ch16. Stornoway operates a safety service on Ch 67 and can be contacted by telephone on ☎01851 702013 and MMSI 002320024.

Lifeboats

All-weather lifeboats are stationed at Castlebay, Leverburgh and Stornoway. The nearest on the mainland and Skye are at Mallaig, Loch Inver and Portree.

Notes on sailing directions & plans

Arrangement

These *Directions* are written starting at the south end of the Outer Hebrides chain and progress northwards up the east coast as far as Stornoway and including in turn the two principal passages leading to the Atlantic: the Sounds of Barra and Harris.

Crossings to the Outer Hebrides are dealt with in the chapters describing each of the various landfalls. These comprise:

The Sea of the Hebrides between the mainland of Scotland in the vicinity of the Point of Ardnamurchan to Barra and northwards to Loch Skipport in South Uist (p.17)

The Little Minch between Skye, North Uist and Harris (p.106)

The North Minch between the mainland from Gairloch in the South to Lochinver in the North across to Lewis (p.120)

The final chapter deals with the west coast of the Outer Hebrides proceeding northwards from Barra to the Butt of Lewis and round to Stornoway and finishes with the outliers, St Kilda and the Flannan Islands.

Each chapter begins with general information relating to the whole: tides, shelter, marks, dangers and lights come first; then any passage directions, sometimes including certain anchorages where it is necessary to relate these to plans associated with the passages; then any branches from the main passage; and finally individual harbours and anchorages, usually in the same south to north sequence and all described as approached from seaward.

It should be noted that marks and dangers are listed in separate paragraphs only in the introductory sections, which usually cover large expanses of water across which yachts may be passage making in many different directions. In describing narrow lochs, sounds and the approach to anchorages and harbours, any dangers and marks are included under the heading *Directions* in the order that they will encountered on passage. This reduces repetition.

Bearings & distances

All bearings, both in text and on the plans, are from seaward and always refer to true north. All plans are orientated with true north at the top as the plan is read.

Distances are given in nautical miles and cables (tenths of nautical mile); distances of less than a cable are generally expressed in metres.

Depths & heights

These are given in metres to correspond with the current Admiralty charts. Depths are related to the current chart datum which is generally lower than that on older charts. This datum is the lowest level to which the surface of the sea is expected to fall owing to astronomical causes (LAT). If high barometric pressure and/or strong offshore winds coincide with a low spring tide the water may fall below this level, in which case there will be less depth than shown on the chart, or sketch plan.

Heights are now given as the clear height above the highest astronomical tide (HAT) which is higher than the previously quoted MHWS used on older charts and previous editions of the *Sailing Directions*.

Tides

Heights of tides are represented by five figures; these are: Mean High Water Springs, Mean High Water Neaps, Mean Tide Level, Mean Low Water Neaps, Mean Low Water Springs. The word Mean is important because (for example) Low Water Springs in any particular fortnight may be substantially higher or lower than the mean.

If you have tide tables which give heights of tides at Ullapool you will be able to relate the height of tide on any particular day to the mean figures there (5·2 3·9 3·0 2·1 0·7 for Ullapool) and judge whether the rise and fall is greater or less than the mean.

The difference between times of tides at Ullapool and at Dover may vary by as much as 40 minutes, so that local tide tables will give more accurate results than those for Dover. In addition to Admiralty tide tables and commercial almanacs, pocket tide tables for Ullapool are supplied by local chandlers, boatyards and marinas.

References to tidal constants and timing of streams give the nearest Standard port first followed by the Dover equivalent in brackets. If times refer to neither a Standard port nor Dover they relate to local HW or LW.

Introduction

Plans

Plans of anchorages and passages in these *Directions* are often at a larger scale than those on current charts, and the information in them is compiled from many sources. These include the Admiralty's original surveys; Antares charts, Ordnance Survey, air photographs, observations and surveys by other yachtsmen and, latterly, Google Earth. Some of them are based directly on British Admiralty charts, with the permission of the Hydrographer of the Navy.

Generally the conventions used on Admiralty charts have been followed so that these *Directions* may be used in conjunction with them. Symbols used on plans are illustrated on the right and also on the front cover flap.

All plans are drawn with north at the top and all depths are in metres. None of the plans is to a recognised scale and the drawn scale should be used to estimate distances. Only information relevant to the size of craft for which these *Directions* are written is given and they are intended as an illustrated guide to the text and should not be used for navigation.

Background information

In previous editions of the *Sailing Directions* a note regarding items of special or historic interest was often included but this has now been omitted as a result of the publication in 2010 of the Club's Companion to the Sailing Directions, *Cruising Scotland*. This well-illustrated hardback book sets out to provide the cruising yachtsman with much of the supplementary information that would ideally be included within the *Sailing Directions* but has often been left out due to shortage of space. Page references to *Cruising Scotland* are given throughout.

Place names

In some cases the popular name for a place, or its spelling, differs from that on Admiralty charts. The latter is usually given, and both where appropriate. The spelling of many names appears to vary greatly – see the Gaelic Glossary in the Appendix – and throughout these *Directions* and on the plans we have endeavoured to use that shown on the Admiralty chart.

Changes, corrections, and supplements

Despite appearances, things do change in the Outer Hebrides. Buoys, lights, piers, pontoons and many shoreside facilities slowly evolve. Readers are asked to bear this in mind and to make sure that they have the latest amendments issued at intervals on the CCC and Imray websites, and also to report any discrepancies, or even uncertainties, which may be further investigated by other readers.

This is greatly appreciated not only by the Club and publishers, but also by the Hydrographic Office to whom any relevant information is forwarded.

Principal chart symbols

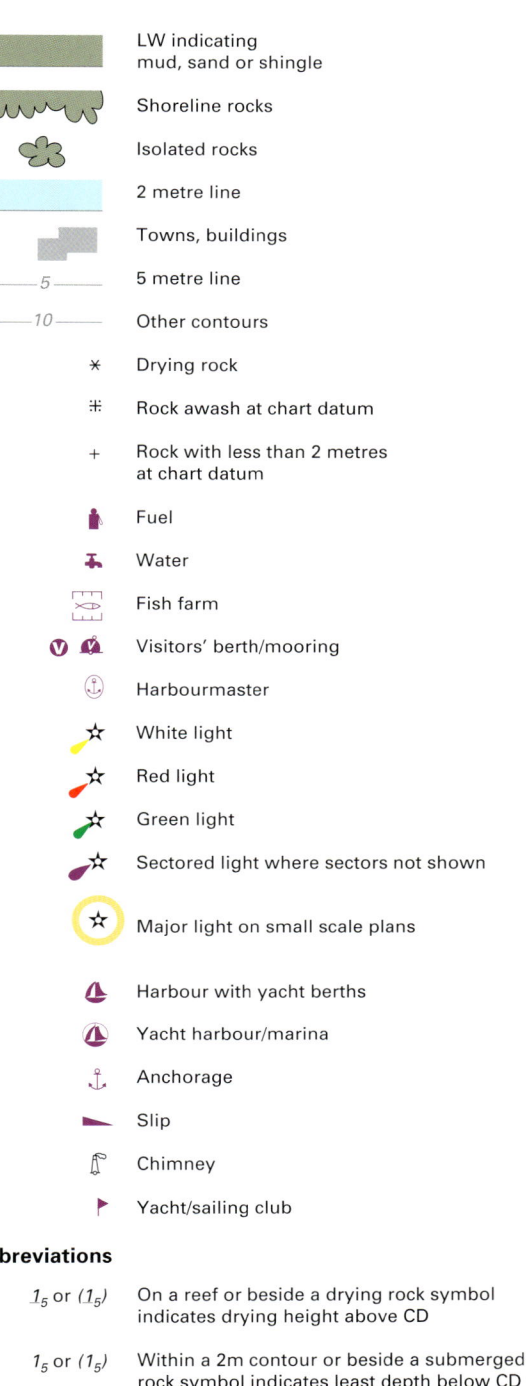

	LW indicating mud, sand or shingle
	Shoreline rocks
	Isolated rocks
	2 metre line
	Towns, buildings
5	5 metre line
10	Other contours
✳	Drying rock
✳	Rock awash at chart datum
+	Rock with less than 2 metres at chart datum
	Fuel
	Water
	Fish farm
V /	Visitors' berth/mooring
	Harbourmaster
☆	White light
☆	Red light
☆	Green light
☆	Sectored light where sectors not shown
☆	Major light on small scale plans
	Harbour with yacht berths
	Yacht harbour/marina
	Anchorage
	Slip
	Chimney
	Yacht/sailing club

Abbreviations

1_5 or (1_5)	On a reef or beside a drying rock symbol indicates drying height above CD
1_5 or (1_5)	Within a 2m contour or beside a submerged rock symbol indicates least depth below CD
5 or (5)	On or beside a rock or islet indicates height above MHWS
M	Miles on land (1760 yards) Miles at sea (6080 feet)
m	Metres
c	Cable (1/10 nautical mile)
bn	Beacon

CCC Sailing Directions and Anchorages

1. Barra Head to Eriskay

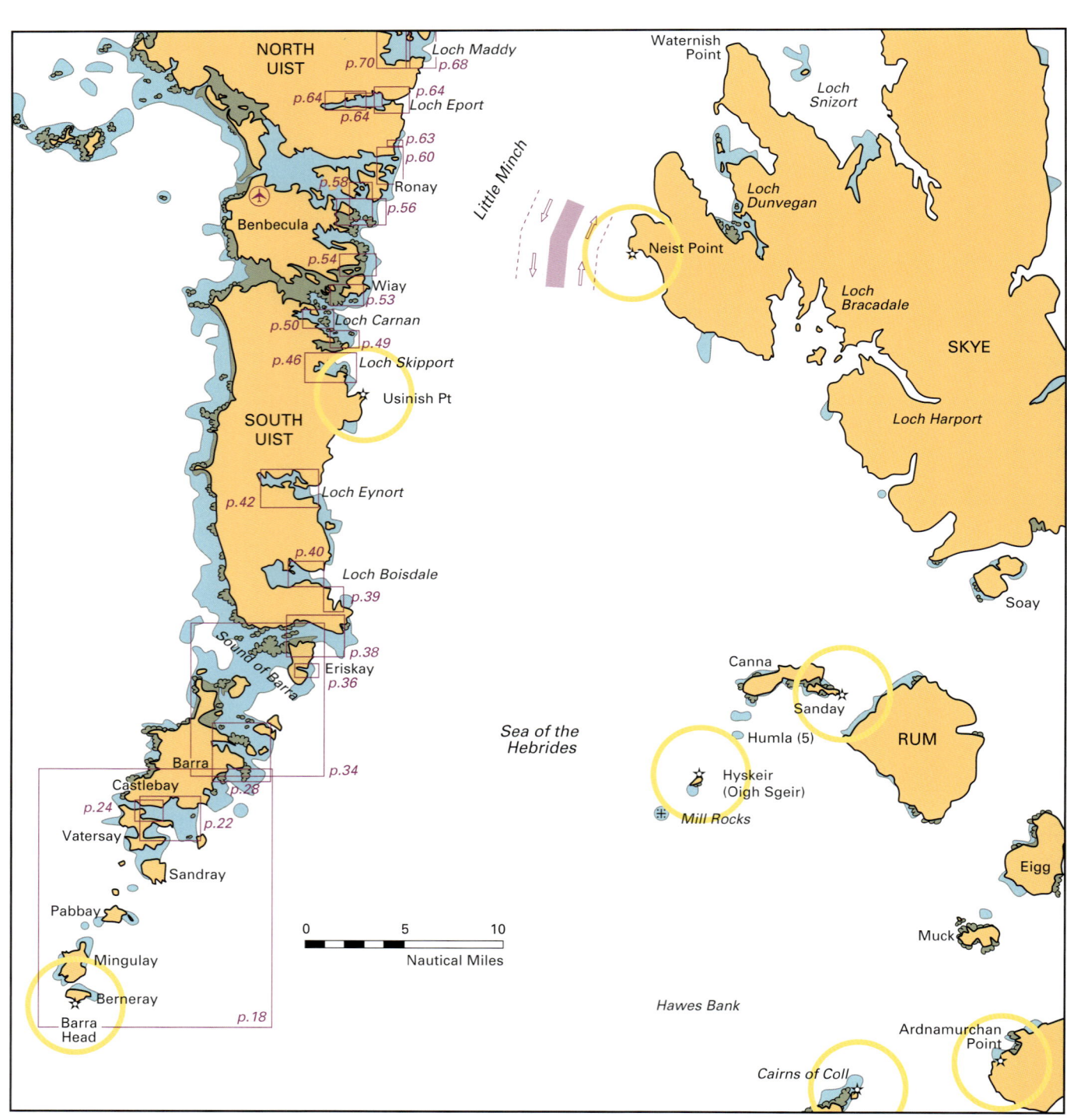

SEA OF THE HEBRIDES KEY PLAN

16   CCC Sailing Directions and Anchorages

1. Barra Head to Eriskay

Crossing the Sea of the Hebrides

This is the crossing favoured by boats coming from the south, it being the shortest route to the Outer Hebrides for the majority. It also allows Canna to be used as a convenient staging post for a passage across the Sea of the Hebrides and Canna Harbour is an ideal anchorage to await the right weather for a crossing. Its location allows advantage to be taken of almost any wind direction, if a landfall anywhere between Barra and Loch Maddy is acceptable.

All the hazards are marked and lit, making a night passage perfectly feasible. The bottom of the Sea of the Hebrides is very uneven and steep seas may be encountered throughout the area. The Admiralty Pilot states that the Sea of the Hebrides, between Tiree and Barra 'is about twice as rough in a given wind as the Minch'. However, in reasonable conditions the passage is straightforward enough.

Distances
Sound of Mull to Castlebay, Barra 50 miles
Sound of Mull to Canna 25 miles
Canna to Castle Bay, Barra 35 miles
Canna to Eriskay 26 miles
Canna to Loch Boisdale 25 miles
Canna to Loch Skipport, South Uist 30 miles
Canna to Loch Maddy, North Uist 40 miles
Gunna Sound to Castle Bay, Barra 36 miles

Tides
Tidal streams in the Sea of the Hebrides are generally weak except around Hyskeir
The north-going stream begins +0550 Ullapool (+0130 Dover)
The south-going stream begins –0010 Ullapool (–0430 Dover)
Around Humla the spring rate is 2½ knots with overfalls over all the rocks around Hyskeir. The sea breaks heavily up to 15 miles southwest of Hyskeir particularly in heavy weather and when wind and tide are opposed.

Dangers
Cairns of Coll, above water and drying, extend 1½ miles north of Coll. A white tower, 8 metres in height, stands on Suil Gorm an islet ½ mile north of Coll, but a reef which dries 4 metres lies ½ mile further NNE.
Hyskeir (Oigh Sgeir), a rocky islet 5 miles southwest of Canna with a white lighthouse 39 metres in height.
Mill Rocks, awash and submerged, lie up to 2¼ miles southwest of Hyskeir; the north point of Eigg open south of Rum bearing 085° leads 1½ miles south of Mill Rocks.
Humla, a rock 5 metres high, 2 miles SSW of the west end of Canna, with rocks close west of it as well as between Humla and Canna, is marked by a green conical light buoy on its west side.

Directions
From Gunna Sound: the passage is as from the Sound of Mull, without the hazard of the Cairns of Coll, but heavy overfalls may be encountered at the windward end of Gunna Sound.

Returning by this route, Gunna Sound is difficult to locate, but a radio mast on Ben Hough, 8 miles WSW of the Sound makes a good landmark.
From Sound of Mull to Castle Bay: Cairns of Coll must be watched for and the passage lies across Hawes Bank which rises to 18 metres from more than 100 metres. Barra is identified by Heaval, which is 382 metres high and Muldoanich Island (151m) one mile east of Vatersay. In poor visibility the 30 metre contour is absolutely as close as it is safe to approach Barra without being certain of your position. The Bo Vich Chuan south cardinal buoy, Q(6) + LFl.15s, gives warning of dangers in the approach.
From Sound of Mull to Loch Boisdale: it may be desirable, if any sea is running, to pass north of Hyskeir to avoid Mill Rocks and the potential overfalls which can extend some distance SW of Hyskeir (see chart 1796).

In good visibility three groups of three hills are visible on South Uist. From south to north these are: the hills south of Loch Boisdale, the Boisdale Hills between Loch Boisdale and Loch Eynort and the more massive Beinn Mhor range at the north end of South Uist.
From Sound of Mull to Loch Maddy: pass north of Hyskeir to avoid Mill Rocks (see above). Eaval, south of Loch Eport, is noticeably wedge-shaped, and the prominent North Lee and South Lee, south of Loch Maddy help to identify the landfall.

If making for Canna as a jumping-off point, the passage east and north of Rum may be preferred for shelter and interest and it is only about 4½ miles longer.

Prominent landmarks when returning are: Small Isles (especially Rum), Hyskeir lighthouse, Ardnamurchan lighthouse, Cairns of Coll light beacon. For details of the Small Isles and Skye see CCC *Sailing Directions & Anchorages, Ardnamurchan to Cape Wrath*.

Lights
Ardnamurchan Lt Ho Fl(2)20s55m24M
Cairns of Coll Lt bn Fl.12s23m10M
Canna (East end of Sanday) Fl.10s32m9M
Hyskeir (Oigh Sgeir) Lt Ho Fl(3)30s41m24M
Humla Lt buoy Fl.G.6s
Barra Head Lt Ho (Berneray) Fl.15s208m18M
Ushenish Lt Ho Fl.20s54m19M
Neist Point Lt Ho (Skye) Fl.5s43m16M

At night the approaches to Castle Bay, North Bay Barra, Eriskay, Loch Boisdale, Loch Carnan and Loch Maddy are well enough lit to be approached on a clear night.

Shelter
Shelter, easily approached in reasonable visibility, can be found at Canna, Vatersay Bay, Castle Bay, North Bay, Eriskay, Loch Boisdale, Loch Skipport and Loch Maddy.

Admiralty Chart
1795, 1796
Admiralty Leisure Folio
5616. 11, 12, 13A, 14
Imray Chart
C65, C66
Cruising Scotland
p.173

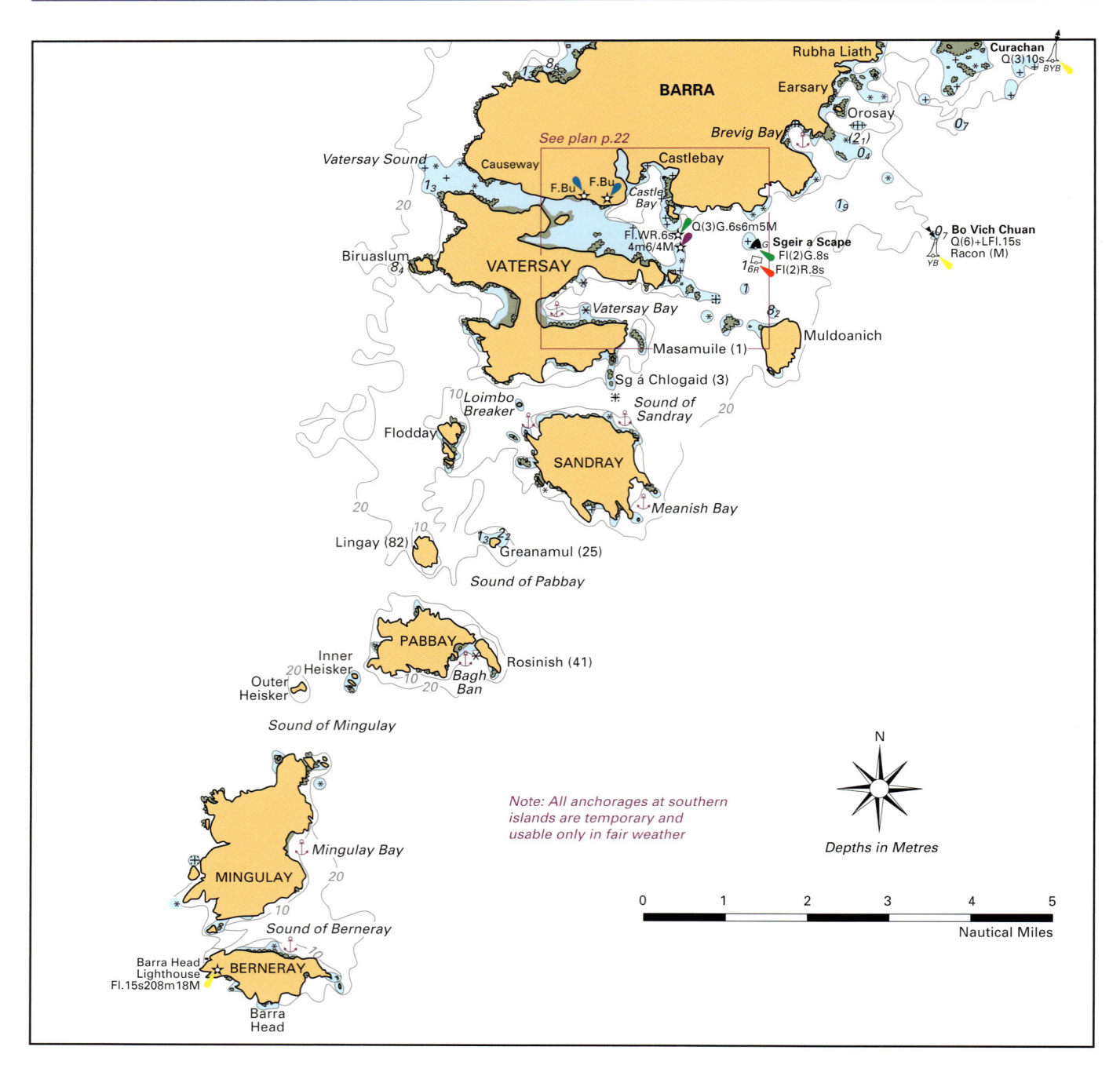

Outer Hebrides

BARRA AND THE ISLANDS TO THE SOUTH

Admiralty Chart
1796, 2769
Admiralty Leisure Folio
5616. 13A
Imray Chart
C65
Ordnance Survey
31
Cruising Scotland
p.174, 175

Islands to the South of Barra

A chain of islands extends about 10 miles SSW of Castle Bay to Berneray. Of these islands, only Vatersay is inhabited offering, in Vatersay Bay, anchorage sheltered from most winds and free from swell at its head. The other islands, Sandray, Pabbay, Mingulay and Berneray provide, in settled conditions, a choice of anchorages off some spectacular sandy beaches, each offering various degrees of shelter from wind and swell. These islands and the sounds between them present a fascinating blend of land and sea with their birdlife and awe-inspiring views of cliffs within a comparatively short distance of secure anchorages in Barra or Vatersay Bay.

Tides

Constant −0110 Ullapool (−0530 Dover)

Height in metres

MHWS	MHWN	MTL	MLWN	MLWS
4·1	3·0	2·4	1·6	0·7

From the east side of Berneray in the south to East Loch Tarbert, Harris, in the north, the tidal flow closer in to the coast differs greatly to those in the Sea of the Hebrides. Three to four miles east of the coast those inshore tidal currents change to those more normal to the Sea of the Hebrides. (See Admiralty Tidal Atlas NP 218.)

On the east side near the coast from Berneray to the Sound of Barra the streams begin two hours earlier than off Barra Head and run in the general direction of the coast as follows:
NE-going stream begins +0520 Ullapool (+0100 Dover)
SW-going stream begins −0400 Ullapool (−0500 Dover)

In each of the sounds the tidal stream runs at between 2½ and 4 knots with turbulence at the down-tide end of the sounds and heavy overfalls with an opposing wind.

18 CCC Sailing Directions and Anchorages

1. Barra Head to Eriskay

In strong wind over tide conditions this can cause breaking seas at either end. At the west end, with strong westerly winds and swell, the seas can be extremely dangerous to small vessels.

Lights
Barra Head Lt Ho (Berneray) Fl.15s208m18M

Berneray & Sound of Berneray
Berneray has a distinctive wedge shape with a lighthouse on the west side near its highest point. There are rugged cliffs on its south end. Barra Head is the most southerly part of Berneray. Approaching Berneray in low cloud the loom of Barra Head Light may not be visible even at ½ mile.

It is less than a mile across the Sound of Berneray from Mingulay to Berneray and it narrows to about 3 cables at its west end, which can be affected by swell meeting tidal flow, resulting in very heavy seas (see above). Shelter Rock (dries 2·4m) lies ¾ cable off the north side of Berneray.

Tides
Constant –0105 Ullapool (–0525 Dover)

Height in metres

MHWS	MHWN	MTL	MLWN	MLWS
4·0	3·0	2·4	1·8	0·8

Tidal streams in the Sound of Berneray and close south of Berneray run at 2–2½ knots
The east-going stream begins –0600 Ullapool (+0205 Dover) and runs for 4¼ hours
The west-going stream begins –0145 Ullapool (–0605 Dover) and runs for 8¼ hours
At a point 3½ miles south of Berneray the east-going stream begins an hour earlier and runs for 6½ hours, and the rate in each direction is 1½ knots.

Anchorage
Berneray Anchor in 8m sand out of the tidal streams, just off the storehouse on the north side of Berneray, about 2½ cables southeast of Shelter Rock which, as its name implies, can reduce the swell in the anchorage. This anchorage is untenable when a heavy sea is running. Land at the slip opposite the shed, but beware that this landing is no longer maintained by the NLB.

Mingulay & Sound of Mingulay
This is perhaps the most spectacular of the southern islands with its six small compact peaks and, on the west side, high steep cliffs filled with birdlife. These are very impressive and it is worth sailing round the island, but only in moderate weather.

Directions
On a passage round Mingulay a considerable swell may be experienced which is accentuated by tidal conditions on the west side of the Sound of Berneray. Heading northwards, give the Twin Rocks, a little over a cable west of the most westerly point on Mingulay, a wide berth and, once past Sunk Rock 5 cables further north, there are no dangers if a distance off of 1 cable is kept until the Sound of Mingulay is reached. Pass south of the Outer and Inner Heisker to enter the Sound of Mingulay which is clean. During the east-going stream a heavy race extends 3½ cables east from the north point of Mingulay.

Tides
In the Sound of Mingulay the streams run as follows:
East-going stream begins +0505 Ullapool (+0045 Dover). 3 knots springs.
West-going stream begins –0140 Ullapool –0600 Dover). 2–2½ knots springs.

Anchorage
Mingulay, has a temporary anchorage off the middle of a sandy beach on the east side of the island, but even in the most apparently calm weather there is often enough swell to capsize a dinghy; if you can get ashore it may be difficult to launch a dinghy again. The best landing places are at either end of the beach. When landing is difficult in the swell, Skipisdale, about a mile southwest around the shore on the Sound of Berneray, may offer a better landing or taking off place.

Pabbay & Sound of Pabbay
Less visited than Mingulay, Pabbay is also worth circumnavigating in settled weather.

Directions
A passage can be made between Inner Heisker and the southwest end of Pabbay but note Sloch Glansich (dries 3·2m) 1 cable west of the middle of Pabbay. Once through the channel between Inner Heisker and Pabbay, keeping about 2 cables off clears all dangers including a drying rock 1 cable off the most northerly point on Pabbay. Thereafter, the sound is clean and should present no problems in moderate weather.

Tides
In mid-channel in the Sound of Pabbay:
East-going stream begins +0505 Ullapool (+0045 Dover) 3½-4 kn. springs.
West-going stream begins –0140 Ullapool (–0600 Dover)
The east-going stream is strongest during its first 3 hours. The west-going stream is weaker than the east-going. Eddies form both north of Pabbay and south of Sandray in the Sound and these streams begin close inshore 3 hours earlier than in mid-channel.

Anchorage
Bagh Ban at the southeast end of Pabbay is only suitable for temporary anchorage in calm conditions. Its eastern arm, Rosinish, has many submerged rocks for at least 1 cable off its south end. Give Rosinish a wide berth on entering Bagh Ban, approach with care and hold to the western half of the bay, anchoring in 4m, sand, off a small headland named Sumula on chart 2769.

Outer Hebrides

Admiralty Chart
1796, 2769
Admiralty Leisure Folio
5616. 13A
Imray Chart
C65
Ordnance Survey
31
Cruising Scotland
p.176

Sandray & Sound of Sandray

Being closer to Castle Bay, and having a slightly more sheltered anchorage, an excursion to Sandray is a good alternative if time or conditions do not allow a visit to Mingulay.

Directions

The Sound of Sandray needs more care than the other sounds; it is partly blocked by a line of rocks which extend south from the east end of Vatersay to Sgeir a' Chlogaid, 3 metres high, in the middle of the east end of the sound.

Kerr Patch, a drying rock, lies 1½ cables SSW of Sgeir a'Chlogaid and Scare Kerks, two further drying rocks, lie ¾ cable off the north side of Sandray. At the west end of the sound Loimbo Breaker, which dries 1·1 metres, lies in mid-channel.

Making a passage through the Sound of Sandray from the west, note that the entrance is narrowed by a shoal bank extending 3 cables north of Flodday, over which seas often break, and another extending 3 cables off the southwest shore of Vatersay. These shoals make the safe channel a little over 2 cables wide. Heading east, Loimbo Breaker, 3½ cables NW of Sandray, must be avoided and left to starboard.

Tides

Tidal Streams in the Sound of Sandray:
East-going stream begins +0505 Ullapool (+0045 Dover) 3 kn springs.
West-going stream begins –0140 Ullapool (–0600 Dover). 2–2½ kn springs.

Anchorage

Meanish The bay SW of Meanish offers temporary anchorage in settled conditions. Approaching from the south Sgeir Leehinish can be passed on either side but beware an uncharted rock (LD 1·1m) in the centre of the bay just over 3 cables due north of Sgeir Leehinish. Anchor off the beach at the head of the bay in 4m.

Bagh Ban on the northeast of Sandray provides good temporary anchorage, but approaching from the west note Scare Kerks and, in winds from east to southeast, the bay on the northwest of Sanday is clean and gives good holding.

Vatersay Bay

This bay has the finest sandy beach on the east side of the Outer Hebrides. In addition to the natural beauty of Vatersay Island the bay itself provides excellent shelter except in easterly winds.

Directions

From the open sea the bay should be approached by the south side of Muldoanich as rocks are scattered northwest of that island. Sgeir Vichalea, a detached drying rock 2 cables from the south side of the bay, is unmarked.

From Castle Bay pass south of Sgeir Dubh and close north of the red can Lt. buoy Fl(2)R.8s before turning SE to pass round the east side of Muldoanich. Keeping 2 or 3 cables off the south side clears all dangers.

Then head for the centre of the bay to clear Sgeir Vichalea (dries 1·5m) off the south shore, formerly marked by a beacon which has now collapsed and is not visible at HW. Opposite this, note also a rock (dries 0·2) a cable off the north shore. From Castlebay round the east side of Muldoanich to the anchorage in Vatersay Bay is about 7 miles.

Vatersay Bay looking southwards towards Barra Head

Martin Lawrence

20   CCC Sailing Directions and Anchorages

1. Barra Head to Eriskay

The Fisherman's Passage from the east with Vatersay Sound and the causeway in the background

The **Fisherman's passage** is an alternative to avoid going east of Muldoanich and is used by the majority of small boats. This deep water passage lies close west of Snuasimul (17). The apparently broad passage east of Sgeir na Muice is encumbered with several dangerous rocks. It should be noted that the islet Uinessan is separated from Vatersay only at HW.

When approaching the passage from Castlebay pass south of Sgeir Dubh with the Rubha Glas leading beacons in line astern on course 115°. Do not turn south until the beacon on Sgeir Dubh and the ruins on the SW side of Orosay bear 335°. Steer 155° until the deep water channel west of Snuasimul opens out.

With Beinn nan Carnan (150m) under the east shoulder of Heaval astern bearing approximately 023°, steer about 203°. The channel lies close west of Snuasimul but at its northern end it is narrowed to 50m by a drying rock NW of Snuasimul. In the approach identify Snuasimul and the islet roughly halfway between it and Uinessan. Aim to pass through in the centre of the eastern half of the gap between them.

When nearing Snuasimul identify a rock which rarely covers, shown on the plan as a small islet lying close NW of Snuasimul, and pass approximately 20m west of this rock, maintaining a course of 203° or thereby. If, due to abnormally HW or swell, either this rock or the islet in the centre is not visible the passage should not be attempted.

If proceeding north through the passage from Vatersay Bay to Castlebay note the channel width as described above and maintain a course of 023° towards Beinn nan Carnan until the leading line on Rubha Glas bears 295° in order to avoid the extensive rocks north of Uinessan. From Castlebay to the anchorage in Vatersay Bay is less than 4 miles using the Fisherman's passage.

Anchorage

Vatersay Bay Anchor at the head of the bay in 5m, clear of moorings. The best shelter is in the southwest corner of the bay, where there is a jetty, but this is uncomfortable in winds between northeast and southeast. The bottom is clean sand.

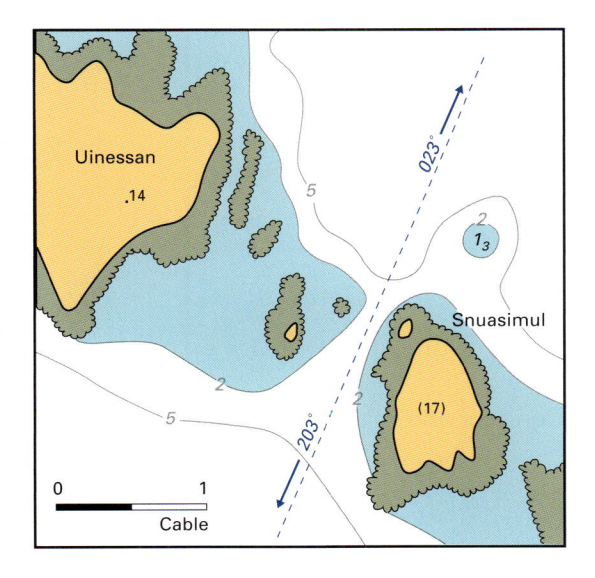

THE FISHERMAN'S PASSAGE

CCC Sailing Directions and Anchorages 21

Outer Hebrides

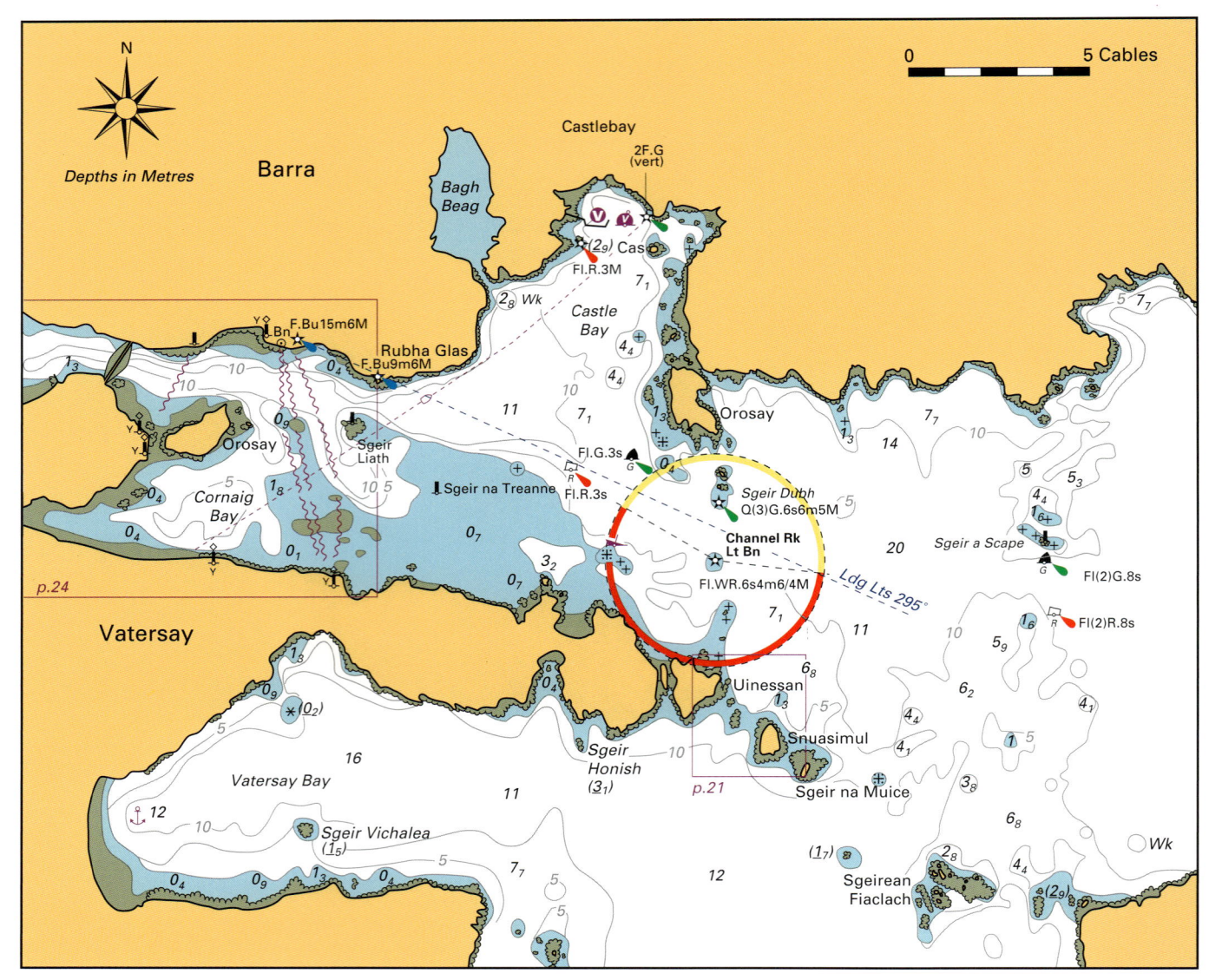

CASTLE BAY, BARRA & VATERSAY BAY

Admiralty Chart
2769
Admiralty Leisure Folio
5616. 13A, 21A, 21B
Imray Chart
C65
Ordnance Survey
31
Cruising Scotland
p.177

Castle Bay, Barra

Castlebay is the centre of the community on Barra and is a good base from which to explore Barra itself or the islands to the south. The bay is a popular anchorage and well-provided with pontoons and moorings. However, it is very exposed to the south and SW and if strong winds from this quarter are forecast it is recommended that shelter is sought in the lee of Vatersay in Cornaig Bay (see p.24).

Tides

Streams are probably insignificant on account of the new causeway

Constant –0110 Ullapool (–0530 Dover)

Height in metres

MHWS	MHWN	MTL	MLWN	MLWS
4·3	3·0	2·4	1·6	0·5

Dangers and marks

Heaval, the main hill on Barra, together with Muldoanich, helps to identify the approach.

Bo Vich Chuan, a drying rock, 1½ miles southeast of Barra, is marked by a south cardinal light buoy which serves as a landfall buoy.

A pair of lateral light buoys about 2 miles west of Bo Vich Chuan marks rocks on either side of the fairway. Sgeir a' Scape, which dries, close north of the green light buoy, has the stump of a thin cylindrical beacon (or thick post) on it with a radar reflector.

Sgeir Dubh light beacon, 1 mile west of the red light buoy, is a conspicuous cylindrical tower with a platform at the top, near the south end of a drying reef.

Channel Rock light beacon marks drying rocks on the south side of the channel south of Sgeir Dubh. Submerged and drying rocks west of Orosay, northwest of Sgeir Dubh, are marked by a stbd-hand light buoy. Submerged and drying rocks lie up to 1½ cables offshore north of the buoy.

A port-hand light buoy, 2 cables west of the stbd-hand light buoy above, marks the edge of shoals on the south side of Castle Bay.

22 CCC Sailing Directions and Anchorages

1. Barra Head to Eriskay

The whole of the south side of the Sound of Vatersay is shoal, mostly sand with occasional submerged rocks. A post, 2m in height, stands on Sgeir na Treanne, which dries 2m, ¼ mile SE of Sgeir Liath.

Leading beacons (white lattice towers 4 metres in height with orange triangular topmarks) stand on the south shore of Barra north of Sgeir Liath.

A light beacon stands on a drying reef on the west side of Castle Bay.

Directions

Pass south of Bo Vich Chuan light buoy, and steer to bring Sgeir Dubh light beacon in line with Sgeir Liath 283° and between the port and starboard hand buoys. Pass between Sgeir Dubh and Channel Rock beacons and then between the port and starboard hand buoys SW of Orosay. If making for the moorings or anchorage off the village, give the east shore of Castle Bay a good berth as rocks lie up to 3 cables off it.

If making for the causeway or Cornaig Bay (see p.24) note the submerged rocks south of the leading line established by the beacons on Rubha Ghlas.

Lights

Bo Vich Chuan Q(6)+LFl.15s4M
Port-hand Lt buoy Fl(2)R.8s
Stbd-hand Lt buoy Fl.G.8s
Sgeir Dubh Q(3)G.6s6m6/4M
Channel Rock Fl.WR.6s4m 5M
Stbd-hand Lt buoy Fl.G.3s
Port-hand Lt buoy Fl.R.3s
Ldg bns Rubha Glas 295° F.Bu.9m/15m6M
Reef W of Castle Fl.R.2s2m3M
Ferry terminal 2F.G(vert)3M

At night pass south of Bo Vich Chuan light buoy and steer with Sgeir Dubh light beacons in line 283°.

After passing north of the red light buoy, pass between Sgeir Dubh and Channel Rock beacons with the Rubha Glas leading lights in line bearing 295°.

Pass south of the stbd-hand light buoy and steer north to head between the reef light beacon and the ferry terminal. If making for the west end of the Sound keep on the leading line to avoid shoals and submerged rocks south of the fairway.

Anchorages

Castlebay A pontoon with finger berths has been established (2017) on the west shore of the bay and there are 8 visitors' moorings between the pontoon and the ferry pier. If no mooring is available, anchor clear of the moorings, roughly midway between them and the reef, dries 2·9 and lit Fl.R.2s, on the west side of the bay, keeping at least 1½ cables clear of the ferry pier. Particular care must be taken to dig in the anchor, as the bottom is soft mud over hard sand. There is a good landing slip behind the linkspan.

The pontoons, moorings and anchorage are wide open to winds from the south and SW and if strong winds from that quarter are forecast, better shelter must be found in Cornaig Bay or Vatersay Bay.

Bagh Beag on the west side of Castle Bay has a narrow entrance with a sill which dries about 1·5 metres at its east side. Keep to the east side of the channel to avoid a rock which dries 2·6 metres in mid-channel.

A rock which dries 1·7 metres lies near the head of the inlet. There is nothing to prevent a yacht anchoring in Bagh Beag but at the top of a neap tide there will not be enough height of tide over the rock sill entrance for most cruising yachts.

Supplies and services

Water and electricity at pontoons. General store, butcher and filling station with petrol, road and marine diesel pumps. PO bank, Tourist Office, restaurant and telephones, 2 hotels, craft shops and heritage centre with café in Castlebay. Co-op supermarket, leisure centre with showers, swimming pool and a library with internet access are near the pontoons at the west end of the town. Calor gas from Barra Island Stores, opposite Co-op. Car and bicycle hire on the island. Golf course.

Car ferry to Oban. Air service 6 days to Glasgow with Sunday flights introduced recently July & August only. Regular bus service round island 6 days including Vatersay and airport.

Castle Bay, Barra before the installation of the pontoons

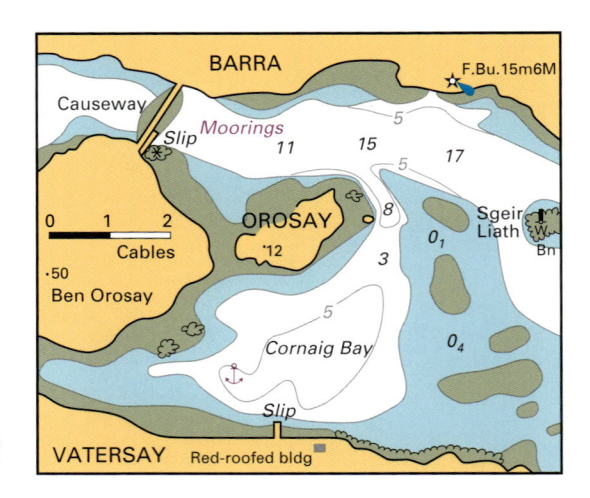

Outer Hebrides

VATERSAY SOUND & CORNAIG BAY

The causeway and slip, Vatersay. Diesel tank on the extreme left

Sound of Vatersay

A causeway connects Vatersay to Barra and prevents passage through the Sound of Vatersay out to the west. The eastern side of the causeway offers good shelter, as does Cornaig Bay to the south. Both provide a good alternative to the exposed visitors' moorings in Castlebay in fresh to strong southerly winds.

Directions

From the east maintain course 295° from Sgeir Dubh until about 2 or 3 cables from the front orange triangle of the leading lights on Rubha Glas and the channel north of Sgeir Liath with its white beacon has opened up, then proceed to the causeway.

Anchorage

Causeway anchorage The bay on the east side of the causeway is a convenient anchorage, but there are fishing boat moorings; anchor clear of the moorings off either shore. There is a slipway at the causeway, and yachts can go alongside after half flood where diesel (key fob needed) and water is available by hose.

Cornaig Bay Pass north of Sgeir Liath and head west towards the causeway. Do not turn south until the small islet to the east of Orosay bears due south. Identify a small building with a red roof on Vatersay with a prominent rock on the shoreline in front of it.

Head towards the islet keeping the red-roofed building over its centre. Aim to leave the islet close to starboard, about 20-25m off, then follow it round and, once it is abeam, keeping the west gable of the red-roofed building open of the rock on the shore and maintaining a distance of about 80m off the Orosay shore will bring you into the bay. Anchor about 75m west of a slipway which lies west of the red-roofed building.

With sufficient rise of tide the bay may be approached by the south of Sgeir Liath, passing north of a post ¼ mile off the Vatersay shore which marks Sgeir na Treinne.

Edward Mason

24   CCC Sailing Directions and Anchorages

1. Barra Head to Eriskay

The Vatersay causeway from the east

Kisimul Castle from the moorings

Outer Hebrides

Admiralty Chart
2769, 2770, 1796
Admiralty Leisure Folio
5616. 13A
Imray Chart
C65
Ordnance Survey
31
Cruising Scotland
p.177

Coastal passage from Castle Bay to Sound of Barra

The southeast side of Barra has many drying rocks and shoal patches and it should not be approached except with great care. Most vessels use the Outer passage but a course further inshore, as described below, has been taken at a suitable rise of tide, in quiet weather and good visibility and with no swell. It would be as well to plot the passage on the chart before attempting it.

However, if navigating in this area it is essential to use the latest edition (Sept 2013) of chart 2769. Not only are the locations of rocks more accurate than those given on older charts but often there is much less water over them than shown previously: eg. Bo na Clerich used to be shown with a LD of 1·9m. It is now given as 0·9m. If using a GPS plotter special care should be taken to check that the chart displayed is based on the latest edition.

Marks

Bo Vich Chuan, a drying rock (which on older charts has a LD of 0·7), 1½ miles southeast of Barra, is marked by a south cardinal light buoy.
Curachan, a rock 10 metres high 9 cables southeast of Bruernish, together with Red Rocks, a patch of submerged and awash rocks NNE of it, are marked by Curachan light buoy.

Outer passage

Because of the many inshore rocks, the safe course is to pass southeast of Bo Vich Chuan and steer to pass east of Curachan and Curachan light buoy. Ben Scrien on Eriskay, open east of Gighay 015°, leads east of Curachan and surrounding dangers.

Inshore passage

From Castle Bay pass south of Sgeir Dubh and a cable southeast of Rubha Charnain and Rubha Mor, keeping Sgeir Dubh beacon just in sight for the next ½ mile and then steer for Curachan until the reefs inshore of Curachan have been identified. Some of them appear to cover more than the figures on the chart indicate, so that a passage at the top of springs would be hazardous, although the clear passage between the reefs and Curachan is ½ mile wide.

From north to south pass a cable west of Curachan and a cable southeast of Sgeir Fiaclach Beag; steer to pass a cable southeast of Rubha Mor with Am Meall at the southeast point of Vatersay just open of Rubha Mor and, when Sgeir Dubh comes open of Barra, head towards it, keeping a cable offshore.

Anchorage

Brevig Bay If exploring the southeast coast of Barra, this bay offers an occasional anchorage with good holding in sand and gives shelter from SW veering to north. It is exposed to the east and in southerlies swell can enter the bay. Enter from the south using chart 2769.

Lights

Bo Vich Chuan Q(6)+LFl.15s4M
Curachan Lt buoy Q(3)10s
Eriskay Ldg Lts 285° both Oc.R.6s10m4M
Binch Rock Lt buoy Q(6)+LFl.15s

Brevig Bay from the southwest

1. Barra Head to Eriskay

Ardveenish and Bay Hirivagh, North Bay, Barra (p.28) from the east. Taken before the new harbour was built NE of Ardveenish

Sgeirislum anchorage (p.29) from the east

CCC Sailing Directions and Anchorages **27**

Outer Hebrides

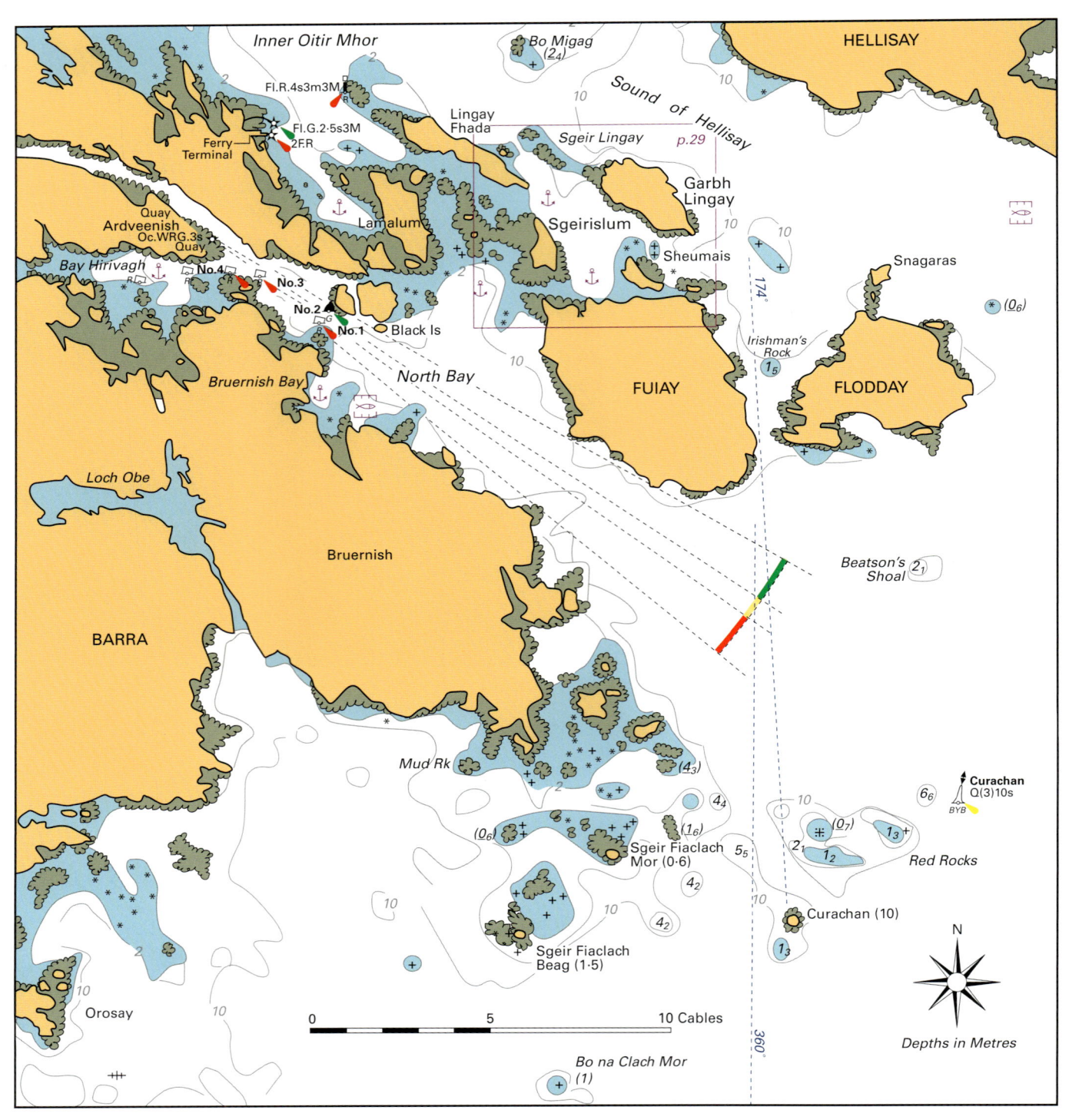

NORTH BAY, BARRA & SGEIRISLUM

Admiralty Chart
2770
Admiralty Leisure Folio
5616. 13A
Imray Chart
C65, C66
Ordnance Survey
31
Cruising Scotland
p.177

North Bay, Barra

An alternative to Castle Bay, especially in southerly or westerly winds, offering good shelter and good holding.

Tides

Constant −0110 Ullapool (−0530 Dover)

Height in metres

MHWS	MHWN	MTL	MLWN	MLWS
4·3	3·1	2·4	1·7	0·6

Dangers and marks

Curachan, **Red Rocks**, and **Curachan light buoy** are described on p.26.

Beatson's Shoal, 4 cables south of Flodday, has a depth of 2·3 metres.

A fish-processing factory stands at Ardveenish, the north point of Bay Hirivagh.

Directions

From the south pass east and north of Curachan light buoy (alternatively pass 1 cable west of Curachan if following the inshore route) heading for the east side of Fuiay 360° until the factory is open of the southwest side of the channel.

From the north, Beatson's Shoal is a hazard if a heavy sea is running and the tide is low.

CCC Sailing Directions and Anchorages

1. Barra Head to Eriskay

The approach to Ardveenish is marked by light buoys, as well as perches around the quay and slipway. No.1 port-hand buoy lies SW of Black Isles, and No.2 starboard-hand buoy west of Black Island. Nos.3 and 4 are port-hand buoys further west. Mid-channel leads safely into North Bay. A new fishing boat quay lies northeast of Ardveenish but yachts should use Bay Hirivagh, where fishing vessels also use the old quay. When this bay opens up, keep to the north side to avoid drying reefs off the south point and anchor as below.

Anchorage

Bay Hirivagh gives the best protection of all but the others are alternatives with less traffic and fewer moorings.

Bay Hirivagh Two unlit red buoys mark the safe manoeuvring limit for larger vessels. Anchor SW of the quay, not too far south of a line between the red buoys, and avoiding moorings. Keep clear of traffic to the quay which is accessible at all stages of tide. At the slipway there is 1 metre at the outer end at MLWS but beware of a rock sill below slipway. A tripping line is recommended.

Black Island Anchor in 10m in the bay east of Black Island but note the drying reefs extending a cable east of Black Island.

Bruernish Bay Off the west shore of the bay in 4m mud. Provides good shelter except from the east. Hold to the NW side of the bay to avoid the rocky patch (0·9m).

Supplies

Water and a public telephone are available at the quay, also diesel (large quantities only). Hotel (meals and internet café), mobile shop, post bus to Castlebay twice daily. Airport at Traigh Mor 2 miles north.

Lights

Curachan Lt buoy Q(3)10s
Ardveenish Oc.WRG.3s 6m 9-6M
Ardveenish quay 2F.G(vert)
No.1 buoy Fl(2)R.8s
No.2 buoy Fl.G.2s
No.3 buoy Fl.R.2s
No.4 buoy Fl(3)R.5s

Sgeirislum

This small area of water north of Fuiay and west of Garbh Lingay, described in the Admiralty Pilot as an inlet, is bounded by a number of islands and islets which give good shelter from most directions. It is likely to contain a number of fish cages.

Directions

Eastern channel; From the Sound of Hellisay keep initially in mid-channel to avoid a rock (dries 0·6m) 2 cables NE of Flodday then head for the north side of Garbh Lingay, turning south only when the east side of Fuiay is in line with Curachan to avoid a rock 2 cables NE of Fuiay. Pass east and south of Garbh Lingay. The passage between Garbh Lingay and Eilean Sheumais is wide but restricted by reefs extending over 100m north from Eilean Sheumais and an isolated rock (LD 1·3) 70m south of Lingay. Hold well towards the Lingay shore to avoid them.

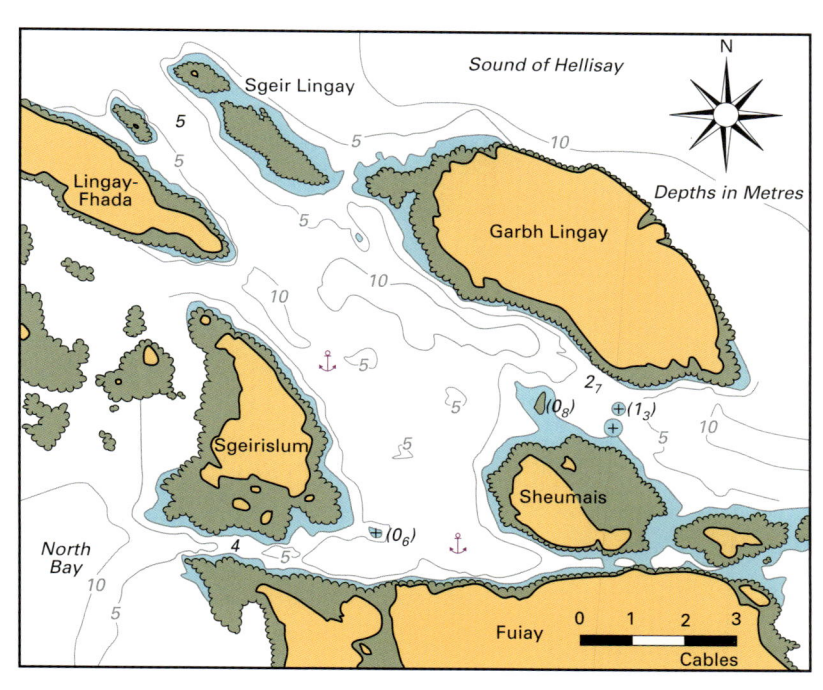

From the south enter between Fuiay and Flodday keeping to the Fuiay third of the channel to avoid Irishman's Rock (LD 1·5m) mid-way between Fuiay and Flodday. Keeping Curachan open of the east shore of Fuiay will clear the reefs extending NE of Fuiay before heading towards Garbh Lingay and following the passage described above.

Western channel; There is a narrow, 35m wide, passage between the Sgeirislum anchorage and North Bay with a least depth of 4m, which is used by local fishermen. Rocky shelves extend from both shores and in the approach from the east a rock, (LD 0·6), lying 150m southeast of Sgeirislum must be avoided.

Leaving the anchorage steer through the passage on a course of approximately 275° keeping midway between the small islet on the north side of the channel and Fuiay. Do not alter course until North Bay is wide open to avoid the large area of reefs lying west of Fuiay.

Northwestern channel; This leads to the Inner Oitir Mhor and has a least depth of 5m. Holding close to the SE point of Linghay-Fhada and the small islet off its northeastern side will avoid the extensive drying reef southeast of Sgeir Lingay.

The channels west of Garbh Linghay and south of Sheumais are not recommended.

Anchorage

Anchor where shown on the plan. Good holding in mud can be found but areas of rock are also present. A tripping line is advisable.

SGEIRISLUM ANCHORAGE

CCC Sailing Directions and Anchorages

Outer Hebrides

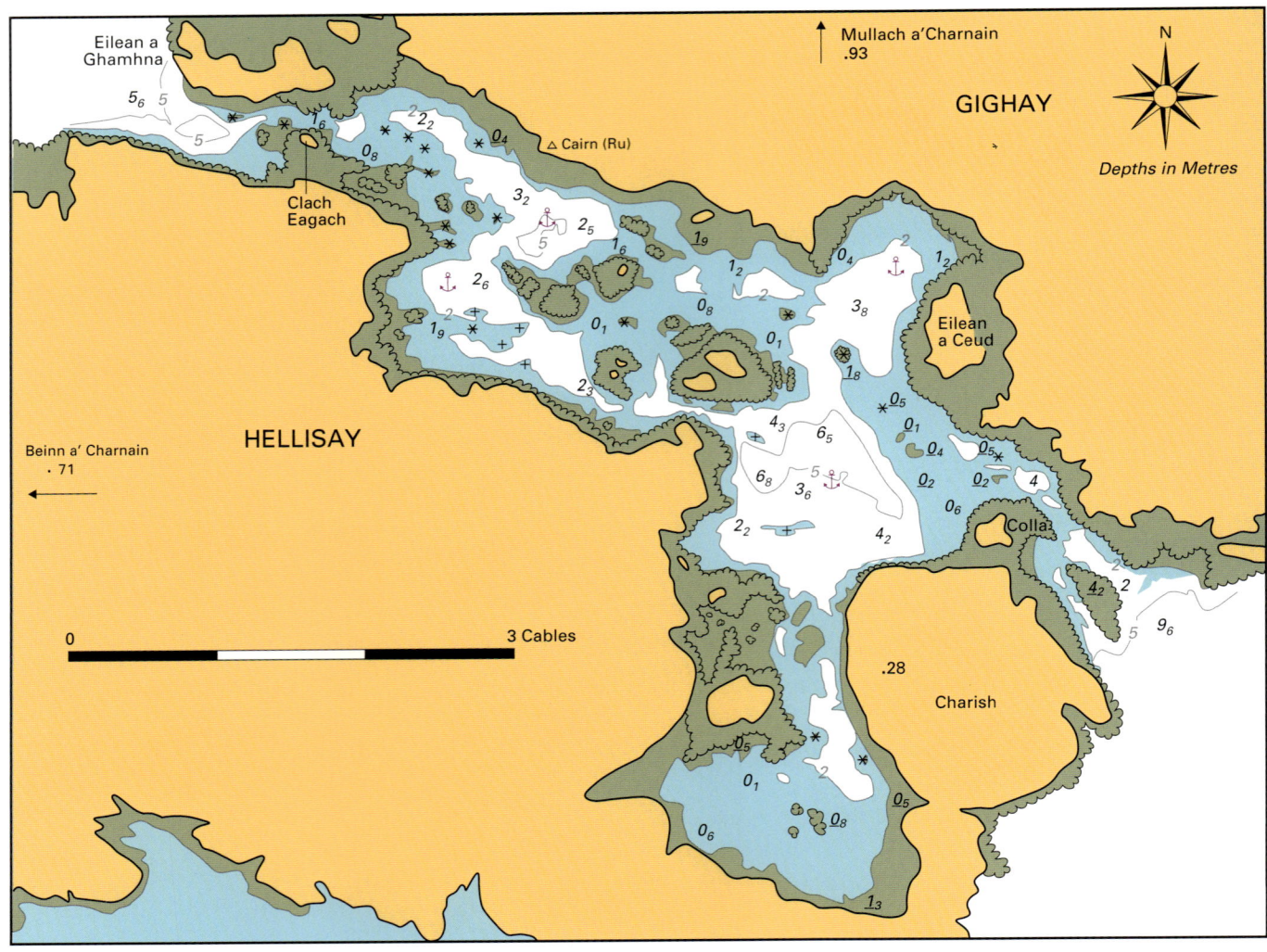

HELLISAY & GIGHAY

Hellisay and Gighay

Admiralty Chart
2770
Admiralty Leisure Folio
5616. 13A
Imray Chart
C66
Ordnance Survey
31
Cruising Scotland
p.178

About 9 miles from Castlebay, the sound between Hellisay and Gighay provides a challenge for the adventurous yacht skipper. This well sheltered anchorage can be reached from either the east or west side through narrow channels badly restricted by rocks.

Inside, the whole sound is littered with rocks but, if manoeuvring, these should be fairly easily seen in contrast to the sandy bottom. Entry should be considered only if no sea is running. Do not assume that all existing rocks are shown on the plan.

Tide

Const. –0057 Ullapool (–0517 Dover)

Height in metres

MHWS	MHWN	MTL	MLWN	MLWS
4·3	3·1	2·4	1·7	0·6

The flood sets into, and the ebb out of, both entrance channels at the same time. The current may reach 2 kn sp. during the first 2 hours of the flood and the ebb.

Directions

Southeast entrance; this is relatively straight, but drying rocks east and north of Colla must be avoided. A sandbank, NW of Colla, across the inner end of the passage is awash at chart datum. Further in, two detached drying rocks a cable and ½ cable west of Eilean a' Ceud cover at about ¼ flood. This entrance might best be used above half flood on a rising tide and only if there is no onshore sea.

In the approach to the narrows pass to the east side of the large rock (drying 4.2m) east of Charish and then maintain a course slightly east of mid-channel to pass clear of the rocks east of Colla. Follow round the north shore of Colla to enter the large pool NW of Charish.

Northwest entrance; This is best approached round the north of Gighay; keeping a cable off will clear all dangers. If approaching from the south careful chartwork is needed to pass through the 1½ cable wide channel between shallows (LD 1.4) extending 1½ cables west of Hellisay and Bull's Rock. Note also the 1·9m rock 2 cables NW of Hellisay.

The entrance is narrow, and seaweed covered rocks extend from both shores particularly where it narrows between Clach Eagach on the south shore and the east side of Eilean a' Ghamhna to the north. The navigable channel is very narrow with a least depth of about 1·5m and should be approached on a rising tide with a lookout at the bow.

30 CCC Sailing Directions and Anchorages

1. Barra Head to Eriskay

Steer initially for Clach Eagach, then northwest of it to follow, but not too close in, the Eilean a'Ghamhna shore. The heading when approaching the narrowest part should be approximately towards Mullach a'Charnain, the west side of the highest point on Gighay.

When past Eilean a'Ghamhna close the shore of Gighay to avoid rocks east of Clach Eagach before turning southeast to avoid a drying rock ½ cable west of a cairn (not easily seen) near the shore on Gighay. When past the cairn turn to head southwest, keeping ½ cable from the west side of the bay on Hellisay, to avoid drying rocks both inshore and further east.

Anchorages

Northwest of Eileen a Ceud under the cliffs of Gighay. This may be squally in northerly winds.

Northwest of Charish is probably the best place. Anchor in 7m wherever offers the best shelter.

Western anchorages Anchoring with restricted swinging room is possible in both pools at the western end of the sound, where indicated. A kedge over the stern might be useful in these anchorages to prevent swinging over rocks.

There is a relatively clear passage along the Hellisay shore south of the islets. A through passage on the north side is a matter of picking a way between rocks which, like the northwest entrance, is best done on a rising tide and with a lookout on the bow.

'Northern Whistler' slowly enters the Hellisay anchorage through the southeastern channel. The 4·2m drying rock beyond her very rarely covers

Hellisay and Gighay from the SE

Outer Hebrides

The northwest entrance from Gighay with Hellisay beyond

The southeast entrance from Gighay

1. Barra Head to Eriskay

Outer and Inner Oitir Mhor

A wide area of sheltered water, rarely more than 10m deep, fringed by the sweeping sands of Barra, the Oitir Mhor is an interesting place to spend some time exploring in settled weather, although on no account should a yacht attempt to enter the Sound of Fuday without local knowledge.

Whilst the east end of Outer Oitir Mhor is free of dangers, the west and south sides have many rocks including the extensive reefs near Greanamul and Bull's Rock. Though there is safe passage from Outer to Inner Oitir Mhor to the Sound of Hellisay, it should be piloted with care as there are many unmarked isolated rocks. The latest edition (August 2013) of Chart 2770 must be used as many of the soundings are less than those shown on older editions.

The buoys shown on the plan (p.34), which mark the route taken by the ferry between Eriskay and Barra, greatly assist navigation in this area.

If heading westwards from the west entrance to the anchorage between Hellisay and Gighay keep at least 2 cables north of a line between the entrance and Greanamul to avoid dangerous unmarked rocks east of Greanamul.

Anchorages

In settled weather there is a number of places where occasional anchorage might be found.

Cordale Beag at the south end of Fuday where there is a fresh water stream. Approach from the SE but note the rock in the middle of the bay.

Weavers Castle, 290° leads eastward of Binch Rock

Corran Ban (Fiaray) just open of Ru Hornish (Fuday) 277°

Views in the Sound of Barra (see overleaf) taken from a 19th century chart

Ferry terminal; Anchor in the bay west of Lamalum (see plan p.28), keeping clear of the ferry slip and the reef extending 1½ cables west of Lamalum. A red perch marking the reefs 2 cables NW of Linghay-Fhada marks the entrance to the bay.

The Sound of Barra from Scurrival

Charles Tait

CCC Sailing Directions and Anchorages 33

Outer Hebrides

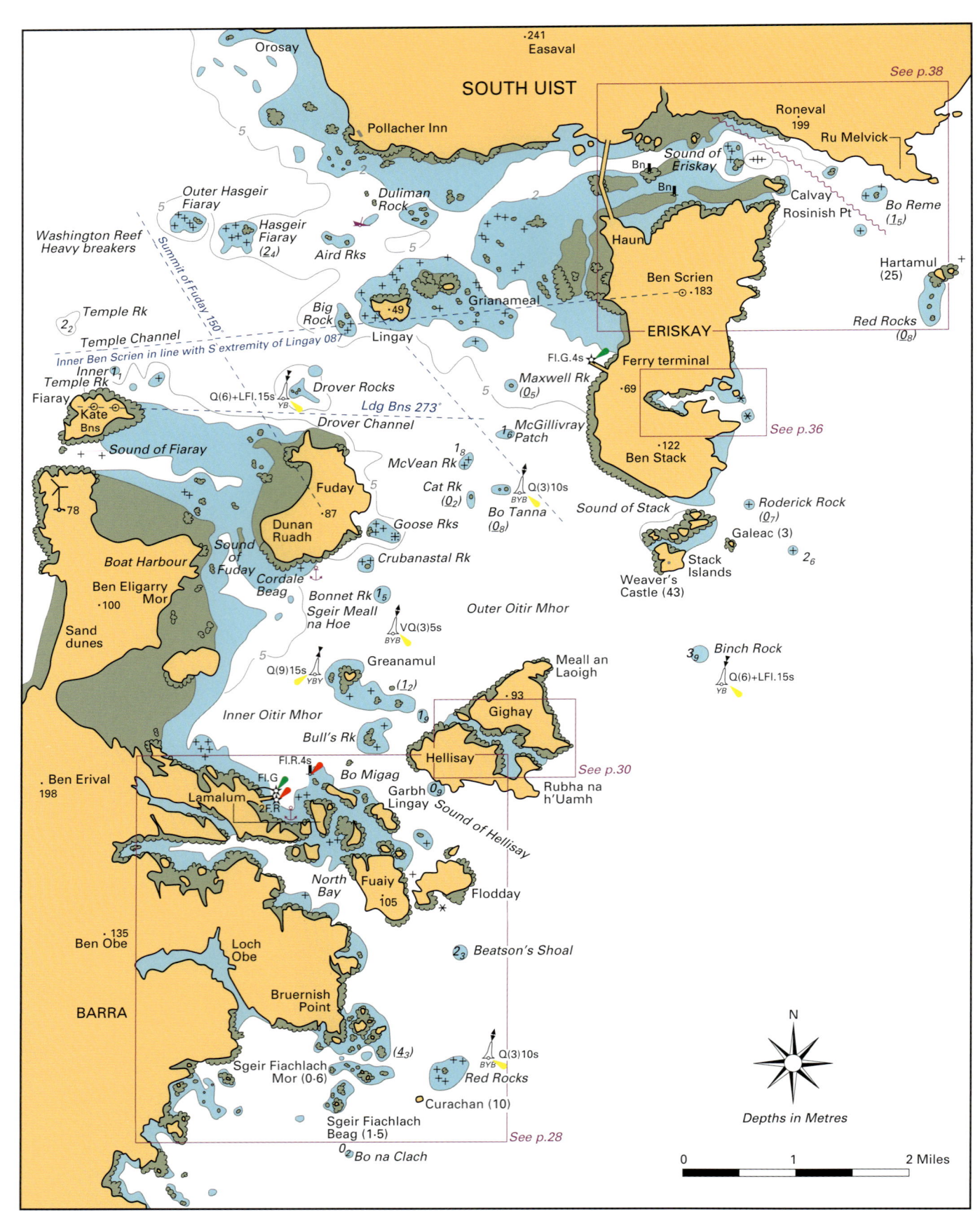

SOUND OF BARRA

1. Barra Head to Eriskay

Sound of Barra

The Sound of Barra is shallow with many isolated rocks and great care must be taken to identify the marks mentioned in the text. It should not be attempted in unfavourable sea conditions nor in poor or marginal visibility. Before making passage through for the first time the course should be plotted on the chart and all adjacent dangers noted. In variable visibility it would also be prudent to plot GPS waypoints in advance and keep an eye on the cross track error if visibility worsens. In good visibility transits should be watched at all times to avoid being set off course.

Chart 2770, of which the latest edition must be used, shows an elaborate sequence of courses for deeper draught vessels. The course described in these *Directions* is similar to these, but slightly simplified, and makes use of the buoys recently established for the ferry. However, other courses are possible as, for instance, by keeping ¼ mile from Fuday yachts can avoid the rocks further east. The drawback to this course is the overfalls which can occur northeast of Fuday with a southeast-going tide; that is, the in-going tide referred to below.

Tide

The incoming tidal streams run in from both the west and east ends of the Sound of Barra simultaneously. The out-going streams behave similarly leaving both ends simultaneously. These streams which are weak and variable meet and separate in Oitir Mhor and west of Eriskay.

In-going streams begin +0530 Ullapool (+0110 Dover).
Out-going streams begin –0045 Ullapool (–0505 Dover).

The strongest tidal flow in the Sound is experienced in the Drover Channel, north of Fuday. The NW-going stream sets towards Drover Rocks. The SE-going stream sets towards Fuday with overfalls extending for ½ mile eastwards.

Directions

Westward Passage; Coming from the Sea of the Hebrides the Binch Rock south cardinal is a useful landfall buoy. Enter the sound between Stack Islands and Gighay and identify the islands of Fuday and Lingay. Steer a course to leave the Bo Tanna east cardinal buoy to port and from a position close east of this buoy head for the left hand edge of Lingay.

Keep on this course for at least ¾ mile until the leading line of the white Kate beacons on Fiaray, bearing 273°, is acquired. (Note the SE going tidal set and overfalls mentioned above). Turn on to this course and proceed westwards through the Drover Channel leaving Drover Rocks south cardinal buoy to starboard and Fuday to port.

When Dunan Ruadh, the most westerly point on Fuday bears due south alter course to steer 330°, with the summit of Fuday bearing 150° astern. To avoid the Inner Temple Rock do not turn into Temple Channel (course 267°) until Ben Scrien is in line with the southern end of Lingay, bearing 087° astern (See below).

Pass through the Temple Channel and, if bound for the Monach Islands, keep on this course until well west of Fiaray before heading north, so as to clear the Washington reef and its associated breaking seas. Alternatively, if sea conditions are calm, the Temple Channel need not be used but maintain a course of 330° to pass inside the Washington Reef.

Eastward Passage; Approaching from the SW or west, the sound is not easily identified but a wind turbine at the north point of Barra is now a valuable landmark. When the sound is well open the sharp peak of Ben Scrien on Eriskay should be seen showing north of Fiaray. Approaching from the NW keep well clear of Washington Reef by keeping seaward of 7°30' until Benn Scrien, Eriskay, is in line with the south end of Lingay bearing 087° (See below)

Follow this course and proceed through the Temple Channel, north of Fiaray, leaving Temple Rock to port and Inner Temple Rock to starboard until the summit of Fuday bears 150°. Turn on to this course and approach Fuday until the beacons on Fiaray are in line. Turn east and follow course 095° through the Drover Channel, heading for Ben Stack on Eriskay.

When the east side of Lingay bears due north, alter course to starboard on to 132° aiming to pass 1 cable NE of Bo Tanna buoy. From close NE of this buoy, course can then be set for the Sea of the Hebrides or, if making for Outer Oitir Mhor, the Sgeir Meall na Hoe east cardinal buoy.

Alternatively if heading to the Outer Oitir Mhor, once through Drover Channel follow round the northeast side of Fuday at a distance off of about ¼ mile and steer for the highest point on Gighay. Keep on this course until south of Fuday when, if making for the Inner Oitir Mhor, course may be altered to pass close east of Sgeir Meall na Hoe and west of Grianamul cardinal buoys.

Lights

Binch Rock S Cardinal buoy Q(6)+LFl.15s
Bo Tanna E Cardinal buoy Q(3)10s
Drover Rocks S Cardinal buoy Q(6)+LFl.15s
Sgeir Meall na Hoe E Cardinal buoy VQ(3)5s
Grianamul W Cardinal buoy Q(9)15s

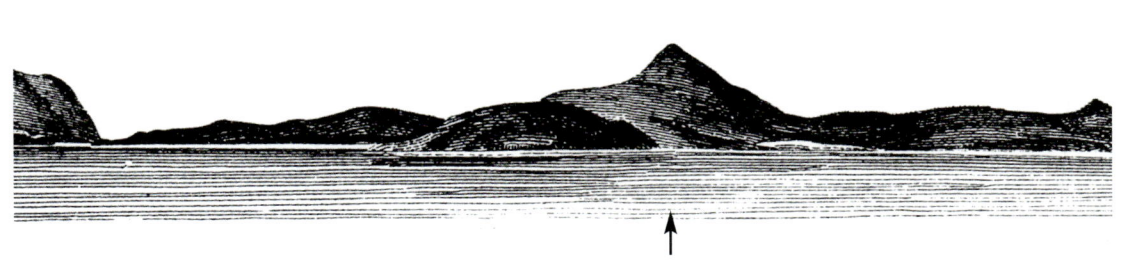

Admiralty Chart
1796, 2770
Admiralty Leisure Folio
5616. 13A
Imray Chart
C66
Ordnance Survey
31
Cruising Scotland
p.178

Ben Scrien on Eriskay over the south side of Lingay bearing 87°. This drawing, taken from a 19th-century chart, illustrates the key transit used in the Temple Channel described above. Drawings on the previous page illustrate other useful landmarks

CCC Sailing Directions and Anchorages

Outer Hebrides

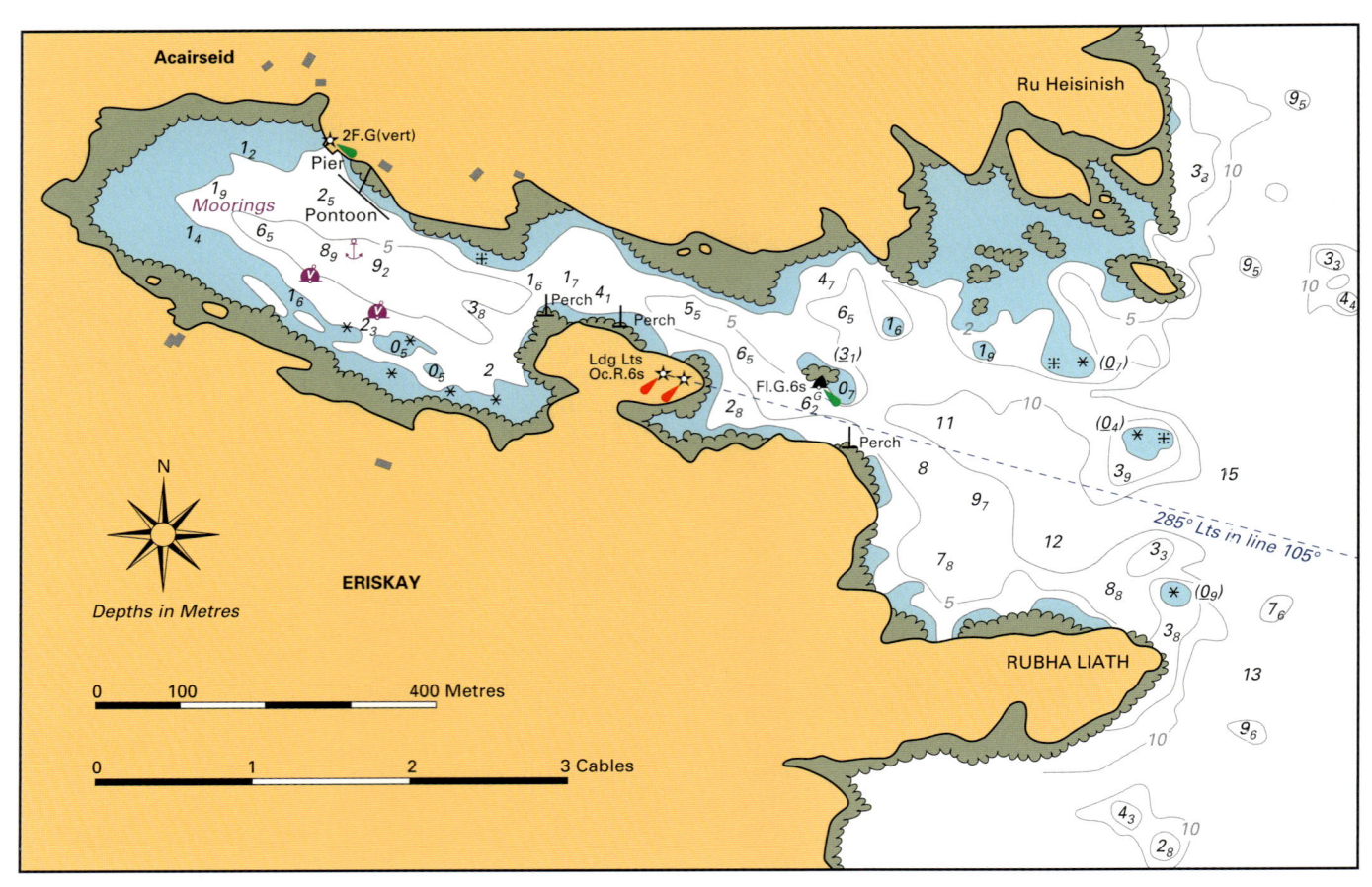

ACAIRSEID MHOR, ERISKAY

Admiralty Chart
2770
Admiralty Leisure Folio
5616. 13A, 13B
Imray Chart
C65
Ordnance Survey
31
Cruising Scotland
p.180

Acairseid Mhor, Eriskay

Nine miles from Lochboisdale, South Uist, Acairseid Mhor on the east side of Eriskay offers protection from all directions and is an outstanding natural harbour. It is also one of the few which is lit, making a night approach possible.

Tides

Constant –0032 Ullapool (–0442 Dover)

Height in metres

MHWS	MHWN	MTL	MLWN	MLWS
4·2	3·2	2·5	1·8	0·6

Directions

Approaching from the south keep mid-channel between Stack Islands and Galeac, a 3m high rock with a further rock (drying 0·6) 1½ cables NNW of it. Eilean Leathan, the most southerly of the islands, has Weaver's Castle (43m), a fairly conspicuous ruin, on its SW end. Maintain this mid-channel course 2 cables off the islands and Eriskay shore to leave Roderick Rock (drying 0·7m) 2 cables to starboard. Alternatively keeping a little over 1 mile off the Eriskay shore clears all dangers until Acairseid Mhor opens up.

When east of Rubha Liath there is a choice to be made to clear the drying rocks in the approach; either steer to pass 30m north of Rubha Liath, which is steep-to, to pass inside the drying rock (drying 0·9m) 60m to the north, or to keep well off until picking out the leading line, bearing 285°, on the transit beacons indicated on the plan. This latter course passes between two drying rocks. However, the beacons, white boards on steel columns, are not easily seen against the evening sun and the inshore course may be preferred.

Once west of the entrance rocks and heading for the inner anchorage, proceed mid-channel leaving the rock in the centre of the channel, (dries 3·1m) and marked by a starboard hand buoy Fl.G.6s, well to starboard. There is a rock ridge, with a least depth of 1·5m, north of mid-channel at the entrance to the anchorage (see plan). Three perches on the south shore mark rock ledges but they are not at the extremities. Pass 25-30m off all of them.

From the north, pass 2 cables NW of Hartamul (25m) and head towards Eriskay keeping Stack Islands open of Rubha Liath 210° until the leading beacons are in line 285° to avoid drying rocks on the north side of the entrance. If passing east and south of Hartamul keep at least ¾ mile off to avoid the Red Rocks (drying 0·3m) which extend up to 5 cables south of Hartamul.

Anchorage

Two visitors moorings have been laid on the south side of the harbour. Alternatively anchor as convenient clear of moorings and shoal water, but the bottom is soft mud and is reputed to be foul with old moorings.

1. Barra Head to Eriskay

There is a pontoon and yachts can also go alongside the old stone quay to take on diesel. Both are in frequent use by fishing boats and overnight or unattended berthing is not advised.

Lights
Leading lights **Oc.R.6s**
Starboard hand G buoy Fl.G.6s
Quay 2F.G(vert)

Supplies
Water by hose at the pontoon. Diesel at quay (key card needed, see p.11). Telephone. PO, pub. Stores and Calor gas from the shop at Haun (1M). Shower at ferry terminal. Causeway for vehicles links Eriskay with South Uist. Ferry service to Barra across the Sound of Barra.

The entrance channel to Acairseid Mhor from the east, taken before the pontoon was installed

The approach to Acairseid Mhor, Eriskay. The house in this photograph and above no longer has a red roof

CCC Sailing Directions and Anchorages 37

Outer Hebrides

SOUND OF ERISKAY

Eriskay Sound from the southwest

Sound of Eriskay

The Sound of Eriskay has been closed as a navigable channel by the causeway between Eriskay and South Uist. The sound has many reefs, sandbanks and shoal patches but can, with care and after half flood on a rising tide, be approached from the east. If a yacht can reach the pool off Haun she should be able to lie afloat at anchor in comfort in about 3m.

It would be dangerous to approach the causeway from the west without local knowledge.

Directions

The approach from the south is straightforward. From the north two detached drying rocks lie 1½ cables off the north shore between Hartamul and Calvay.

At Calvay a drying spit extends 1½ cables northwest towards Calvay Rock which covers 1 metre at HW springs (is awash at HW neaps), 3 cables from the island. If Calvay Rock cannot be seen, sound your way round the spit and steer west for Stag Rock beacon, about 1 mile distant and almost in line with the bridge in the middle of the causeway.

Identify Bank Rock beacon and keep it on the port bow. When it is abeam, turn to port and aim to pass Bank Rock beacon close on your starboard side, heading southeast, and then come round to southwest to head just north of the church. Keep a lookout for a reef extending from the southeast shore, as well as Haun Rock in the middle of the pool. Anchor between Haun Rock and the ferry slip.

Except for shoal-draught yachts, do not approach until Bank Rock is awash. This anchorage should not be attempted without chart 2770 (2013 Edition) but be aware that since the causeway was built, the charted depths may well be much less, especially in areas away from the main channel.

Supplies

See Acairseid Mhor (p.37) The walking distance to Haun is considerably less from here.

2. South Uist

Rubha Melvick to Loch Skipport
For a key plan of this stretch of coast see p.16.

South Uist has an east coast which is of rugged appearance with mountains, hills and vertical cliffs to the sea. The west side of South Uist is flat and inhabited. The steep rocky shores of the east side are penetrated by three sea lochs each in its own way providing anchorage. Loch Boisdale offers safe anchorage with facilities. Of the two remote lochs, Loch Eynort is wild and somewhat inaccessible except in favourable weather and tidal conditions, whilst Loch Skipport is easy of access and offers many well protected anchorages.

Tides
Off Loch Boisdale tidal streams run at up to 2 knots off salient points
The north-going stream begins +0520 Ullapool (+0100 Dover)
The south-going stream begins –0040 Ullapool (–0500 Dover)
At Rubha Melvick a tidal eddy, present only in the NE-going stream, causes a permanent set to the SW between Rubha Melvick and Rubha na h'Ordaig, extending almost a mile offshore.

Directions
Keeping 1 mile east of a line from Rubha na h'Ordaig south of the entrance to Loch Boisdale, to the headland at Usinish and the landfall safe water buoy at Loch Carnan, clears all dangers. Between Rubha Melvick and Rubha na h'Ordaig there are rocks extending about 4 cables off-shore.

North of Loch Boisdale, Stuley Island lying 1 mile south of the entrance to Loch Eynort has rocks extending 4 cables off its SE and east shores. The Broad Rocks extend 3 cables north of Stuley. South of Stuley Island lies Sgeir an Fheidh (3m) close inshore with a drying rock ½ cable offshore.

Further dangers are described in the approach to each of the principal anchorages.

Lights
Ushenish Lighthouse Fl.20s54m19M
Loch Carnan landfall buoy L.Fl.10s
Note: Ushenish refers to the light, Usinish is the point itself.

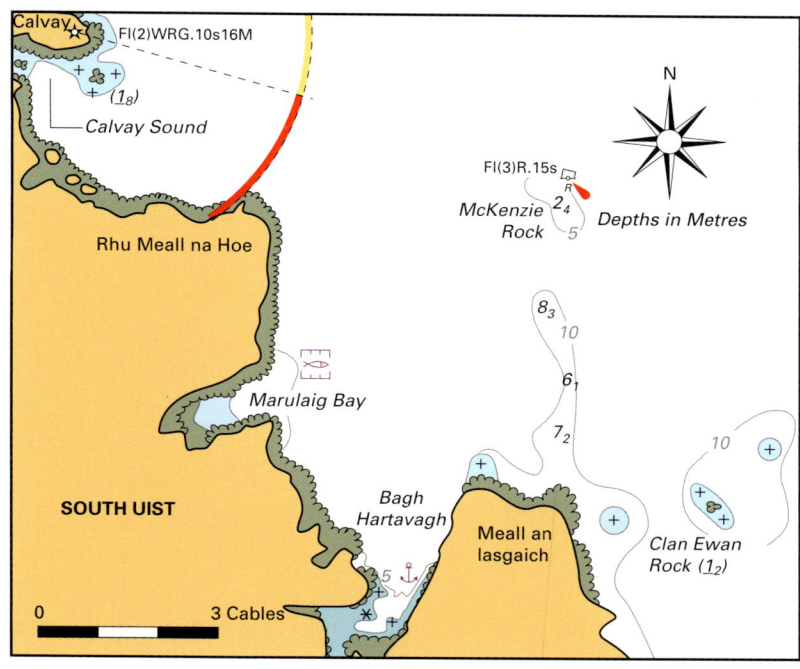

Anchorages
In addition to the anchorages described in the following pages, the two below offer good shelter from the prevailing wind whilst necessitating only a slight deviation from the direct route.

Bagh Hartavagh A small inlet, 1½ miles south of Loch Boisdale. Shoals and drying reefs extend 4 cables east of Meall an Isagaich, the point forming the east side of the inlet. Shoal patches also extend 4 cables north from Meall an Isagaich. Although these latter shoals have a least depth of 6m, they make the entrance to Bagh Hartavagh dangerous in bad weather and in these conditions it is best approached from McKenzie Rock buoy Fl(3)R.15s. Some shelter may be found up to 2 cables within the entrance. Anchor in 3m. Exposed to the NE.

Mol a' Tuadh (Shepherds' Bight) A good passage anchorage, sheltered from SE to NW, just north of Usinish Point. Although eclipsed by the better known anchorages in nearby Loch Skipport it is a useful alternative and offers a footpath to the headland and lighthouse. Use chart 2904 and anchor near the head of the bay.

BAGH HARTAVAGH

Admiralty Chart
1795, 2904, 2770, 2825
Admiralty Leisure Folio
5616. 13A, 11
Imray Chart
C66
Ordnance Survey
31, 22
Cruising Scotland
pp.181-183

For a key plan of South Uist and further description of its appearance, see pp.16,17)

CCC Sailing Directions and Anchorages 39

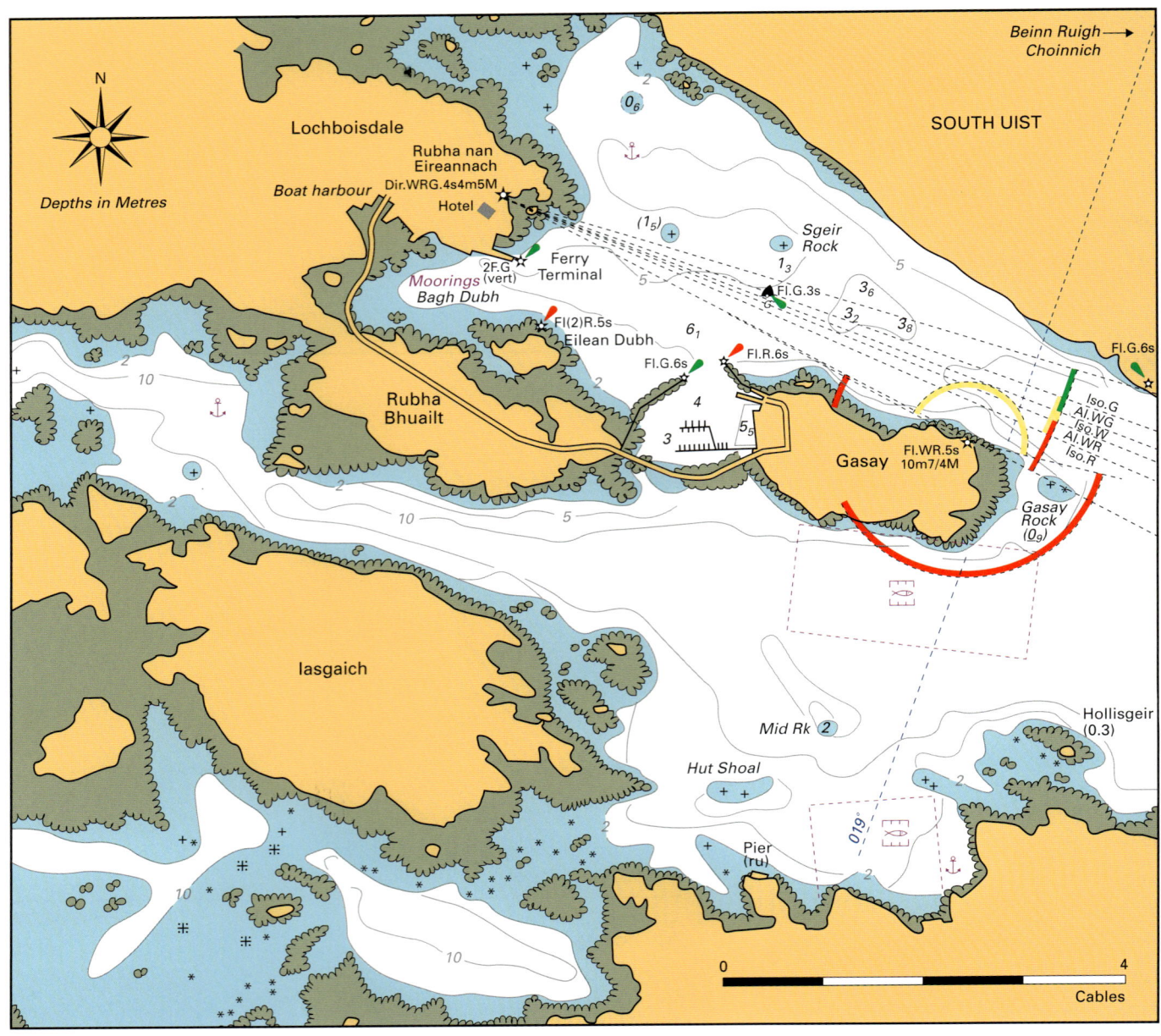

Outer Hebrides

LOCH BOISDALE

Loch Boisdale

Lochboisdale, one of the main centres of population on South Uist, is situated on the north side of Loch Boisdale about 21 miles north of Castlebay. The greater part of the loch westward of Lochboisdale consists of countless islands and reefs, most of which dry and little of it is navigable.

Admiralty Chart
2770
Admiralty Leisure Folio
5616. 13A, 22
Imray Chart
C66
Ordnance Survey
31
Cruising Scotland
p.181

Tides

Constant –0045 Ullapool (–0505 Dover)

Height in metres

MHWS	MHWN	MTL	MLWN	MLWS
4·3	3·0	2·4	1·6	0·5

In Loch Boisdale the in-going stream begins +0530 Ullapool (+0110 Dover). The out-going stream begins –0045 Ullapool (–0505 Dover)

Directions

It is important not to confuse Loch Eynort with Loch Boisdale, both having low skylines at their entrances. Approaching from the east, the south shore is comparatively flat near sea level at the entrance whilst the north side is much steeper with rugged rocky ravines rising from the entrance shore to the prominent cone shaped Beinn Ruigh Choinnich (272m).

From the north the approach is straightforward but from the south, to avoid rocks and shoal patches, it is best to keep at least 1 mile east of Rubha na h'Ordaig until Loch Boisdale opens up north of McKenzie Rock buoy. Turn west to pass north of this buoy and Calvay. If tacking beware of rocks extending 2 cables west of Calvay and one cable east of Gasay further in.

The approach is north of Gasay. Leave the Fl.G.3s buoy marking Sgeir Rock to starboard and open up the marina entrance before turning to port. If making for the anchorage note the 1·5m patch midway between the buoy and Rubha nan Eireannach.

40 CCC Sailing Directions and Anchorages

2. South Uist

Loch Boisdale Harbour

As well as being a ferry port, Loch Boisdale is used by other large vessels and the channel north of Gasay has been declared a restricted channel. Vessels over 20m LOA or 3m draught will broadcast their intentions on Ch.16 and all smaller vessels must give way them.

When 3 red lights are displayed on the marina breakwater vessels are prohibited from leaving the marina.

Anchorage and berthing

Marina A new harbour area and pontoon facility has been created north of a causeway linking Rubha Bhuailt and Gasay. Visitors' berths with water and electricity. Diesel in limited quantities by can.

Bagh Dubh Although there are fewer moorings here now there is still the possibilty of fouling old mooring tackle and the holding in the centre of the bay is reported as being poor.

East of Rubha nan Eireannach The previous visitors' moorings have been taken up and this area is now available for anchoring. Anchor in 5m, well clear of the 1·5m patch.

West of Rubha Bhuailt Approach from the south of Gasay and then head to pass between Rubha Bhuailt and Iasgaich. Do not alter course north into the bay until clear of extensive reefs off the SW corner of Rubha Bhuailt. At LW note the submerged rock NW of Iasgaich. This is a quieter anchorage than Bagh Dubh but, again, holding has been found to be poor (see Antares chart).

South Loch Boisdale Submerged and drying rocks lie up to a cable off the south shore west of Hollisgeir, an extensive reef, part of which is just above water. The east end of Gasay under the peak of Beinn Ruigh Choinnich 019° astern leads close west of these rocks.

A ruined pier lies 3 cables WSW of Hollisgeir, with drying rocks close northwest of it. Hut Shoal lies ¾ cable north, and Mid Rock 1½ cables NNE, of the jetty. Anchor where indicated in the larger bay to the east of the jetty, clear of a small fish cage.

Lights

McKenzie Rock Lt buoy Fl(3)R.15s
Calvay Island Lt bn Fl(2)WRG.10s16m7-4M, showing red over McKenzie Rock, and a narrow green sector towards submerged rocks at the north side of the entrance
Gasay Lt bn Fl.WR.5s10m7/4M shows red over Gasay Rock
Lt bn on N shore, ENE of Gasay Fl.G.6s3m3M
Sgeir Rock Lt buoy Fl.G.3s
Directional Light (295°) DirWRG.4s4m5M
Ferry terminal linkspan 2F.G(vert)
Eilean Dubh Fl(2)R.5s

At night, approach in the white sector of Calvay light beacon, and in the white sector of the Directional light (292.5°), passing south of the Fl.G.3s light buoy, then head towards the lights at the pier.

Supplies and services

At Lochboisdale: At marina (☏ 01878 700830): Water, diesel by can, toilets and showers. Hotel, shops, PO. Tourist information Centre with shower facilities, Bank. Water at pier. Car hire. Car ferry to Mallaig. Bus to Benbecula Airport. Golf course.

The new marina at Loch Boisdale

Edward Mason

CCC Sailing Directions and Anchorages

Outer Hebrides

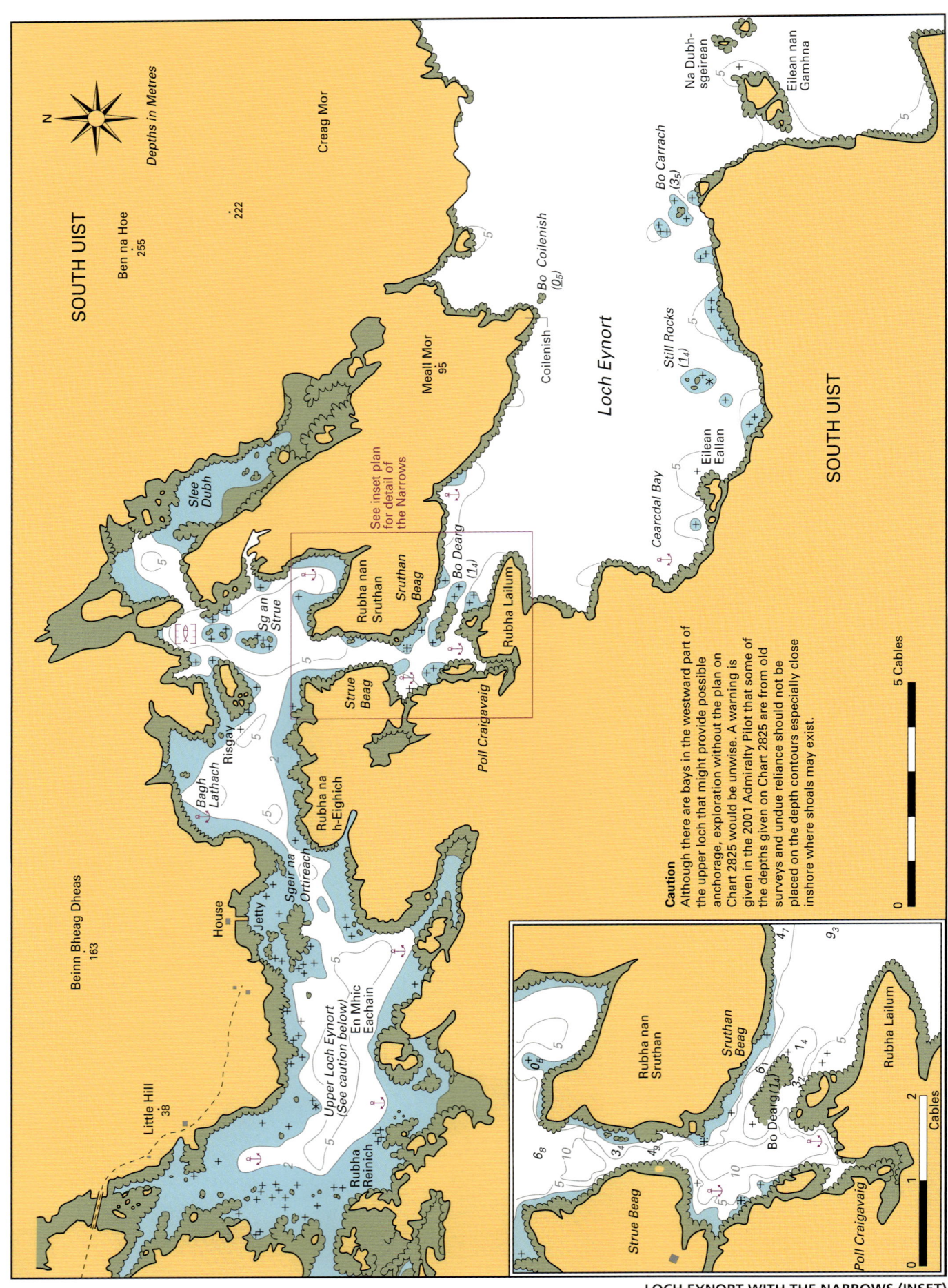

Caution
Although there are bays in the westward part of the upper loch that might provide possible anchorage, exploration without the plan on Chart 2825 would be unwise. A warning is given in the 2001 Admiralty Pilot that some of the depths given on Chart 2825 are from old surveys and undue reliance should not be placed on the depth contours especially close inshore where shoals may exist.

LOCH EYNORT WITH THE NARROWS (INSET)

2. South Uist

Loch Eynort

Loch Eynort offers views of barren slopes in wild isolation. The upper loch is difficult and at times even dangerous to enter. The outer loch is not protected from easterly winds. If awaiting the tide for entry to Upper Loch Eynort there are anchorages in the Outer Loch in Caercdal Bay and in a bay on the north shore.

Tide

Constant –0035 Ullapool (–0455 Dover)
Height in metres

MHWS	MHWN	MTL	MLWN	MLWS
4·3	3·0	2·4	1·6	0·5

At the entrance to Loch Eynort:
In-going stream begins +0545 Ullapool (+0125 Dover).
Out-going stream begins –0035 Ullapool (–0455 Dover).

Nowhere in the outer part of Loch Eynort do streams gain any perceptible strength except at Sruthan Beag, the narrow channel leading to Upper Loch Eynort. (For details see below.)

Directions

Although Loch Eynort, like Loch Boisdale, has a low skyline in the vicinity of its entrance the latter's shores are steep-to particularly on the north side. Loch Eynort's skyline is low at the entrance to the upper loch.

From the south give Glas-eilean Mor and Dubh-sgeir Mhor, both islets 2 cables east of Stuley, a fair berth to avoid a drying rock off their north shores. Once clear of Cleit a'Ghlinn-mhoir and Na Dubh-sgeirean, both islets on the south side of the entrance, head for Meall Mor whose slopes end in distinctive vertically indented cliffs and mark the entrance to the upper loch. If tacking, beware of Bogha Coilenish (dries 0·5m) ½ cable off the north shore and Bogha Carrach (dries 3·5m) and the Still Rocks (drying 1·4m) ½ and 1 cable respectively off the south shore. Once clear of these hazards, head for the anchorages or, if tide and conditions are suitable, make the passage into the upper loch.

From the north head to pass midway between Bogha Coilenish (dries 0·5m), ½ cable off the north shore and Bogha Carrach (dries 3·5m) ½ cable off the south shore. Once clear of Still Rocks (drying 1·4m) on the south shore, head for the anchorages with due regard to the tide and weather conditions.

Anchorages in the Outer Loch

Caercdal Bay is an occasional anchorage in the SW corner of the outer loch about 1 cable west of Eilean Eallan off the burn. If closer to the island beware of the submerged rocks off its west end. Exposed to the east.

Bay east of Sruthan Beag Occasional anchorage on the north shore in 4m out of the tide. Good holding but exposed to the SE.

Upper Loch Eynort

The entrance channel, Sruthan Beag, is difficult and could be dangerous unless care is taken to ensure that tidal conditions are favourable. The 1894 Admiralty Pilot gives LW as the best time for entering the upper loch and just before HW for leaving to return to the outer loch.

Tide

In-going stream begins –0605 Ullapool (+0200 Dover)
Out-going stream begins –0010 Ullapool (–0430 Dover)

The spring rate in both directions is reported to be between 5 and 7 knots. There are overfalls in the channel and eddies at either end. During the out-going stream the flow runs strongly across Bo Dearg until it uncovers. In the upper loch tidal flows are weak.

Directions

As will be seen from the plan, the Sruthan Beag channel is extremely narrow and encumbered with rocks the largest being Bo Dearg (dries about 1·4m), a large flat seaweed-covered rock. To pass through the narrows on the north side of Bo Dearg follow the north shore between 40-50m off the rock face until clear of Bo Dearg then, soon after the inner leg of the channel leading northwards begins to open, head west to clear an awash rock lying about ¼ cable west of the SE side of the entrance. Once the inner channel is fully open, head north into it maintaining a mid-channel course until the Upper Loch is reached.

Alternatively instead of making for the Upper Loch turn south when well clear of Bo Dearg to enter Poll Craigavaig where, out of the main tidal flow, the inner half of Sruthan Beag may be observed before completing the passage.

On the outward passage beware of the above-mentioned awash rock at the SE end of the inner channel and guard against being swept towards Bo Dearg if it is covered.

Anchorages

Poll Craigavaig in the SE corner, west of the first narrows, provides anchorage in moderate depths. Alternatively the NW corner, southwest of the entrance to Strue Beag, provides anchorage in 4-5m.

Upper Loch Eynort the first bay east of the inner narrows has a rock at the centre of its entrance. Pass north and east of this rock. Well sheltered anchorage in 4 to 7m in shingle. Do not be tempted to proceed north when leaving the narrows as this is an area strewn with rocks. Moving westwards from the narrows to Bagh Lathach, which provides anchorage in 3 to 5m, avoid the reefs and rocks extending up to 1 cable SW off Risgay.

See the Caution on the plan opposite for anchorage and exploration of the westward part of the Upper Loch.

Admiralty Chart
1795, 2825
Admiralty Leisure Folio
5616. 11, 23A
Imray Chart
C66
Ordnance Survey
22
Cruising Scotland
p.181

CCC Sailing Directions and Anchorages   43

Outer Hebrides

Loch Eynort, entrance to the upper loch from SE

Loch Eynort, the east end of the upper loch from the west

44 CCC Sailing Directions and Anchorages

2. South Uist

HIDDEN HARBOUR

Hidden Harbour
(Acarsaid Fhalach)

A very occasional anchorage, suitable for small boats only, about ¾ mile south of Ornish Island which lies in the mouth of Loch Skipport. The plan is part of an old chart with soundings in fathoms. Note that the current chart shows several submerged rocks NE of the entrance.

The inlet is difficult to discern from seaward and care must be taken to identify the entrance before making an approach. Rubha Rossel, south of Hidden Harbour is a prominent rounded hillock darker in colour than the surrounding landscape.

Note Rubha Rossel is shown as Russel Pt. on the plan, and En Cireach as Ciaray I.

Directions

Approaching from the south identify Rubha Rossel and steer midway between it and En Cireach, keeping the eastern extremity of Ornish Island open east of the eastern extremity of En Cireach 350°.

Approaching from the north steer for Rubha Rossel keeping a minimum of 2 cables offshore to avoid foul ground to the north of Bo na Sgeir Liath, with Ornish Island open east of En Cireach astern 350°, as above.

Midway between En Cireach and Rubha Rossel look for a break in the coastline with a small shingle beach in the northwest corner of the main entrance. Bo na Sgeir Liath covers about half tide, and is usually identifiable; keeping slightly to the north of this rock while heading for the shingle beach will take you into the main entrance. The shingle beach has been found difficult to identify at LW, being hidden behind a skerry.

There is plenty of water close in to the south shore of the main entrance. Just before the shingle beach, the channel turns southwards and narrows. At the first turn keep mid-channel with a tendency towards the north shore, to avoid a drying rock in the entrance to the small inlet to port. There are rings on the shore and a sternline will be needed. Depths within the anchorage itself are uncertain and, if intending to stay for any length of time, check carefully that there will be sufficient water at all heights of tide.

Hidden Harbour from the south east. Best entered on a rising tide and just before Bo na Sgeir Liath, lower right, covers

CCC Sailing Directions and Anchorages 45

Outer Hebrides

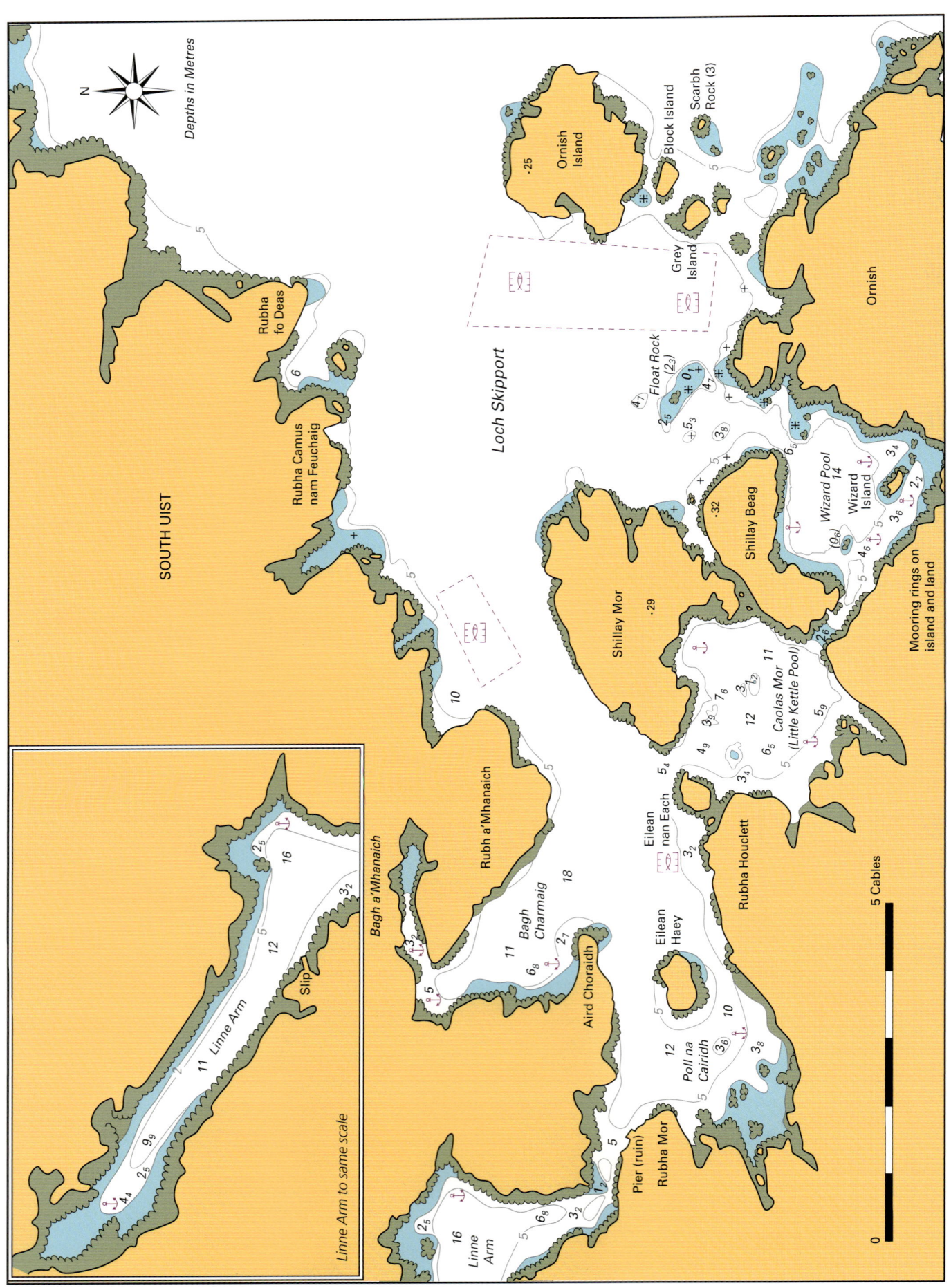

Depths in Metres

N

SOUTH UIST

Rubha fo Deas

Rubha Camus nam Feuchaig

Loch Skipport

Ornish Island

Block Island

Scarbh Rock (3)

Grey Island

Ornish

Float Rock (2₁)

Shillay Mor

Shillay Beag

Wizard Pool 14

Wizard Island

Mooring rings on island and land

Caolas Mor (Little Kettle Pool)

Rubh a'Mhanaich

Bagh a'Mhanaich

Bagh Charmaig

Aird Choraidh

Eilean nan Each

Eilean Haey

Rubha Houclett

Poll na Cairidh

Pier (ruin)

Rubha Mor

Linne Arm

Linne Arm to same scale

Linne Arm

Slip

5 Cables

LOCH SKIPPORT

46   CCC Sailing Directions and Anchorages

2. South Uist

Loch Skipport

A popular, well sheltered and easily entered loch in spectacular surroundings under the slopes of Hecla, which can send down some awesome gusts in fresh SW or SE winds. It offers a choice of several excellent anchorages.

Tides
Constant –0052 Ullapool (–0602 Dover)

Height in metres

MHWS	MHWN	MTL	MLWN	MLWS
4·6	3·3	2·5	1·7	0·5

Tidal streams are slight except in narrow channels, including the entrance to Linne Arm. The in-going stream begins +0545 Ullapool (+0125 Dover). The out-going stream begins –0035 Ullapool (–0455 Dover)

Directions
From the south, keeping a mile offshore clears all dangers and keep even further off the headland at Usinish in wind against tide conditions. The entrance to Loch Skipport is about 2 miles north of Ushenish Lighthouse, which together with Hecla make excellent landmarks if crossing the Sea of the Hebrides.

To enter do not use the false entrance south of Ornish island but pass to the north. Once within the loch the approaches to the anchorages are free of danger except for Float Rock (dries 2·3m) at the north entrance to Wizard Pool. In general the shores can be closely approached. However, fish cages can be found in several locations and must be guarded against at night time as they are frequently moved and not always in the charted positions.

From the NE or east, as the land to the north and west of Loch Skipport is low-lying, locate the Benmore Mountains and Ushenish Lighthouse and proceed as from the south.

Anchorages
Wizard Pool Float Rock, between Shillay Mor and Ornish, dries 2·3 metres, and fish cages lie east of the rock. To avoid Float Rock steer towards Shillay Mor until within a cable of that island. Pass the east end of Shillay Beag to the west of mid-channel to avoid drying rocks off Ornish and then pass closer to Wizard Island to avoid a drying rock east of the south end of Shillay Beag.

Anchor anywhere around the sides of the pool. Very soft holding south of Wizard Island but generally good elsewhere. Water may be had from a burn south of Wizard Island. If anticipating fresh to strong SW or SE winds with their violent gusts, more shelter could be had by anchoring as close as possible to the south shore west of Wizard Isle. In addition a line ashore might add to peace of mind. A slop is experienced in this anchorage when the wind is north or NE.

It is possible to pass from Wizard Pool into Caolas Mor (Little Kettle Pool) south of Shillay Beag. Keep towards the south side of the channel where the least depth is 2·6m.

Caolas Mor (Little Kettle Pool) Approaching from west of Shillay Mor the entrance is straightforward. Note the two groups of submerged rocks shown on plan. Anchor in suitable depth. Wizard Pool is less subject to gusts in fresh to strong winds from the southerly quarter. For passage between the two pools see above.

Poll na Cairidh (photo p.48) in the southwest corner of the loch has drying rocks more than a cable from the shore but they are easily avoided by keeping outwith the 5 metre line; this bay has been found to provide excellent shelter in a southerly gale.

Linne Arm When entering the narrows west of the pier of Rubha Mor keep closer to the south shore to avoid a 1·3m patch off the north shore. Anchor anywhere in suitable depth but note rocks dry up to ½ cable offshore in some parts of the arm. The bottom in Linne Arm is stony and the holding may not be good; anchor chain will be noisy in unsettled weather.

Bagh Charmaig (McCormack Bay) on the north side of the loch is reasonably clean but the holding is poor in soft mud. Anchor at the head of bay in 5m, or in 3m just within Bagh a'Mhanaich (Mannoch Arm) which shoals further in.

Admiralty Chart
2825, 2904
Admiralty Leisure Folio
5616. 11, 23B
Imray Chart
C66
Ordnance Survey
22
Cruising Scotland
p.183

Wizard Pool, Loch Skipport. Wizard Island is beyond the anchored yacht

Martin Lawrence

CCC Sailing Directions and Anchorages

Outer Hebrides

Poll na Cairidh, Loch Skipport, from the west

Caolas Luirsay from the ENE

48 CCC Sailing Directions and Anchorages

2. South Uist

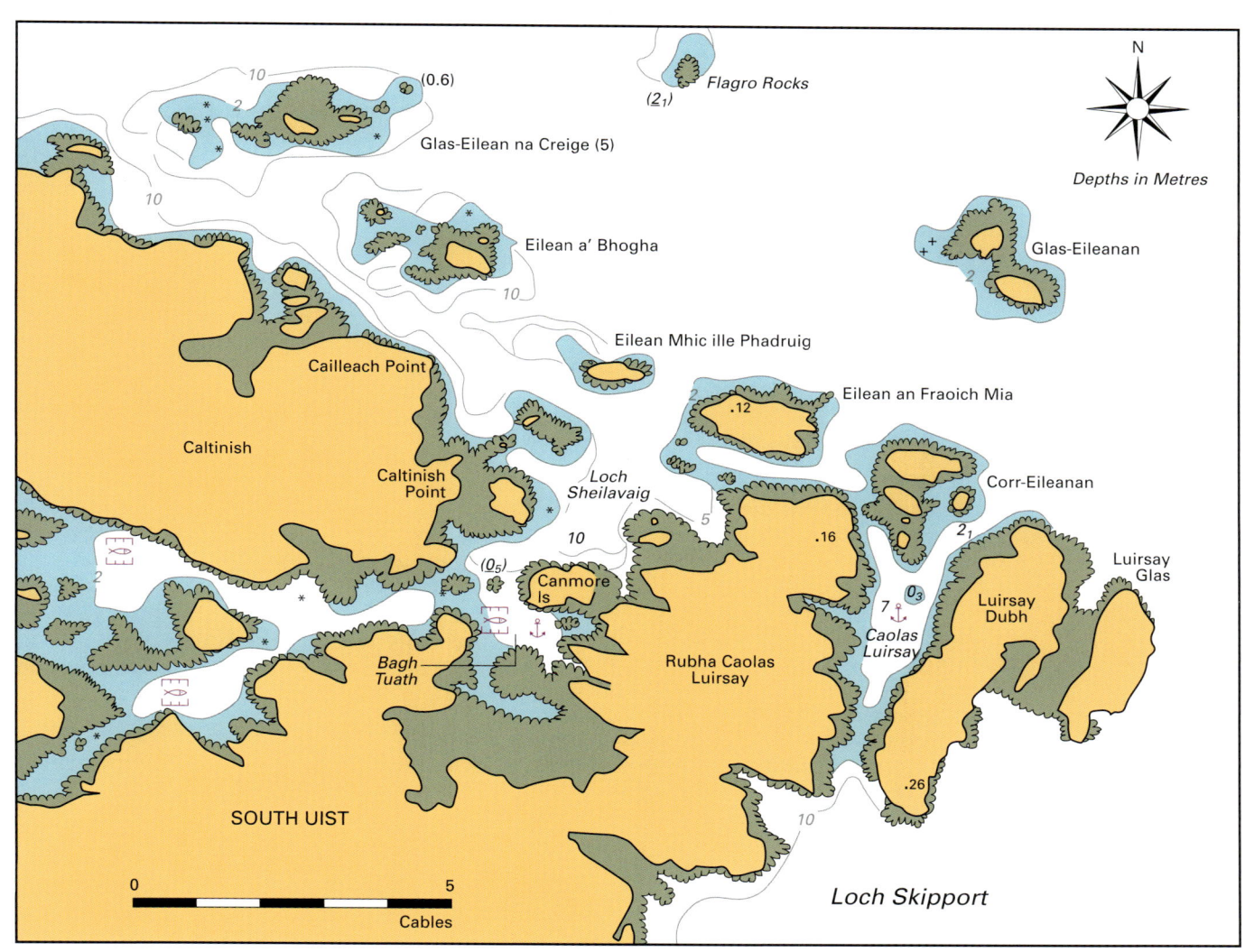

CAOLAS LUIRSAY & LOCH SHEILAVAIG

Loch Skipport to Loch Carnan

From Luirsay Glas to Loch Carnan, a distance of about 3 miles, a large number of islets, reefs, rocks and channels extend from the NE coast of South Uist as much as a mile into Bagh nam Faoileann. Chart 2904 is essential when approaching the anchorages on this short length of coast.

If heading further north, passing east of the Loch Carnan landfall buoy and keeping Luirsay Glas well open east of Wiay clears all dangers.

Tides
The tidal streams are weak and nowhere exceed 1·5 knots. See also *Loch Carnan*

Marks
Loch Carnan Power Station, a long low, twin chimney building visible from north of Luirsay Dubh is conspicuous
Loch Carnan Landfall RW pillar buoy LFl.10s

Anchorages
Caolas Luirsay At the north side of the entrance to Loch Skipport, this is a narrow channel between Luirsay Dubh and the South Uist shore. Neither the south or NE entrances would be easy in waves of any significant size as they are narrow with a depth of only 2·1m in the NE channel and less in the south. Note a submerged rock 0·3m towards the north end of the pool. Not recommended except in settled weather. Anchor in 7m mud.

Loch Sheilavaig ½ mile west of Caolas Luirsay, is a rather featureless loch with several fish cages, but it is full of rocks and provides an interesting challenge.

The entrance, between Eilean Mhic ille Phadruig and Eilean an Fraoich Mia, is most easily found by taking a bearing astern on Glas-Eileanan (062°). Pass about 50 metres west of Canmore Island, named on Chart 2904 as En a' Chinnbhaoraigh, so as to pass east of a drying rock ½ cable from the island as well as a shallow rocky patch which extends almost to the west shore of the narrows, and anchor south of Canmore Island in 4m mud. Beware of the reef in the east half of this bay.

Outer Hebrides

Admiralty Chart
2825, 2904
Admiralty Leisure Folio
5616. 11, 23C
Imray Chart
C66
Ordnance Survey
22
Cruising Scotland
p.185

Loch Carnan

Loch Carnan, about 5 miles from Loch Skipport, is the northernmost anchorage on South Uist before South Ford, an impenetrable barrier for all but the smallest craft. The power station for the Uists with its oil terminal stands here and the loch has a buoyed and lit approach. A few yachts are kept on moorings there.

Tide

Constant –0020 Ullapool (–0440 Dover) at springs;
–0110 Ullapool (–0530 Dover) at neaps

Height in metres

MHWS	MHWN	MTL	MLWN	MLWS
4·5	3·2	2·6	1·9	0·7

The in-going stream begins +0535 Ullapool (+0115 Dover)
The out-going stream begins –0025 Ullapool (–0445 Dover)

Approach

Using the buoyed channel
From the south keep on a northerly course until 1 mile past the Luirsay Islands, leaving Glas Eileanan to port.

From the north keep 2 cables off Dubh Sgeir a' Tuath and Dubh Sgeir a' Deas, each 1 metre high and lying 2 cables from the southeast shore of Wiay, to avoid drying and submerged rocks to seaward of them.

The landfall buoy provides useful confirmation of one's position. Identify Outer No.1 buoy lying north of Grey Island Rocks, pass north of it and pass the subsequent buoys on the appropriate hand.

Passage south of Gasay
It is essential to identify each island correctly to avoid various hazards. The key to this passage is the most southerly islet on the north side of the passage, 3 metres in height and well separated from the other islets south of Gasay.

The main hazards are a rock which dries 0·6 metre a cable northeast of Glas-eilean na Creige and a submerged rock at a depth of 1·2 metres, a cable southwest of the 3-metre islet.

Pass south of Glas-Eileanan (see plan p.49) and ¼ mile outside the string of islands along the south shore heading towards Gasay, to pass between Flagro Rocks, ½ mile WNW of Glas-Eileanan, and drying reefs north of Glas-eilean na Creige. Steer for the 3-metre islet (see plan below) and pass south of it, and from there towards the oil wharf.

Anchorage

Anchor 2 cables NW of the quay avoiding shoal water and a reef extending 1 cable south from Direy, the southern extremity of which may be marked with a perch, or alternatively in 8m in suitable depth clear of moorings. The inner section of the loch is studded with reefs. Anchorage space usually available in 4-5m east of the quay but note the 0·9m patch shown on the plan NE of the power station.

Supplies

None except for water at quays. Supermarket 4 miles. Restaurant 1 mile.

Lights

Landfall buoy LFl.10s
Channel buoys and Leading Lights as plan below.

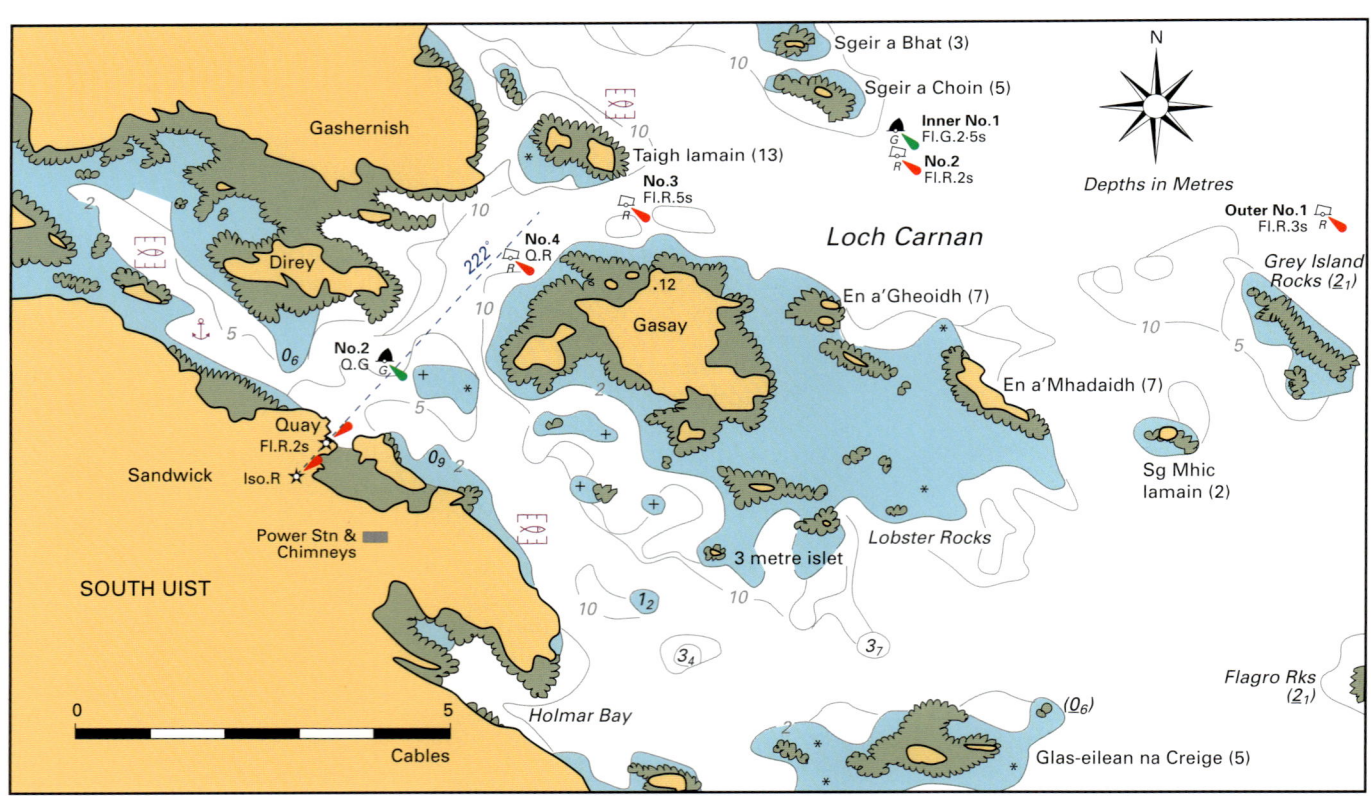

LOCH CARNAN

50 CCC Sailing Directions and Anchorages

2. South Uist

Loch Carnan from the west

Loch Carnan from the ESE. The rock lower left of centre is the drying rock WNW of the '3-metre islet'

CCC Sailing Directions and Anchorages 51

3. Benbecula

Admiralty Chart
2904
Admiralty Leisure Folio
5616. 11
Imray Chart
C66
Ordnance Survey
22
Cruising Scotland
p.185

Peter's Port to Flodday Sound

For a key plan of this stretch of coast see p.16.

The coastline between South Uist and North Uist is occupied mainly by the Island of Benbecula. This is a much indented shore with many islands such as Wiay, Ronay, Floddaymore, Floddaybeg and lochs such as Loch a'Laip, Loch Keiravagh, Loch Uiskevagh and innumerable islets, reefs, rocks and narrow channels extending east from Benbecula.

Passage

Between Hecla (604m), South Uist and Eaval (345m) on North Uist the coast outline is low lying and lacks dominant features. Keeping a mile off shore from Luirsay Glas, Loch Skipport, along this coast easily clears all hazards. The coast should not be approached in poor visibility or in easterly winds which are fresh to strong as many of the entrances are difficult or even dangerous. In such conditions it is far better to head for Loch Skipport, South Uist or Loch Maddy, North Uist and explore this fascinating coast in settled conditions and in good visibility. The distance from Loch Skipport to Loch Maddy is about 18 miles.

Tides

Offshore the tidal streams run as follows:-
N-going stream begins +0520 Ullapool (+0100 Dover)
S-going stream begins –0040 Ullapool (–0500 Dover)

Inshore the tidal streams run as follows:-
Between South Uist and Benbecula at South Ford:
In-going stream begins +0535 Ullapool (+0115 Dover).
Out-going stream begins –0025 Ullapool (–0445 Dover).

Loch Uiskevagh:
In-going stream begins +0550 Ullapool (+0130 Dover)
Out-going stream begins –0020 Ullapool (–0440 Dover)

Between Benbecula and North Uist at North Ford:
In-going stream begins +0535 Ullapool (+0115 Dover)
Out-going stream begins –0025 Ullapool (–0445 Dover)

Marks

All the following require good visibility for correct identification:

Dominant features which can be seen from afar (from S to N): Hecla (604m) at NE end of South Uist; Eaval (345m) at SE end of North Uist.

Features of some distinction not obviously seen (from S to N): Usinish Point on NE end of South Uist; Ben Tarbert (166m) near head of Loch Skipport; The summit of Wiay, Beinn a'Tuath (100m) a smooth gently rounded outline; Rueval (123m), Benbecula, low outline and Stiaraval (52m) very low outline; Beinn Rodagrich (97m), South end of Ronay; Beinn an t-Sagairt (113m); Ronaybeg (72m), North end of Ronay.

Islets to help identify entrances (from S to N)
Greanamul Deas (10m) for Loch a'Laip, Loch Keiravagh and Loch Meanervagh. This islet has a green rounded shape.

Greanamul (16m) for identification of Loch Uiskevagh, Caolas Wiay Beag to the west, and the approaches to Kallin from the south.

Dangers

Dangers less than a mile off shore for entrances (from S to N)
- An Dubh-sgeir a Deas (1m) and Du'Sgeir a'Tuath (1m) both at SE coast of Wiay
- Bo Greanamul, with associated tidal rip, 3½ cables SE of Greanamul Deas (10m)
- Morrison's Rock lies ½ mile south of Ronay and 4 cables ENE of Maragay Mor
- Ritchie Rock lies 4 cables SE of Ronay and 7½ cables ENE of Rubha na Rodagrich.
- The reefs and rocks 1½ cables off Eileen an Fheidh and close to the E side of Ronay

Admiralty Pilot Bearings to clear the above dangers (from S to N)

Bo Greanamul:– Luirsay Glas bearing 193° and well open east of Wiay leads east of Bo Greanamul

Morrison's Rock:– The summit of Wiay bearing 200° and open east of Greanamul leads east of Morrison's Rock.

Approaching anchorages at Kallin – Steer for Rubha na Rodagrich, Ronay on a bearing of not more than 313° until clear of Morrison's Rock. Rueval, Benbecula bearing 268° and open north of Maragay Beag also leads north of this rock.

Ritchie Rock:– Rueval (123m) Benbecula bearing 263° and open south of Rubha na Rodagrich leads south, and Madadh Mor, North Uist bearing 013° and open east of Floddaymore, leads east of both Ritchie Rock and Morrison Rock.

Eilean an Fheidh reefs and rocks, Ronay:– The east extremity of Floddaymore bearing 013° leads east of these dangers.

3. Benbecula

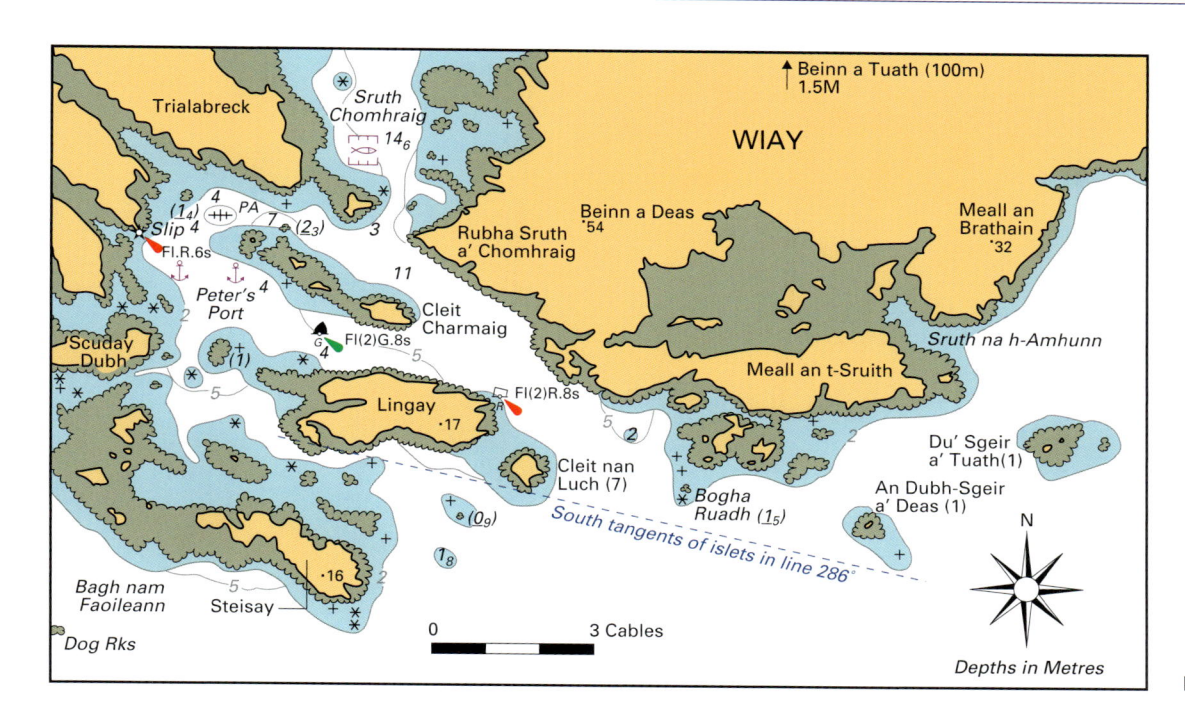

PETER'S PORT

Peter's Port

The remote and isolated quay was built at Peter's Port earlier last century because the mainland authorities were unable to agree whether to build a new quay to serve communities further north or further south; so they built it in the middle of nowhere. A modern slip has been added and it now serves local fishermen and fish farms.

Tides
Constant –0040 Ullapool (–0500 Dover)

Height in metres

MHWS	MHWN	MTL	MLWN	MLWS
4·6	3·3	2·5	1·7	0·5

Directions
From the south, make for Beinn a'Tuath (100m), the summit of Wiay. When crossing the entrance to Bagh nam Faoileann, alter course for Beinn a Deas (54m) on SW Wiay. The entrance is between Bogha Ruadh (dries 1·5m) and an islet to the west, Cleit nan Luch (7m). A shallow patch extends ½ cable south of Bogha Ruadh. Enter closer to Cleit nan Luch leaving it to port.

From the north, keeping ½ mile off the SE coast of Wiay clears both Du Sgeir a'Tuath (1m) and An Dubh-sgeir a Deas (1m) and their off-lying rocks. Heading for the south end of Steisay till the entrance opens, clears Bogha Ruadh (dries 1·5m) and the shallow patch ½ cable south of it. Enter between Bogha Ruadh and Cleit nan Luch, an islet 3 cables to the west keeping closer to the islet.

The channel into the anchorage, between Lingay and Cleit Charmaig, is buoyed. Passing north of Cleit Charmaig is to be avoided due to the drying rocks and the tidal stream, also the presence of a wreck (see below).

Anchorage
Anchor as convenient, SE of the slip, but keeping the approach to the slip clear, as it is used by fishing boats. The wreck lies close southeast of the rock which dries 1·4 metres about a cable ENE of the slip; on older charts the wreck is shown further SE and it would be unwise to pass west and north of the rocks west of Cleit Charmaig, even if the wreck is uncovered, without careful investigation or use of GPS and the Antares chart.

A reef lies parallel with the south face of the slip and 15 metres from it. The slip is marked at its outer end by a light beacon.

Lights
Port-hand buoy Fl(2)R.8s
Stbd-hand buoy Fl(2)G.8s
Bn at slip Fl.R.6s2M

Peter's Port from the SSE. The fish farm service vessel is heading out through the channel north of Cleit Charmaig towards the pens in Sruth Chomraig; not recommended without local knowledge or the Antares chart

Martin Lawrence

CCC Sailing Directions and Anchorages 53

Outer Hebrides

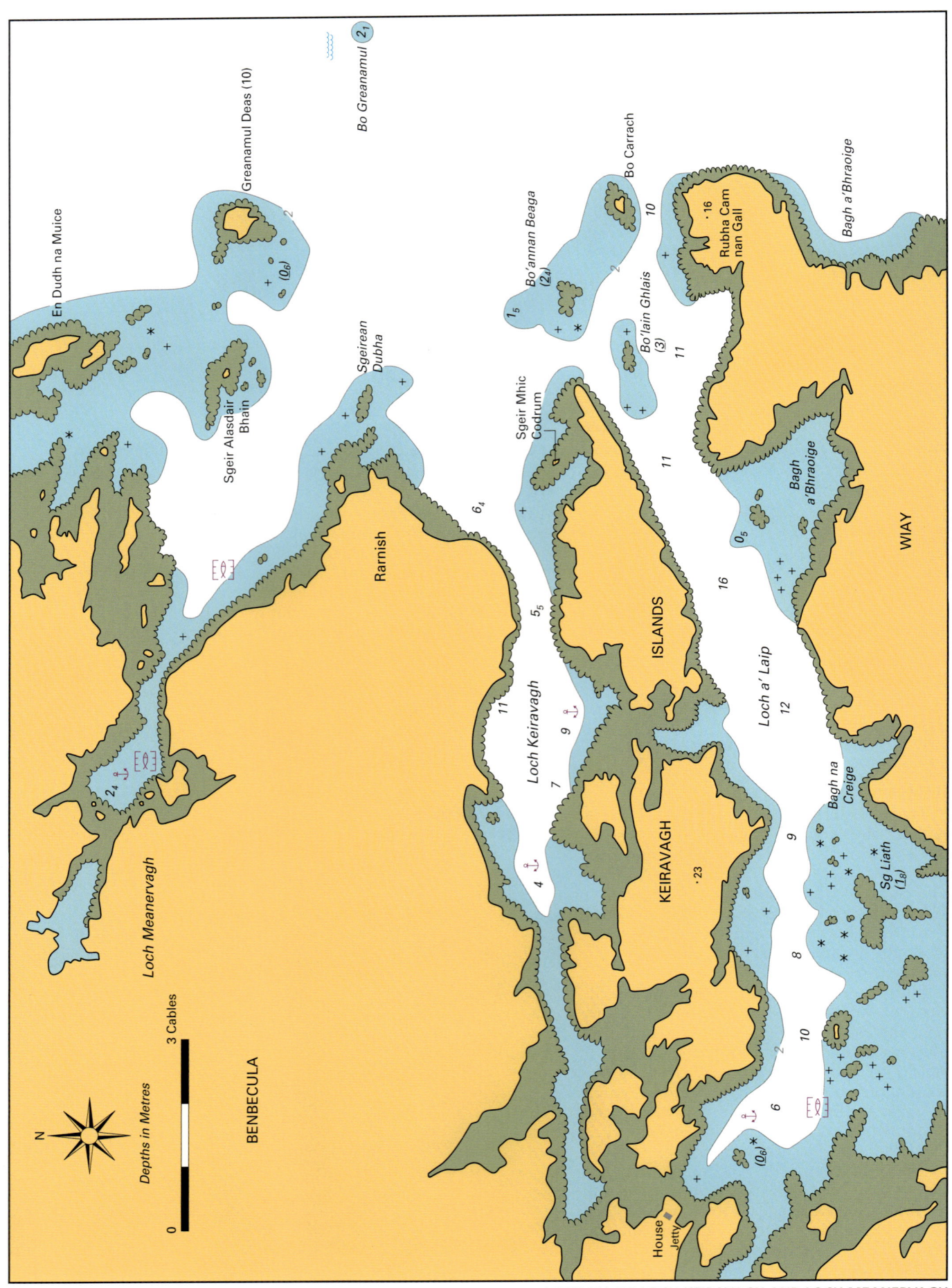

LOCH A' LAIP, LOCH KEIRAVAGH AND LOCH MEANERVAGH

3. Benbecula

Loch a'Laip & Loch Keiravagh

The Keiravagh Islands lie close north of Wiay. Anchorage in adjacent lochs can be found both south and north of the Keiravagh Islands, in Loch a'Laip and Loch Keiravagh respectively.

The lochs share the same approach directions and the entrances have many rocks and islets to negotiate. Greanamul Deas (10m), a rounded green islet, is north of the entrances and helps to identify them.

Tides
Const. −0040 Ullapool (−0500 Dover)
Height in metres

MHWS	MHWN	ML	MLWN	MLWS
4·6	3·3	2·5	1·7	0·5

Approach
From the south, keeping more than ½ mile off the south of Wiay clears both An Dubh-sgeir an Deas (1m) and Du'Sgeir a'Tuath (1 m) and off-lying rocks. Once past these, the east side of Wiay can be approached to a cable off until Rubha Cam nan Gall, its NE extremity, is reached. Note Greanamul Deas (10m) and Bo Greanamul (see below).

From the north, identify, but do not yet approach, Greanamul Deas (10m) in line with Beinn a'Tuath (100m), the summit of Wiay bearing 208°. Note the dangerous submerged rock, Bo Greanamul with 2·1m over it and associated tide rips, 3½ cables east of Greanamul Deas (10m). To pass to the east of this, keep Luirsay Glas, the north entrance to Loch Skipport, well open of Wiay bearing 193°. Open up either loch for the final approach.

Alternatively, keep 2 cables east of Maaey Glas and approach the loch entrances close east of Greanamul Deas leaving Bo Greanamul to seaward.

Loch a'Laip
Best entered before half tide when Bo'annan Beaga and Bo'lain Ghlais will show.

Directions
Pass south of Bo Carrach and keep mid-channel. Tend to the north shore only when entering the inner loch north of Sgeir Liath with its extensive outcrops of rocks. *Note*: On leaving Loch a'Laip it helps to identify Greanamul Deas (10m), the rounded green islet, correctly before proceeding north along this rocky and much indented coast.

Anchorage
Near head of loch in 3m mud in NW arm avoiding rock (dries 0·6m). Southeast of this rock in deeper water allows more swinging room, with the south point of the entrance just closed behind Keiravagh Island. Excellent shelter but some tidal stream.

Bagh na Creige is a possibility for shoal draught vessels but it is poorly charted and should be entered with great care.

Martin Lawrence

Loch Keiravagh
A more straightforward loch but, as with Loch a' Laip, it is best entered before half tide when Bo'annan Beaga will show.

Directions
From the south pass well clear east then NE of Bo Carrach to avoid Bo'annan Beaga (dries 2·4m) and the shallow patch of rock (1·5m) extending NW for 1 cable.

Coming from the north keep closer to Greanamul Deas (10m) to avoid Bo Greanamul but avoid rocks extending a cable south of Greanamul Deas. The outer entrance to Loch Keiravagh, 1½ cables wide, is between submerged rocks extending 1 cable north from Bo'annan Beaga and 1 cable south from Sgeirean Dubha.

When 1 cable southeast of Greanamul Deas steering a course of about 235° towards Sgeir Mhic Codrum, an above water rock in the reef strewn north bay of the eastmost island, will lead safely between the submerged rocks. When due north of Sgeir Mhic Codrum tend to the Rarnish shore to avoid the reef and rock extending NW more than 1 cable from Sgeir Mhic Codrum.

Anchorage
Once through the first narrows, anchor in 10m at the opening between the islands. Better protection may be had anchoring in 4m just east of the second narrows.

Loch Meanervagh
Although this loch offers good shelter from all directions it is restricted by fish farming equipment and is shallow with a narrow entrance. It is only suitable for small shoal draught boats and not recommended for yachts.

Loch a' Laip from the ENE. Keiravagh Islands on the right of the picture

Admiralty Chart
2904
Admiralty Leisure Folio
5616. 11
Imray Chart
C66
Ordnance Survey
22
Cruising Scotland
p.185

CCC Sailing Directions and Anchorages 55

Outer Hebrides

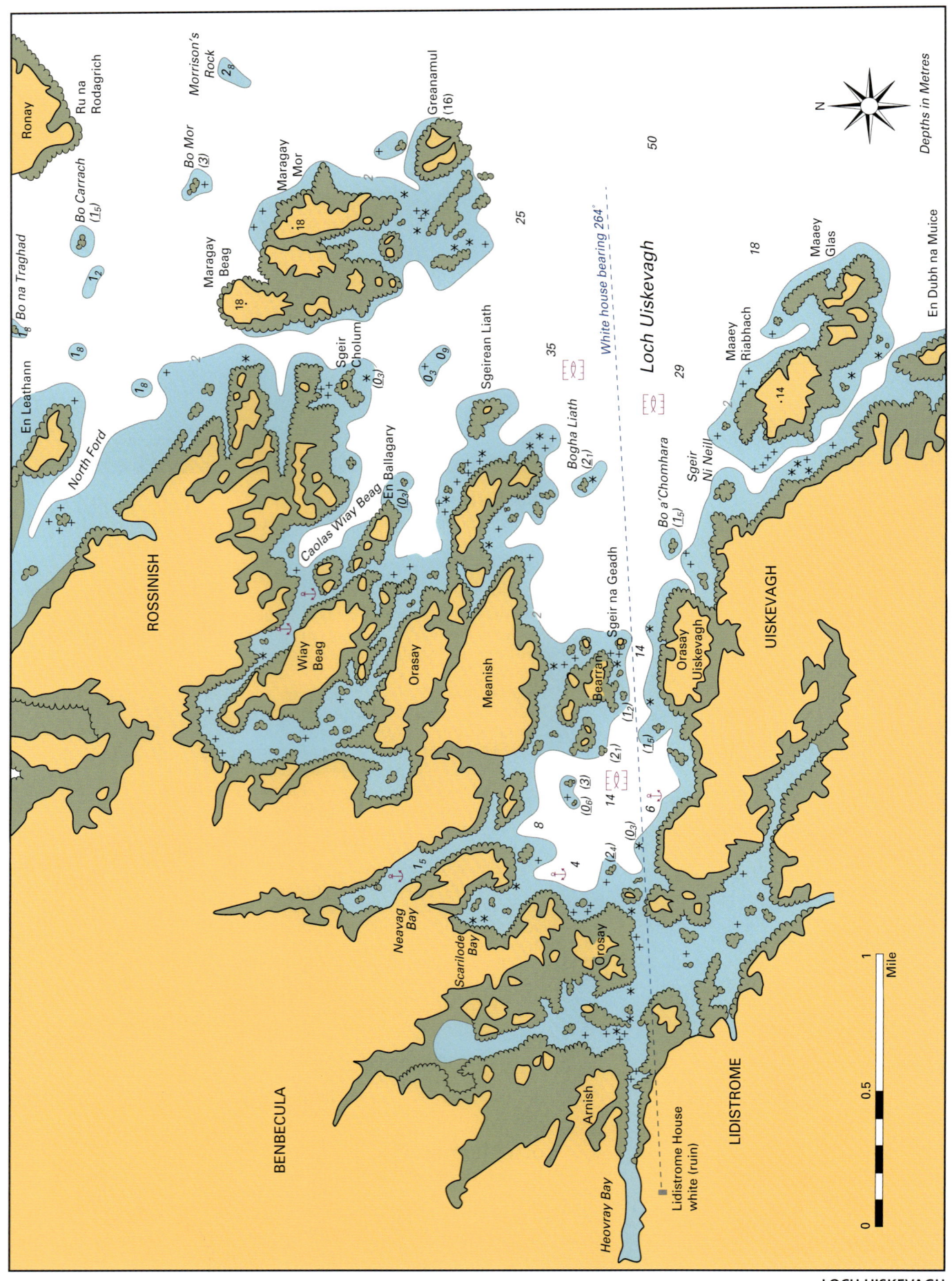

LOCH UISKEVAGH

56 CCC Sailing Directions and Anchorages

3. Benbecula

Loch Uiskevagh

Loch Uiskevagh, midway between Loch a' Laip and Kallin, is the innermost extent of the sea's penetration of the east side of Benbecula with innumerable islets, reefs and rocks and narrow channels. Great care must be exercised to reach its well sheltered but isolated anchorages. At HW Loch Uiskevagh appears as a broad open firth encumbered with green islets and which, at LW, becomes an almost continuous ridge of bare rocks.

Entry is made between Bearran and Orosay Uiskevagh, a passage ½ cable wide. Once within, careful pilotage is needed to avoid the many reefs and drying rocks extending from all shores.

Tides

Const. –0040 Ullapool (–0500 Dover)
Heights in metres

MHWS	MLWN	ML	MLWN	MLWS
4·8	3·6	2·8	1·9	0·7

The streams are weak everywhere in the loch.

Directions

From the south keep a cable east of a line through Rubha Cam nan Gall, the NE point of Wiay, Greanamul Deas and Maaey Glas, the most easterly of the Maaey group of islets. This clears all hazards off this shore except Bo Greanamul, (see p.55). The outer loch is entered between the Maaey group of islets in the south and Greanamul (16m) group to the north.

From the north, keep at least ½ mile off the Ronay shore to avoid Ritchie Rock and giving Greanamul (16m) a good berth, head SW and aim to pass between two large fish farms which lie either side of the leading line and pick up the bearing 264° on the white house at the head of the loch which is shown on the chart.

This bearing may be difficult to see. If so, Sgeir na Geadh at the north side of the narrows is recognisable and should be approached on a bearing of 270° until close south of it. At this point, alter to port on to 264° (the white house bearing) until through the narrows. Continue on this bearing passing south of another fish farm in the inner loch. When past the west end of the pens steer NW towards the anchorages in the northern part of the loch or south towards the anchorage in the bay west of Orasay Uiskevagh.

Anchorage

Neavag Bay may be approached when its west side bears 350° or so. Approach with caution as reefs extend into the ever narrowing entrance. Well protected but the bottom is very soft mud.

Bay west of Orasay Uiskevagh Anchor where indicated on plan keeping clear of reefs and drying rocks. Anchoring close to the south shore with kedge anchor to prevent swinging might offer better protection from SW winds.

Caolas Wiay Beag

Wiay Beag, an island 1 mile NE of Loch Uiskevagh close south of Rossinish, the NE extension of Benbecula, provides good shelter in isolation on the NE side of the island.

Tides

Const. –0040 Ullapool (–0500 Dover)
Range: 3·9m Sp, 1·3m Np.

Directions

From south and north it is best to approach from well south of the Greanamul group of islets with their west extending reefs. A large area of submerged rocks is situated ½ mile from the outer anchorage. They lie between a large reef, Sgeirean Liath, a small part of which always shows, and the large reefs west of Greanamul. Passing 1 cable east of Sgeirean Liath on a NW course (315°) clears dangers including a rock (dries 0·3m) a cable SE of Eilean Ballagary at the south side of the entrance. Maintain this course heading for the Rossinish shore until entrance opens out. Once within the outer anchorage north of Eilean Ballagary head to pass east then north of the 2 islets protecting the inner anchorage. Keep mid-channel as reefs extend particularly from the north shore.

Anchorage

Anchor NE of Wiay Beag, where shown on the plan in about 8m. Fish farms shown on the chart are longer present. The area has been surveyed by Antares making a circumnavigation of Wiay Beag a possibility using GPS.

Admiralty Chart
2904
Admiralty Leisure Folio
5616. 11
Imray Chart
C66
Ordnance Survey
22
Cruising Scotland
p.185

Loch Uiskevagh with Scarilode Bay in the foreground

Martin Lawrence

CCC Sailing Directions and Anchorages   57

Outer Hebrides

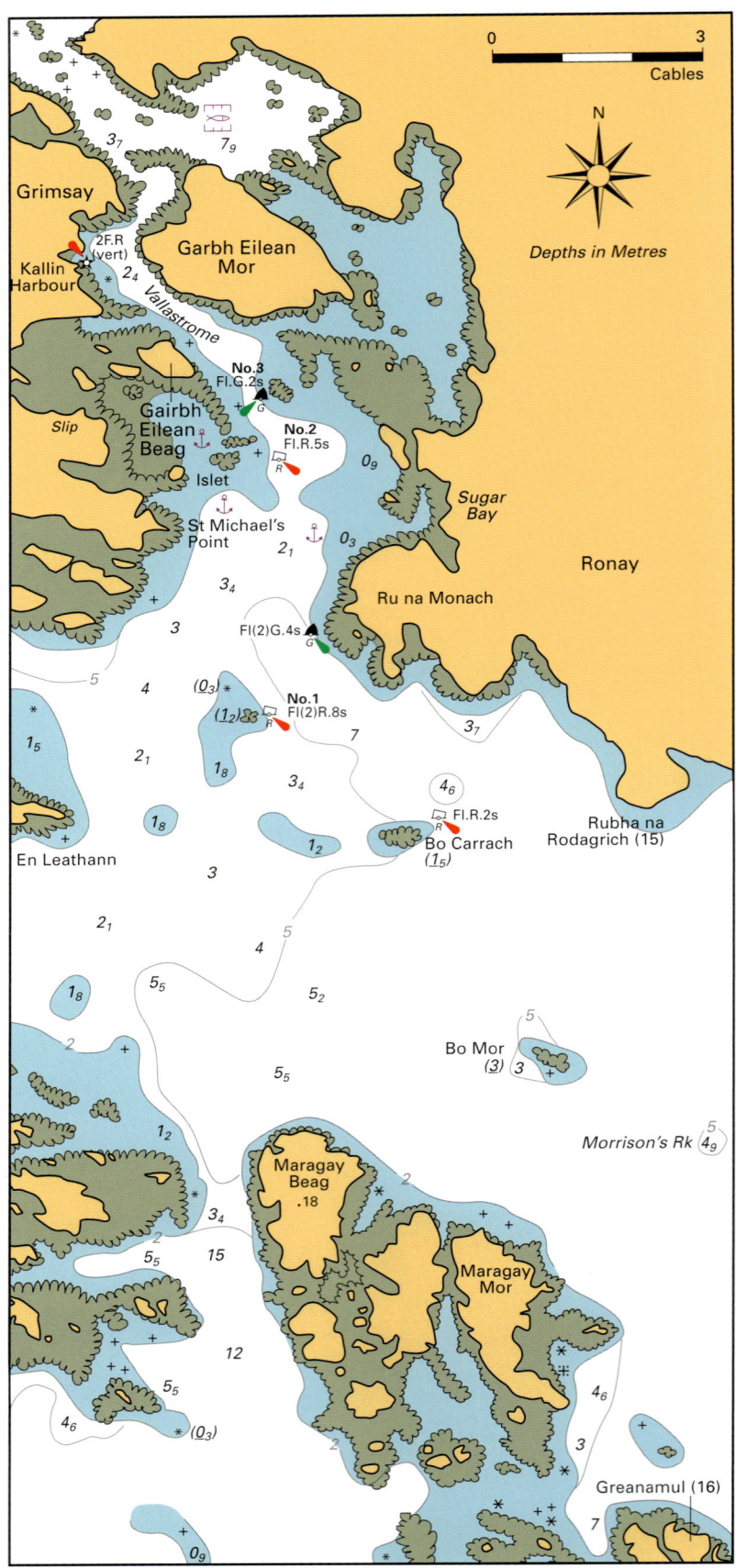

KALLIN AND APPROACHES

Kallin

A small community principally occupied with lobster fishing and working in summer on the Atlantic coast. Smaller boats from Kallin pass regularly under a bridge in the causeway at North Ford, which has a headroom of 2·4 metres. The area east and north of Kallin has now (2016) been surveyed by Antares charts, making a circumnavigation of Garbh Eilean Mor and even Ronay, given sufficient rise of tide, a possibility using GPS.

Tides

Constant –0040 Ullapool (–0500 Dover)

Height in metres

MHWS	MHWN	MTL	MLWN	MLWS
4·8	3·6	2·8	1·9	0·7

The in-going stream begins +0535 Ullapool (+0115 Dover)
The out-going stream begins –0025 Ullapool (–0445 Dover)

Directions

From the south keep the summit of Beinn a' Tuath on Wiay open of the east side of Greanamul astern 200°, to clear Morrison's Rock which lies up to 4 cables SE of Bo Mor. When the Bo Carrach port hand buoy bears 300° steer to leave it to port and pass between No.1 red can light buoy and the starboard hand buoy marking the reef southwest of Rubha na Monach. From this point follow the buoyed channel northwards and enter the Vallastrome.

Alternatively, having identified Greanamul, pass west of the Maragay islands, but note the various submerged and drying rocks on the west side of the passage. Head to pass close to the east end of Eilean Leathann, to avoid a submerged rock lying a cable east of that island and from there make for No.2 buoy, passing midway between No.1 red can light buoy and islets off St Michael's Point to port to clear the drying rock SW of that buoy.

From the north keep ½ mile off the east side of Ronay to avoid Ritchie's Rock (for clearing marks see Passage notes above, page 52) and pass a cable south of Ronay then follow the buoyed channel as above.

When entering the Vallastrome keep mid-channel between Garbh Eilean Mor and Garbh Eilean Beag and beyond, all the way up to the harbour at Kallin. The tide runs strongly in Vallastrome and care is needed when manoeuvring.

Anchorages and berthing

Kallin Harbour is small and usually well filled with local boats but the recently completed pier allows more room for visiting yachts provided they are prepared to raft alongside fishing vessels. Depth alongside the pier is 4m. Anchoring off the pier can cause obstruction and is not recommended as the tidal stream is troublesome.

NW of Ru na Monach. The bay north of Ru na Monach is shoal and anchoring in the channel is almost inevitable.

58 CCC Sailing Directions and Anchorages

3. Benbecula

Admiralty Chart
2904
Admiralty Leisure Folio
5616. 11
Imray Chart
C66
Ordnance Survey
22
Cruising Scotland
p.185

Kallin Harbour and the newly extended pier

St Michael's Point. Anchoring off the west shore in 4m is preferable. Shoal-draught yachts, and others at neaps, can anchor in the pool north of the islet which lies north of St Michael's Point (below centre); pass 20 metres northeast of the islet to avoid the drying reef which extends south from Gairbh-Eilean Beag. Land at a slip WNW of the islet.

Lights
Bo Carrach port hand light buoy Fl.R.2s
No.1 light buoy Fl(2)R.8s
Starboard hand light buoy off Ru na Monach Fl(2)G.4s
No.2 light buoy Fl.R.5s
No.3 light buoy Fl.G.2s
Pierhead, 2F.R(vert)

Supplies
Water by hose on pier. Diesel at harbour (key fob needed); limited fishermen's chandlery. Mains electricity outlet at harbour. Travelling shop twice weekly. Sea food factory.

Kallin approaches. The Vallastrome is in the upper right centre and Ronay in the foreground

CCC Sailing Directions and Anchorages

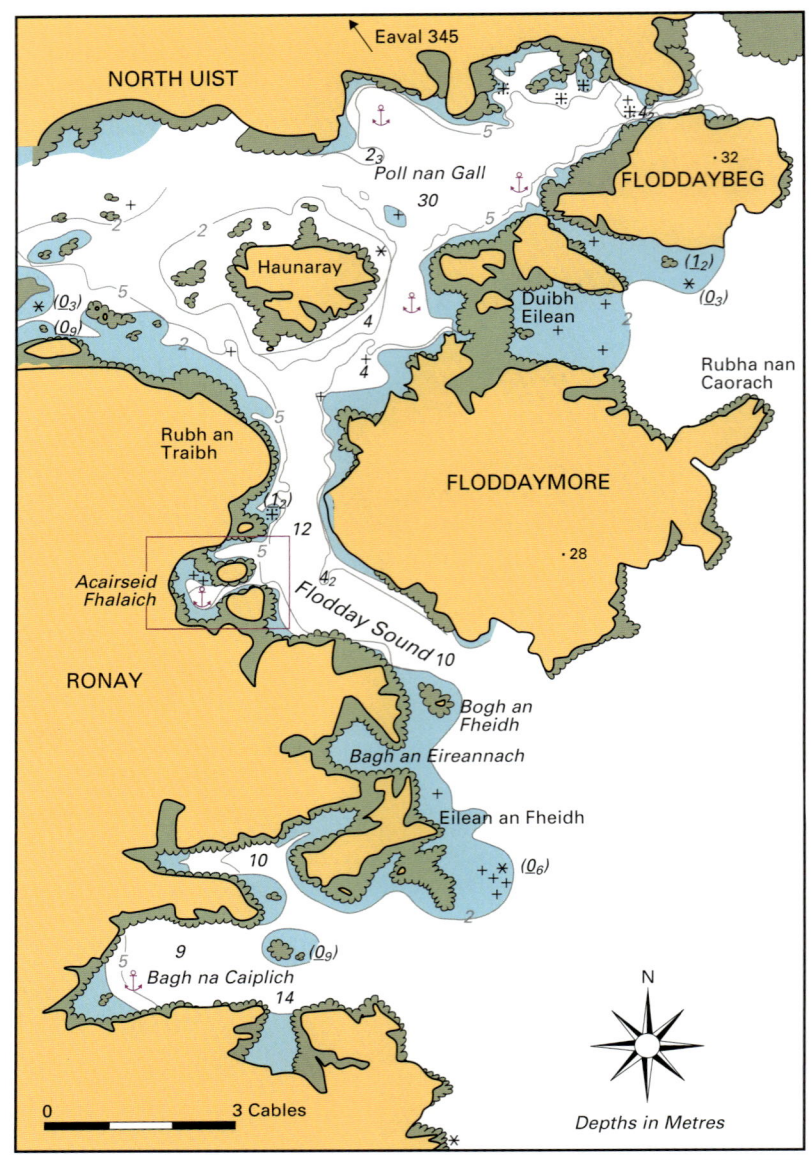

Outer Hebrides

Flodday Sound

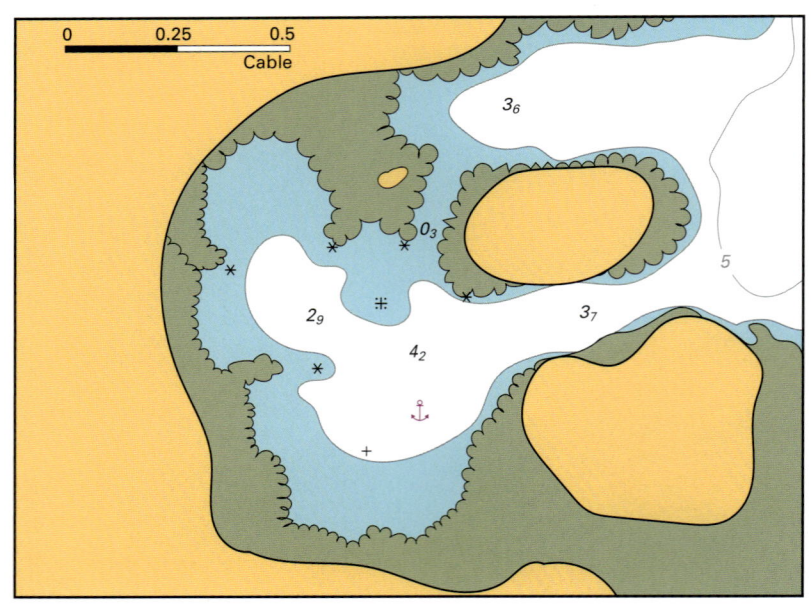

This narrow inlet between Ronay and Floddaymore provides several possible anchorages which can be reached only by way of the Sound of Flodday. The entrance north of Floddaybeg can be used with care and with the Antares chart of Flodday Sound. Eaval (345m), a mountain on the SE end of North Uist, indicates the general direction of Ronay and Floddaymore Islands.

Tide

As Kallin p.58

The tidal flow in the sound is not strong but off the entrance a sea is set up even in moderate winds. This makes the entrance uncomfortable during the out-going stream and even dangerous in strong winds.

Directions

From the south keep at least ½ mile off the Ronay shore to avoid Ritchie Rock and its associated tidal rip. As reefs and rocks extend 2 cables east from Eilean an Fheidh at the south side of the entrance, do not alter course for the entrance to the sound until it is well open. Proceeding north in Flodday Sound keep to the Floddaymore side until abeam Rubh an Traibh. Beyond this point keep to the Haunaray side of mid-channel but not too close as reefs extend from there also.

Anchorages

Poll nan Gall on the North Uist shore. Anchor where indicated but note the rock lying 150m NE of Haunaray. The passage at the west entrance to Poll nan Gall is less than ½ cable wide and is not recommended without the Antares chart of Haunaray Sound. This chart will enable the sound to be explored for about a mile further westward, giving access to several remote anchorages.

Acairseid Fhalaich on the west side of Flodday Sound, can be entered with caution between the two islets at the entrance where there is a depth of 3·7m notwithstanding that Chart 2904 indicates that the entrance is closed by a drying reef. Inside the bottom is soft mud, depth 3m but with several, almost vertical, rock heads. These lie mainly on the north side of the pool so anchor towards the south side. The anchorage is restricted but offers perfect shelter for a single yacht.

Bagh na Caiplich on the east side of Ronay about 1 mile south of the entrance to the Sound of Flodday has offered shelter to generations of fishermen. Once inside the bay the shores are steep-to and the hazards obvious, provided an approach is made from the SE to avoid the reefs and rocks extending 2 cables east of En an Fheidh. Hold to the south shore to avoid the mid channel reef and rock (dries 0·9) but beware drying rocks off the outer headland in the approach. Anchor in 6–9m. Exposed to the east.

FLODDAY SOUND

ACAIRSEID FHALAICH

60   CCC Sailing Directions and Anchorages

3. Benbecula

Entrance to Flodday Sound from southeast; Acairseid Fhalaich is at top, centre left

Admiralty Chart
2904
Admiralty Leisure Folio
5616. 11
Imray Chart
C66
Ordnance Survey
22
Cruising Scotland
p.186

Acairseid Fhalaich, Flodday Sound

CCC Sailing Directions and Anchorages **61**

4. North Uist

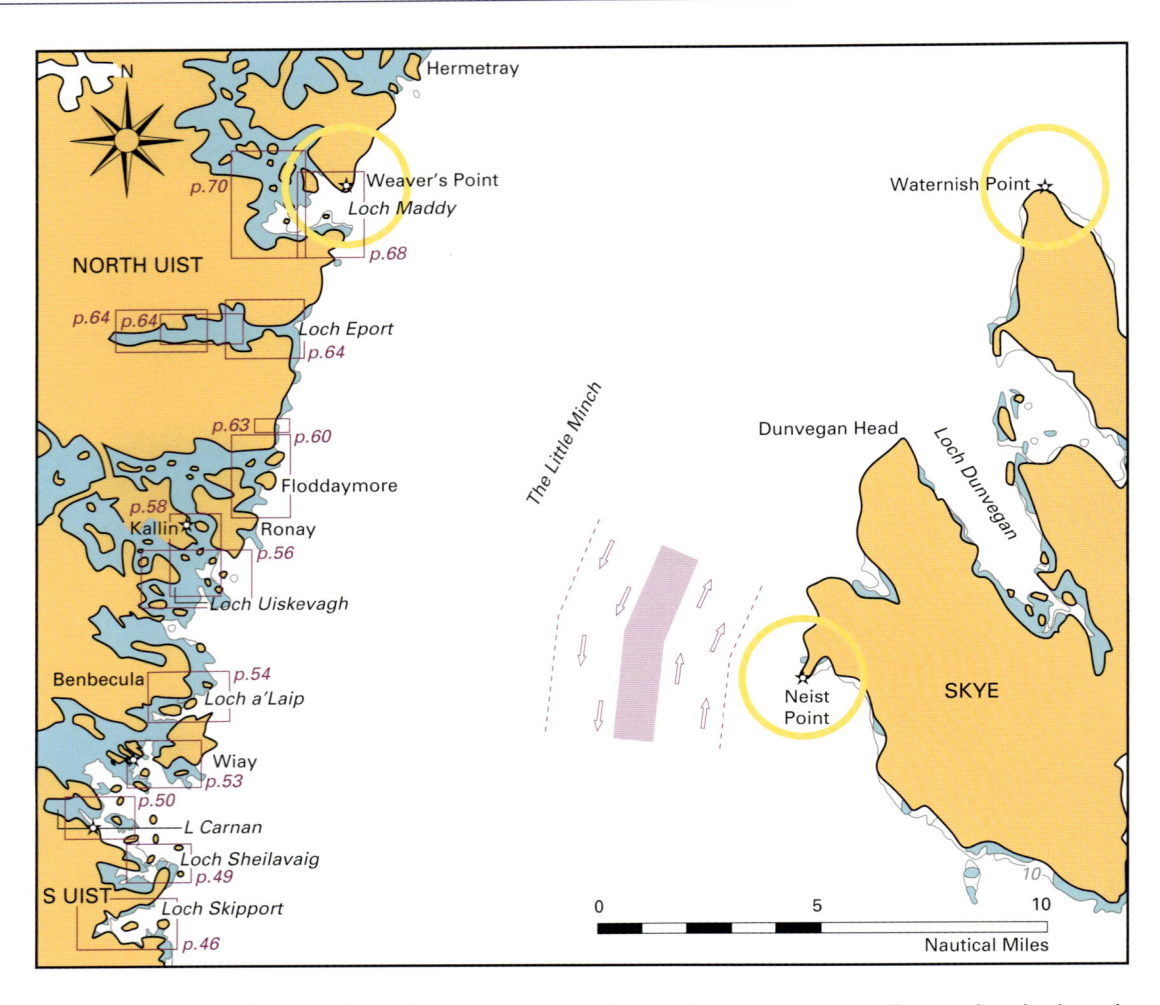

NORTH UIST AND BENBECULA KEY PLAN

Admiralty Chart
2825, 1795, 2904
Admiralty Leisure Folio
5616. 11
Imray Chart
C66
Ordnance Survey
18, 22
Cruising Scotland
p.186

East coast of North Uist

North Uist is similar to South Uist, having steep shores and relatively high ground on its east side. The west side, particularly the NW side, is low lying and well populated. The gently rising wedge shape of two hills, South Lee (279m) and North Lee (260m) lie between Loch Eport to the south and Loch Maddy to the north. Eaval (345m) also wedge shaped and the only mountain on North Uist, lies to the south of the entrance to Loch Eport. The distance from the SE end of North Uist to Loch Maddy is about 5 miles.

The east coast of North Uist, given a reasonable berth, is free from offlying dangers. The approach to the entrance to Loch Eport is free of danger except on the south side though strong easterly winds might make the seas at the entrance dangerous. Loch Maddy may be entered in all weathers.

Tides

Off the east coast of North Uist run as follows:
N-going stream begins –0550 Ullapool (+0215 Dover)
S-going stream begins +0035 Ullapool (–0345 Dover)

The spring rate in each direction off the salient points is 2 knots but is less between the points and the streams become weaker farther seaward.

Lights

Weaver's Point, Loch Maddy Fl.3s24m7M
Neist Point, West Skye Fl.5s43m16M
Waternish Point, NW Skye Fl.20s21m8M

4. North Uist

Bagh Moraig (Moraig Harbour)

A fascinating but remote landlocked anchorage (57°30.8'N, 7° 09'W) at the extreme SE corner of North Uist 2½ miles south of Loch Eport and 4 cables north of Floddaybeg. Ben Eaval is 1 mile to the NW. It would be dangerous to attempt the entrance except in favourable conditions. As the holding is poor this is an anchorage to explore in settled weather only.

BAGH MORAIG

Tide

Const. –0040 Ullapool (–0500 Dover)

Height in metres

MHWS	MHWN	ML	MLWN	MLWS
4·8	3·6	2·8	1·9	0·7

Directions

The entrance is set-in between two minor headlands. It appears to be closed because of the small isthmus projecting from the south shore thus forming a 'chicane' entrance with tight turns that could prove awkward for a vessel over 10m. The approach is deep and clear allowing you to examine the entrance without committing yourself to enter.

It is necessary to enter at or near slack HW when there will be ample depth at the 'bar' inside, and only a weak or nil stream at the narrow chicane. At mid-tide the stream can run strongly at this point and could take charge. Keep slightly towards the north shore on the first bend, then keep towards the south shore when turning west to cross the bar, leaving the large seaweed-covered rock (dries 3m) to starboard. The middle of the bar dries 1·6m and accordingly, although more depth exists either side of the middle, it is advisable to await sufficient rise of tide before crossing the bar.

Anchorage

The bottom is mainly soft mud with poor holding. There is a deep hole towards the north shore about half-way along with heavy weed on the bottom. The NW and west end of the main loch are shoal but moderate depths for anchoring can be found in the west third of the main pool.

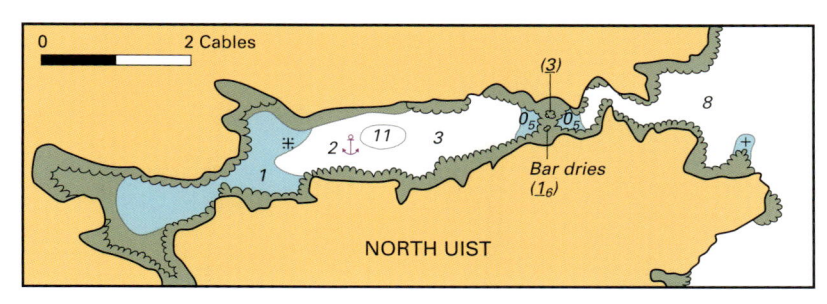

The North Uist coastline from seaward

Bagh Moraig | Eaval (345m) | Entrance to Loch Eport | Ben Lee

Bagh Moraig from SW at LW showing drying sill

R Arnold

CCC Sailing Directions and Anchorages   63

Outer Hebrides

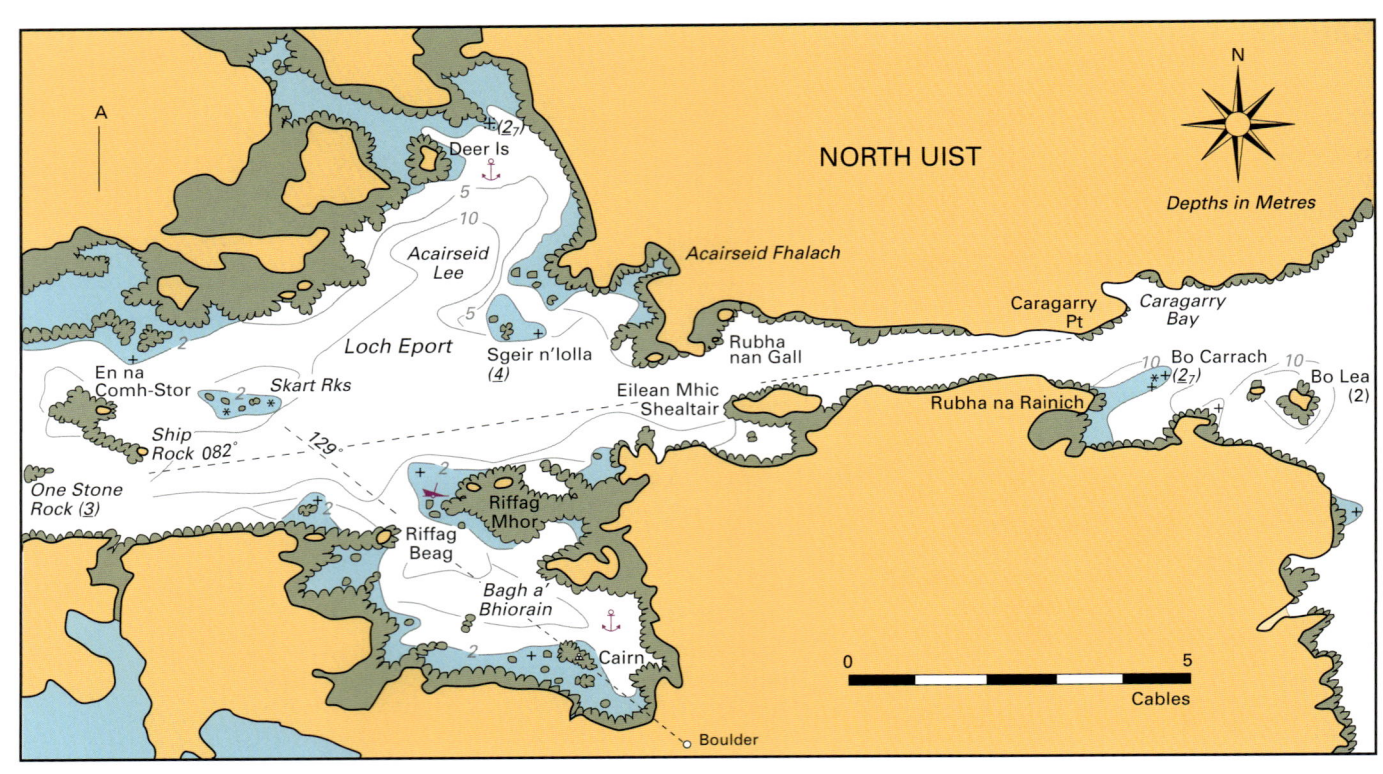

LOCH EPORT ENTRANCE

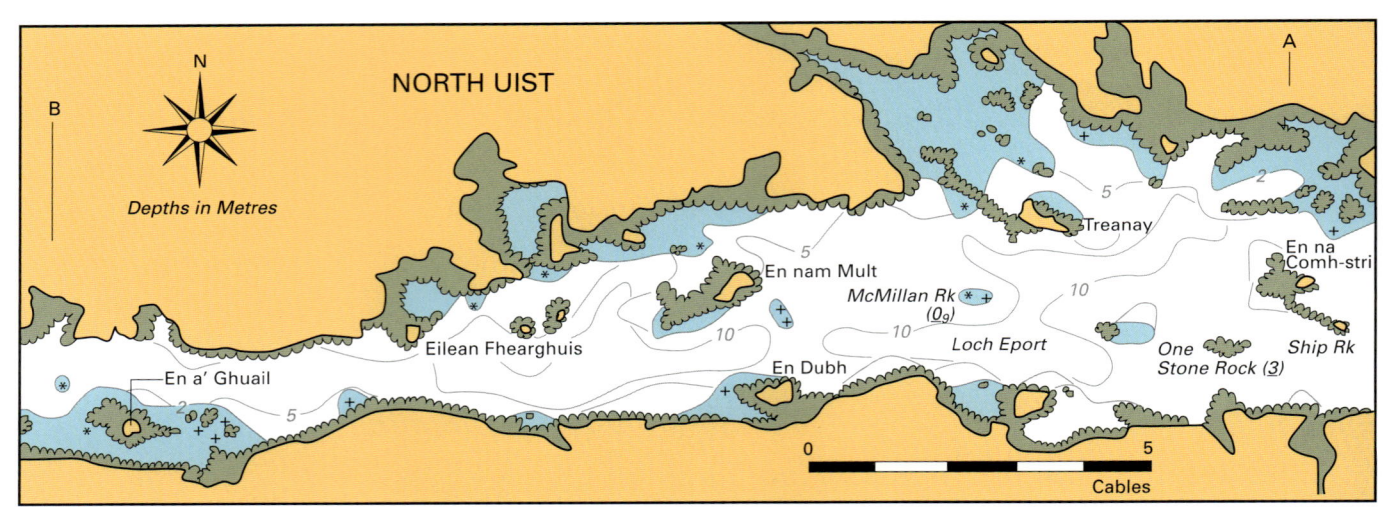

LOCH EPORT MIDDLE PART

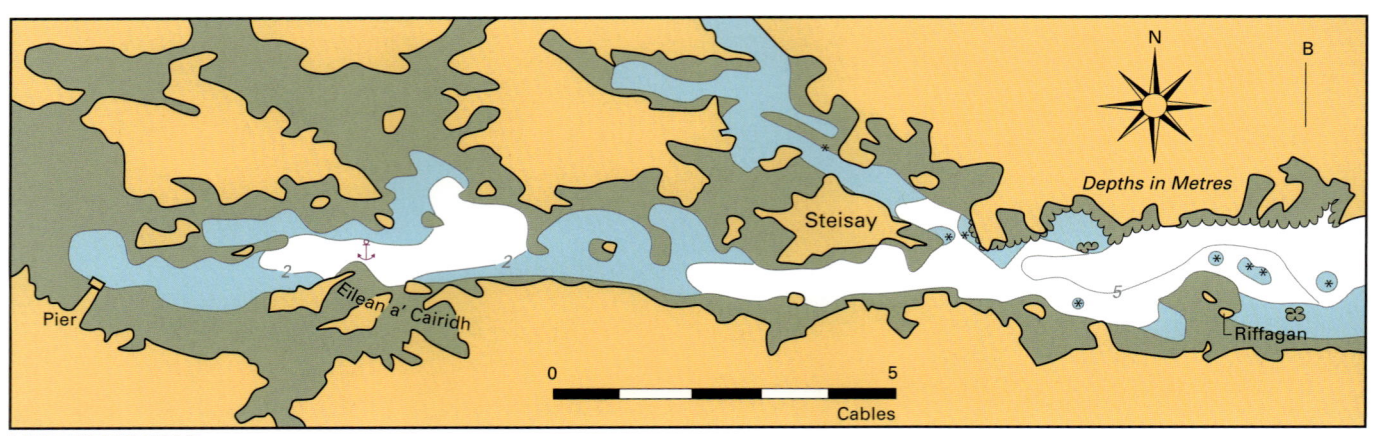

LOCH EPORT HEAD

64 CCC Sailing Directions and Anchorages

4. North Uist

Loch Eport

A long, narrow loch, rather featureless in its upper reaches, Loch Eport is entered through a canal-like passage leading to two anchorages immediately inside the narrows. Eaval, the wedge-shaped hill 345 metres high, lies 1½ miles south of the entrance.

Tides

Constant −0040 Ullapool (−0500 Dover)

Height in metres

MHWS	MHWN	MTL	MLWN	MLWS
4·8	3·6	2·8	1·9	0·7

The spring rate in the narrows is 3 knots
The in-going stream begins +0550 Ullapool (+0130 Dover)
The out-going stream begins −0020 Ullapool (−0440 Dover)

Directions

Bo Lea, 2 metres high, stands on the south side of the entrance with drying rocks further west. The entrance channel is clean but the inner parts of the loch are full of rocks.

Maintain a mid-channel course from the outer entrance until the loch opens out west of Eilean Mhic Shealtair (McCalter Island). The north point of the entrance just open of this island, 082° astern, clears all rocks as far as One Stone Rock.

Anchorages

The principal anchorages are on either side of the loch immediately west of the narrow entrance channel.

Bagh a' Bhiorain is entered between Riffag Mhor, at the west end of which lies a drying wreck, and Riffag Beag, a drying reef at the west side of the entrance with an islet on its east end.

A cairn on a rock near the head of the bay in line with a white boulder on the hillside 129° leads between these obstructions, but if this line is not seen pass close northeast of Riffag Beag. Anchor between the cairn and the east shore of the bay in 5m, poor holding in soft mud.

Acarsaid Lee on the north side of the loch is less sheltered. It is best approached when Sgeir n' Iolla, which dries 4 metres, about 1¼ cable southwest of the east point of the entrance, is showing.

A rock drying 2·3 metres stands at the south end of a reef which extends ½ cable south from the shore northeast of Deer Island. Anchor east of Deer Island. The holding has been found to be poor, with weed and soft mud.

A small inlet entered a couple of cables east of Sgeir n'Iolla, dries 4m, south of the entrance to Acarsaid Lee and marked on the old chart as Acarsaid Fhalach, may have attractions for a yacht of shallow draught.

Upper loch

The passage further up the loch is best undertaken when One Stone Rock (covers 2½ hours before HW) is showing, when it may be passed on its south side; then keep about ½ cable off the south shore as far as Eilean Fhearghuis, after which keep about ½ cable from the north side, and note especially the extensive drying rocks on the south side of the channel extending for about a ½ to ¾ mile west of Eilean Fhearghuis.

A drying reef extends south from the east end of Steisay more than halfway across the channel. After Steisay there are patches with depths of 1 metre, but apparently no submerged rocks, in the fairway as far as the pier at the head of the loch.

Anchorages

NE of Eilean a'Cairidh Anchor in 4 metres. The area between Eilean a'Cairidh and the pier is reported to be now too shallow for most yachts to anchor there. The bottom is soft mud so that a long keel yacht would sink in; care is needed to dig in the anchor securely.

Other anchorages may be found with chart 2825, although it does not cover the head of the loch. The channel leading northwestwards from Steisay has also been surveyed by Antares and presents another option.

Supplies

Shop, PO at Clachan, 1 mile west from pier. Mermaid Fish, just past the shop, supplies peat-smoked salmon. Hotel 1½ miles north from the pier.

Admiralty Chart
2904, 2825
Admiralty Leisure Folio
5616. 11, 23D
Imray Chart
C66
Ordnance Survey
18, 22
Cruising Scotland
p.186

The leading line into Bagh a' Bhiorain; it is unlikely that either of the two marks will stand out as well as those in the picture, though the cairn in the foreground can usually be seen

John Trythall

Outer Hebrides

Loch Eport entrance from the east (p.65)

The head of Loch Eport at LW (p.65)

66 CCC Sailing Directions and Anchorages

4. North Uist

Loch Maddy looking north; the fish farm (right centre) has been removed (p.71)

Loch Maddy before pontoons installed; ferry pier left of centre (p.71)

Outer Hebrides

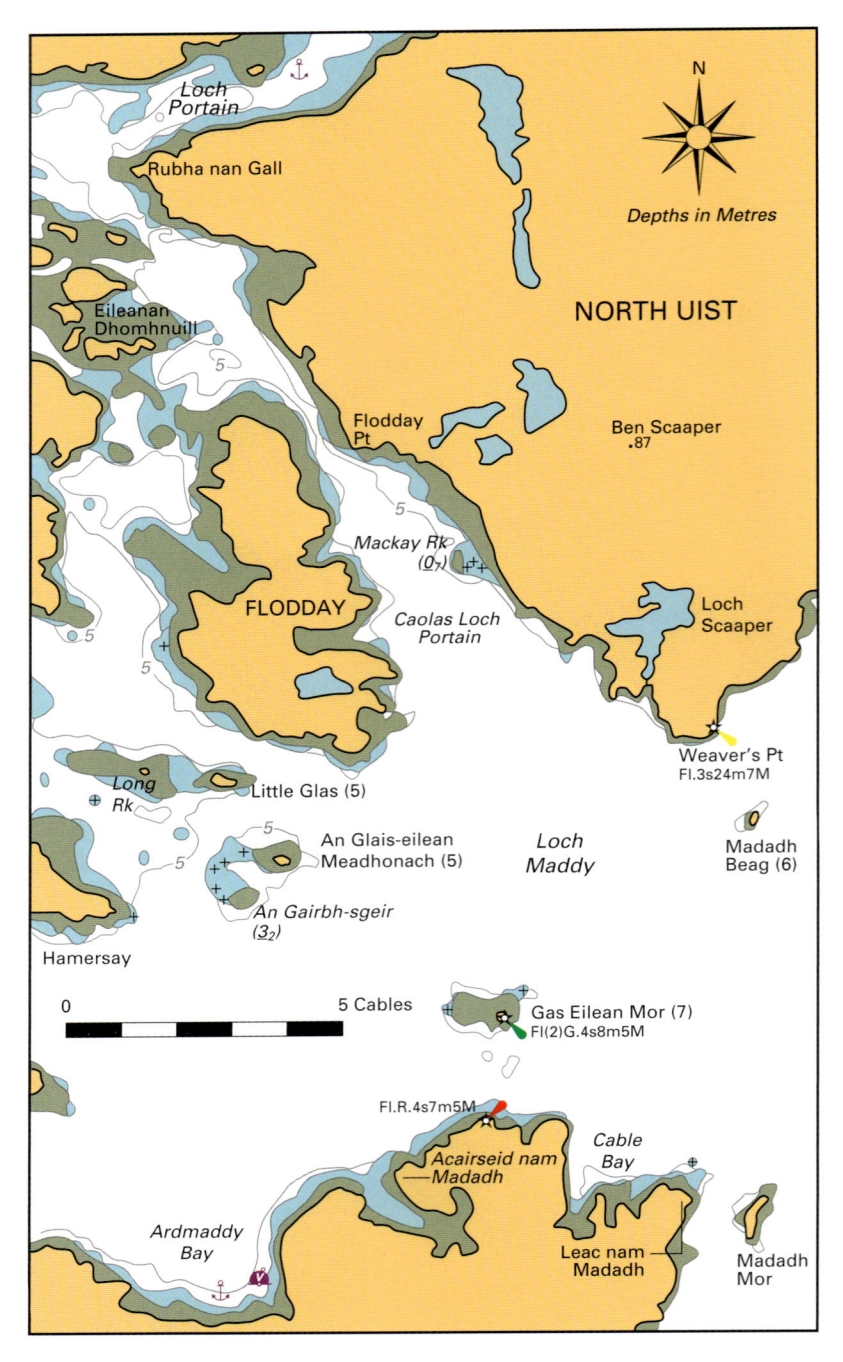

OUTER LOCH MADDY

Admiralty Chart
2825
Admiralty Leisure Folio
5616. 11, 24
Imray Chart
C66
Ordnance Survey
18
Cruising Scotland
p.186

Loch Maddy (Outer)

A broad loch littered with islands and rocks but well marked and lit for the needs of car ferries. Loch Maddy is identified by the gap in the hills at the entrance, and the conspicuous angular islets, Madadh Mor and Madadh Gruamach on the south side of the entrance and Madadh Beag on the north side.

Tides

Constant –0040 Ullapool (–0500 Dover)

Height in metres

MHWS	MHWN	MTL	MLWN	MLWS
4·8	3·6	2·8	1·9	0·7

The in-going stream begins +0555 Ullapool (+0135 Dover)
The out-going stream begins –0025 Ullapool (–0445 Dover)
Owing to the influence of the tidal streams along the coast, the in-going stream turns to run northeast between Weaver's Point and Madadh Beag, and the out-going stream sets strongly along the south shore.

Directions

From the south, when passing west of Madadh Mor note the submerged rock ½ cable north of Leac nam Madadh. Passing east of Madadh Mor, note reefs extend north from it. Pass south of Glas Eilean at the entrance to the loch and Ruigh Liath if making for the moorings in the vicinity of Lochmaddy Ro-Ro Terminal. (VHF Ch 16 and 12 'Loch Maddy Harbour')

From the north, pass Madadh Beag on either hand and if heading for the moorings near the Ro-Ro Terminal pass at least 1 cable west and NW of Glas Eilean Mor and leave An Glais-eilean Meadhonach and An Gairbh-sgeir (dries 3·2m) at least 1 cable to starboard. The Ro-Ro Terminal may be approached either south or north of Ruigh Liath and Faihore. Give both a wide berth as reefs extend in all directions.

In strong winds, with wind against tide, the seas at the entrance may be very bad, particularly off Weavers Point and Leac nam Madadh. It may be better in such circumstances to enter the loch in mid-channel.

Lights

Weaver's Point Lt Bn Fl.3s24m7M
Glas Eilean Mor Fl(2)G.4s8m5M
Ardmaddy Point Lt Bn Fl.R.4s7m5M
Ruigh Liath Lt Bn Q.G.6m5M
Red spar buoy NW of Faihore Fl.R.3s4M
Vallaquie Island Lt Bn DirFl(3)WRG.8s11m5/8M
Port entry light Dir Iso.WRG.2s9m6M
Ferry terminal pierhead 2F.G(vert)8m4M
Marina pontoon Fl.R3s2·5m2M

Anchorage

Ardmaddy Bay (Bagh Aird nam Madadh) Situated just inside the south entrance to the loch this bay provides excellent anchorage. Anchor in 3 to 5m but preferably in the SE corner where no swell is felt even in easterly winds. Squally in strong SW winds and exposed to the north. Two visitors moorings. (See also p.71 for temporary anchorages.)

Loch Portain

This secluded loch forms the NE arm of Loch Maddy and provides good shelter although in parts the mud is soft and care is worth taking to obtain good holding.

Directions

Pass mid-channel straight through Caolas Loch Portain, NE of Flodday. Just before Rubha nan Gall turn to port to keep a cable off the point. Turn to starboard and enter Loch Portain only when its south shore opens. Pass south of the islet and anchor in 2 to 3m, mud, but not further in than 2 cables.

Anchorage

Holding is reported as good in thick grey mud particularly in mid-channel ½ cable ESE of the islet, so it is worthwhile seeking this as certain areas are reported as poor.

68 CCC Sailing Directions and Anchorages

4. North Uist

Loch Maddy looking over Ardmaddy Bay towards the entrance

Loch Maddy from the south

Outer Hebrides

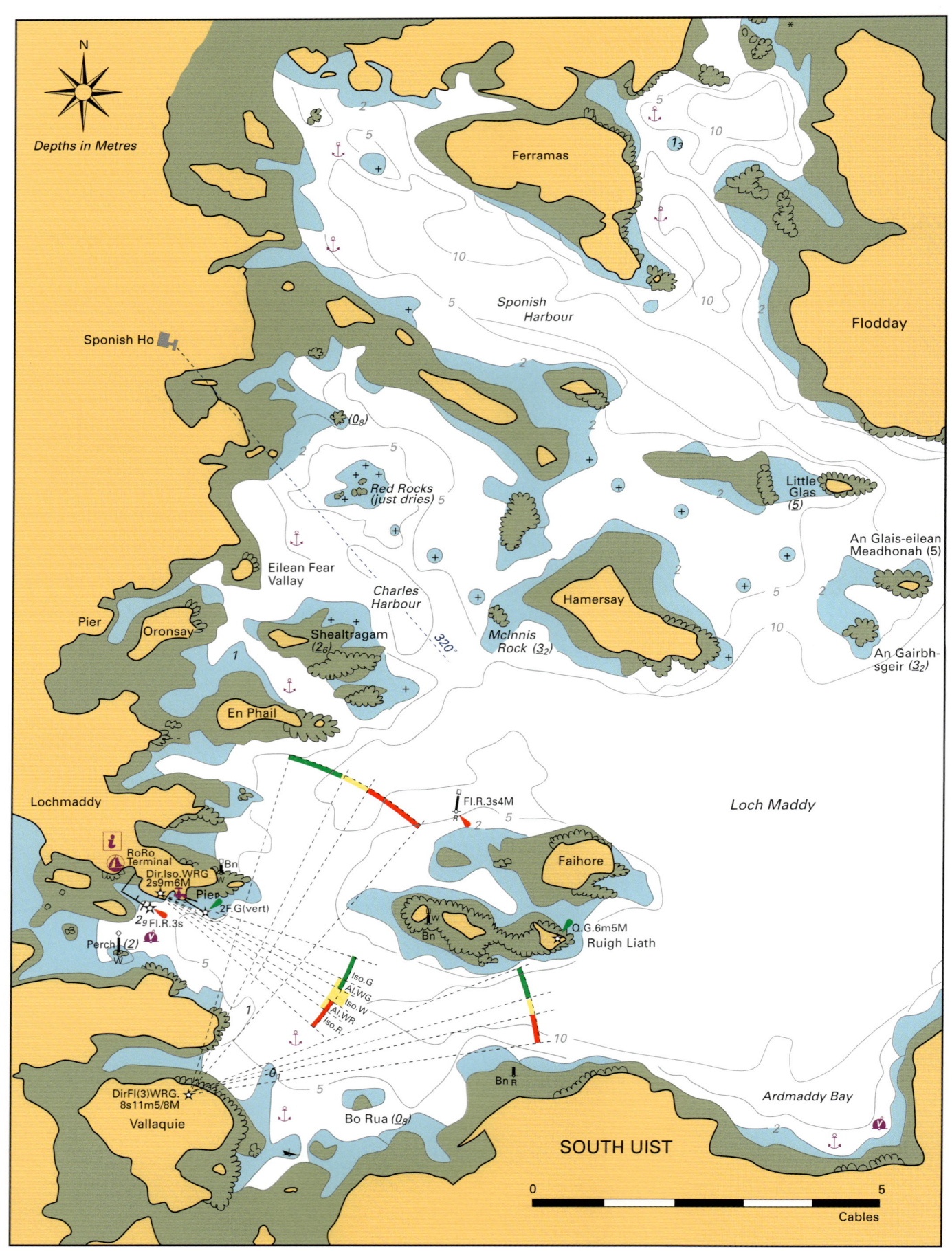

INNER LOCH MADDY

70 CCC Sailing Directions and Anchorages

4. North Uist

Loch Maddy (Inner)

For the approach to the outer loch, tidal information and lights, see p.68.

Directions

Having passed Glas Eilean Mor and heading for the ferry terminal, pass either south of Ruigh Liath or north of the red spar buoy which lies northwest of Faihore.

Anchorages

Marina There is a small 26 berth marina in the bight to the west of the Ro-Ro pier. The pontoons are serviced with water and electricity. Depth is limited at the inner berths and 2m is found only at the outer third of the pontoon. Larger craft should berth at the hammerhead and approach it from the south. Contact marina on ☏ 07828 105 423.

Near the Ro-Ro terminal So as to keep clear of ferries and the approach to the marina do not anchor northwest of a line between the pierhead and the two visitors' moorings. Anchor in 3-4m southeast of the visitors' moorings but note the reef to the SW (dries 1·7m), marked by a perch with a topmark.

Alternatively, it is possible to tie up to the north (inner) side of the pier as near to the sheds as depth will allow. A fender board and lines ashore may be necessary to keep off the pier. Keep well clear of the ferry when it is manoeuvring at the round-head.

Vallaquie 4 cables SSE of ferry terminal. Note Bo Rua, which dries 0·8m, to the east of it. Weaver's Point in line with the SE side of Ruigh Liath leads north of Bo Rua.

A wreck which covers, and two drying rocks, lie towards the head of the bay; anchor north of the wreck but keeping clear of a submerged reef which extends a cable north from the east end of Vallaquie.

Oronsay This small enclosed area NW of Oronsay is well sheltered but shallow with little or no room to anchor, being fully occupied by moorings of local boats.

The pier, with 2m at HW Neaps and which dries out, may be laid alongside temporarily. Enter from Charles Harbour north of Shealtragam and between Eilean Fear Vallay and Oronsay. Anchorage can be found between En. Phail and Shealtragam where the fish farm shown on the chart has now been removed. Water at the pier.

Charles Harbour (Acarsaid Nighean Thearlaich on the chart), northwest of Hamersay, is obstructed by drying and submerged rocks and much of the bottom is either rock or soft mud. The best anchorage is northeast of Eilean Fear Vallay; local boats have moorings there, but there is still space for visitors to anchor.

Approach from the southeast, keeping mid-channel and heading 320° for Sponish House, a conspicuous three-storey building. Keep 1½ cables off Hamersay to avoid McInnis Rock which dries 3·2m, until east of Eilean Fear Vallay; then turn west towards the anchorage.

Sponish Harbour is cleaner than Charles Harbour, but the holding is poor. Enter between Flodday, a large island on the northeast side of the loch, and Little Glas, less than a cable off its south side.

Ferramas On the west side of the pool between Flodday and Ferramas. The best shelter is northeast of Ferramas, but drying reefs extend more than 1½ cables northwest from Flodday, and a submerged rock lies ½ cable east of the northeast point of Ferramas.

Temporary anchorages in the outer loch that could be used in suitable weather for a scramble ashore are:

Cable Bay (Bagh Chlann Neill), just inside the south point of the entrance, SE of Glas Eilean Mor.

Acarsaid nam Madadh SW of Glas Eilean Mor (very shoal) - avoid low spring tide.

Lighthouse beach northwest of Weaver's Point light beacon; Loch Scaaper close to shore is good for drinking, swimming, and catching trout.

Flodday A bay on the east side of Flodday west of Mackay Rock. The inviting-looking inlet further south dries and is foul.

Services and supplies

Shops (EC Wednesday) at Lochmaddy and supermarkets at Sollas and Balivanich, PO, telephone, bank, two hotels, doctor. Petrol and diesel from garage, water at pontoon and at the pier inside Oronsay. Calor Gas (ask at tourist office). Sports centre, excellent Visitor Centre with restaurant, Taxi/mini-bus. Showers/baths may be had at the hotels, youth hostel and sports centre. Piermaster (VHF Ch 12) ☏ 01876 500337. Car Ferry daily to Uig, Skye and Tarbert, Harris. Bus to airport on Benbecula and Sollas. Tourist Information Centre ☏ 01876 500321. Marina ☏ 07828 105 423.

Loch Maddy marina

5. Sound of Harris

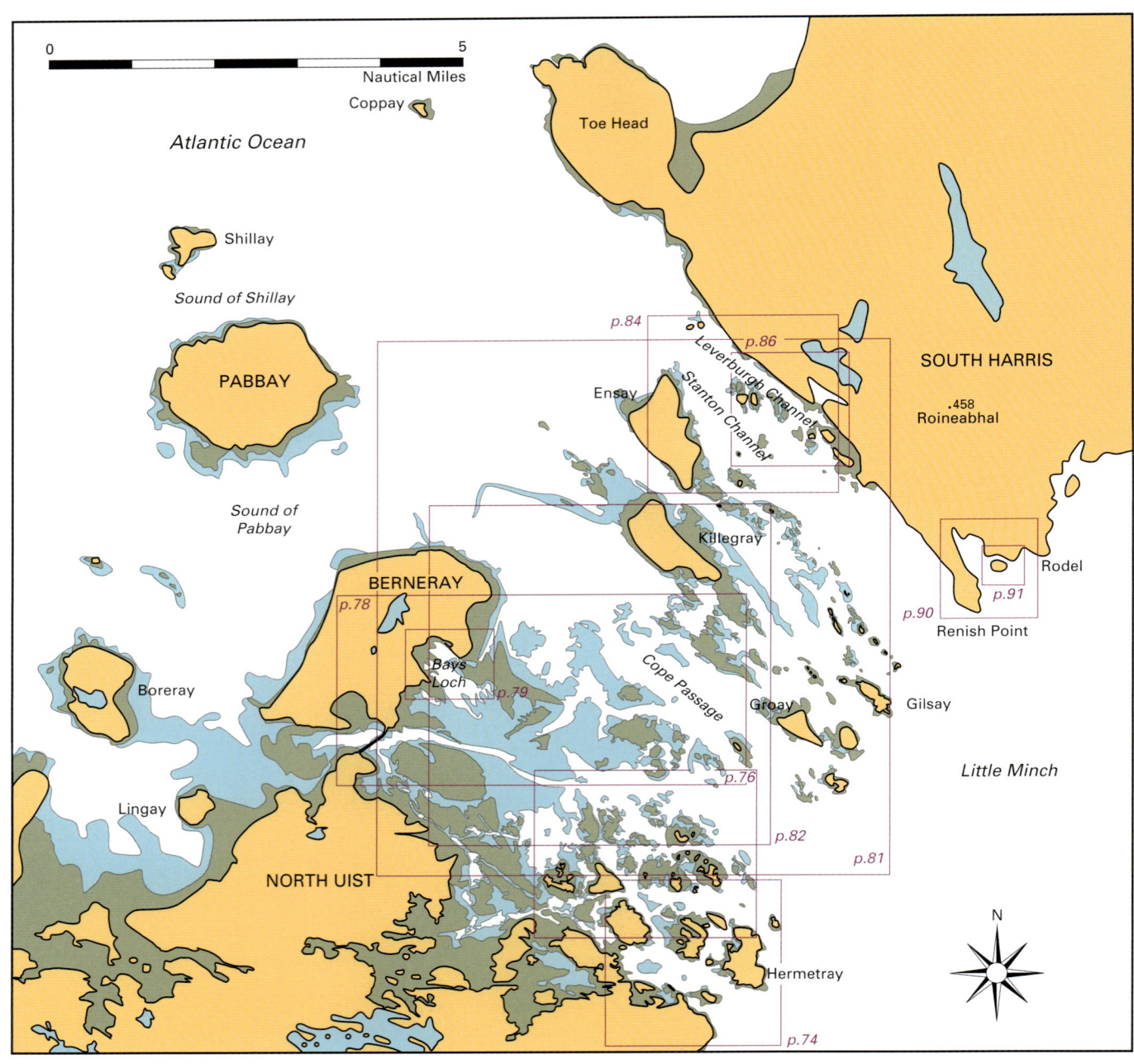

SOUND OF HARRIS KEY PLAN

5. Sound of Harris

Sound of Harris

The Sound of Harris which separates the largest island of the Outer Hebrides, Lewis and Harris from North Uist, runs from SE to NW for about 8 to 9 miles and has many reef and rock hazards. Until recently there was a choice of marked channels: the deeper but more tidal Stanton Channel between Ensay and South Harris on the northern side or the shallower Cope Passage between the Hermetray and Groay groups of islands at the SE entrance to the sound and between Berneray and Killegray at the NW entrance.

The removal of the majority of the buoys marking the Cope passage now means that for all practical purposes there is one main channel through the sound. This can be varied by deviating towards Leverburgh and following the Harris shore for some distance. Outer sections of the Cope Passage are still used by vessels visiting Bays Loch on Berneray but most of the NW part of this channel is not marked and the lack of suitable shore marks means that it can be navigated only with local knowledge or the use of GPS and in fair weather.

Two groups of islands and islets, the Hermetray and Groay groups, are situated at the SE side of the Sound. The former, lying close to the coast of North Uist, offers a number of anchorages and provides a base from which to explore the intricate channels between North Uist and Berneray.

The central area of the Sound is occupied by three larger islands, Berneray, Killegray and Ensay. The tide is strongest in the channels between these islands. In Caolas Skaari between Ensay and Killegray, the spring rate achieves 5 knots and as the channel is narrow, with many reefs, rocks and shoal patches on either hand, it is dangerous and cannot be recommended.

The introduction of a vehicle ferry service between Leverburgh on South Harris and a terminal at the causeway between Berneray and North Uist has required the positioning of many perches and buoys to mark the intricate route across the sound. These must be distinguished from the buoys marking the SE entrance to the Cope Passage. Provided the buoys and perches marking the ferry route are identified the approach from the Cope Passage to the Bays Loch is greatly simplified.

The NW entrance to the Sound is readily recognised by the islands of Pabbay and Shillay to the west and by Coppay and Toe Head (named Cape Difficulty on old charts and the diagram below) on South Harris to the north. Approaching from the west it should be entered between Shillay and Coppay.

Tides

Tidal streams throughout the Sound of Harris are very variable not only between springs and neaps, but also between day and night and between summer and winter. The notes here should only be taken as a rough guide.

In the greater part of the Sound the flood runs eastward but, near the southwest shore, the flood runs inward from both ends towards Loch Mhic Phail and Loch Aulassary on North Uist.

In Caolas Skaari, between Ensay and Killegray, which is about as central to the Sound as you can get, the SE-going (flood) stream begins +0545 Ullapool (+0125 Dover) and ends –0025 Ullapool (–0445 Dover). Generally the NW-going stream runs for the remainder of the time, but at neaps in summer the stream runs to the southeast during the day and to the northwest by night.

On the bar northeast of Berneray the tides turn about half an hour earlier.

Around the Hermetray group at the south point of the Sound, the NW-going (flood) stream begins –0535 Ullapool (+0230 Dover) and the SE-going tide begins +0035 Ullapool (–0345 Dover).

In narrow channels associated with Caolas Skaari the streams may reach 5 knots, and elsewhere 3 knots. In many places the streams may be diverted at right angles to the main channel by rocks and islets, and a constant watch must be kept to see that one is not being carried off course.

Admiralty Chart
2802, 2841
Admiralty Leisure Folio
5616. 10 (part only)
Imray Chart
C66
Ordnance Survey
18
Cruising Scotland
pp.188-9

Approach to Sound of Harris from SE

Approach to Sound of Harris from NW

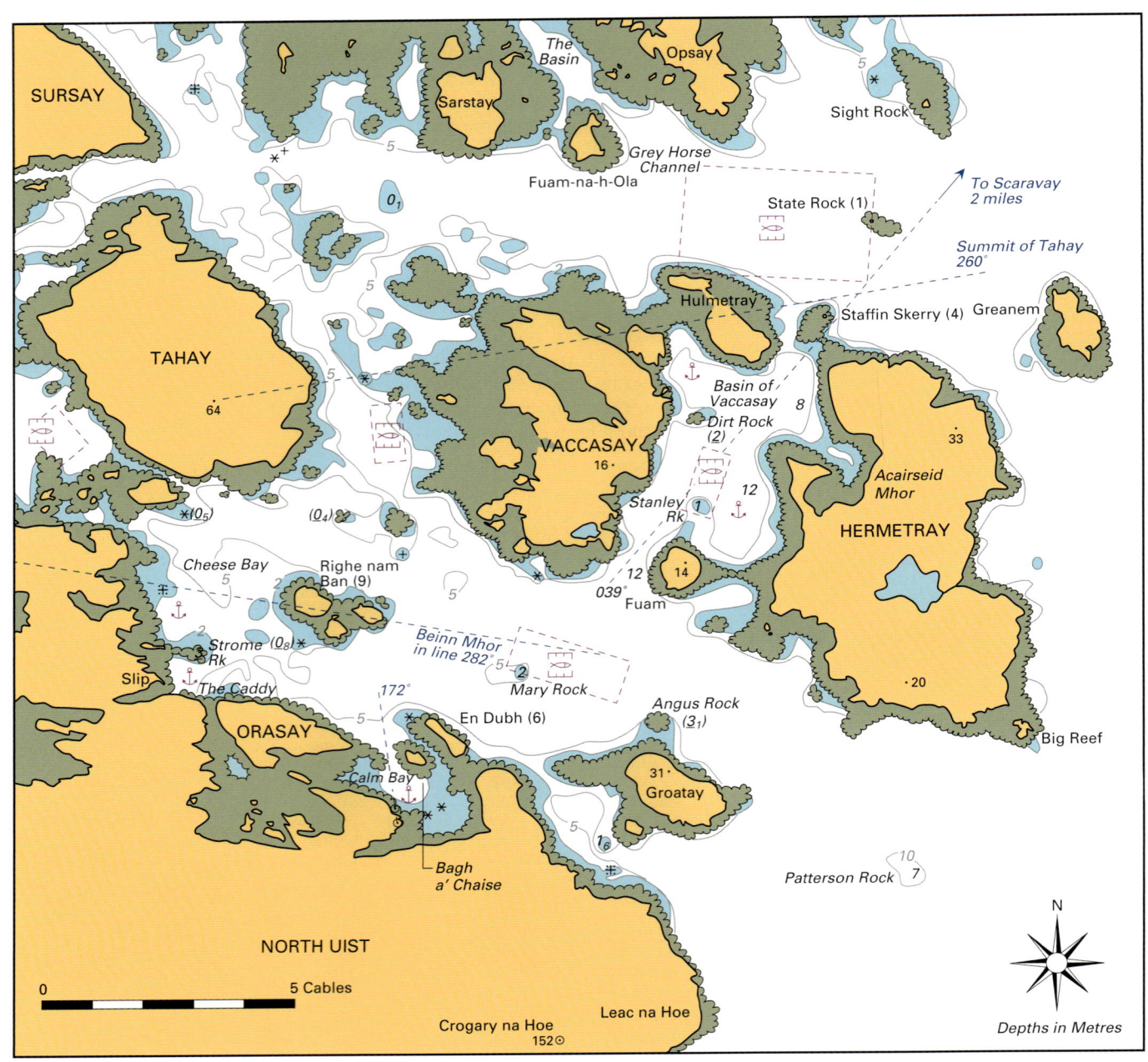

Outer Hebrides

HERMETRAY GROUP

Hermetray Group of Islands

Admiralty Chart
2802
Imray Chart
C66
Ordnance Survey
18
Cruising Scotland
pp.188-9

Hermetray is the most southerly island in the Sound of Harris with Vaccasay on its west side. Several sheltered and easily accessible anchorages lie within a mile of Vaccasay. Tahay (64 metres), west of Vaccasay is the highest island of the group.

Tides

Tidal streams among the Hermetray Group run as follows:
The southeast-going stream begins about –0535 Ullapool (+0230 Dover)
The northwest-going stream begins +0035 Ullapool (+0345 Dover)
Streams in the narrower channels may reach 3 knots

Directions

From the south make for the middle of Hermetray. Then alter course to pass midway between Groatay and Hermetray as reefs extend up to a cable from each. When the east end of Groatay is abeam, bringing the summit of the Righe nam Ban group of islands ahead in line with Beinn Mhor 282° leads north of Angus Rock and Mary Rock, but a large fish farm may prevent this line being followed precisely. Mary Rock is charted as 2 metres, but tangle (weed) has been seen breaking the surface at a very low tide.

From the north either pass east of Hermetray and then approach as from the south or, if the visibility is good, identify Greanem 3 cables NE of Hermetray and steer to pass 1 cable north of it on a course of 260° to the summit of Tahay. Alter course to pass between a large fish farm and Staffin Skerry which, in contrast to other rocks in the area, is sharp and angular and enter Vaccasay Basin by passing west of Staffin

5. Sound of Harris

Vaccasay Basin from the WNW with Hermetray beyond. Dirt Rock is clearly visible. The fish cages will almost certainly have been moved since this photograph was taken

Looking westward over the Hermetray group

Skerry, midway between the skerry and Hulmetray – with care as reefs extend some way off either side.

Anchorages
Calm Bay on North Uist is nearer habitation and is said to be sheltered from all winds and Cheese Bay to the west has good holding. Vaccasay Basin is a more remote alternative but has many fish cages. Opsay Basin, a mile north from Vaccasay Basin, is entered from the east through the Grey Horse Channel (see p.76). It is completely surrounded by low islets and reefs and is open to the sky and wind.

Vaccasay Basin, from the south pass west of Fuam, between Fuam and Vaccasay.

Dirt Rock, a cable east of Vaccasay, is charted as drying 2 metres and fish cages are moored south of it.

Stanley Rock, over which the depth is 1 metre, lies a cable northeast of Fuam at the south end of the basin. Staffin Skerry in line with the southeast point of Scaravay, the most southeasterly island north of Cope Passage, bearing 039°, clears both these rocks. Anchor in the northwest or southeast corners of the basin.

Shoal-draught boats can anchor in the inlet on Hermetray known as Acarsaid Mor, but this is shallow and rather constricted, with weed on the bottom, although the innermost part of the inlet is said to be free of weed. Water may be available from a spring near the east shore of Hermetray.

Calm Bay (Bagh a' Chaise) Noting the position of Mary Rock with 2 metres over it, alter to port but give En. Dubh a wide berth to avoid the drying rock WNW of the island, as the marks leading clear of this, and the reef off Orosay, are reported (2017) as obscured or missing. Keep in the eastern third of the entrance passage to avoid the drying reef extending eastwards from Orosay more than halfway across the entrance. Anchor in 2-3m between the islet SW of Eilean Dubh and the shore where the leading marks are shown. Good shelter and holding in mud with shells.

Orasay Anchor off a concrete slip on North Uist, WNW of Orasay. Approach by the south of Righe nam Ban, keeping closer to Orasay, and look out for Strome Rock which dries 3 metres, more than a cable northeast of the slip.

Cheese Bay It is also possible to anchor north of Strome Rock in Cheese Bay but beware of the awash rock in the northern half of this bay and the shallow patches up to a cable SW of Righe nam Ban. Although not a snug anchorage it provides a large area of reasonable depth for anchoring in good holding, mud.

CCC Sailing Directions and Anchorages

Outer Hebrides

GREY HORSE CHANNEL

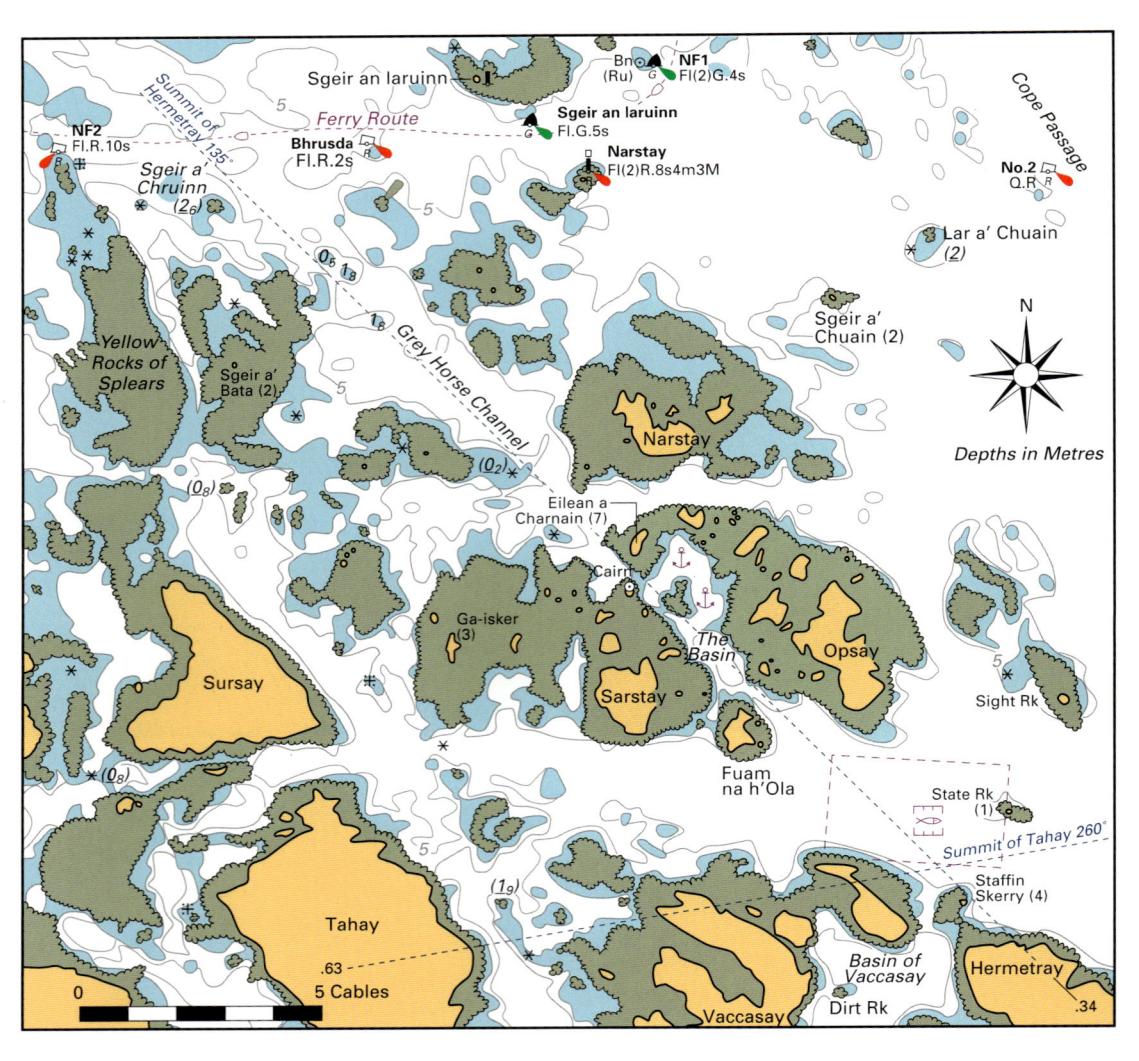

Grey Horse Channel

Admiralty Chart
2802
Imray Chart
C66
Ordnance Survey
18
Cruising Scotland
pp.188-9

The Grey Horse Channel runs between Hermetray and Greanem to Opsay Basin where it narrows between many islets. It continues NW through a narrow passage north of the Cairn and finds its way amidst shoals and rocks to Bays Loch, Berneray. Because there is now a well marked ferry route from the Cope Passage to Bays Loch (see p.78) there is now no requirement even to consider using the Grey Horse Channel except to prove to oneself that it can be done! However the following directions, when used with Chart 2802 and extreme caution, may be of interest.

The tide runs strongly across the passage and such marks as there are must be constantly watched to check that the yacht is not being carried sideways.

Directions

The NW section of the Grey Horse Channel, northwards from Opsay Basin, should only be attempted in clear settled weather and with a rising tide, preferably beginning around LW or as soon as the rise allows passage over the bar northeast of the Grey Horse Cairn (charted as 0·5m but local knowledge suggests that a narrow channel of 1·5m exists), so that some of the dangers are visible. However, bear in mind that access to Bays Loch from the Ferry Route will be delayed until after half tide (see p.78).

From Opsay Basin pass north of the Grey Horse ('Cairn' on chart) and keep the highest part of Hermetray astern over the passage north of the Grey Horse on a bearing of 135°. For the first cable or so keep a little south of this line until clear of drying rocks NW of Eilean a'Charnain. After a mile Sgeir a'Chruinn (dries 2·6m) is left to port. This rock may show white when covered at half tide. After this point the flood tide sets strongly to the SW and must be allowed for when joining the ferry route to Berneray.

Anchorage

Opsay Basin At the outer entrance keep mid-channel to avoid reefs extending 1 cable SW from Opsay. The entrance is not narrow but be sure to turn into the basin only when clear of extending reefs on either hand. Anchor east of the drying reef NE of Sarstay in 6m. Some weed. Further north a bottom of mud and shells can be found in 3-4m. The rocks east and south of the cairn (The Grey Horse) dry about 3-4m.

5. Sound of Harris

Looking northwest along the Grey Horse Channel

Loch nam Ban; Berneray Causeway on far right

CCC Sailing Directions and Anchorages 77

Outer Hebrides

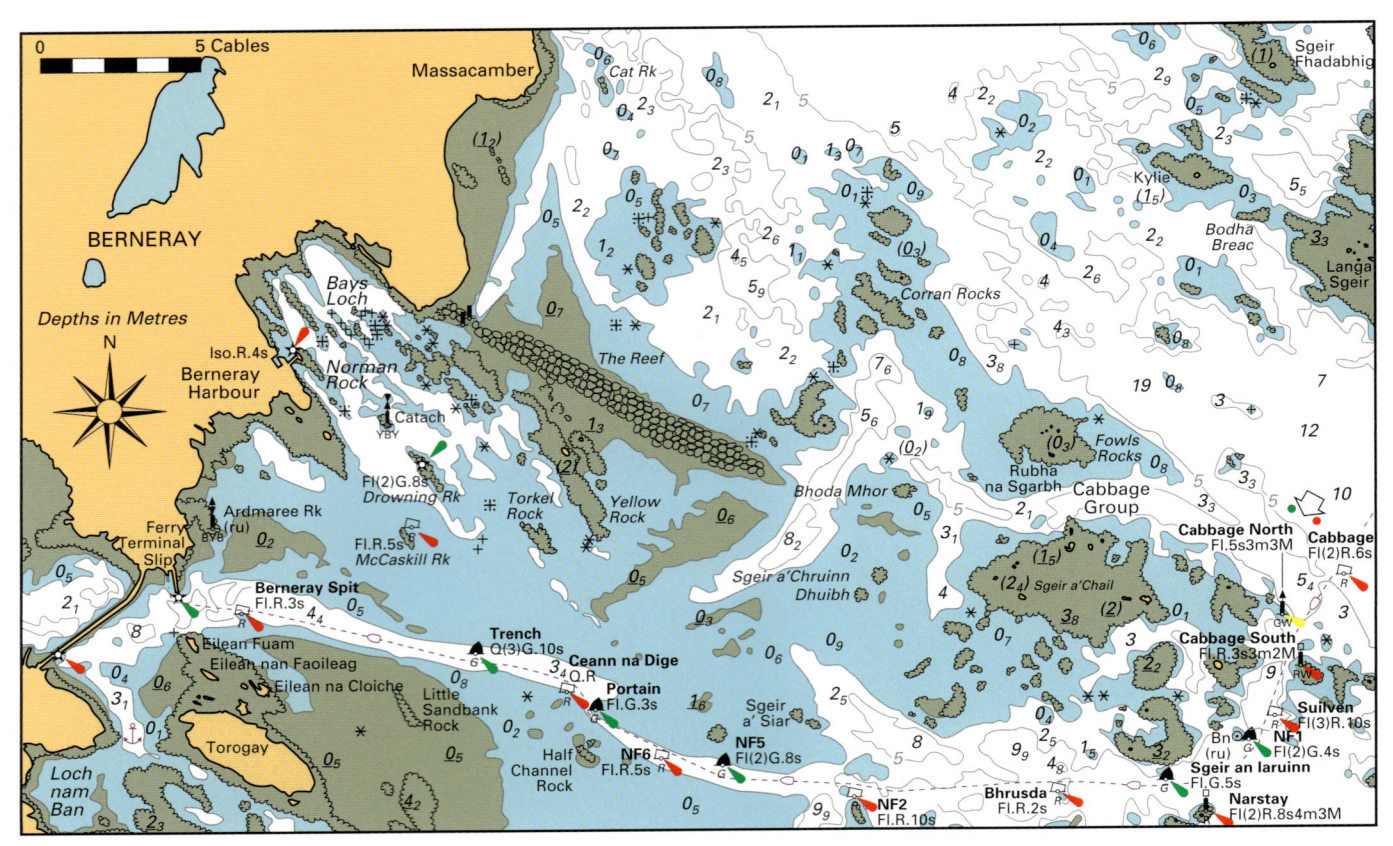

APPROACHES TO BERNERAY

Admiralty Chart
2802
Imray Chart
C66
Ordnance Survey
18
Cruising Scotland
pp.188-9

Berneray

Berneray, well within the Sound of Harris, is close north of the northernmost extremity of North Uist. The west and north coasts have extensive sand dunes. Its east side has an anchorage in Bays Loch which can be approached either by following the ferry route or by the Reef Channel but in both cases an adequate rise of tide is needed. Berneray is no place to make for in bad weather or poor visibility.

Tides

Constant −0046 Ullapool (−0506 Dover)

Height in metres

MHWS	MHWN	MTL	MLWN	MLWS
3·9	3·5	2·4	1·6	0·7

Tides in passage through The Reef Channel
The southeast-going stream begins +0515 Ullapool (+0055 Dover)
The northwest-going stream begins −0125 Ullapool (−0545 Dover)
The stream runs at least 4 knots.

Directions

From the south by the Ferry Route:
This straightforward approach uses the SE (buoyed) part of the Cope Passage (pp.82, 83) and then follows the ferry route. Do not leave the ferry route until the half tide rock (Half Channel Rock on the chart) is covered.

If intending to join the Ferry Route from the Cope Passage, proceed NW after passing port hand buoy No.4 (see plan p.81) until the Cabbage North perch on the ferry route bears less than 240°, and the perch on Cabbage South is identified. This turning point is near port hand buoy, 'Cabbage', Fl(2)R.6s. Alter course to port and then follow the ferry route precisely until reaching a point just before the Trench buoy; then alter course to leave the Trench and McCaskill Rock buoys to port and Drowning Rock and Catach, both marked by perches, to starboard during the final approach either to the harbour or to the anchorage in the NW corner of the loch (see plan opposite).

From the north by The Reef Channel:
The alternative approach to Bays Loch is through the extremely narrow, 15–20m wide, channel between the reef extending eastwards from the Berneray shore and the area of rocks known as 'The Reef'. This channel should be used only above half tide and preferably at slack HW because of strong cross-currents that can be encountered at other times. If in doubt, the buoyed Ferry Route approach should be used.

From a position at the northwest end of the Cope Channel, 2½ cables off the Berneray shore with Beinn Shliebhe bearing 270°, steer southwards holding to the Berneray shore and passing not more than 1½ cables off Massacamber and inside Cat Rock.

Thereafter make for the two tall wood piles which resemble telephone poles which stand on the east extremity of the reef on the Berneray side of the channel (see photograph p.80). The poles must be left to starboard and passed within 5-7m. Do not alter to starboard immediately after passing the southernmost pole but when about 10–15m past it to bring that pole on a line astern on a distant 6 mile transit of 090° with Dun-aarin (a distinctive island the

5. Sound of Harris

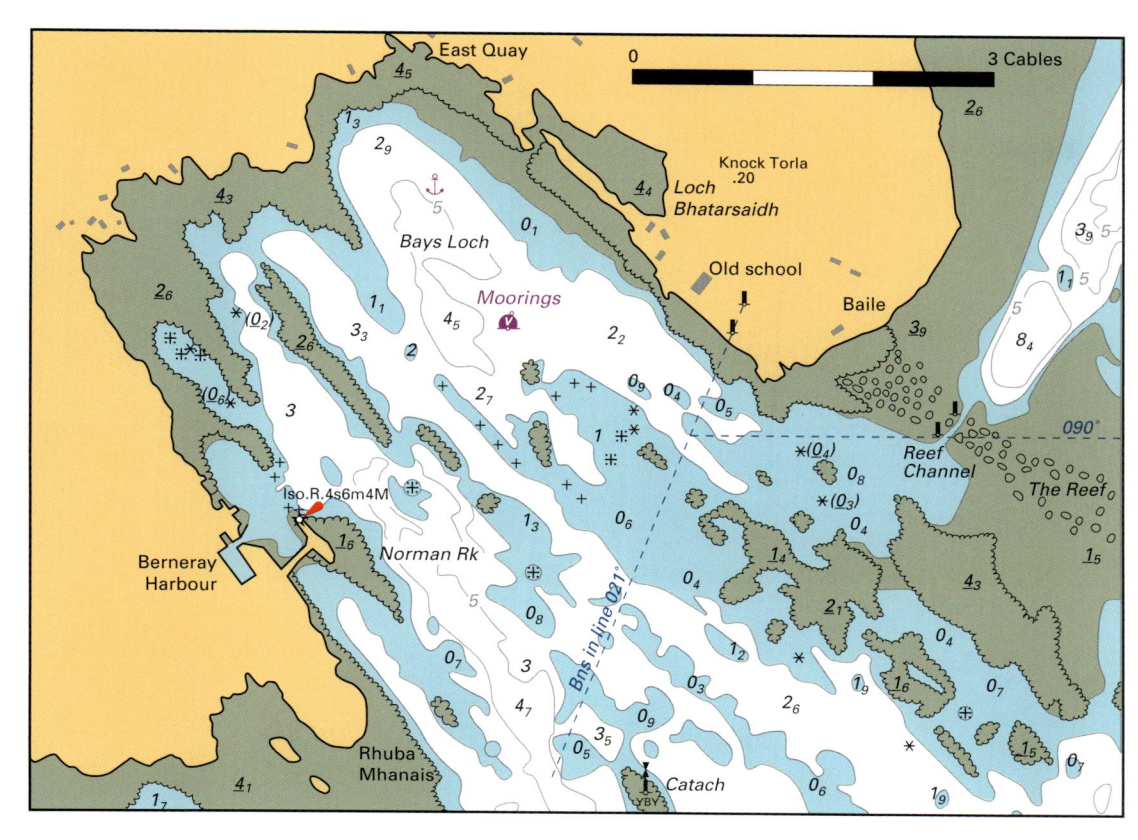

BAYS LOCH, BERNERAY

shape of a small Ailsa Craig). This leading line will lead clear of shoal water on either side until making a turn towards the northern area of Bays Loch. Continue to maintain a close watch for shoal water (see plan above).

Bays Loch

Bays Loch is the only secure anchorage on Berneray but it is shallow and reef strewn. Visitors' moorings and anchorage can be found in the northern part and the secure harbour is on the southwest side. Crossing between the two is only possible above half tide.

Directions

Crossing Bays Loch the transit triangles on the NE shore on a bearing of 021° must be used. To make for the harbour, steer to pass 60m off the end of the breakwater.

Anchorages

North side Anchor in 4m. There are also two visitors' moorings.

The harbour has 2·0m at LW. The immediate approaches northwest of Norman Rock may dry. The entrance is narrow and on entry a sharp turn to port is required.

Loch nam Ban On north Uist, south of Berneray. Approach from the ferry route by steering 280° and leave Trench buoy to starboard, taking care not to stray from the straight and narrow into shoal water on either side. Pass north of Eilean Fuam. Reefs dry one cable off either side of the entrance, and drying rocks lie in the middle of the loch.

Anchor in the mouth of the loch or, at neaps, further in, taking care to avoid the drying rocks. The bottom is soft mud so that a long keel yacht would sink in; care is needed to dig the anchor in securely.

Temporary anchorage for a brief daytime visit to Berneray in settled weather can be found off the sandy beach, at least 1½ cables north of the Reef Channel beacons so as to be out of the worst of the tide. Approach as Reef Channel directions opposite.

Lights and marks

Reef Channel No.1 Unlit
Reef Channel No.2 Unlit
Drowning Rock Lt Bn Fl(2)G.8s2m2M
McCaskill Rock Lt buoy Fl.R.5s
Harbour Iso.R.4s
Berneray ferry slip 2F.G(vert)6m3M
Leac Bhan ferry slip 2F.R(vert)6m3M
Newton jetty root 2F.G(vert)9m4M
Trench Lt buoy Q(3)G.10s
Berneray Spit Lt buoy Fl.R.3s

For lights and marks on the Ferry route see the adjacent plan and Chart 2802. These are frequently changed and it is important to have an updated copy. In the 3 miles from the Cope Passage to the Trench buoy there are 13 buoys or beacons and it is vital that they are checked off methodically as they are passed.

Supplies

Water hose, toilets, shower and telephone at Berneray Harbour. Diesel (key fob needed). Post Office and small shop in village on NW side of Bays Loch. Licensed stores and tearoom at Ardmaree, close to ferry terminal. Calor gas up the Borve road on the left.

CCC Sailing Directions and Anchorages

Outer Hebrides

The small landlocked harbour at Bays Loch, Berneray

The Reef Channel, Berneray looking southwest. The poles should be passed within 5–7 metres

Looking ENE from the summit of Beinn Shliebhe on Berneray over the Cope Passage towards Ensay and Killegray with Harris beyond.

5. Sound of Harris

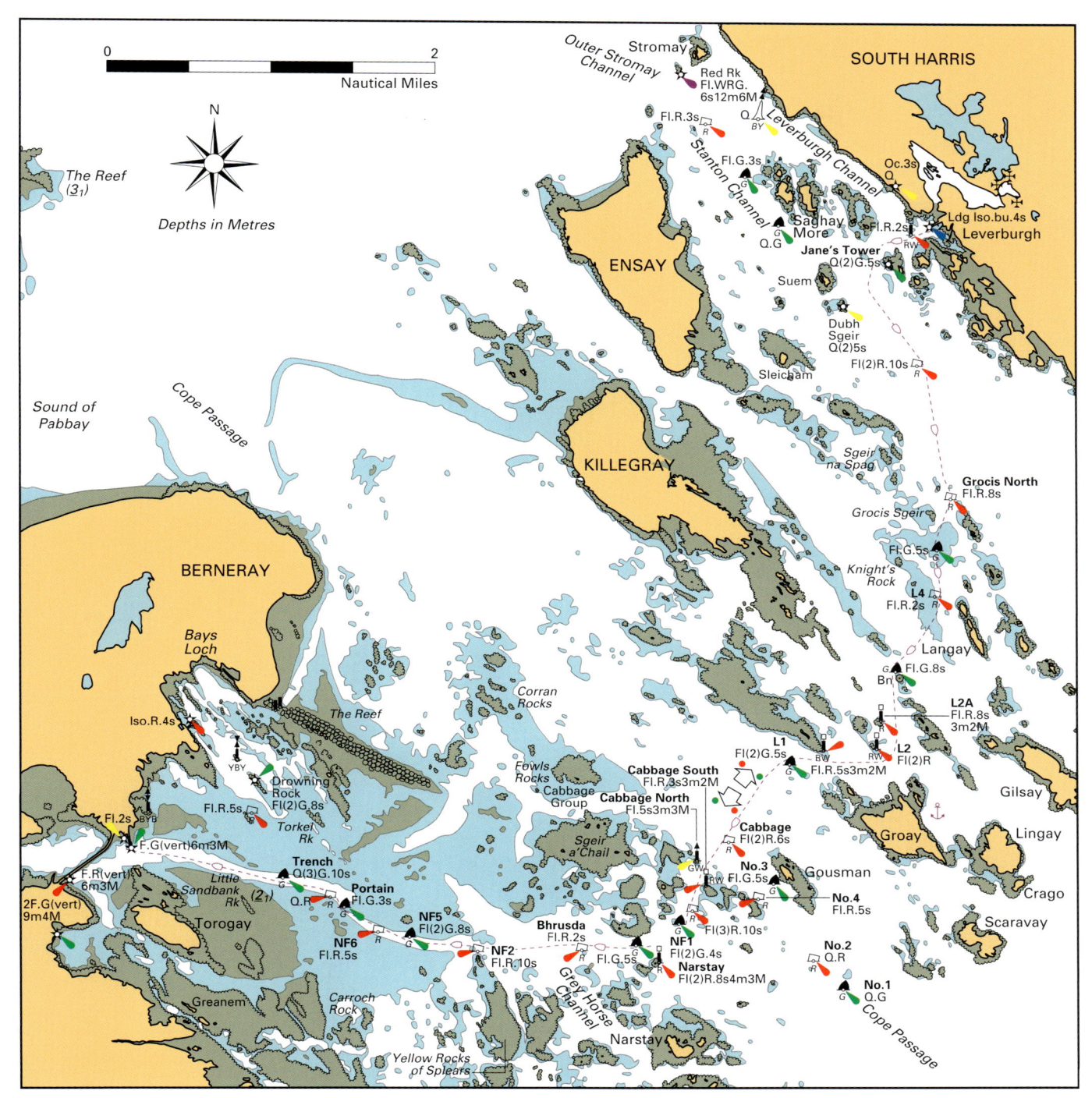

Passages in the Sound of Harris

In the following pages the Cope Passage, the Stanton Channel and the Leverburgh Channel are described in detail. The remaining passage, the Ferry Route, was partially covered in the approaches to Berneray on p.78. The NE section of this, from Grocis North buoy to the Cabbage buoy, is very rarely used by yachts, who, if not heading for Berneray, are usually on passage through the sound.

The Ferry Route is not covered in detail in these *Directions* but, as it is very well marked, no difficulty should be encountered. Yachts who do use it should note the change in direction of buoyage of the Ferry Route at its junction with the Cope Passage and take great care to check off all marks as they are passed.

Anchorage

There are few anchorages in the Sound of Harris, although depths are such that temporary anchorage might be found almost anywhere.

Groay is probably the best occasional anchorage in the sound and is easily approached from between Lingay and Gilsay or, with care, from the Ferry route. Fish farm cages may be encountered.

CCC Sailing Directions and Anchorages 81

Outer Hebrides

COPE PASSAGE

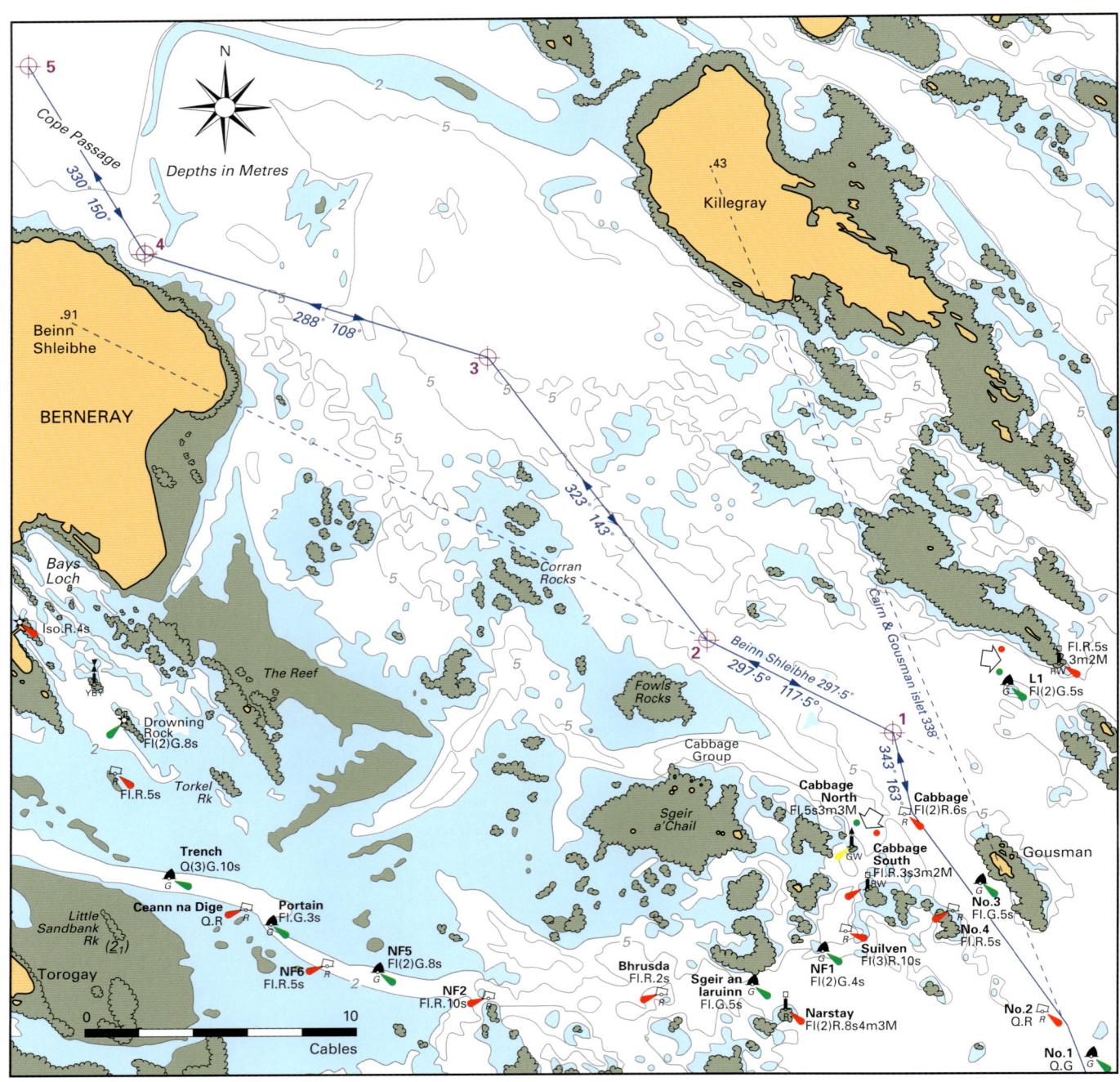

Cope Passage

Admiralty Chart
2802
Imray Chart
C66
Ordnance Survey
18
Cruising Scotland
pp.188-9

The passage was originally laid by Stanley Cope in 1957 for shallow draft Army vessels supplying the base at St Kilda, so as to avoid the strong tidal streams of the Stanton Channel. From its SE entrance a stable channel, with weak streams and previously well marked by lit buoys, leads NW between isolated rocks to a position NE of Berneray. Beyond this point the route passes across the WSW end of a shifting sand bar.

Following the buoying of the Stanton channel by the NLB in 2007 the usage of the Cope Passage, then no longer needed by the Army, was monitored and in 2010 the decision was taken to remove all buoys apart from four SE of the Ferry route. Parts of the passage are still well used: the SE, buoyed, section by vessels approaching Bays Loch, Berneray from the Little Minch (pp.78, 79) and the extreme NW end for vessels approaching Bays Loch from the Atlantic through the reef channel.

The unbuoyed channel, NW of Cabbage buoy, leads very close to many shoal patches through a featureless area which has few landmarks and, even with local knowledge, its navigation would be hazardous without assistance from GPS. For those with faith in their electronics the directions below, giving waypoints that approximately follow the previously buoyed passage, are included. The original advice, that the passage should only be attempted in fair weather by vessels drawing no more than 2m and with a suitable rise of tide, is still very much applicable.

82 CCC Sailing Directions and Anchorages

5. Sound of Harris

Tides
Constant: –0040 Ullapool (–0500 Dover)

Height in metres

MHWS	MHWN	ML	MLWN	MLWS
4·7	3·5	2·7	1·8	0·6

Tidal streams seldom exceed one knot; it is believed that rates are generally ½ knot or less.

NB. Since 1974 the *Admiralty Pilot* has given specific stream data 'on the bar NE of Berneray', as repeated in previous editions of these *Directions*. This was an editorial error, as the data was in fact for a quite different location.

The Bar - Caution
Based on information in the Admiralty Pilot

A bar, consisting of loose shifting sand, extends north from Berneray and then east to Killegray. Chart 2802 shows the approximate position and form of this bar in 2004. The NW part of the main shoal bank had a steep slope on its seaward side and during surveys across the bar, in freshening onshore winds, heavy breakers were suddenly encountered close seaward of this steep slope. These had developed within 40 minutes. Such breakers would be dangerous, particularly as they might not be seen from seaward until craft are upon them.

The precise track given in the directions below leads through a channel close to the Berneray coast. Available data and reports (as recently as 2016) indicate that this channel has been reasonably stable. To allow for the uncertainty of shifting sands, it is recommended that the passage should not be taken with less height of tide than the draught of the vessel. Extreme caution is required and vessels should not attempt passage over the bar in adverse weather conditions. The bar should only be approached in conditions such that the vessel could readily reverse its course and adopt an alternative passage plan.

Directions
Passage from SE to NW

It should be noted that the general direction of buoyage for the Sound of Harris is NW. Thus when approaching the Cope Passage from SE, all red can buoys must be left to port and all green conical buoys to starboard. The best track is made by passing all these lateral marks at a distance of ½ cable. If leaving the Cope Passage to follow the Ferry route, note that the local direction of buoyage on the Ferry route changes at the point where it crosses the Cope Passage (see plan opposite). Care is needed not to confuse the lighted marks on these two routes, particularly at night or in reduced visibility.

Enter the Cope passage from a position approximately 3 cables NE of Greanem (not shown on the plan opposite) on a course of 338° with the conspicuous cairn on Killegray in line with the summit of Gousman. Follow this track until No.1 G buoy is identified. Pass SW of this buoy and NE of No.2 R buoy. When abeam No.2 R buoy, alter course to pass midway between No.3 G and No.4 R buoys, keeping well clear of the reefs which extend almost 3 cables SE from Gousman. The Cabbage R buoy marks the crossing of the Ferry route and the Cope Passage, being a port-hand mark for both and the last of the lateral marks for the Cope.

From a position 100m east of Cabbage buoy steer a course of 343° for the cairn on the summit of Killegray towards Waypoint No.1. When this is reached alter to port and with the summit of Beinn Shliebhe bearing 297·5° head towards Waypoint No.2, a distance of approximately ¾ mile. From this point onwards there are no landmarks that are of assistance.

At Waypoint No.2 alter course to starboard on to 323° and head towards Waypoint No.3, which lies approximately midway between Berneray and Killegray. When this is reached it is necessary to head towards Berneray in order to avoid the shallowest part of the sand bar.

From Waypoint No.3 the track leads 288° for a distance of 1⅓ miles to Waypoint No.4, close by the Berneray shore. Here it turns on to 330° and out to Waypoint No.5 which is clear of the bar. From here continue NNW into the Atlantic, noting The Reef, extending more than 2 cables east of Pabbay, and Halo Rock (LD 3·7) to starboard. If heading west through the Sound of Pabbay, be aware of the extensive shoals and reefs between Berneray and Pabbay which are described for the eastbound passage on p.134 and shown on Chart 2841.

Note that this precise track across the shifting bar has been derived from 2004 survey data. Depths should be observed frequently and compared to those charted as a precaution against subsequent changes.

On most of the legs of the passage the track leads within a cable of drying rocks or shoals charted at less than a metre. It is essential that a vessel's cross track error is constantly monitored.

Passage from NW to SE

As for SE to NW but in reverse. The approximate reciprocal courses are shown on the plan. If in any doubt about the conditions at the bar north of Berneray use either of the main channels, Stanton or Leverburgh, both at the NE side of the Sound of Harris (see p.84).

Waypoints

No.1	57° 42'·44N	007° 04'·04W
No.2	57° 42'·79N	007° 05'·32W
No.3	57° 43'·87N	007° 06'·83W
No.4	57° 44'·28N	007° 09'·20W
No.5	57° 45'·00N	007° 10'·00W

Lights
From SE entry to Cope Passage to Ferry Route

No 1 Stbd-hand Lt buoy QG
No 2 Port-hand Lt buoy QR
No 3 Stbd-hand Lt buoy (SW of Gousman) Fl.G.5s
No 4 Port-hand Lt buoy (SW of Gousman) Fl.R.5s
Cabbage Port-hand Lt buoy Fl.(2).R.6s

Outer Hebrides

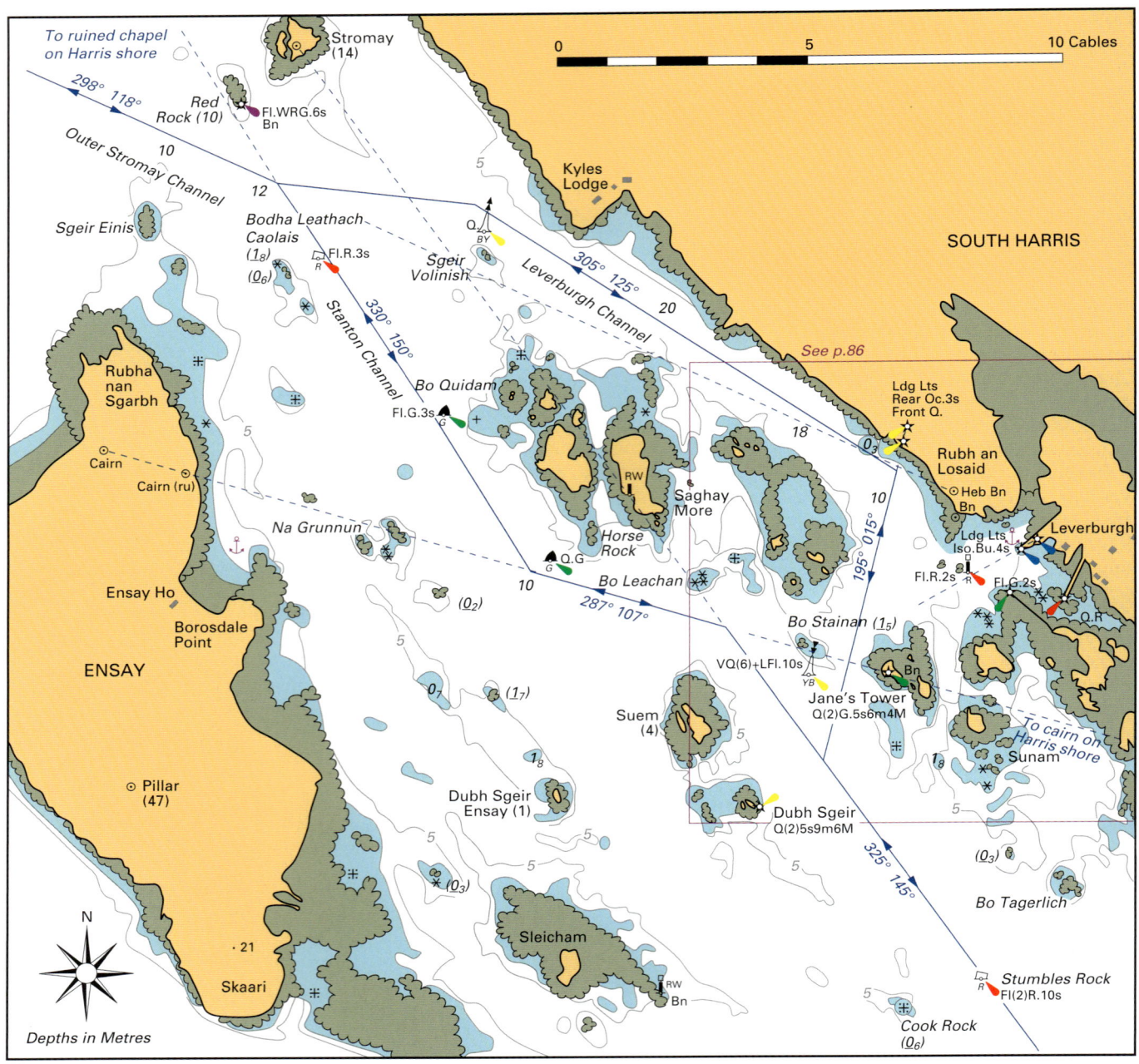

STANTON CHANNEL

Admiralty Chart
2802, 2841
Admiralty Leisure Folio
5616. 10 (part only)
Imray Chart
C66
Ordnance Survey
18
Cruising Scotland
pp.188-9

Stanton Channel

The main channel through the Sound of Harris is the Stanton Channel. Although nowhere in the channel is the width of safe water less than 1½ cables, the dangers on either side and the need to cross tidal streams demand that the track shown and transits given are carefully followed and, if using GPS in poor visibility, it is essential to monitor the cross-track error.

Some of the transits, which were formerly the prime navigational aids before the channel was buoyed in 2007, are shown on the chart and the above plan to provide a degree of guidance in clear weather. An alternative route through the sound is the Leverburgh Channel which passes NW of Jane's Tower but in places it is restricted in width to little over half a cable and it is necessary to follow the transits carefully. Both channels join up with the Outer Stromay Channel between Ensay and Stromay.

Tides

Constant: –0040 Ullapool (–0500 Dover)

Height in metres

MHWS	MHWN	MTL	MLWN	MLWS
4·6	3·5	2·6	1·9	0·6

In the channels between Ensay and Harris, including the Stanton Channel and Leverburgh Channels, the streams are remarkable. The SE-going stream begins +0545 Ullapool (+0125 Dover) and the NW-going stream begins –0025 Ullapool (–0445 Dover). This is the norm. However during the summer at neaps it has been observed that the SE-going stream runs during the day and the NW-going stream at night. The spring rate south of Saghay More is 4 knots.

84 CCC Sailing Directions and Anchorages

5. Sound of Harris

Directions

Passage from SE to NW

Enter the Sound from the Minches between Renish Point, South Harris and Dun-aarin, the most easterly of the Groay group of islands and readily identified by its height (26m) and angular profile. In wind against tide conditions give Renish Point a good offing. Make for the R buoy marking the Stumbles Rock or, if it cannot be made out, head between Jane's Tower and the beacon on Dubh Sgeir. Jane's Tower is under the peak of Chaipaval at the NW point of the Sound and Dubh Sgeir beacon resembles a disused lighthouse and is the more conspicuous, having open water behind it. The Stumbles buoy must be left to port.

From the Stumbles buoy pass between Jane's Tower and the beacon on Dubh Sgeir on a course of 325° towards the stone beacon on Saghay More. When past Suem alter towards the G buoy SW of Horse Rock. Note that the transit of 287° on the plan may not be easily recognised as the lower cairn on Ensay has almost totally collapsed. The tidal streams may be strong here.

When the Horse Rock buoy is abeam alter to starboard towards the Red Rock lattice beacon (see photograph below) leaving the G buoy west of Bo Quidam to starboard and the R buoy east of Bodha Leathach Caolais to port. At a distance of 1 cable from the Red Rock beacon alter to a course of 298° to pass northwestward out through the Outer Stromay Channel leaving the R buoy (9 cables WNW of Red Rock Bn.) marking Colasgeir (dries 2·2m) close to port. Doing so will avoid Irishman Rock (dries 0·6m) lying 5 cables NE of Colasgeir.

If heading north after leaving the Sound of Harris, Red Rock beacon in line with the summit of Saghay More astern 135° leads close south of Inner and Outer Temple Rocks off the Harris shore.

Passage from NW to SE

From the north and NW Beinn a'Charnain on Pabbay is conspicuous, as is Chaipaval on Harris. Pass to the west of Coppay and at least 1 mile to the south before identifying the Colasgeir R buoy and lining up with the Outer Stromay Channel. From the west it is best to pass through the Sound of Shillay to approach the Outer Stromay Channel.

If the Colasgeir R buoy is difficult to see, keeping the lattice beacon on Red Rock in line with the N Cardinal buoy marking Sgeir Volinish will avoid any dangers until close enough to identify the Colasgeir buoy and also the Heb Beacon on Rubh 'an Losaid.

Leaving the Colasgeir R buoy to starboard enter the Outer Stromay Channel with the Heb Beacon bearing 118°. Maintain this course, passing south of Red Rock Beacon, until 1 cable beyond it before turning to starboard on to a course of 150°. Leave the R buoy marking Bodha Leathach Caolais to starboard and follow the track on the plan leaving both the G buoy west of Bo Quidam and the second G buoy SW of Horse Rock to port. Avoid straying towards the Na Grunnun group of rocks.

After passing the Horse Rock buoy, course can be altered to pass between Suem and the S cardinal buoy marking Bo Stainan. Thereafter proceed to pass east of the Stumbles Rock buoy.

Anchorage

Ensay Approach from the NW is best, from the direction of Sgeir Volinish, noting carefully the hazards on either hand. Anchor in the bay on NE side, off the large house.

Alternatively approach from Stumbles Rock R buoy (in conditions of good visibility), pass south of Dubh Sgeir Ensay and on a course of 331° keeping the south tangent of the Harris shore below the slopes of Chaipaval just open of the north tangent of Ensay, the hazards are cleared on either hand. Maintain this course passing between the reefs off Borosdale Point and those round Na Grunnan. Do not turn into the anchorage until the house bears 225°. The anchorage is sheltered from the east through south to NW. Note the reefs extending from either side of the bay especially from the east.

Lights

Dubh Sgeir Beacon Q(2)5s9m6M
Jane's Tower Beacon Q(2)G.5s6m4M
Stumbles Rock Lt buoy Fl(2)R.10s
Bo Stainan Lt buoy VQ(6)+LFl.10s
Horse Rock Lt buoy QG
Bo Quidam Lt buoy Fl.G.3s
Sgeir Volinish Lt buoy Q
Bodha Leathach Caolais Lt buoy Fl.R.3s
Red Rock Lattice Beacon Fl.WRG.6s
Colasgeir Lt buoy Fl.(2)R.8s

Red Rock beacon at the northwest end of the Stanton Channel; Chaipaval on the left

J Ferguson

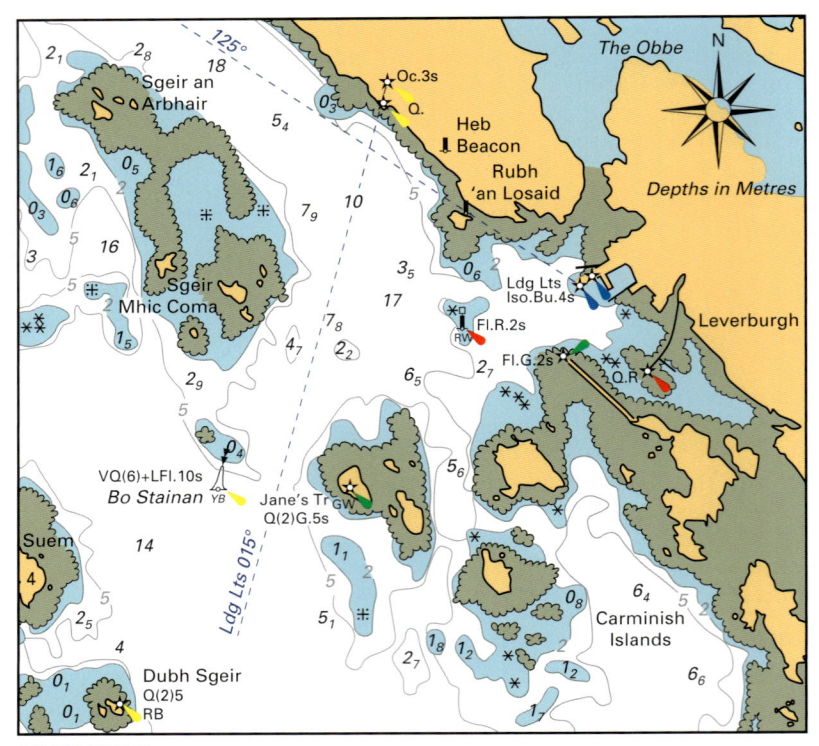

Outer Hebrides

LEVERBURGH

Admiralty Chart
2802
Admiralty Leisure Folio
5616. 10 (part only)
Imray Chart
C66
Ordnance Survey
18
Cruising Scotland
pp.188-9

Jane's Tower from the south with the Heb beacon to the right and the two beacons for the Leverburgh channel, with a white painted mark above them, to the left

Leverburgh Channel

This channel, an alternative to the west part of Stanton Channel (see p.84), offers more shelter and less tide and is a useful option in bad conditions.

Directions

From SE to NW

Approach as described for the Stanton channel towards the stone beacon on Saghay More on a course of 325°. Alter course to starboard, just before Jane's Tower, when the white transit marks NW of Rubh'an Losaid are in line bearing 015°. Keep on this transit until fairly close to the shore then turn to port to bring a small iron beacon on the shore (below the Heb beacon) in line with the Leverburgh pierhead astern bearing 125°. Steer 305° to pass north of the N Cardinal buoy marking Sgeir Volinish. After passing Sgeir Volinish steer to pass south of the lattice beacon on Red Rock and join the Outer Stromay channel then follow the directions for the Stanton/Outer Stromay channels (p.85).

From NW to SE

Approach and follow the Outer Stromay channel as described for the Stanton channel (p.85). Pass a cable south of the Red Rock beacon and when about a cable beyond it steer to leave Sgeir Volinish N Cardinal buoy to starboard. When the small iron beacon and Leverburgh pierhead (described above) are in line, turn to starboard and steer 125° on this transit. Turn to starboard again only when the white transit marks on the Harris shore can be brought to bear 015° astern. Pass west of Jane's Tower on this transit on a heading of 195°. Once between the beacon on Dubh Sgeir and Jane's Tower, turn to port and steer to leave the Stumbles Rock buoy to starboard.

Leverburgh

Tides

Constant –0040 Ullapool (–0500 Dover)

Height in metres

MHWS	MHWN	MTL	MLWN	MLWS
4·6	3·5	2·6	1·9	0·6

Directions

As described for the Leverburgh Channel but leave the transit (white marks on Rubh'an Losaid in line 015°) when the R&W perch on the reef is in line with the head of the pier. Turn towards the pier and leave the perch to port. If the perch is missing it may be replaced by a R can buoy.

Anchorage

Anchor either side of the pier and clear of moorings but keep clear of the ferry turning area. There are two breakwaters south and SE of the pierhead giving protection to the ferry berth and small craft moorings. This area should not be entered without local knowledge. A pontoon has been installed on the north side of the pier for small boats. Visiting yachts should leave the outer berths clear for trip boats.

Carminish Bay on the SE side of Carminish Peninsula, Harris, 2 miles NW of Renish Point. Approaching 1 cable off shore clears all dangers including Leade Rocks 3 cables south of the peninsula. Enter the bay avoiding the rock (dries 1·7m) off the east shore. Anchor in 5m. Exposed to west, south and SE.

Lights

Leverburgh leading Lts. Front: Iso.Bu.4s
Rear: Iso.Bu.4s
Leverburgh perch Fl.R.2s
Outer breakwater Fl.G.2s5m3M
Inner breakwater Q.R.5m3M

Supplies

Shop, PO, petrol and road diesel at shop, Calor gas, water at pier or pontoon. Diesel (key fob needed, see p.11). Craft shop. Bank (Thursday only), Car hire. Tearoom/Restaurant at craft shop. Vehicle ferry service to Berneray and North Uist. Bus service to Stornoway.

86 CCC Sailing Directions and Anchorages

5. Sound of Harris

Leverburgh; the moorings, upper right, are now protected by two breakwater and a pontoon has been installed on the north side of the main pier

Leverburgh approaches, Saghay More, lower left

CCC Sailing Directions and Anchorages **87**

6. South Harris

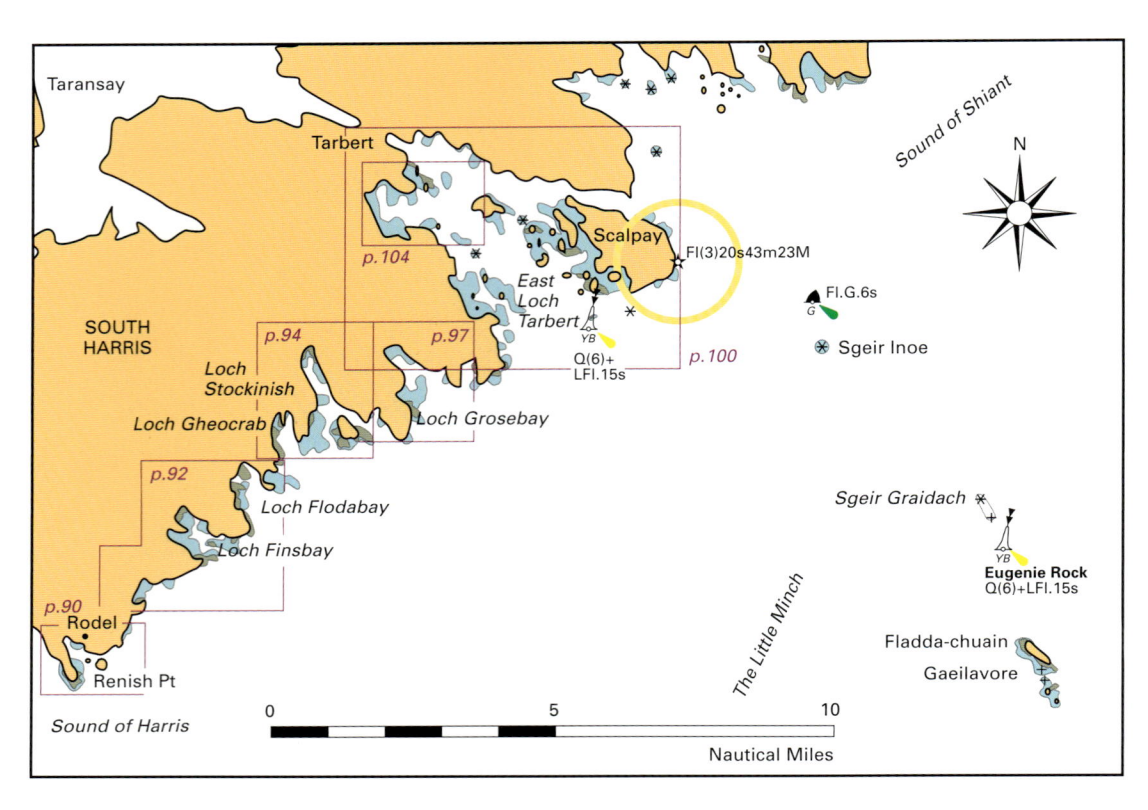

SOUTH HARRIS
KEY PLAN

Sound of Harris to East Loch Tarbert

The coastline from Renish Point at the Sound of Harris to Rubha Bhocaig, at the south entrance to East Loch Tarbert, is a distance of 10 miles and is indented with many lochs which offer anchorage. These include Loch Rodel, Lingara Bay, Loch Finsbay, Lochs Gheocrab and Beacravik, Loch Stockinish and Lochs Grosebay and Scadabay all of which can be used in suitable conditions as shelter or as interesting places to visit.

Admiralty Chart
1757, 1795, 2802
Admiralty Leisure Folio
5616. 10
Imray Chart
C66
Ordnance Survey
14, 18
Cruising Scotland
pp.190-192

Directions

To clear this coast and remain free of hazards including Nun Rock and Bogha Bhocaig both off Rubha Bhocaig, keep at least ½ mile SE of a line from Renish Point to Rubha Bhocaig. In poor visibility the fact that Rubha Chluar (plan p.97) is dark and steep to with no offlying islands may be the only distinguishing feature.

There are no large scale charts, and the plans in this book are based on Admiralty surveys from about 1860 at a scale of 1:10,560, supplemented by individual observations, and are indicative only of the hazards which may be met. It is emphasised that careful pilotage is essential.

Tides

(Interpolated between Leverburgh and Tarbert)
Constant –0035 Ullapool (–0455 Dover)
Height in metres

MHWS	MHWN	MTL	MLWN	MLWS
4·8	3·8	2·8	2·0	0·7

NE-going stream begins –0335 Ullapool (+0430 Dover)
SW-going stream begins +0250 Ullapool (–0130 Dover)
Off the headlands the tidal rate may reach 2 knots sp. but the streams are very weak in the lochs.

Lights

There are none southwest of the entrance to East Loch Tarbert, but the following will be of some help:
Eilean Glas, Scalpay Fl(3)20s43m 23M
Neist Point, Skye Fl.5s43m16M
Waternish Point, Skye Fl.20s21m8M

6. South Harris

Rodel from the east

Rodel from the NW

CCC Sailing Directions and Anchorages 89

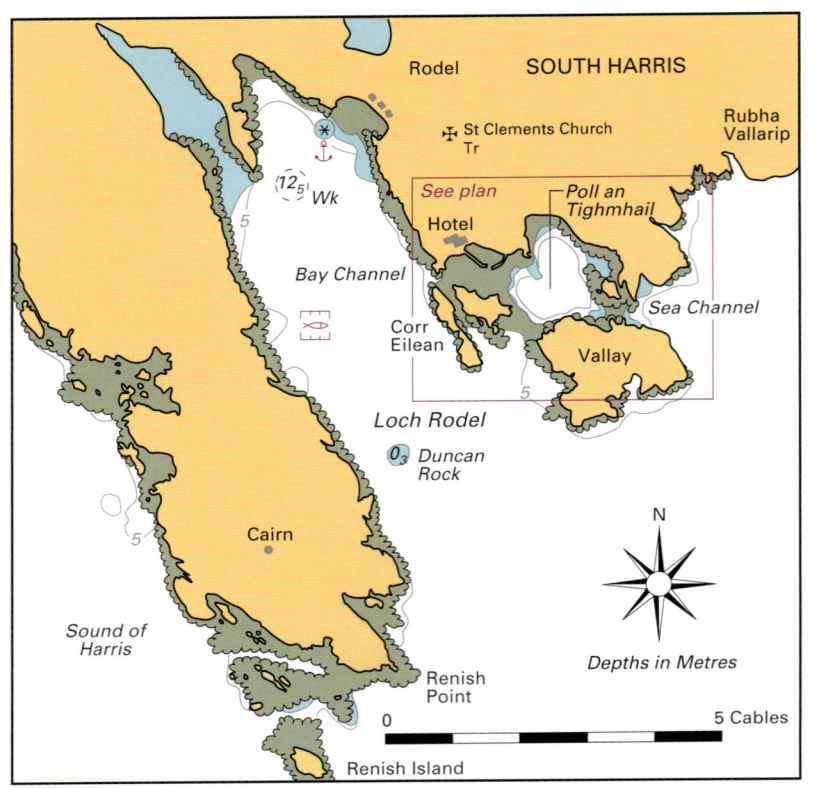

Outer Hebrides

LOCH RODEL

The Sea Channel, Poll an Tighmhaill at LW

Tides
Const. –0040 Ullapool (–0500 Dover)

Height in metres

MHWS	MHWN	MTL	MLWN	MLWS
4·6	3·5	2·6	1·9	0·6

Directions
From the Sound of Harris give Renish Point a good offing and beware of vigorous wind against tide conditions which may be present here even in moderate winds. The square tower of St Clement's Church on the east side of the loch forms a good landmark. When entering Loch Rodel keep at least 1 cable off the SW side to avoid Duncan Rock (0·3m over it) near the entrance. There is a wreck whose position is uncertain, and a rock near the northern corner of the loch.

Anchorage
Temporary anchorage whilst waiting for the tide to enter Poll an Tighmhail may be had SW of the shingle beach on the NE side of Loch Rodel. Take care to avoid a drying rock about 100m offshore towards the northern end of the shingle beach. Anchor in 8m, weed. The submerged wreck off the point at the head of the loch is now charted as being well covered.

Loch Rodel
The entrance to the loch lies just north of Renish Point. The main part of the loch is exposed to the south and provides temporary anchorage only. Poll an Tighmhail (see opposite) provides better anchorage although entry is only possible when there is sufficient rise of tide.

90 CCC Sailing Directions and Anchorages

6. South Harris

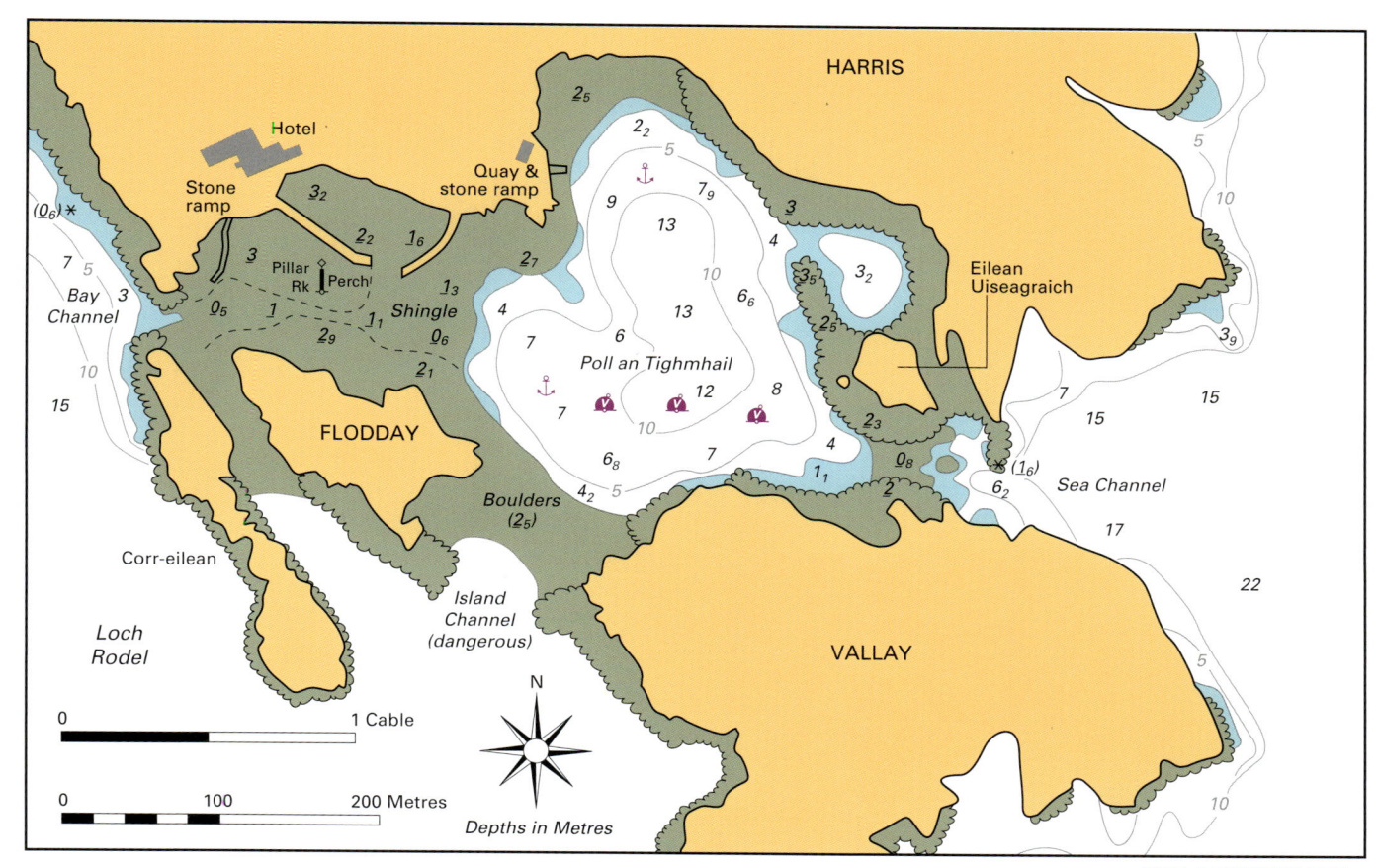

Rodel (Poll an Tighmhail)
A deep pool on the east side Loch Rodel, enclosed by three islets Vallay, Flodday and Corr-eilean which give perfect shelter. Access is governed by the height of the tide as all the channels between the islets dry.

Approach
Bay Channel, which dries 1·1m, is the best entrance. Making entry keep slightly south of mid-channel and steer to pass 15m south of Pillar Rock on which there is a perch, then head towards the north side of the Sea Channel. When the top of the rectangular Pillar Rock is awash there is 3·1m in the channel. When the base of that rock is awash there is 1·9m in the channel.

Sea Channel entrance dries 0·8m with a flat sill covered by heavy kelp. The channel is 20m wide but it must be used with caution if any swell or wave surge is present. Care is required to avoid the rock (dries 1·6m) at the east end of the channel.

Island Channel dries and due to the rock strewn bottom is dangerous at any state of the tide and should not be used.

Anchorage
The centre of the pool is deep with poor holding but 3 visitors moorings are available on the south side. Anchorage is possible in the north of the pool off the quay and stone ramp in 5m. Swinging is restricted and a kedge may be necessary. It is reported that the restricted space in the NE corner behind a rock (dries 3·5m) offers anchorage in 3·2m for small vessels. A survey by dinghy or the help of local knowledge is advisable before entering this part of the pool. Anchor bow and stern, taking a line ashore if necessary. Holding ground is reported poor throughout the pool.

Services
Hotel (closed in 2016, re-opening date uncertain). Shops, PO and fuel at Leverburgh 2½ miles.

POLL AN TIGHMHAILL

Admiralty Chart
2802, 1757
Admiralty Leisure Folio
5616. 10A, 10B
Imray Chart
C66
Ordnance Survey
18
Cruising Scotland
p.190

Pillar Rock in the Bay Channel, Poll an Tighmhaill. The topmark was reported missing in 2015

Edward Mason

CCC Sailing Directions and Anchorages 91

Outer Hebrides

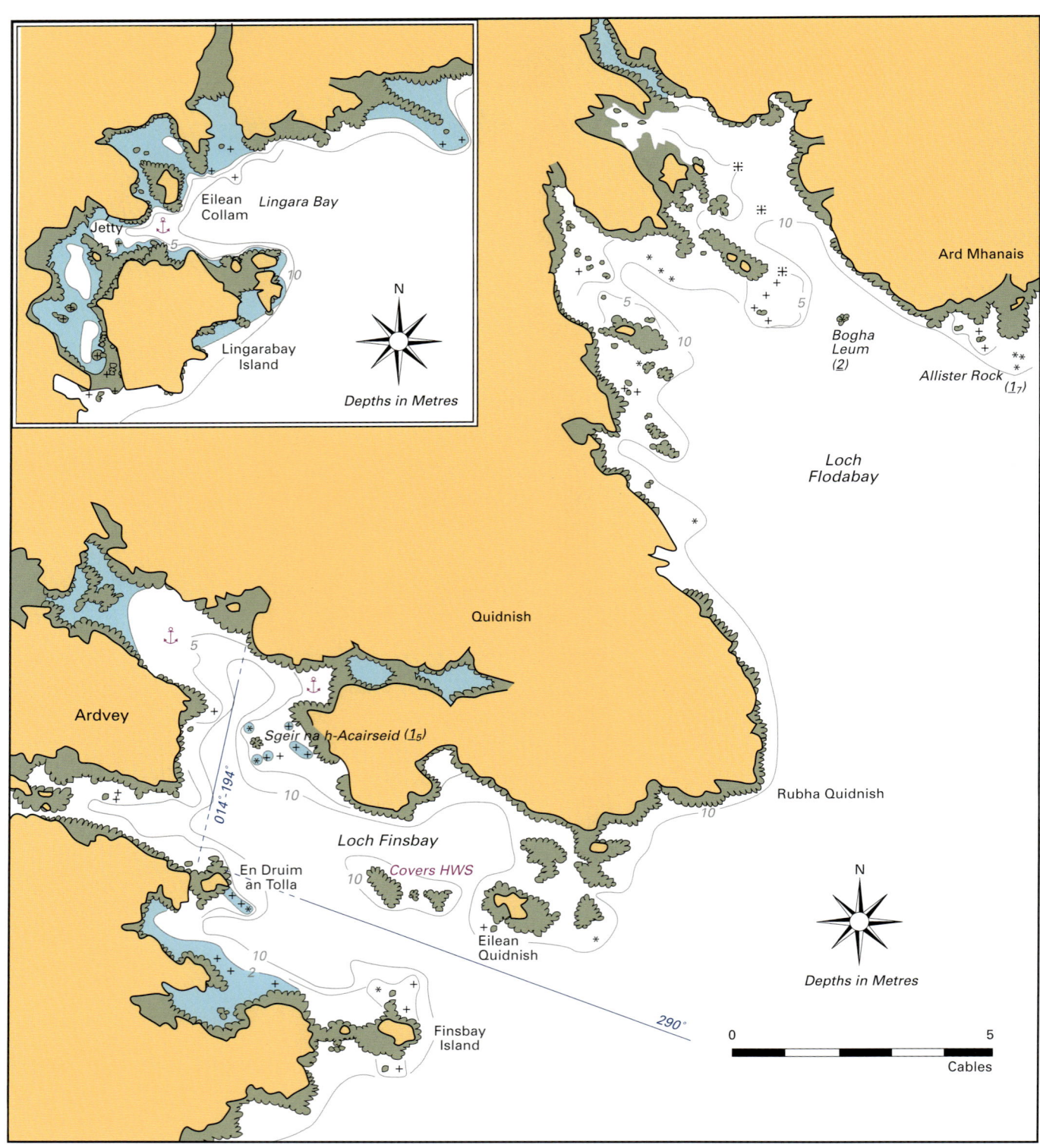

LOCH FINSBAY AND LOCH FLODABAY WITH LINGARA BAY (INSET)

Lingara Bay

About 2 miles NE of Loch Rodel. Sheltered by Lingarabay Island and islets.

Approach

The east entrance is wide and hazard free but if approaching from the NE note rocks extending 1½ cables offshore 4 cables east of the entrance.

Anchorage

Anchor just past the south side of Eilean Collam in 5m. The inlet beyond is inaccessible as it is encumbered with rocks. Excellent shelter in winds from the south round by west to north but untenable in easterly weather.

6. South Harris

Loch Finsbay

This loch, a mile in length, provides good sheltered anchorage which is relatively easy of access.

The entrance lies ¾ mile southwest of Rubha Quidnish, between Finsbay Island, which is 17 metres high, steep-sided with grass on top, on the south side, and Eilean Quidnish which is 13 metres high with a sharper peak.

Drying and submerged rocks lie up to a cable north of Finsbay Island, and drying reefs and submerged rocks lie up to 2 cables ESE and ENE of Eilean Quidnish.

Directions

From the south, do not turn into the loch until about midway between the two islands.

From the northeast keep Ard Mhanais open east of Rubha Quidnish 032° astern to clear the rocks east of Eilean Quidnish.

Inside the loch, keep the north side of Eilean Druim an Tolla, which is at the tip of a promontory on the south side, bearing 290° to avoid drying rocks on the north side of the channel, then pass a cable north of Eilean Druim an Tolla.

Turn to starboard and steer with the promontory off which Eilean Druim an Tolla lies bearing 194° astern, and the conspicuous bluff on the east side of an inlet ahead bearing 014° (not the inlet further east), passing about ¾ cable east of Ardvey, between Sgeir na h-Acarsaid which dries 1·5 metres and drying reefs off Ardvey.

Anchorage

Ardvey Anchor north of Ardvey in 4 metres, rather soft mud. Telephone. Some private moorings. Alternatively, the small bay on the east side gives better protection from that direction.

Loch Flodabay

This loch is encumbered with below water rocks and is not particularly recommended. There appears, from an old Admiralty Survey, to be a clear passage, following the NE shore, to the head of the loch leaving Bogha Leum (dries 2m) to port. Note two further rocks awash near the head of the loch. All three rocks are about 1 cable from the NE shore and should all be left to port.

Several rocks lie off Aird Mhanais, a low lying headland. These include Allister Rock (dries 1·7m) and Earr Manish (dries 2·3m). Accordingly, when passing Aird Mhanais, give it a wide berth of 5 cables.

Loch Finsbay: the anchorage north of Ardvey is beyond the reef in the foreground

Admiralty Chart
1757
Admiralty Leisure Folio
5616. 10A
Imray Chart
C66
Ordnance Survey
14
Cruising Scotland
p.192

The anchorage in Loch Beacravik (p.95) from the NW. The salmon hatchery is left of centre and has now been extended and is green

CCC Sailing Directions and Anchorages

Outer Hebrides

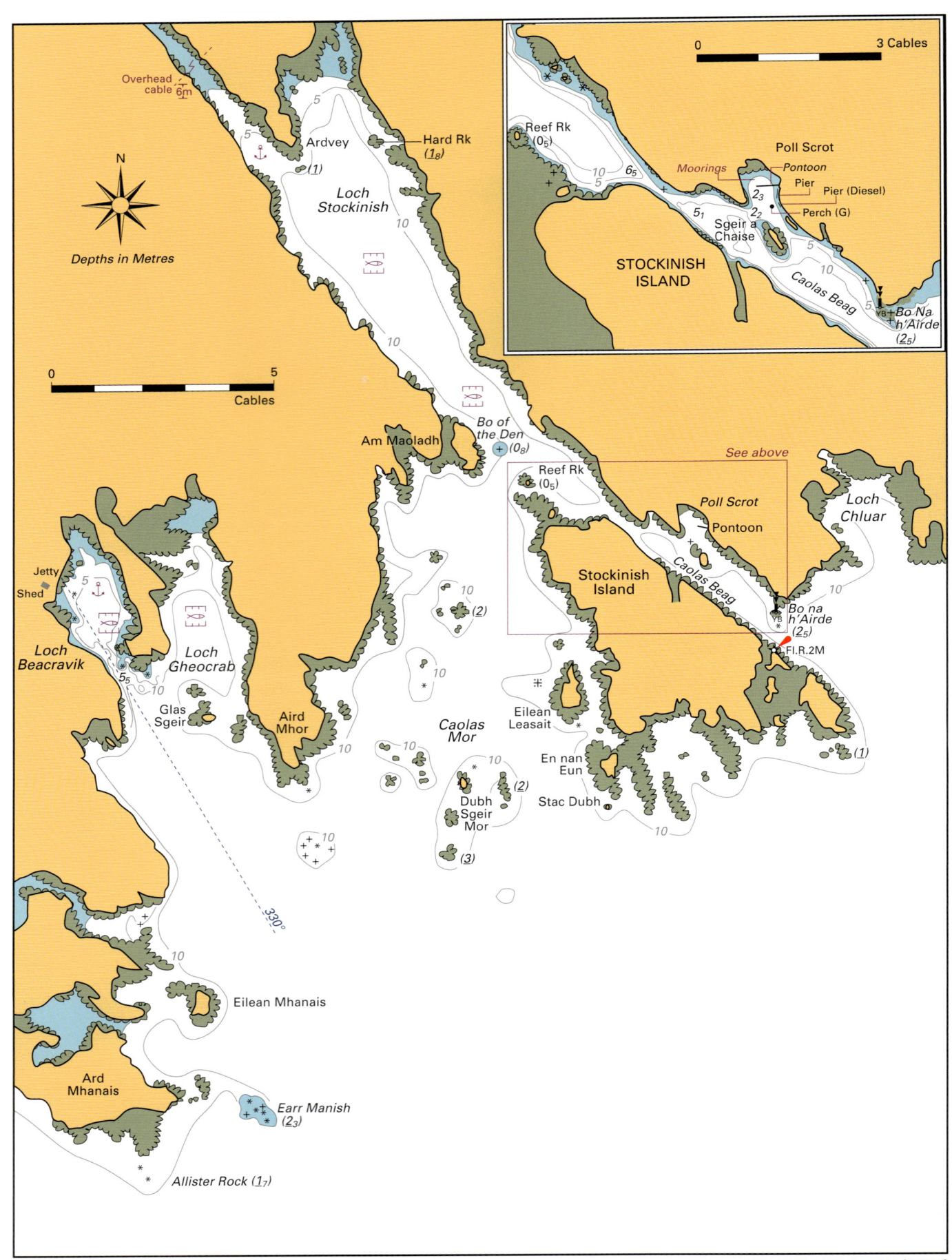

LOCH BEACRAVIK, LOCH GEOCRAB AND LOCH STOCKINISH WITH POLL SCROT (INSET)

6. South Harris

Loch Beacravik
About 3 miles from Loch Finsbay, Loch Beacravik offers good shelter. Loch Gheocrab to the east is not recommended and the following directions are for Loch Beacravik only.

Tides
Const. –0035 Ullapool (–0455 Dover)
Height in metres

MHWS	MHWN	MTL	MLWN	MLWS
4·8	3·8	2·8	2·0	0·7

Directions
From the south note the drying rocks south and east of Aird Mhanais (p.93) and keep 5 cables off that point. A large stone fronted shed at the head of Loch Beacravik is conspicuous and when this is in sight it is clear to alter towards the entrance to Loch Beacravik.

Approach the shed on a bearing of 330° to clear the rocks south and west of Aird Mhor. Beyond Glas Sgeir, at the mouth of Loch Gheocrab, a reef (dries 1·5m) partially blocks the entrance to that loch. In the entrance to Loch Beacravik rocks dry more than half of its width from the east side; keep a quarter of the width from the west side.

From the east or NE head for Ard Mhanais then Eilean Mhanais. It is important to note the rocks (one of which dries 0·3m) 3 cables south of Aird Mhor and also those rocks south of Dubh Sgeir Mhor and Stockinish Island. A clearance bearing of the south end of the Shiant Islands in sight south of Rubha Chluar leads south of all of them. (If heading NE out of Loch Beacravik this bearing is particularly useful). Once the shed bears 330° head towards it as above.

Anchorage
Centre of the basin, off the jetty in 9m. Rocks extend off the burn on the west side and at the head of the basin. Within the loch there are shoal rocky patches which give poor holding so that the anchor needs to be placed with care. Some fish cages are laid on the east side of the loch.

Loch Gheocrab provides little shelter, apart from a pool at the head of the loch behind a drying reef, and is also obstructed by fish cages.

Loch Stockinish
The outer part of Loch Stockinish between Aird Mhor and Stockinish Island, known as Caolas Mor, is rock encumbered and, with only Dubh Sgeir Mhor above water, requires great care in pilotage (see below). It is not recommended as the principal approach channel to the inner loch. At LW or in a heavy sea the rocks in Caolas Mor show or are marked by breakers. NE of Stockinish Island, Caolas Beag provides a straightforward passage to the Inner Loch. Loch Chluar which lies immediately to the north of Loch Stockinish cannot be recommended as an anchorage.

Tides
Const. –0027 Ullapool (–0447 Dover)
Levels as for Loch Beacravik

Directions
Caolas Beag although only 27m wide at its narrowest has a least depth of 3·7m. Bogha na h'Airde (dries 2·5m) lies at the NE side of the entrance to the narrows. This rock, which shows below half tide, is marked by a S cardinal perch. In any event keep to the Stockinish side at the entrance to the narrows.

If making for Poll Scrot pass east of the islet in the narrows and leave the perch off the north end of the islet to starboard before altering towards the pontoon.

Heading into Loch Stockinish from the narrows, keep the channel open astern for 4 cables to clear Bo of the Den, a rock with 0·8m over it which lies ½ cable east of Am Maoladh, a prominent tidal island on the west side of the entrance to the inner loch. The inner loch is clear up to its head where Hard Rock (dries 1·8m) lies 1 cable east of the point which divides the loch. Note particularly the rock drying 1m extending 1 cable SE from this point.

Caolas Mor demands great care. From the south aim to pass between Dubh Sgeir Mhor, which always shows, and Eilean nan Eun. The passage to the inner loch is best made within 2½ hours of LW when the reefs which dry 2m will show. The main dangers are extensive reefs 1 cable east (dries 2m) and over 2 cables south (dries 3m) of Dubh Sgeir Mhor. Further in, a rock awash west of Eilean Leasaid and an extensive reef (dries 2m) 4 cables north of Dubh Sgeir Mhor must also be watched.

To avoid these pass a cable west of Eilean nan Eun and associated islets then 1½ cables west of Eilean Leasaid. With Eilean Leasaid abeam head midway between Am Maoladh and Reef Rock, leaving the reef (dries 2m) to port. After reaching Reef Rock make for the NE shore in order to avoid Bo of the Den with 0·8m over it. Hold this course until Caolas Beag begins to open up when a turn may be made to port to enter the inner loch.

Anchorage
Poll Scrot NW of Sgeir a Chaise in Caolas Beag in 4m. Anchoring not recommended but there is a pontoon, often busy with working boats, which has a depth of 3m alongside.

Inner Loch Stockinish There is good anchorage just within the entrance to the NW arm of the loch in 7m, sand. If going further in, beware of a cable crossing midway up the NW arm of Loch Stockinish at a height of 6m above sea level.

Supplies
Pol Scrot Water by hose at the pontoon, diesel at quay (key fob needed). Toilet and shower at quay.

Admiralty Chart
1757
Admiralty Leisure Folio
5616. 10A
Imray Chart
C66
Ordnance Survey
14
Cruising Scotland
p.192

Outer Hebrides

Poll Scrot, Caolas Beag, Loch Stockinish (p.95)

Caolas Beag, Loch Stockinish from north (p.95)

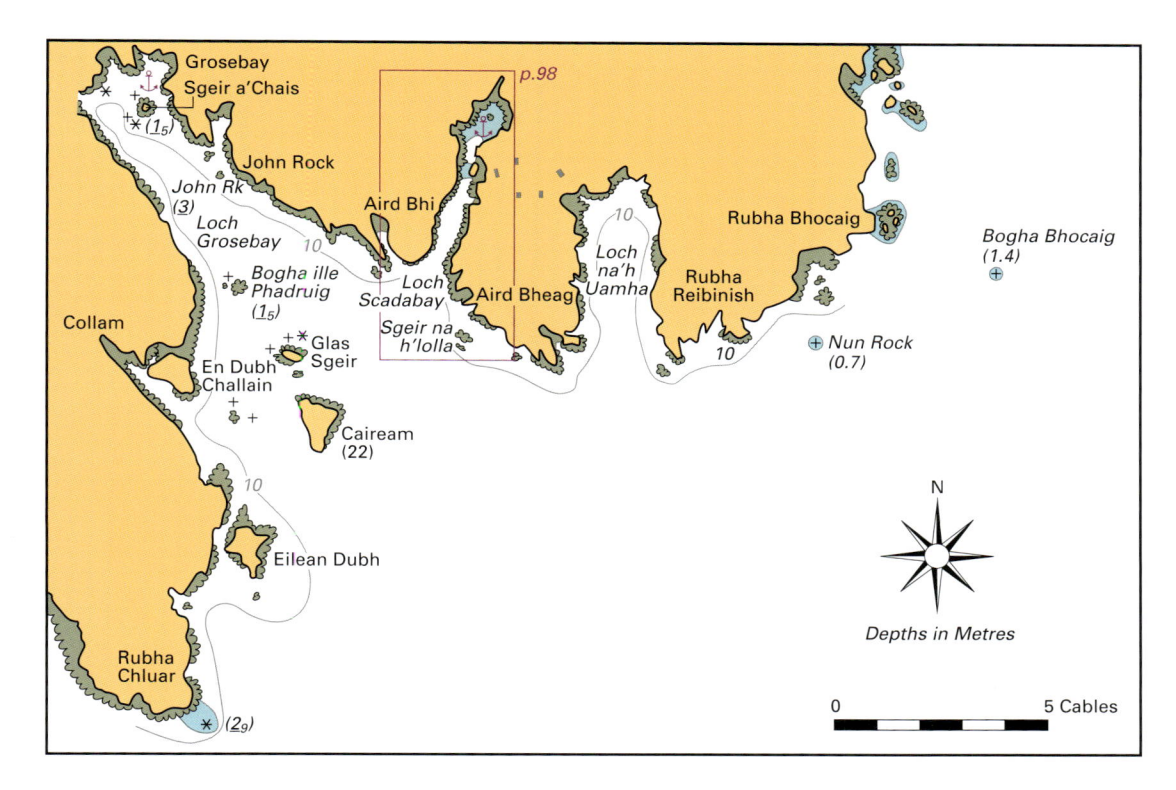

6. South Harris

LOCH GROSEBAY

Admiralty Chart
1757
Admiralty Leisure Folio
5616. 10A
Imray Chart
C66
Ordnance Survey
14
Cruising Scotland
p.192

Loch Grosebay from the north

Loch Grosebay

The main loch offers only moderately good shelter at its head and is exposed to easterly winds but Loch Scadabay, an inlet on the north side, gives excellent all-round protection.

Directions

If coming from the north keep ½ mile off the Reibinish Peninsula to avoid Bogha Bhocaig with 1·4m over it and Nun Rock with 0·7m over it, which lie 4 cables east and south respectively of Rubha Bhocaig. On entry, keep 2 cables off the NE shore of Loch Grosebay to clear Sgeir na h'Iolla at the south side of the entrance to Loch Scadabay. Note that whatever the direction of approach, the islands, islets and reefs off the SW shore of the loch, Eilean Dubh, Caiream, Glas Sgeir and Bogha ille Phadruig (dries 1·5m) should all be left to port. Nearing the head of the loch, tend to the west shore to clear John Rock (dries 3m) and Sgeir a'Chais with its rock (dries 3·0m) which extends SW ½ cable.

Anchorage

North of Sgeir a'Chais in 9m. Not well sheltered.

Supplies

Garage and workshop for repairs at Grosebay village. (K. Maclennan, ☎01859 511253.) Small slipway.

CCC Sailing Directions and Anchorages 97

Outer Hebrides

Admiralty Chart
1757
Admiralty Leisure Folio
5616. 10A
Imray Chart
C66
Ordnance Survey
14
Cruising Scotland
p.192

Loch Scadabay

This well hidden loch offers very good protection and, although the entrance is narrow, it is not difficult to negotiate. It is a little over 2 miles from Poll Scrot, Loch Stockinish to Loch Scadabay.

Tides
Const. –0027 Ullapool (–0447 Dover)

Height in metres

MHWS	MHWN	MTL	MLWN	MLWS
4·8	3·8	2·8	2·0	0·7

Directions
From the east and north keep at least 5 cables off Rubha Bhocaig and the coast south of that headland to avoid Bogha Bhocaig with 1·4m over it, and Nun Rock with 0·6m over it. (see plan p.97)

On altering westwards to acquire the narrow entrance to Loch Scadabay do not be deceived by the first wide inlet, Loch na h'Uamha. Continue keeping 2 cables off shore to avoid Sgeir na h'Iolla. The narrow entrance will open up when Toddun (526m) north of East Loch Tarbert bears 016°.

From the south keep 3 cables off Rubha Chluar and Eilean Dubh and then alter towards the entrance. If Toddun is not visible then the SE side of Cairéam in line astern with Rubha Chluar leads to the west side of the outer entrance clear of rocks.

Within the entrance keep mid-channel and pass west of Eilean an Duine through a narrow cleft 30m wide with steep sides and a least depth of 1·7m over a sandy bottom. Bear to starboard towards the stone jetty to avoid drying rocks off a scree at the foot of the cliff on the port hand and follow the rocky point round to starboard to avoid drying rocks to port which lie on the west side of the pool.

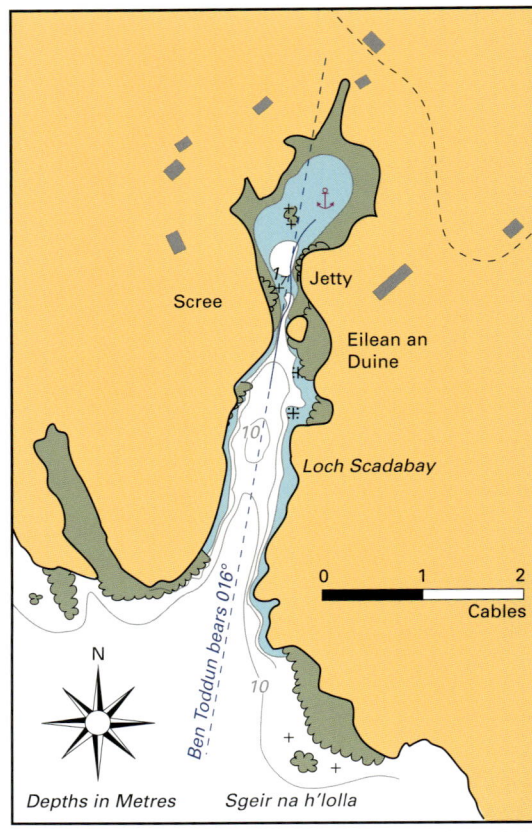

Anchorage
Anchor in the centre of the pool, NE of the rocks, in about 0·5m. The mud is very soft and fin keel yachts will sink in without listing. Note: Loch na h'Uamha is unsuitable for anchorage but an Admiralty survey shows no hidden dangers.

Supplies
Telephone. Water at houses.

LOCH SCADABAY

Loch Scadabay from the south
Martin Lawrence

6. South Harris

The pool, Loch Scadabay, note rocks on the right

East Loch Tarbert taken before the installation of pontoons (p.104)

CCC Sailing Directions and Anchorages 99

Outer Hebrides

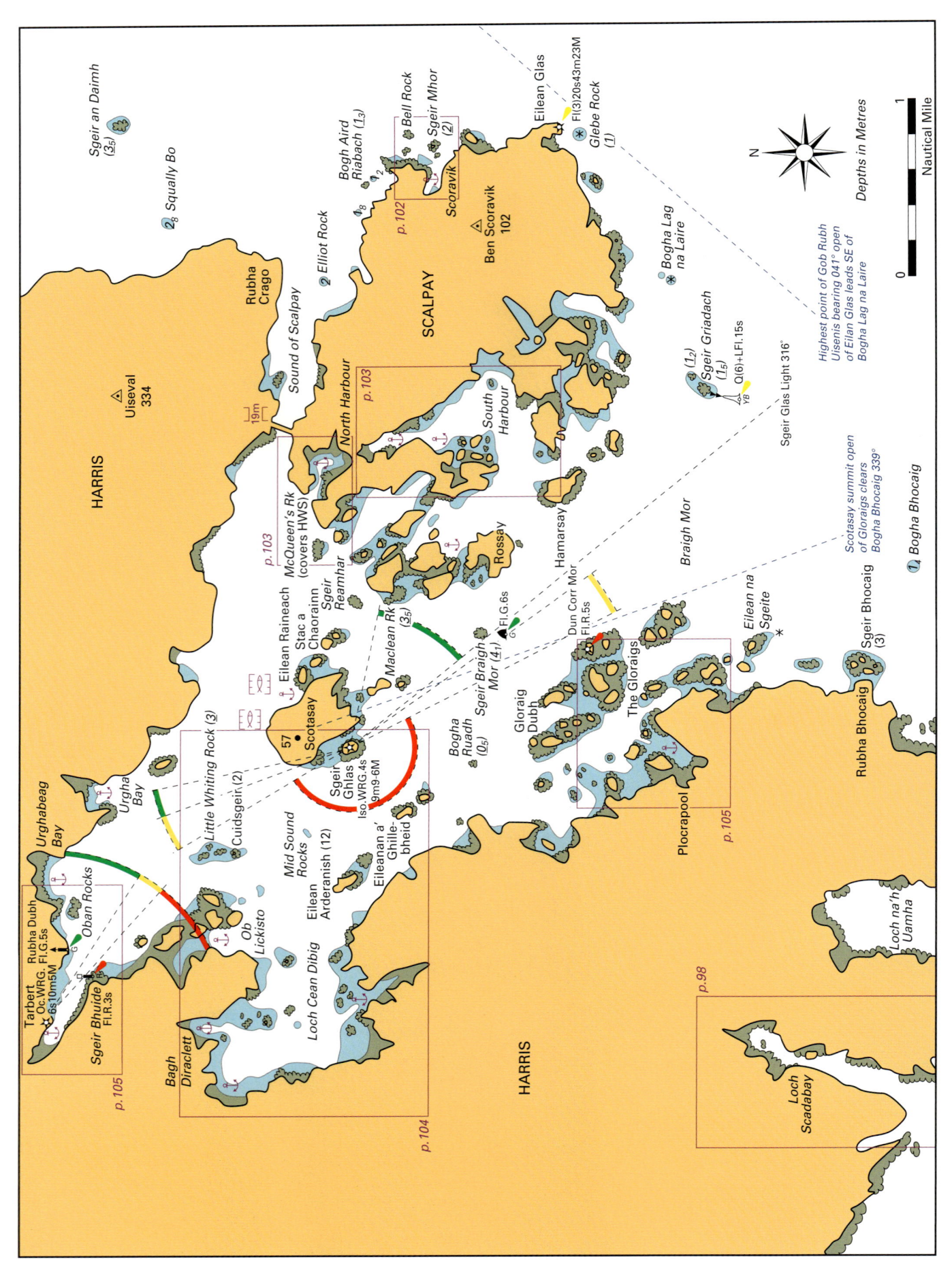

EAST LOCH TARBERT, SCALPAY AND APPROACHES

100 CCC Sailing Directions and Anchorages

6. South Harris

East Loch Tarbert

A broad loch with many bays providing a choice of anchorages. Braigh Mor, the principal approach, has innumerable islands, islets, reefs and rocks and can best be navigated safely with Chart 2905, although it is well marked and lit because of the ferry traffic. Arriving from the north or east, the Sound of Scalpay, spanned by a bridge with 19m clearance, provides an alternative, and simpler, entrance.

It is an excellent place of arrival at the Outer Hebrides from the north of Skye, combining a shorter crossing of the Little Minch with relative ease of access and the recently installed pontoons at East Loch Tarbert and Scalpay now offer much improved facilities with access to fuel and stores.

Tides

Constant –0026 Ullapool (–0446 Dover)

Height in metres

MHWS	MHWN	MTL	MLWN	MLWS
5·0	3·7	2·9	2·1	0·8

The northwest-going stream in Braigh Mor flows round Scalpay to run east in Sound of Scalpay and begins –0520 Ullapool (+0245 Dover). The southeast-going stream (west-going in Sound of Scalpay) begins +0105 Ullapool (–0315 Dover).

Lights

Eilean Glas Lt Ho. Fl(3)20s43m23M
Braigh Mor Entrance Channel
Sgeir Griadach S Cardinal light buoy Q(6)+LFl.15s
Sgeir Braigh Mor Green con light buoy Fl.G.6s
Dunn Corr Mor Lt Bn. Fl.R.5s10m5M
Sgeir Ghlas Lt. Twr. Iso.WRG.4s9m9–6M

At night

From the south keep at least a mile offshore (Eilean Glas bearing not more than 048°) until Dun Corr Mor light is in line with Sgeir Ghlas light and turn to head to the east of Sgeir Braigh Mor light buoy until in the white sector of Sgeir Ghlas light.

From the east or northeast, Sound of Scalpay is the more straightforward approach. North Harbour, Scalpay has a light Fl.G on the buoy northeast of Coddem as well as 2F.G(vert) at the seaward end of the pier, and may be approached by way of Sound of Scalpay if there is less than total darkness.

If approaching by Braigh Mor, the south passage, Sgeir Griadach light buoy must be identified and approached on a bearing of not less than 260°; keep outwith the 40 metre contour until south of this line.

Keep in the white sector of Sgeir Ghlas light beacon passing Dun Corr Mor light beacon to port, and Sgeir Braigh Mor light buoy to starboard. Pass south and west of Sgeir Ghlas light beacon until in its northwest white sector. Continue in that sector until in the white sector of the light at Tarbert pier.

Braigh Mor

Braigh Mor, the main fairway, runs between Scalpay, a substantial island 2½ miles long lying to the NE and the Harris shore on its SW side. Both have many off-lying islets and reefs extending well into the loch which reduce the channel to 3 cables at its narrowest point. Scotasay stands in the middle of the loch, 8 cables west of Scalpay. Tarbert village and ferry terminal are 2 miles further northwest.

Dangers and Marks

Approaching from the south

Nun Rock, described on p.97, is just cleared on its east side by keeping Eilean na Sgaite, 8 cables south of Dun Corr Mor, open of Sgeir Bhocaig, a rock 3 metres high close to Rubha Bhocaig, the southwest point of the entrance, bearing 008°.

Bogha Bhocaig, over which the depth is 1·4 metres, lies 4 cables east of Rubha Bhocaig and may be dangerous in a swell. Dun Corr Mor, the most northeasterly of the Gloraigs, under the summit of Scotasay 342° leads 2 cables east of Bogha Bhocaig. Sgeir an Leum Bhig, the most southeasterly of the Gloraigs, touching Stiughay, east of Scalpay 004°, leads clear west of Bogha Bhocaig.

Approaching from the north and east

Eilean Glas lighthouse at the most easterly point of Scalpay is a white tower with red bands, 30 metres in height.

Bogha Lag na Laire, a group of rocks which just dry, lies 3 cables south of Meall Chalibost, the southern extremity of Scalpay.

Sgeir Griadach, a patch of rocks, part of which dries 1·5 metres, 4 cables south of Scalpay, is marked on its south side by a south cardinal light buoy (not to be confused with Sgeir Graidach, a few miles east in the middle of the Minch).

Approaching from east or northeast, Sgeir Griadach light buoy must be identified and approached on a bearing of not less than 260°; keep outwith the 40-metre contour until south of this line.

Within Braigh Mor

Dun Corr Mor, the most northeasterly of the Gloraigs, on which is an inconspicuous light beacon.

Sgeir Braigh Mor, 6 cables north of Dun Corr Mor, is marked on its south side by a green conical light buoy.

Bogha Ruadh, on the southwest side of the fairway a mile northwest of Dun Corr Mor, dries ½ metre. A pair of islands, Eileanan a' Ghille-bheid, lies ½ mile beyond Bogha Ruadh and a further ½ mile northwest is a larger island, Eilean Arderanish. Eilean Arderanish open northwest of Eileanan a' Ghille-bheid 305° clears the northeast side of Bogha Ruadh.

Sgeir Ghlas, on the southwest side of Scotasay, has light tower 9 metres high showing a sectored light, IsoWRG.4s.

Admiralty Chart
2905, 1794, 1757
Admiralty Leisure Folio
5616. 25, 26
Imray Chart
C67
Ordnance Survey
14
Cruising Scotland
pp.192-193

Outer Hebrides

Scalpay North Harbour. A pontoon has now been established to the left of the pier

Admiralty Chart
2905, 1794
Admiralty Leisure Folio
5616. 25, 26
Imray Chart
C67
Ordnance Survey
14
Cruising Scotland
pp.192-193

Scalpay

The largest island in the loch is well populated and now joined to Harris by a bridge. It possesses the best natural harbour in the area, which is home to a number of working boats, as well as two other anchorages.

Sound of Scalpay

Scalpay Sound provides a straightforward approach to Scalpay North Harbour and Tarbert at the head of East Loch Tarbert. Scalpay Bridge has 19m clearance.

Directions

When approaching Scalpay Sound from the south or east give the east and NE side of Scalpay a fair berth to avoid reefs and rocks extending offshore more than a cable. Open the sound well up before heading west to avoid Elliot Rock.

From the north keep ¾ mile offshore to avoid Sgeir an Daimh (dries 3·5m) about 1 mile NE of Rubha Crago (see plan p.100). Enter the sound following the north shore to avoid Elliot Rock.

After entering the sound note that rocks extend from the north shore at the old ferry slip. Pass under the bridge (clearance 19m). Once through the Sound there is easy access to North Harbour, Scalpay, or to Tarbert at the head of the loch by proceeding in mid channel leaving Cuidsgeir (2) and Little Whiting Rock (dries 3·0m) to port and passing south of the Oban Rocks.

Lights

Bridge Oc.6s (centre of span) and Iso.G (north side) and Iso.R (South side)

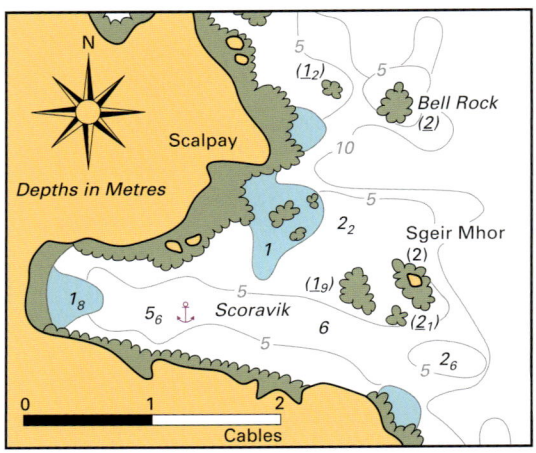

SCORAVIK

Scoravik

This small inlet on the east side of Scalpay, a little over ½ mile north of Eilean Glas Lighthouse, is a useful stopping place during passage making and avoids the extra distance to North Harbour, Scalpay. Enter, keeping closer to the south side, leaving Sgeir Mhor (2) and rocks south and west of it, on the starboard hand. Anchor on the south side in good holding ground in 5m. Well protected from SW through west to north.

Scalpay, North Harbour

Directions

From the Sound of Scalpay give Aird an Aiseig, on the port hand, a berth of ½ cable and keep in mid-channel in the entrance; pass north of the conical light buoy before turning to starboard and heading for the pier.

6. South Harris

From the Braigh Mor channel pass either side of Sgeir Braigh Mor (dries 4·1) and make for Stac a Chaorainn lying 2 cables east of Scotasay. Sgeir Reamhar (covers at HWS) is best left to starboard. Similarly, pass 1 cable west of MacQueen's Rock (covers at HWS) which lies west of the entrance to the North Harbour.

Alternatively pass west and north of Scotasay before altering towards Scalpay North Harbour entrance.

Anchorage and berthing

The outer half of the visitors' pontoon, established in 2017, has a least depth of 2m and can accommodate 8-10 yachts, with the possibility of more with rafting. The inner part is used by small local boats. The stone pier is reserved for fishing boats and should only be used for re-fuelling.

Anchor where indicated on plan, well clear of the fairway to the pier and pontoon but note the 0·5m patch in the centre. Use a tripping line.

Supplies

Water and electricity at pontoon. Diesel by hose at pier (arrangements for payment for diesel and pontoon dues not yet known, 2017). Bistro, showers at Community Hall.

Lights

Lt buoy Fl.G.2s
Pier 2F.G(vert)

Scalpay, South Harbour

Identify Hamarsay and Rossay (the highest of the islands southwest of Scalpay), and pass between them and midway between Raarem and the southeast shore to avoid drying rocks SSE of Raarem. When Raarem is abaft the beam and the promontory on the west shore is well open north of Raarem turn to pass ½ cable from its east side to clear Boundary Rock over which the depth is 0·4 metre and then keep close to the west side at the narrows. Anchor southeast of the islet off the southwest side of the inner loch, clear of a drying rock 50 metres from the shore ½ cable southeast of the islet. There is deep water further in, but more rocks than water, and several moorings. Alternatively anchor south of the narrows in 13m, black mud.

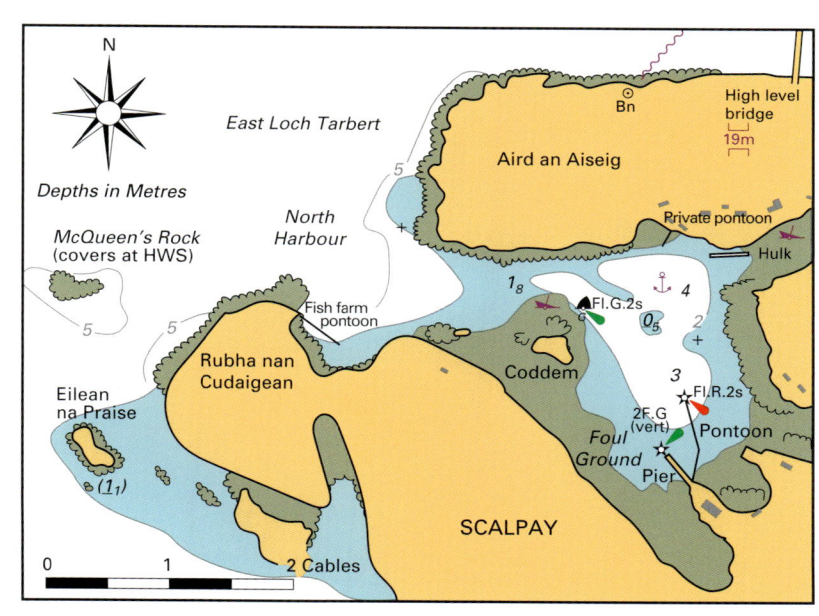

SCALPAY NORTH HARBOUR

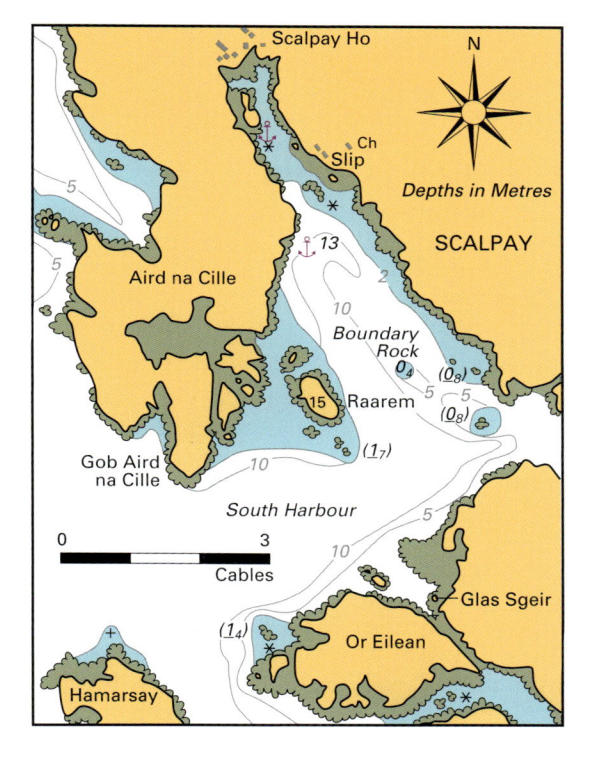

SCALPAY SOUTH HARBOUR

Scalpay South Harbour

CCC Sailing Directions and Anchorages 103

Outer Hebrides

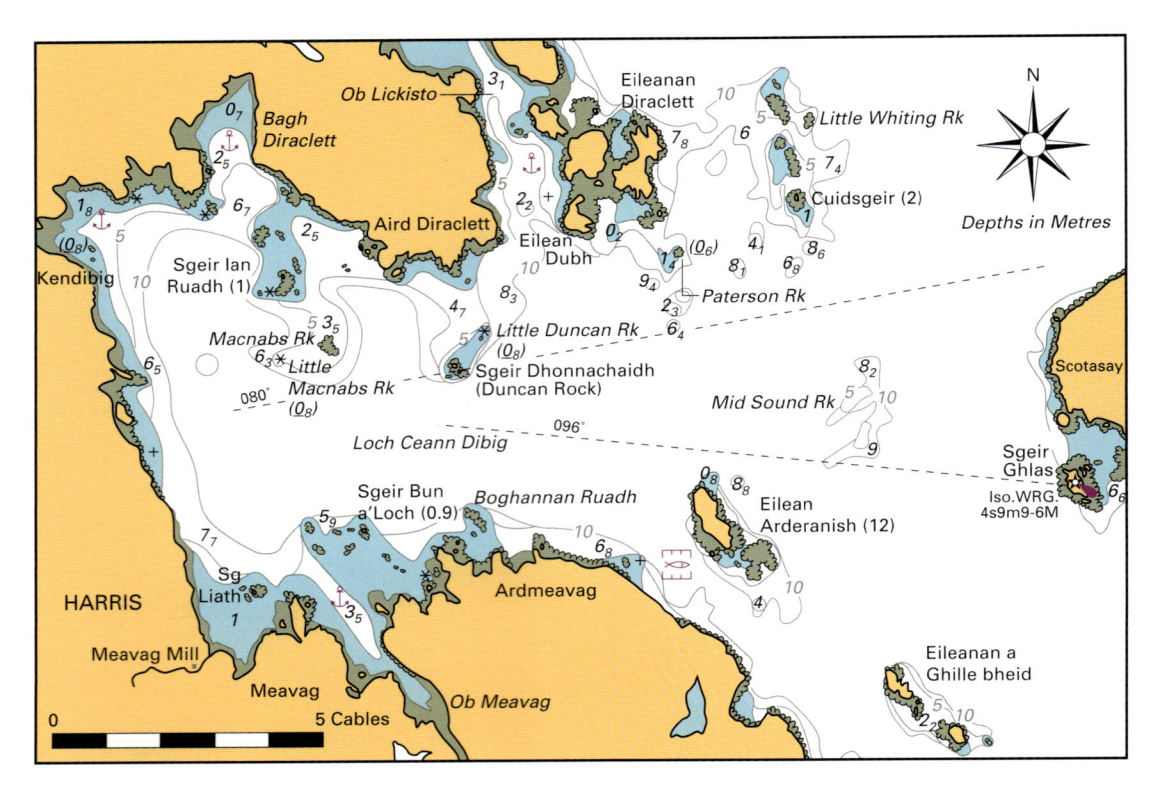

LOCH CEANN DIBIG

Admiralty Chart
2905, 1794
Admiralty Leisure Folio
5616. 25, 26
Imray Chart
C67
Ordnance Survey
14
Cruising Scotland
p.192-193

Loch Ceann Dibig

Loch Ceann Dibig, on the west side of East Loch Tarbert is obstructed by rocks on all sides but has several sheltered anchorages which, despite the symbols shown on the chart, are now clear of fish farms.

Anchorages

Ob Meavag, on the south side of Loch Ceann Dibig is shoal and dries for 2 cables from its head. In the approach keep Sgeir Ghlas light open of Eilean Arderanish to clear the drying rocks which lie over a cable west of Sgeir Bun a'Loch (0·9m high).

To pass beyond these rocks do not turn to port until Meavag Mill bears 200°. Steer on this bearing until Sgeir Bun a'Loch is open north of Eilean Arderanish and then approach from the NW with the head of the inlet bearing 138°. Anchor within the entrance in 3m, mud. Well sheltered with good holding.

Bagh Diraclett is a shallow bay on the north side of Loch Ceann Dibig with rocks above water and drying in the approach. Little Macnab's Rock (dries 0·8m) is cleared by keeping Sgeir Dhonnachaidh, which is just above water, in line with the north side of Scotasay 080°. The rocks either side of the entrance will show within 2 hours of LW.

Kendibig There is an easily approached anchorage in the bay NE of Kendibig, north of the rock which dries 0·8m. Good holding.

Ob Lickisto: Keep 1½ cables south of Eileanan Diraclett to avoid Paterson's Rock and other shoal patches and alter course northwards when the entrance west of Eilean Dubh is open. Anchor as shown on the plan. Good holding.

Tarbert

A narrow inlet with the ferry terminal on its north side, Tarbert now welcomes yachts following the installation of pontoons and visitors' moorings.

Directions

When making for Tarbert pass between Dun Corr Mor and the light buoy south of Sgeir Braigh Mor and steer for Sgeir Ghlas, SW of Scotasay. Pass west of Sgeir Ghlas and head in a northerly direction towards the west side of Urgha Bay. Maintain this northerly course until clear of Cuidsgeir (2) and Little Whiting Rock (dries 3·0m) to port and then turn to port and head for Tarbert keeping mid-channel until well clear of the Oban Rocks to starboard and Sgeir Bhuidhe to port.

Mooring and berthing

There are six fore-and-aft visitors' moorings along the south shore, all with single pickup buoys. The pontoons provide berths for yachts up to 15m LOA in a LD of 2m for the outer third of its length. All are exposed to the southeast when better shelter will be found in Scalpay (see p.102).

Access to and from the pontoons and moorings is prohibited 30 minutes before and after the arrival and departure of a ferry. Anchoring is not feasible and is not permitted.

Lights

Sgeir Bhuidhe Bn. Fl.R.3s
Rubha Dubh Bn. Fl.G.5s
Tarbert Pier 2F.G(vert)10m5M
　　　　　　Oc.WRG.6s10m5M (When ferry expected)
RoRo terminal 2F.G(vert)7m5M

104　CCC Sailing Directions and Anchorages

6. South Harris

Plocrapool from the SE

Facilities
Hotels, shops, PO, bank. Harris Tweed shop. Petrol, diesel and Calor gas at filling station, 3M (see p.139). Water and electricity at pontoons. Car hire and taxi service. Car ferry to Lochmaddy and Uig.

Plocrapool
A snug but shallow anchorage on the southwest side of the entrance to Braigh Mor. Approach by south of Dun Corr Mor (8), which looks a bit like a sugar loaf, and pass northwest of the above water rock, Sgeir Bun a' Loch which is in the middle of the entrance, closer to that rock than to the islands on the west side to avoid drying reefs off them. At spring tides look out for rocks at a depth of less than 2 metres although these are not likely to be a problem at other times. Head well to the east of the houses, steering 210° towards the small headland within the bay, and anchor as far in as the depth allows.

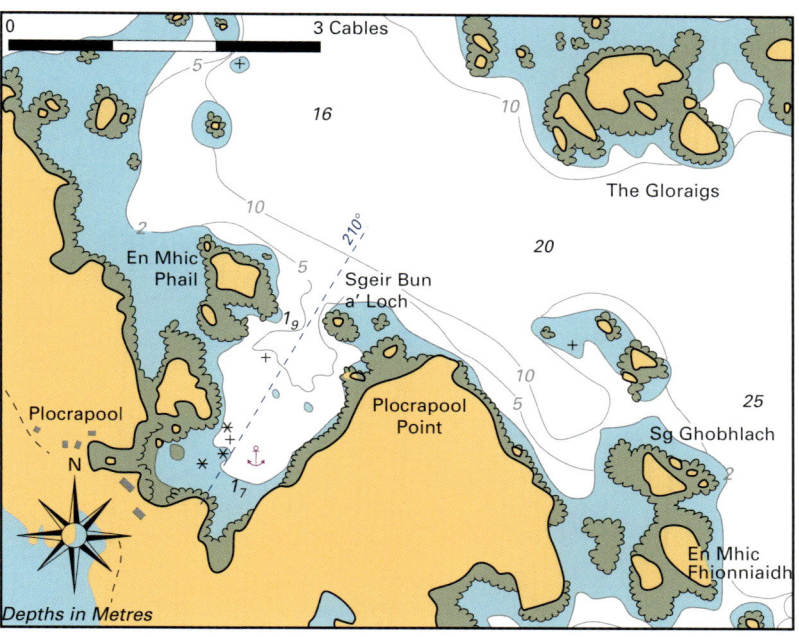

Other anchorages in Loch Tarbert
Urgha Bay on the north shore about 1 mile east of Tarbert. Good holding. Protected from northerly winds (see plan p.100).

Urghabeag Bay a little over ½ mile east of Tarbert (see plan p.100). Note the Oban Rocks and large reef at the west side of the entrance. Anchor near the head of the bay in 2·5m but clear of the drying reefs extending ½ cable on the west side of the bay.

Scotasay on the NE side of the island in the NW part of the bay west of Eilean Raineach in 3m. A drying rock lies NW of Eilean Raineach. Well sheltered from south through to west. There is a large fish farm NE of Scotasay.

Rossay Approach between Rossay and Aird na Cille on Scalpay. Anchor towards the north side of the bay north of Rossay. Drying reefs give some protection from west.

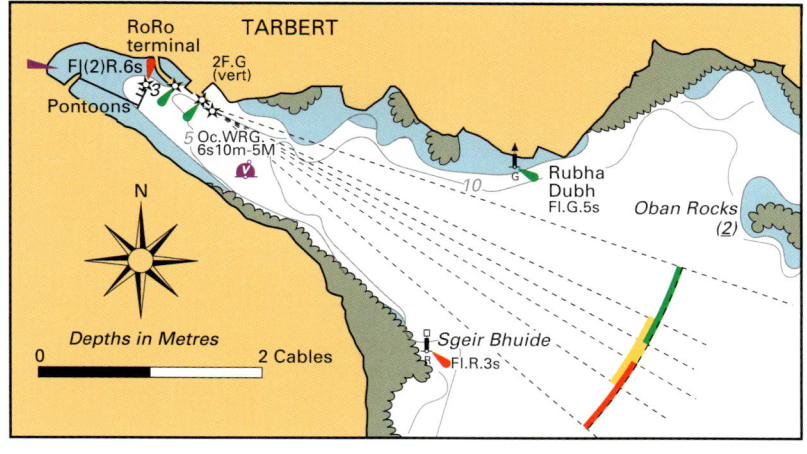

PLOCRAPOOL

TARBERT

CCC Sailing Directions and Anchorages 105

Outer Hebrides

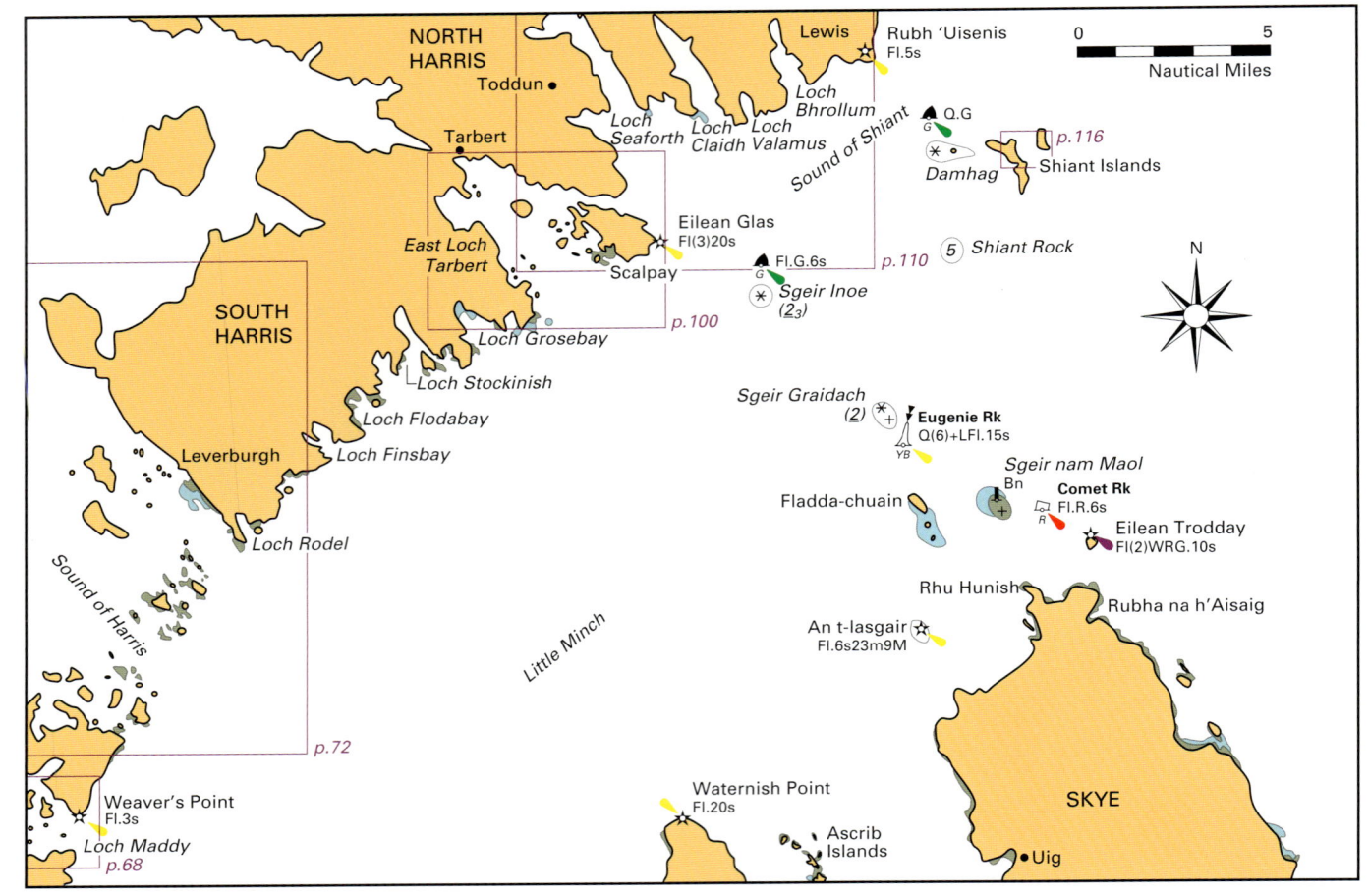

**LITTLE MINCH
KEY PLAN**

Admiralty Chart
1794, 1795, 1757
Admiralty Leisure Folio
5616. 9, 10A
Imray Chart
C66, 67
Ordnance Survey
14, 23
Cruising Scotland
p.173

Crossing the Little Minch

The Little Minch between Skye and Harris is a dangerous area of sea in bad weather conditions. The effect of wind, tidal streams and, in places, the nature of the sea bottom results in steep waves.

Crossing from Dunvegan or Uig presents no particular problem but from the north of Skye to Harris or Lewis passage planning should take particular care to allow for tidal flow in the Minches and the avoidance of hazards.

Distances
North Skye to Tarbert Harris 20 miles
North Skye to Lochmaddy 29 miles.
Loch Dunvegan to Tarbert, Harris 29 miles.
Dunvegan to Lochmaddy 21 miles.
North Skye to Stornoway, Isle of Lewis 30 miles

Tides

Off Rubha Hunish the northeast-going stream begins –0405 Ullapool (+0400 Dover). The southwest-going stream begins +0220 Ullapool (–0200 Dover).

Off Scalpay, Harris, the northeast-going stream begins –0305 Ullapool (+0500 Dover) at springs and –0505 Ullapool (+0300 Dover) at neaps, beginning at NNE and gradually turning to east. The southwest-going stream begins +0320 Ullapool (–0100 Dover) at both springs and neaps. This has the effect that at neaps the NNE-going tide runs for 8½ hours and the southwest-going tide for 4 hours. Northeast-going streams run at 2½ knots at springs, but both streams vary according to the wind direction and strength.

Dangers and marks

(described in sequence from Skye towards Harris)
A group of islets of which the largest is Fladda-chuain lies between 2½ and 3½ miles northwest of Rubha Hunish.

An t-Iasgair, a group of four islets or rocks, the tallest of which (22) is surmounted by a lit beacon, lie 3½ miles south of Fladda-chuain.

Sgeir nam Maol beacon, 12 metres high, with six legs and a cylindrical cage with a cross on top, is at the centre of a patch of rocks 2½ miles NNW of Rubha Hunish.

Comet Rock red can light buoy is more than a mile east of these rocks, which themselves are a 1½ miles east of Fladda-chuain.

Sgeir Graidach (dries 2m), which no longer has a beacon, is 2¾ miles NNW of Fladda-chuain.

Eugenie Rock lies ½ mile SSE of Sgeir Graidach at a depth of 0·9 m. Both are marked by the S cardinal buoy lying a mile SSE of Sgeir Graidach.

Sgeir Inoe, 3 miles ESE of Eilean Glas lighthouse dries 2·3 metres, and is marked by a green conical light buoy nearly a mile NNW of it.

Eilean Glas lighthouse on the east point of Scalpay is a white tower with red bands, 43 metres in height.

106 CCC Sailing Directions and Anchorages

6. South Harris

Large commercial vessels pass through the Little Minch and are recommended to pass between Trodday and Comet Rock buoy in a northeasterly direction, and through Sound of Shiant and northwest of Sgeir Inoe light buoy in a southwesterly direction, but this is not a mandatory separation scheme. A good lookout needs to be kept for vessels following these tracks – as well as for those which ignore the recommendations.

Directions

From North Skye to Tarbert, Harris. The best course is to pass 1 mile north of both Eilean Trodday and Comet Rock light buoy. Maintain course to pass well north of Sgeir nam Maol, The aim is to avoid overfalls, also the Eugenie Rock and Sgeir Graidach (dries 2·0m) lying 3 cables NW of that rock. In good visibility a course towards Toddun, a conspicuous conical hill on Harris, clears these hazards.

Leave the light buoy marking Sgeir Inoe (see below) to port. Once clear of the buoy alter course for the Sound of Scalpay, north of Scalpay, to enter East Loch Tarbert (note that the bridge over the sound has a clearance of 19m).

If making for the Braigh Mor entrance channel, south of Scalpay, Sgeir Inoe (dries 2·3m) which lies almost a mile south of the G conical light buoy marking it, should be left to starboard. Eilean Glas Light Tower in line with the summit of Tiorga Mor (58° 00'N, 6° 59'W), the first hill north of Tarbert, bearing 308° leads 4 cables SW of Sgeir Inoe.

From North Skye to Loch Maddy. Pass between Eilean Trodday and Skye when tidal and sea conditions are suitable. Thereafter the passage to Loch Maddy is straightforward.

From North Skye to Lewis. A course from north Skye to the north part of Lewis passes close to the Shiant Islands which lie between 10 and 12 miles north of Rubha Hunish. If making for Loch Shell heavy seas in the Sound of Shiant are avoided by passing east of the Shiant Islands (see p.116).

From Uig (Loch Snizort, Skye) to Tarbert, Harris. Set a course for the light tower on Eilean Glas, Scalpay for subsequent entry by the Sound of Scalpay but taking into account any tidal set towards Sgeir Inoe.

Alternatively enter East Loch Tarbert through Braigh Mor, south of Scalpay. This entrance requires greater navigational care (see p.101) but there is not the masthead height restriction of 19m at the bridge over Scalpay Sound.

From Loch Dunvegan to Tarbert, Harris. Once clear of Loch Dunvegan, head for Eilean Glas light tower, Scalpay. Then enter East Loch Tarbert as for the passage from Uig (see above).

Lights

Eilean Trodday Fl(2)WRG.10s52m12-9M
An t-Iasgair Lt Bn Fl.6s23m9M
Comet Rock Lt buoy Fl.R.6s
Eugenie Rock Lt buoy Q(6)+LFl.15s
Sgeir Inoe Lt buoy Fl.G.6s
Eilean Glas Lt Ho Fl(3)20s43m23M
Shiants Lt buoy Q.G
Rubh' Uisenis Lt bn Fl.5s24m11M

At night

Look out for large commercial vessels. When crossing from Skye to East Loch Tarbert keep in the white sector of Eilean Trodday light beacon and pass northeast of Sgeir Inoe light buoy; Sound of Scalpay is easier for a stranger at night than the passage south of Scalpay and Tarbert is better lit than Scalpay.

Shelter

Some shelter is to be found in Duntulm Bay south of Rubha Hunish (northwest Skye) and Kilmaluag Bay, south of Rubha na h'Aisaig on the east side of Skye. There is good shelter in East Loch Tarbert, Loch Claidh, Loch Shell, Loch Erisort and Stornoway.

Looking across the Little Minch from Duntulm Bay to the mountains of Harris. The Fladda-chuain group of islets is in the foreground and the rounded summit on the right is Toddun (see text)

Edward Mason

CCC Sailing Directions and Anchorages

7. East Lewis

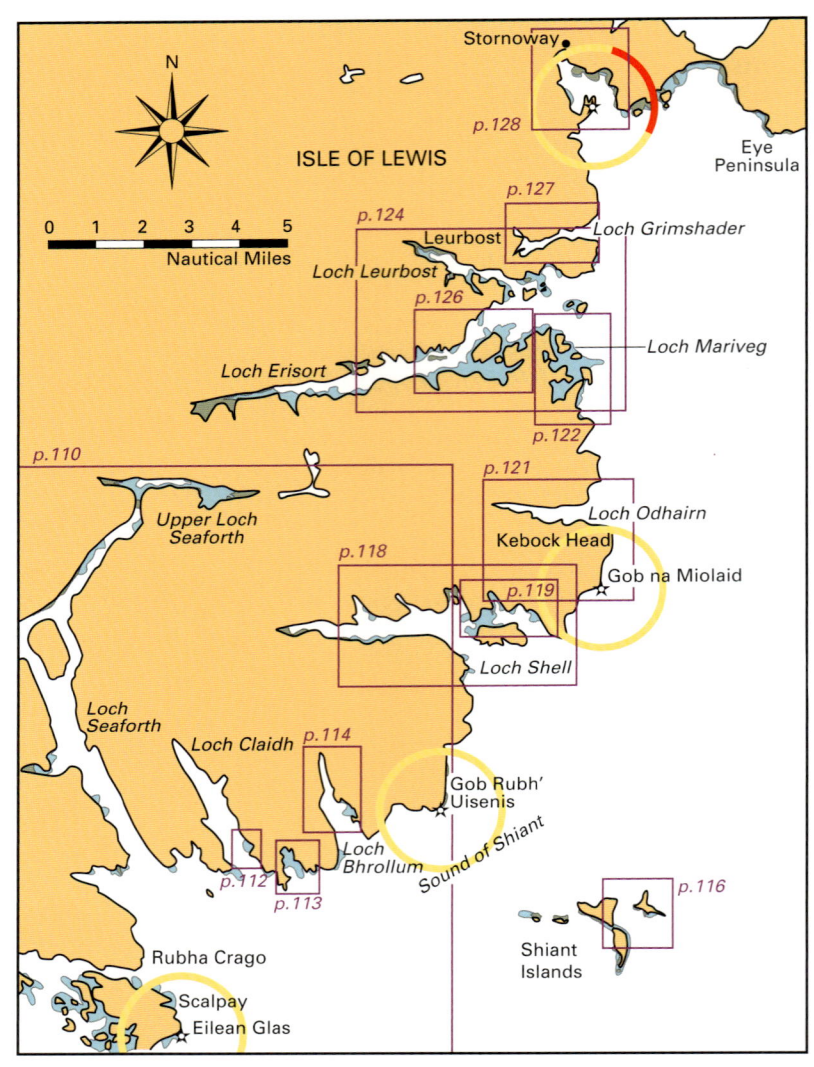

The lochs on the SE of the Isle of Lewis comprising Loch Seaforth, Loch Claidh, Loch Valamus (Bhalamuis) and Loch Bhrollum, reach northwards into a particularly mountainous and isolated part of the Isle of Lewis. They are all exposed to southerly winds and subject to heavy squalls. Protection may be limited. Northwards from Gob Rubh'Uisenis the coast is less dramatic but Loch Shell, Loch Erisort and Loch Mariveg all offer a great variety of fascinating and better protected anchorages.

Tides

Between Gob na Miolaid and Kebock Head and off these headlands the tide reaches 3 knots at springs.

N-going stream begins –0305 Ullapool (+0500 Dover)
S-going stream begins +0220 Ullapool (–0200 Dover)

The tides N of Kebock Head and as far as Tiumpan Head on the Eye Peninsula are weak.

Directions

It is about 27 miles from North Harbour, Scalpay, Harris to Stornoway.

If proceeding northeastwards to cross the entrances to Loch Trollamarig, Loch Seaforth and Loch Claidh, keep southeast of a line from Rubha Crago, the NE side of the Sound of Scalpay, to Rubh 'a Bhaird on the west side of the entrance to Loch Bhrollum. Keeping SE of this line and then a few cables offshore and clear of the entrances to all lochs further north, provides safe passage to Stornoway.

Lights

Eilean Glas Lt Ho Fl(3).20s43m23M
Sgeir Inoe Lt buoy Fl.G.6s
Shiants Lt buoy Q.G
Rubh' Uisenis Fl.5s24m11M
Arnish Point Fl.WR.10s17m9/7M

Shelter

Eilean Thinngarstaigh (Hingerstay) in Loch Claidh and Tob Limervay in Loch Shell are easily approached in daylight and give good shelter in most summer conditions. Further north many secure anchorages are to be found in Loch Mariveg (Mharabhig), Loch Erisort and Loch Grimshader.

EAST LEWIS KEY PLAN

East Loch Tarbert to Stornoway

This section of coast is as bleak and remote as any in the Outer Hebrides. There are neither roads nor houses between Loch Seaforth and Loch Shell.

There are no hazards on a direct passage between Rubha Crago or Eilean Glas and Gob Rubh' Uisenis except for the strength of the tide, with heavy and sometimes dangerous overfalls in the Sound of Shiant.

Admiralty Chart
1794, 1757
Imray Chart
C67
Ordnance Survey
14, 8
Cruising Scotland
pp.193-197

7. East Lewis

Loch Maaruig, looking north up Loch Seaforth

Looking down Loch Seaforth from above Aline Lodge

CCC Sailing Directions and Anchorages **109**

Outer Hebrides

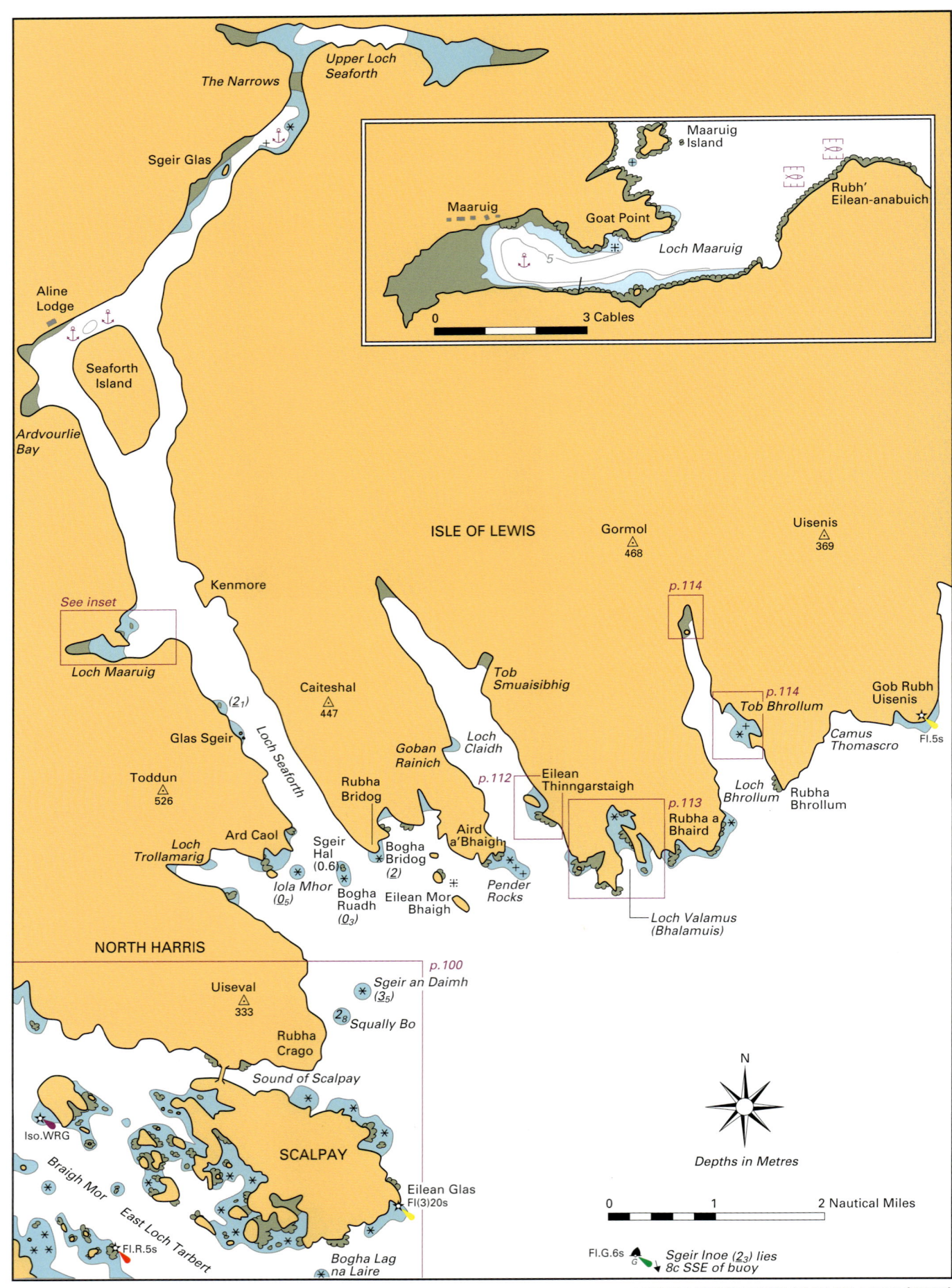

LOCH SEAFORTH WITH LOCH MAARUIG (INSET)

110 CCC Sailing Directions and Anchorages

7. East Lewis

Loch Seaforth

A long narrow loch reaching 9 miles into a mountainous region of Harris and Lewis and, therefore, subject to dangerous squalls from unexpected directions. There are several dangers in the approach but the loch appears to be reasonably clean within, although the plan is to a small scale and does not show all inshore dangers. Accordingly give the shores a generous berth and approach anchorages with great care.

Tides

Constant –0027 Ullapool (–0447 Dover)

Height in metres

MHWS	MHWN	MTL	MLWN	MLWS
5·0	3·7	2·9	2·1	0·8

Tidal streams are generally weak but reach 1 knot in the channels either side of Seaforth Island, turning at local HW and LW. At the narrows to Upper Loch Seaforth, which are impassable to yachts, the streams reach 7 knots.

Directions

In the outer approaches to Loch Seaforth, that is in the area between Rubha Crago at the NE side of the Sound of Scalpay and Aird a'Bhaigh at the west side of the entrance to Loch Claidh, there are a number of islets and rocks most of which can be seen. In particular Sgeir an Daimh lying about 9 cables NNE of Rubha Crago, although charted as 'dries 3·5m', is reported never to cover and to be visible in all conditions except in a flat calm near HW.

On the east side of the entrance to Loch Seaforth a series of above and below water rocks extends 4 cables southwards from Aird a'Bhaigh (the west point of Loch Claidh) terminating in Pender rock (with 0·3m over it). Between Aird a'Bhaigh and Rubha Bridog, the entrance point to Loch Seaforth, are three islets - Eilean Mor a'Bhaigh, Dubh a'Bhaigh and Beag a'Bhaigh.

Sgeir Hal, the key to navigating the entrance to the loch, lies 4 cables SW of Rubha Bridog. It is believed to be about 0·6m high, although charted at 2·0m high, and may be difficult to spot at HW. Bogha Ruadh, lying 1 cable south of Sgeir Hal, dries 0·3m. Bogha Bridog (dries 2·0m) lies 1 cable SSE off Rubha Bridog.

Iola Mhor, about ¼ mile SSE of Ard Caol at the west point of the entrance, dries about 0·5 metre. Loch Trollamarig, to the west of the entrance to Loch Seaforth, is not a safe anchorage.

Approach from the south; When passing Eilean Glas Light tower on Scalpay, the remarkable conical mountain Toddun, indicates the SW entrance to the loch. Pass ½ mile east of Eilean Glas light tower and then steer towards Sgeir Hal, the small islet in the entrance to the loch (see above), passing more than 2 cables east of Sgeir an Daimh, which, as mentioned above, has been reported never to cover.

When approaching the entrance from the south aim to pass either west of Sgeir Hal avoiding Bogha Ruadh (dries 0·3m) lying 1 cable south of Sgeir Hal and Iola Mhor lying 2½ cables south of Ard Caol the west point of the entrance; or east of Sgeir Hal holding close to the NE shore. This latter course is recommended but be aware of Bogha Ruadh, and Bogha Bridog (dries. 2·0m) lying a cable SSE of Rubha Bridog, the east point of the entrance. (*See clearance bearing below**).

Approach from the east; pass south of Eilean Mor a'Bhaigh and then alter towards Rubha Bridog and hold close to the NE shore leaving Sgeir Hal to port. Take care to avoid Bogha Bhridog which lies 1 cable SSE of Rubha Bhridog. *The south point of Loch Maaruig, an inlet on the west side of the loch, open of Rubha Bridog leads close west of Bogha Bridog.

Within the loch the west shore is free from dangers from Ard Caol to Seaforth Island except for a rock 75m offshore which dries 2·1m. This rock lies 3 cables north of Glas Sgeir, an islet 1 mile south of the entrance to Loch Maaruig. The east side of the loch is clear.

Beyond Loch Maaruig the shores are less steep; Seaforth Island, 2 miles further north, can be passed on either side. Two miles beyond Seaforth Island, Sgeir Ghlas stands southeast of the middle of the loch with rocks which dry extending north and west from it. There is a clear passage east of Sgeir Ghlas, and the depth is reasonable for anchoring ½ mile northeast of Sgeir Ghlas in a bay on the southeast shore; a drying rock lies a cable from the southeast shore 3½ cables beyond the south point of the bay.

Three miles northeast of Seaforth Island narrows lead to Upper Loch Seaforth; the narrows are filled with drying rocks which form tidal rapids where the stream runs at up to 7 knots, with only about 5 minutes of slack water, and are not passable except in a kayak or an expendable dinghy.

Anchorages

Loch Maaruig (photo p.109) on the west side of the loch 2½ miles from the entrance. The awash rock SW of Goat point is cleared by keeping Goat Point open of the south point of the entrance. Anchor off Maaruig west of Goat Point in 7m, mud. Well sheltered.

Seaforth Island The two bays on Harris, west of the island, are shoal and drying, but reasonable anchorage can be found off the jetty at Aline Lodge (photo p.109), northwest of Seaforth Island, or in the passage north of the island in about 7 metres, which may be more sheltered.

South of the Narrows in the SE corner ½ mile from the narrows. Approaching from Seaforth Island this NE arm has several dangerous rocks off the NW shore. Leave the islet Sgeir Glas to port. Entering the anchorage there is a rock with only 0·2m over it, a cable east of the point and ½ cable off the shore.

Admiralty Chart
1794, 1757
Imray Chart
C67
Ordnance Survey
14
Cruising Scotland
p.194

Outer Hebrides

Admiralty Chart
1794, 1757
Imray Chart
C67
Ordnance Survey
14
Cruising Scotland
p.194

Loch Claidh

About 2 miles east from Loch Seaforth and 2 miles west of Loch Bhrollum, Loch Claidh has hills of moderate height at its entrance but becomes mountainous at the head of the loch. It can appear desolate, grim and forbidding in appearance but the anchorage behind Eilean Thinngarstaigh is one of the best. Loch Claidh is easier to identify and enter than Loch Bhrollum, and is 3 miles in length and about ½ mile wide at its entrance.

Tides

Constant –0026 Ullapool (–0446 Dover)

Height in metres

MHWS	MHWN	MTL	MLWN	MLWS
5·0	3·7	2·9	2·1	0·8

Directions

The entrance is between Rubha Bhalamuis Bhig on the east side, with rocks extending 100m offshore, and Aird a'Bhaigh on the west side, from which a series of above and below water rocks extends 4 cables southeastwards terminating in Pender Rock (with 0·3m over it). The tidal streams run strongly near Pender Rock resulting in substantial turbulence and should be avoided.

There are two rocks which dry about 3·0m, lying ½ cable west of Sgeir Niogaig, a 5m high rock, which is close off the NE shore, 5 cables WNW of Rubha Bhalamuis Bhig (see plan Loch Valamus). From the south and east the loch should be well open before entering; then keep about 2 cables off the east shore.

Anchorage

Eilean Thinngarstaigh (Hingerstay) on the east side 1 mile within the loch. The passage south of the island is beset by reefs so pass west and north of the island and anchor on the east side in 8m, with good holding in mud and sand.

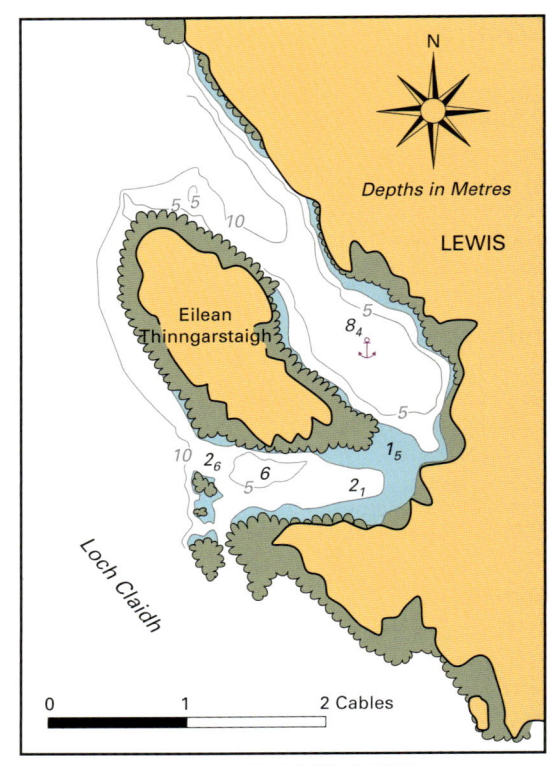

EILEAN THINNGARSTAIGH, LOCH CLAIDH

The shelter is good in southerly and westerly gales though some swell may enter in southerlies.

Tob Smuaisibhig about 2½ miles within the loch on the east side. Good holding in the bay as far into the inlet as depth will allow. A considerable sea sets in during southerly gales.

Goban Rainich, an inlet on the west side 1 mile within the loch provides shelter from the southwesterly gales. With weather from the south or SE the anchorage behind Eilean Thinngarstaigh would be preferred.

The anchorage behind Eilean Thinngarstaigh, Loch Claidh

Andrew Thomson

112 CCC Sailing Directions and Anchorages

7. East Lewis

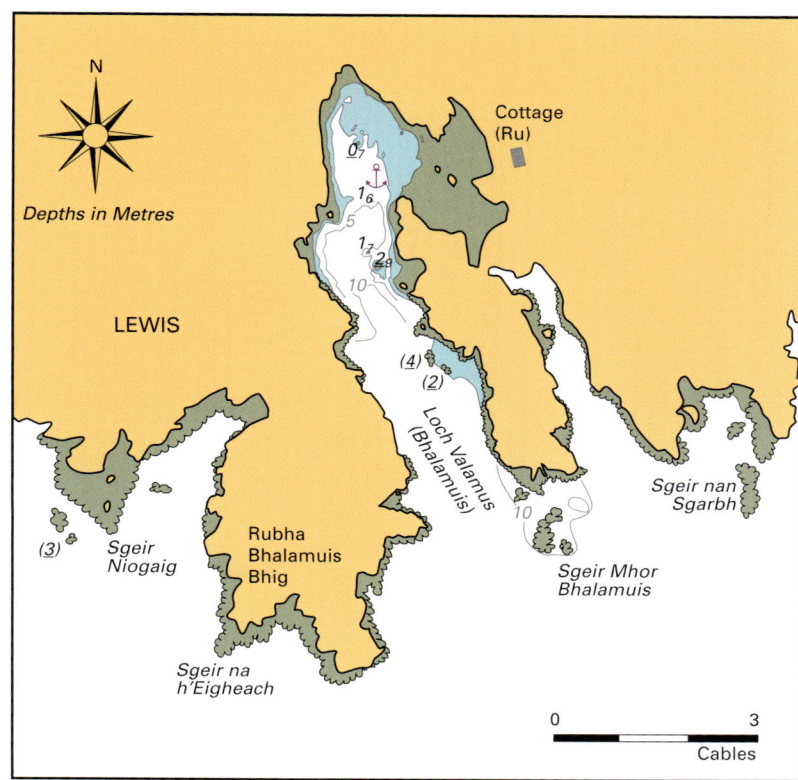

LOCH VALAMUS

Loch Valamus (Bhalamuis)

A small inlet running about ½ mile northwards between Rubha Bhalamuis Bhig, the east entrance point to Loch Claidh, and Rubha a'Bhaird, the west entrance point to Loch Bhrollum.

Tides
As Loch Claidh

Directions
From the east keep at least 3 cables offshore with Rubha Bhalamuis Bhig on the west side of the entrance bearing not less than 250°, until the loch is well open. This will avoid reefs Sgeir nan Sgarbh and Sgeir Mhor Bhalamuis extending 2 cables from the shore east of the entrance. When within the loch hold well to the west side to avoid drying rocks to the east.

Anchorage
Anchor near the head of the loch just beyond the promontory on the east shore clear of the shallows, isolated rocks and drying area indicated on the plan.

Upper left: The anchorage off the ruined cottage in Loch Valamus

Loch Valamus from the southeast

CCC Sailing Directions and Anchorages 113

Outer Hebrides

Admiralty Chart
1794, 1757
Imray Chart
C67
Ordnance Survey
14
Cruising Scotland
p.194

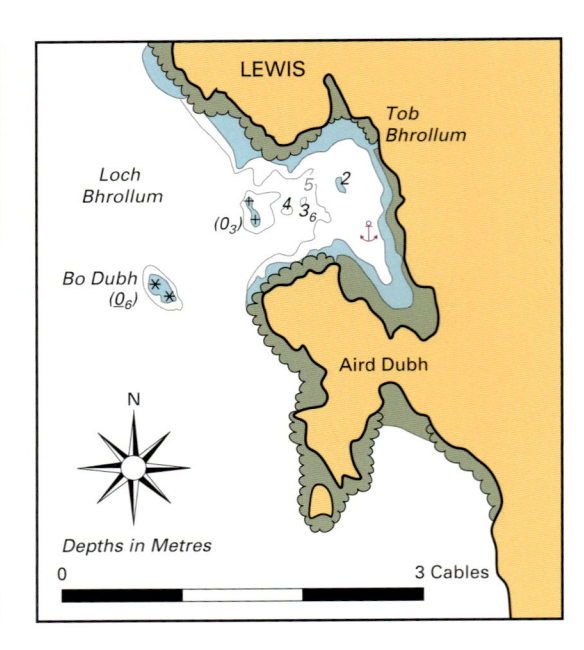

TOB BHROLLUM, LOCH BHROLLUM

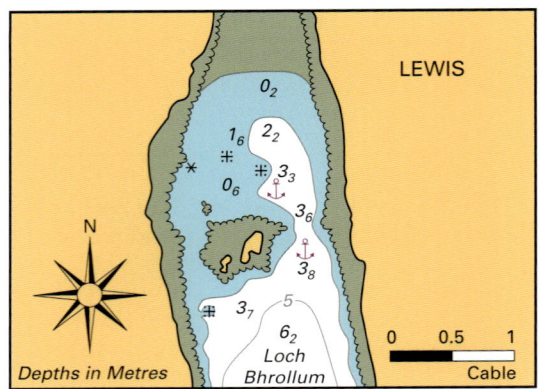

HEAD OF LOCH BHROLLUM

Loch Bhrollum

Extending 2 miles into this desolate mountainous region of Lewis, Loch Bhrollum may be visited whilst awaiting the tide to make passage north round Gob Rubh' Uisenis or when planning to visit the Shiant Islands.

The entrance is between bold headlands, Rubha a'Bhaird and Rubha Bhrollum and is about 2 miles east of the entrance to Loch Claidh and 2 miles west of Gob Rubh' Uisenis.

Tides

Const. –0027 Ullapool (–0447 Dover)
Height in metres

MHWS	MHWN	MTL	MLWN	MLWS
5·0	3·7	2·9	2·1	0·8

Approach

Keep at least a cable from either shore at the entrance to avoid rocks. Once within the loch there are no hidden dangers until Aird Dubh (15m), a grassy peninsula on the east side, 6 cables from the loch entrance.

Anchorages

Tob Bhrollum A small bay north of Aird Dubh. Approach from the south, passing no more than 50m off Aird Dubh to avoid Bo Dubh (dries 0·6m) and another rock with 0·3m over it, a cable NE of Bo Dubh. Some swell enters with southerly winds but the effects may be reduced by moving further into the SE corner, though there is more weed here.

Head of the Loch The loch narrows to a cable north of Meall Mor, the headland on the east side of the loch, north of Tob Bhrollum. There are no hazards but, at the head of the loch, shoals extend eastwards from the north of the island and from the east shore, so keep to mid channel leaving the island to port. Depths gradually decrease north of here but the bottom is soft mud and yachts sink in without listing. There appears to be good shelter, especially behind the island which is used by fishermen in bad weather. Anchor where shown or further in but note the rocks about 100m north of the island.

Tob Bhrollum from the NE

114 CCC Sailing Directions and Anchorages

7. East Lewis

Tob Bhrollum from south

Looking WNW towards Lewis and Loch Bhrollum from the Shiant Islands

CCC Sailing Directions and Anchorages 115

Outer Hebrides

SHIANT ISLANDS

Shiant Islands

A dramatic group of islands to visit in settled weather, the Shiants are usually uninhabited, although occasionally visited by shepherds and the occupants of a holiday bothy. The approach from south is straightforward.

There are three islands, Garbh Eilean, Eilean Mhuire and Eilean an Tighe. Garbh Eilean, joined to Eilean an Tighe, has higher cliffs than Eilean an Tighe but the latter's are more precipitous. There are 2 islets and a drying rock, Galta Beag, Galta Mor (54m) with Damhag (dries 0·3m) extending in a line over 1 mile west from the NW end of Garbh Eilean.

There is a passage about 3 cables wide between Galta Beag and the west side of Garbh Eilean, and also a passage between Eilean Mhuire and the east side of Garbh Eilean. Both may be used in suitable conditions

Tides

Constant (for Loch Shell) –0016 Ullapool (–0436 Dover)

Height in metres

MHWS	MHWN	MTL	MLWN	MLWS
4·8	3·6	2·8	1·9	0·7

Sound of Shiant
NE-going stream begins –0315 Ullapool (+0500 Dover)
SW-going stream begins +0310 Ullapool (–0100 Dover)
The spring rate in each direction is 3 to 4 knots.

The streams around the Shiants are much affected by the wind especially at neaps. The Shiant Islands lie across the direction of the stream, and eddies occur near the islands.

Admiralty Chart
1794, 1757
Imray Chart
C67
Ordnance Survey
14
Cruising Scotland
p.194

There are heavy overfalls in the Sound of Shiant mid-channel area approximately 2 miles west of the Shiants light buoy (Q.G) and about 2 miles SE of the entrance to Loch Bhrollum. This area is particularly dangerous when strong NE winds interact with the NE-going tidal stream.

Directions

From the north pass between Garbh Eilean and Eilean Mhuire. This passage is restricted by a drying reef and a sunken rock extending 1½ cables west from Eilean Mhuire and a sand spit extending ½ cable from Garbh Eilean. Keep slightly west of mid-channel. The tide can reach 3 knots.

From the south, approaching the east sides of Eilean an Tighe and Garbh Eilean is straightforward but note the reef extending 1½ cables from Eilean Mhuire from the middle of the south side.

Anchorages

The usual anchorage in moderate westerly winds is on the east side of Mol Mor, a stony isthmus between the two western islands, but the bottom consists of boulders, with sand at greater depths further from the shore.

An alternative anchorage is the bay 3 or 4 cables north, where the depth is moderate and the bottom is sand with patches of weed.

In moderate easterly winds it is possible to anchor west of Mol Mor, keeping to the north side of the bay to avoid drying rocks off its south side.

116 CCC Sailing Directions and Anchorages

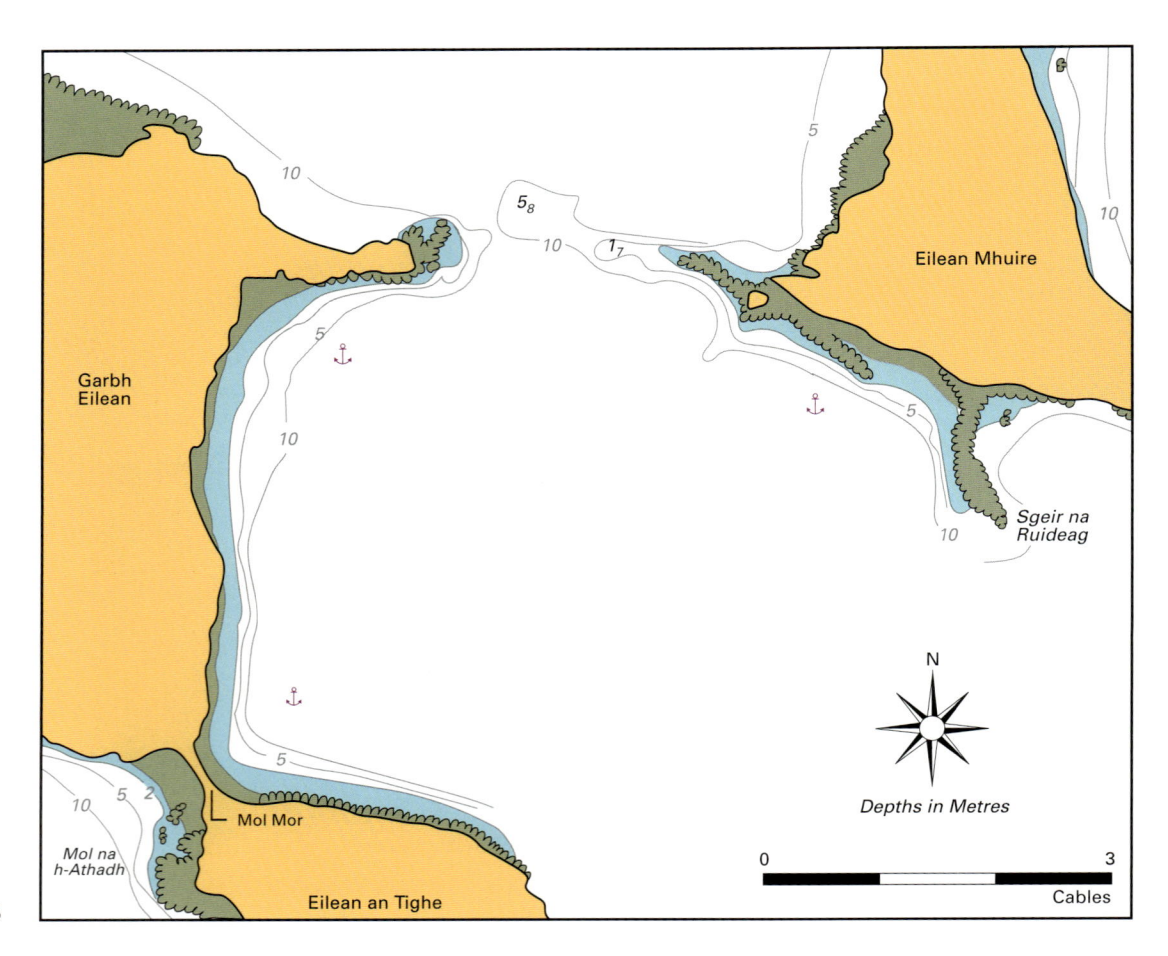

7. East Lewis

Looking north from Eilean an Tighe, Shiant Islands

The Shiants from the southwest

CCC Sailing Directions and Anchorages 117

Outer Hebrides

LOCH SHELL

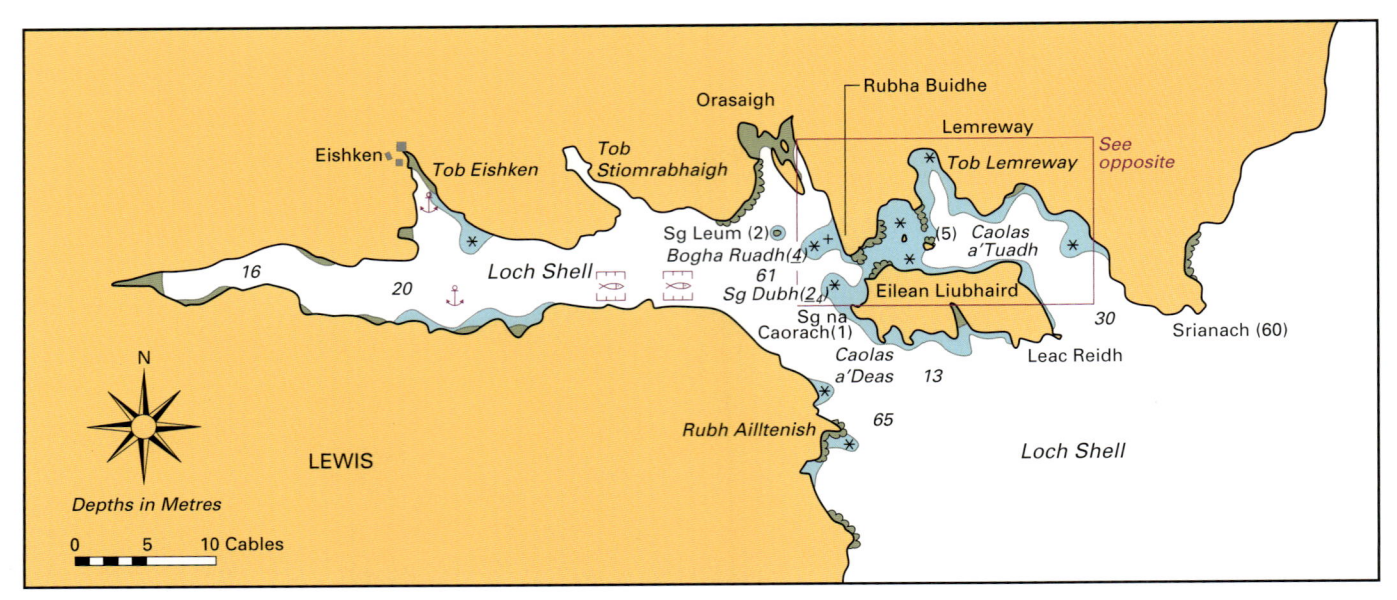

Loch Shell

Admiralty Chart
1794, 1757
Imray Chart
C67
Ordnance Survey
14
Cruising Scotland
p.194

Loch Shell is one of the best and most convenient anchorages on the east coast of Lewis. Its prominent danger-free entrance is easy of access and the loch itself provides good shelter. For those making passage in the North Minch it makes a convenient place of arrival at the Outer Hebrides being about mid-way between Stornoway, Lewis and East Loch Tarbert, Harris; and north of the Shiant Islands and the strong tides in the Sound of Shiant.

The entrance to the loch is between Rubha Ailltenish on the south side and Srianach, a bold headland with a vertical face on the NE side. From Srianach to the head of the loch is 6 miles and to Tob Eishken about 4 miles. The south shore which leads to the inner loch, given a reasonable offing, is free from hazard. The north shore has many indentations which provide some well protected anchorages particularly those in Caolas a'Tuath off the north shore of Eilean Liubhaird, and in the inlet of Tob Lemreway.

Tides

Constant –0016 Ullapool (–0436 Dover)

Height in metres

MHWS	MHWN	MTL	MLWN	MLWS
4·8	3·6	2·8	1·9	0·7

Tob Lemreway

Whereas there are reefs and drying rocks west and north of Eilean Iubhard, Caolas a'Tuath provides a clear approach to Tob Lemreway. In westerly gales Caolas a'Tuath is subject to very violent gusts.

Directions

From the south the long low finger of Leac Reidh, the SE corner of Eilean Liubhaird may be distinguished against the much higher background of the Lewis shore. The entrance to Caolas a'Tuath is between Leac Reidh and Srianach. Note Sgeir Phlathuig (dries 0·6m) 1 cable from the north shore. This rock is off a ravine with large boulders at the mouth where the shore line changes from cliffs to steep hills. The SE point of Eilean Liubhaird in line with Galta Mor (westmost islet (54) of the Shiant Islands) bearing 178° astern leads west of Sgeir Phlathuig. Sron Chrom, the NE point of Eilean Liubhaird in line with Rubha Buidhe leads south of it.

As reefs, terminating in a drying rock, extend more than ½ cable off the east shore at the entrance to Tob Lemreway, head towards Sgeir Fraoich till the entrance is well open. Once within Tob Lemreway keep at least ½ cable off both shores and note that there are drying rocks lying offshore 2 cables from the head of the inlet.

Anchorages

SE of the Lemreway pier is possible for a brief stay but it is restricted by many moorings and fish farm traffic and not recommended.

East side of Tob Lemreway inlet is a better alternative to the pier anchorage. Anchor south of the rocks in 4m.

Off the north shore of Eilean Liubhaird provides more shelter in fresh to strong southerly winds. Anchor close in on a shallow 6m ledge, 3 cables west of the fish cages, but note drying rocks to the west and north. In SE winds this may be subject to swell.

NW of Sgeir Ghlas is a good anchorage providing shelter from most wind directions with good holding in 7-8m. If making passage westwards from Caolas a Tuath hold closer to Sgeir Fraoich and Sgeir Ghlas to avoid the rocks off Eilean Liubhaird but take note of the reef which stretches south from Sgeir Ghlas.

Facilities

Water at pier. Telephone.

7. East Lewis

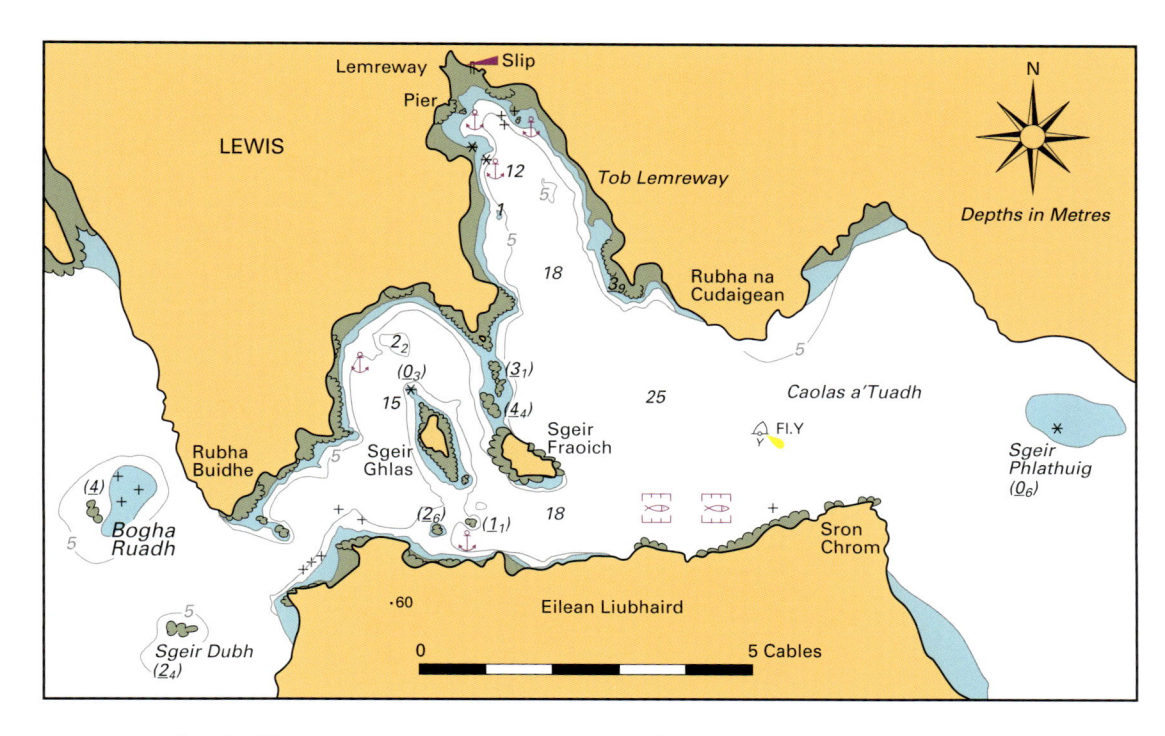

TOB LEMREWAY

Inner Loch Shell

The plans above and on the previous page show most of the hidden dangers. Note also, Sgeir na Caorach, about a cable south of Sgeir Dubh, a metre high and Sgeir Leum, 4 cables WNW of Rubha Buidhe, 2 metres high.

Directions

Enter south of Eilean Liubhaird and, when past that island, its SW side should bear no more than 120° astern to clear rocks west of the island. The south shore is clean beyond 3 cables north of Rubha Ailltenish.

Anchorages

Tob Eishken This inlet lies on the north side of the loch 2½ miles west of Eilean Liubhaird. Note the drying rock lying 1 cable off the NE shore of the entrance and a rock awash ¼ cable from the west side 2 cables south of Eishken Lodge. The anchorage is at the head of the inlet but is reported foul with lost moorings.

Bight on the south shore SE of Tob Eishken, is sheltered from southerly winds. The beach dries off considerably.

The head of the loch is clear and suitable for anchorage but dries out for about 2 cables. It is sheltered except from the east.

Tob Lemreway from the west

CCC Sailing Directions and Anchorages 119

Outer Hebrides

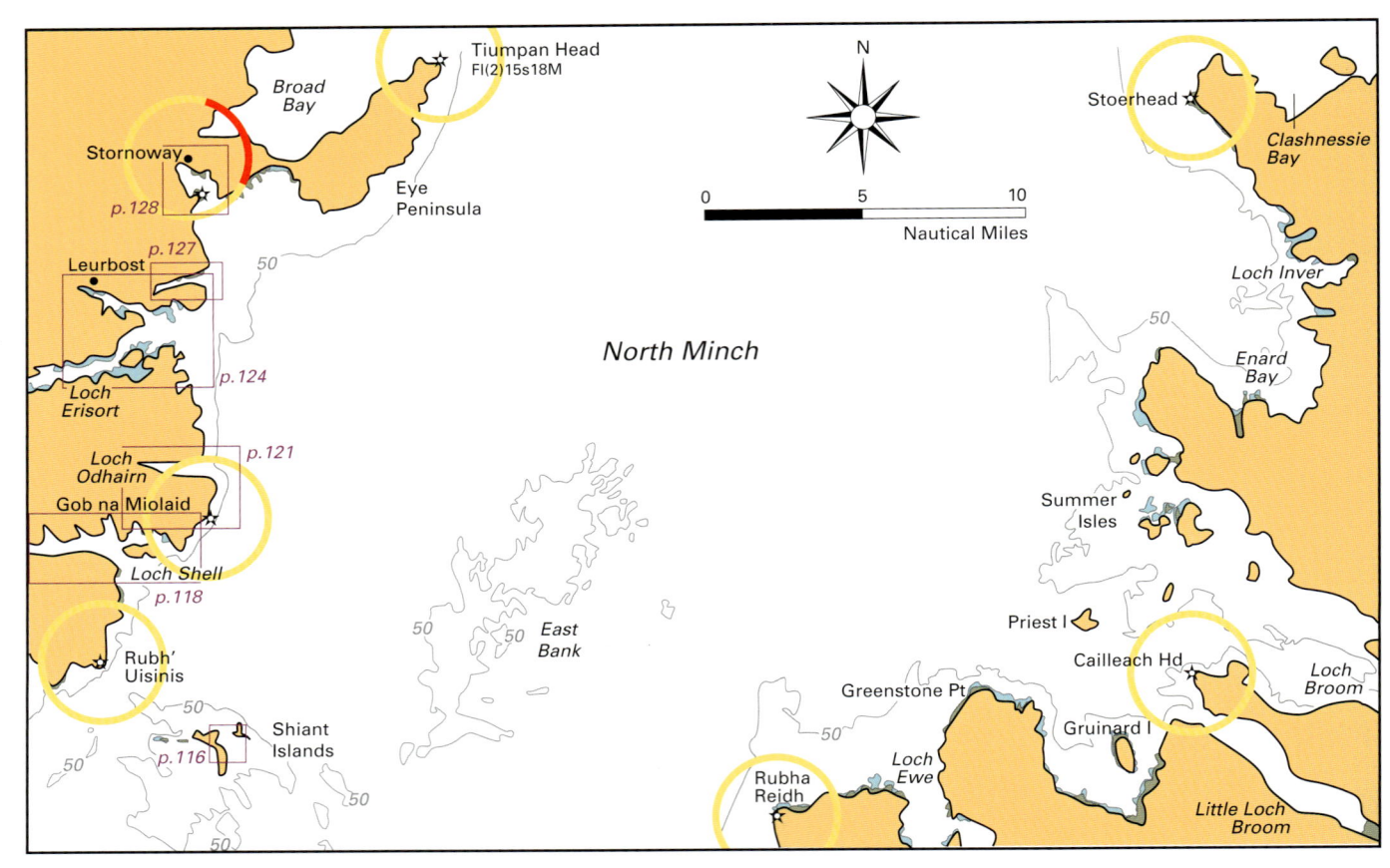

NORTH MINCH KEY PLAN

Admiralty Chart
1794, 1757
Imray Chart
C67
Ordnance Survey
8, 14
Cruising Scotland
p.173

Crossing the North Minch

The distances for the crossing of the North Minch are considerably greater than across the Little Minch but, although much exposed to the weather and swell which is present in strong northerly winds, tidal considerations are significantly less.

Tides

In the southern part of the North Minch
S-going streams begin +0410 Ullapool (HW Dover)
N-going streams begin −0150 Ullapool (−0600 Dover)

In the northern part of the North Minch
S-going streams begin +0510 Ullapool (+0100 Dover)
N-going streams begin −0050 Ullapool (−0500 Dover)

The mean spring rate offshore is between ½ and 1 knot with stronger streams occurring at headlands and particularly in the vicinity of the Shiant Islands

Lights

Mainland
Rubha Reidh Fl(4)15s37m24M.
Stoer Head Fl.15s59m24M
Cape Wrath Fl(4)30s122m22M

Scalpay, Harris
Eilean Glas Fl(3)20s43m23M

North Skye
Eilean Trodday Fl(2)WRG.10s52m12-9M
South Rona Fl.12s69m19M

Lewis
Butt of Lewis Fl.5s52m25M
Tiumpan Head Fl(2)15s55m18M
Gob na Miolaid Fl.15s17m10M
Rubh 'Uisenis Fl.5s24m11M

Distances

From South Rona
  to Loch Shell 33 miles, to Stornoway 47 miles
From North of Skye
  to Loch Shell (passing east of the Shiant Isles) 20 miles
From Badachro (Gairloch)
  to Loch Shell 30 miles, to Stornoway 38 miles
From Loch Ewe
  to Loch Shell 29 miles, to Stornoway 33 miles
From Loch Inver
  to Loch Shell 40 miles, to Stornoway 37 miles
From Kinlochbervie
  to Loch Shell 51 miles, to Stornoway 47 miles

Landfalls

Loch Shell (Isle of Lewis) offers good protection particularly in Tob Lemreway. It is easy of access in all conditions and makes an intermediate point of arrival at the Outer Hebrides between East Loch Tarbert, Harris and Stornoway. From the east a large vertical mark near Rubha Ailltenish, the south entrance point, can be seen from well out to sea.

Loch Odhairn, 1½ miles north of Gob na Miolaid, also makes a good landfall. The entrance is straightforward and the loch offers good shelter.

Stornoway is the best choice if supplies are needed. The approach from the south is straightforward but from the east the Chicken Rock (5m high), lying 3½ miles east of the harbour entrance must be watched. It is marked by a south cardinal buoy. The harbour itself is easy of access in all conditions.

120 CCC Sailing Directions and Anchorages

7. East Lewis

Loch Odhairn

Immediately north of Kebock Head, this loch is free from dangers and runs inland for 2 miles. There are no dangers within, or outwith, the loch and even in easterly winds the sea rarely disturbs the inner part of the loch.

Tides

Constant –0016 Ullapool (–0436 Dover)

Height in metres

MHWS	MHWN	MTL	MLWN	MLWS
4·8	3·7	2·9	2·0	0·7

Anchorage

In the bay on the south side, opposite the pier, just before the loch finally narrows. Some exposure to the east but good otherwise. In SW gales heavy squalls come down the slopes on the south side.

Supplies

PO, telephone 1 mile. Water from the tap at the pier.

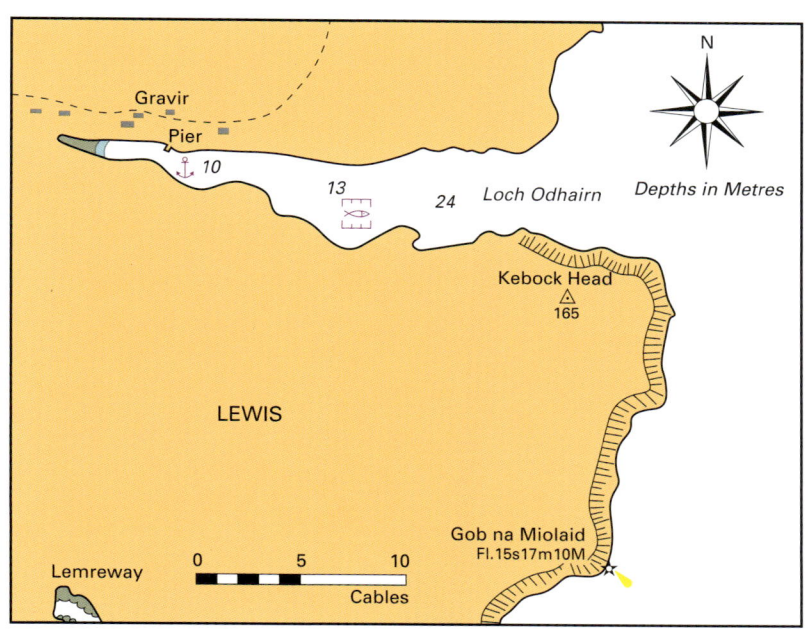

LOCH ODHAIRN

Loch Odhairn, anchorage on right

Loch Odhairn from SW

CCC Sailing Directions and Anchorages   121

Outer Hebrides

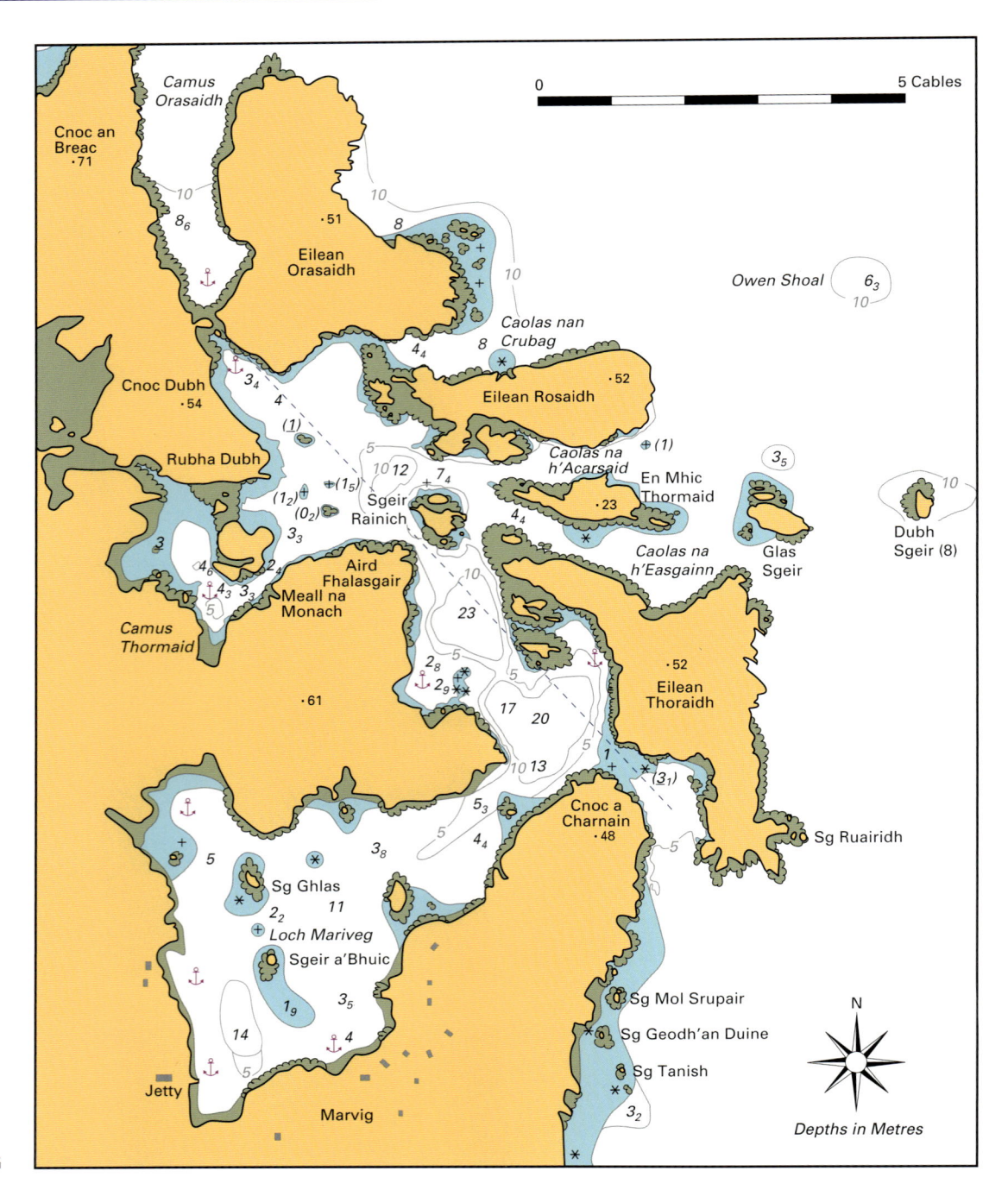

LOCH MARIVEG

Admiralty Chart
2529, 1794, 1757
Imray Chart
C67
Ordnance Survey
14
Cruising Scotland
p.196

Loch Mariveg (Mharabhig)

Lying about 6 miles south of Stornoway Harbour there are two indentations in the coastline on the SE side of the entrance to Loch Erisort which have their entrances almost completely enclosed by three islands and a number of islets. This results in a network of bays giving a surprising variety of sheltered anchorages.

Loch Mariveg is protected by Eilean Thoraidh. North of the entrances to Loch Mariveg, Eilean Orasaidh and Eilean Rosaidh provide anchorages on each side of the drying bar south of Camus Orasaidh.

There are two entrances to Loch Mariveg, one to the south between Cnoc a'Charnain and Eilean Thoraidh and the other, Caolas na h'Acarsaid, 3 cables WNW of Dubh Sgeir (8m), between Eilean Rosaidh and Eilean Mhic Thormaid. Both entrance passages are narrow and could be dangerous to enter in fresh to strong easterly winds.

Tides

Constant –0010 Ullapool (–0430 Dover)

Height in metres

MHWS	MHWN	MTL	MLWN	MLWS
4·8	3·7	2·9	2·0	0·7

Directions

The southern channel, southwest of Eilean Thoraidh, has only 1m but it is the wider entrance. It would be unwise to attempt this passage below half tide.

7. East Lewis

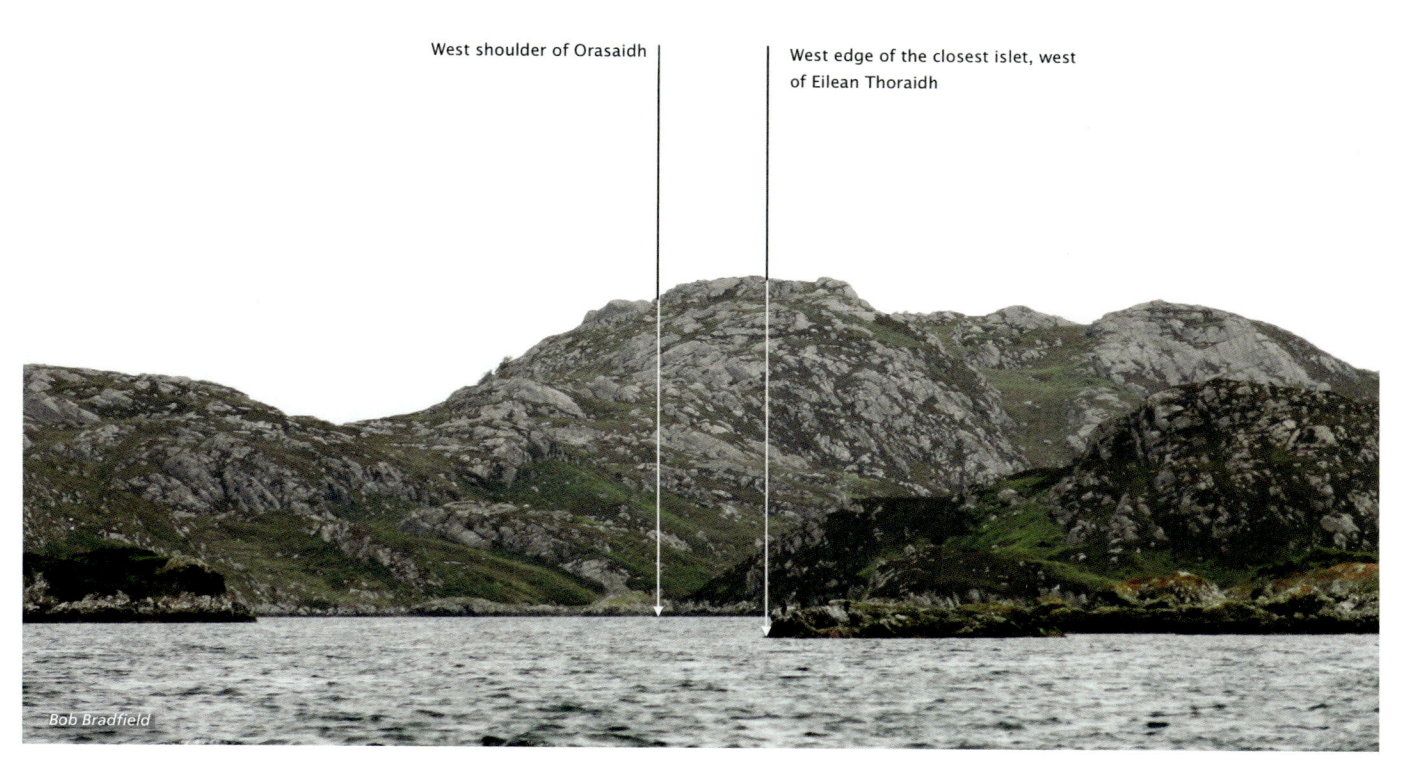

West shoulder of Orasaidh

West edge of the closest islet, west of Eilean Thoraidh

Bob Bradfield

Keep SW of mid-channel to avoid a drying rock (dries 3·1m), which shows white beneath the water, in the narrows. The west shoulder of Orasaidh open of the west edge of the closest islet west of Eilean Thoraidh (photograph above) clears this rock. This line should be identified before entering the channel. At the west end of the channel a rock, LD 0·4m, lies 50m from the north point of Cnoc a'Charnain.

Caolas na h'Acarsaid, the northern channel immediately south of Eilean Rosaidh, although narrow, is less obstructed than the southern channel and has greater depth. The rock SE of Eilean Rosaidh, LD 1m, may be dangerous if a swell is running. Give the NW end of Sgeir Rainich a berth of ½ cable to clear the reef off it before heading for the anchorages within the loch.

Once through either of the entrances and, if heading for Loch Mariveg itself, steer to avoid a reef off the NW shore of Cnoc a'Charnain and keep nearer to the NW shore. Maintain this course until the loch is well open. Within the loch note the drying rock about 1 cable ENE of Sgeir Ghlas and another about ½ cable SW of that islet. There are two more rocks side by side 1 cable WNW of Sgeir Glas. There is also a rock between Sgeir Glas and Sgeir a'Bhuic.

Anchorages

Loch Mariveg The best anchorages are southeast of Sgeir a'Bhuic and in the northwest corner. The SW corner is reported to be foul with chain and there are moorings which reduce the available space. The jetty in the southwest corner dries; there is a water tap at the head of the jetty and a telephone nearby.

Eilean Thoraidh on its west side, east of the mussel farm buoys and clear of drying reefs which extend 50 metres southeast of the southernmost islet.

Aird Fhalasgair in the bay ¼ mile south of the point. A drying rock lies ¼ cable off the south point of the bay.

Camas Thormaid (known to local yachtsmen as the Witches' Pool), southwest of Aird Fhalasgair. Keep 20 metres from the south shore to avoid a drying rock 60 metres off, with further rocks to the north of it, and anchor southwest of the 20-metre islet, in heavy clay. The pool further north can be used but it shoals to the west and is full of weed.

South or SW of Orasaidh A rock, drying 1m, ¾ cable from the west shore is cleared by keeping the west side of Sgeir Rainich in line the east side of Cnoc a Charnain, bearing 143°.

Southern entrance to Loch Mariveg from the SE showing the marks for clearing the drying 3·1 rock

Camas Thormaid anchorage, centre left. (see also p.9 for Loch Mariveg photograph)

Edward Mason

CCC Sailing Directions and Anchorages 123

Outer Hebrides

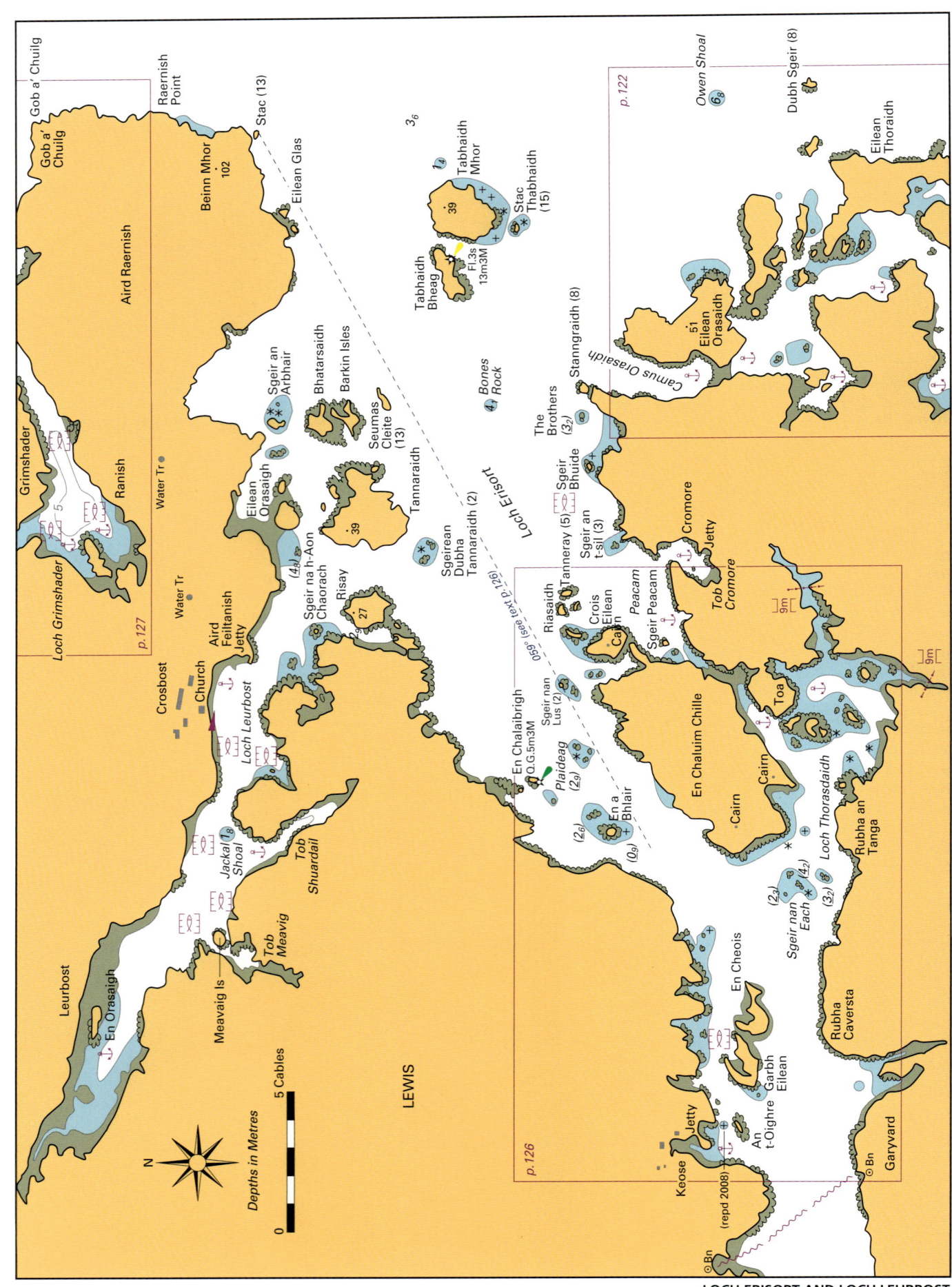

LOCH ERISORT AND LOCH LEURBOST

7. East Lewis

Loch Erisort

Loch Erisort, whose entrance is a little over a mile wide, runs westwards for 9 miles, 7 miles of which are navigable. This is a well inhabited part of Lewis. The south side of the loch entrance has some sheltered anchorages which are easy to enter. The north side of the entrance leads to Loch Leurbost, an arm of the sea reaching 2½ miles NW which is well sheltered from all directions.

Within Loch Erisort itself there are many islets, reefs and rocks but, with the use of Chart 2529, all dangers may be avoided. All rocks show at LW except Bones Rock (depth 4·1m) in the outer part of Loch Erisort and Jackal Shoal (depth 1·8m) in Loch Leurbost.

Tabhaidh Mhor and Tabhaidh Bheag are islands which lie in the centre of the approach to the loch. Barkin Isles, with the castellated quarried Seumas Cleite (13) and Tannaraidh to the west, shelter the entrance to Loch Leurbost. A large island, Eilean Chaluim Chille joined to the south Lewis shore at LW, narrows Loch Erisort considerably. The inner loch is entered north of this island.

Tides
Constant –0010 Ullapool (–0430 Dover)

Height in metres

MHWS	MHWN	MTL	MLWN	MLWS
4·8	3·7	2·9	2·0	0·7

Tidal streams are insignificant.

Directions
Approaching from the south Owen Shoal (LD 6·8) lies 3 cables north of Dubh Sgeir (8m) near the entrance to Loch Mariveg. If making for Peacam, pass between Bones Rock (LD 4·1) and The Brothers (dries 3·2m) 1 cable west of Stanngraidh.

From the north or east the approach is straightforward as Tabhaidh Bheag and Tabhaidh Mhor can be passed on either hand but beware a shoal patch (LD 1·4m) 150m off the NE side of Tabhaidh Mhor and a further patch (LD 3·6) approximately 3c off. Note also Bones Rock (LD 4·1).

If making for Loch Leurbost the straightforward approach is between the west side of Tannaraidh and Sgeirean Dubh Tannaraidh (2). Keep closer to the SW end of Tannaraidh to avoid reefs to port.

Anchorages (Outer Loch Erisort)
Camas Orasaidh lies south of Stanngraidh on the west side of Eilean Orasaidh. Hold well over to the west side of the bay on entry as rocks extend 40m off the east shore. Good holding in mud. Exceptionally this bay is subject to swell in northerly winds or easterly gales. It is said that when The Brothers (dries 3·2m - see above) are covered, a small vessel can make passage south from the head of Camus Orasaidh into the north basin of Loch Mariveg. Keep to the east side of the narrows.

Peacam (Cromore Bay) From Rubha Stanngraidh keep 1½ cables offshore to avoid The Brothers (dries 3·2m) and leave the above water rocks, Sgeir Bhuidhe and Sgeir an t-sil (3m) to port. Anchor in 4m south of Sgeir Peacam.

Tob Cromore A shallow pool with a cable wide entrance on the SE side of Peacam. Clay bottom, shoal towards the head. Note the drying rock ⅓ cable from the NW shore. Anchor in 2·5m as soon as the pool opens out. There is an increasing number of moorings but space to anchor should be available.

Loch Leurbost

Approach
Loch Leurbost is best entered SW of Tannaraidh, keeping close to that island to avoid drying rocks east of Sgeirean Dubh Tannaraidh. After passing west of Tannaraidh head round to port to enter the loch. Entry can also be made north of Barkin Isles and Tannaraidh. Note the rock (dries 4·8m) which lies 1 cable west of Eilean Orasaigh on the north shore. This rock rarely covers.

Anchorages
Head of the loch Anchor not much beyond Eilean Orasaigh, in 3m mud.

Tob Shuardail Jackal Shoal (LD 1·8m) lies at the east side of the entrance. Anchor in 2·5m as far within the inlet as depth and size allow.

Crosbost Anchor clear of moorings in the wide bay between the church and the jetty on Aird Feiltanish, in 8m.

Risay The basin west of Risay, on the south side of the entrance to Loch Leurbost, is shallow (see Antares chart) with depths of 2-3 metres, soft mud. Enter from the north and anchor where indicated on plan.

Lights
Tabhaidh Bheag Fl.3s13m3M
Eilean Chalaibrigh Q.G.5m3M

Camus Orasaidh anchorage showing the artificial boat passage at HW leading to Loch Mariveg

Admiralty Chart
2529, 1794
Imray Chart
C67
Ordnance Survey
14
Cruising Scotland
p.196

Outer Hebrides

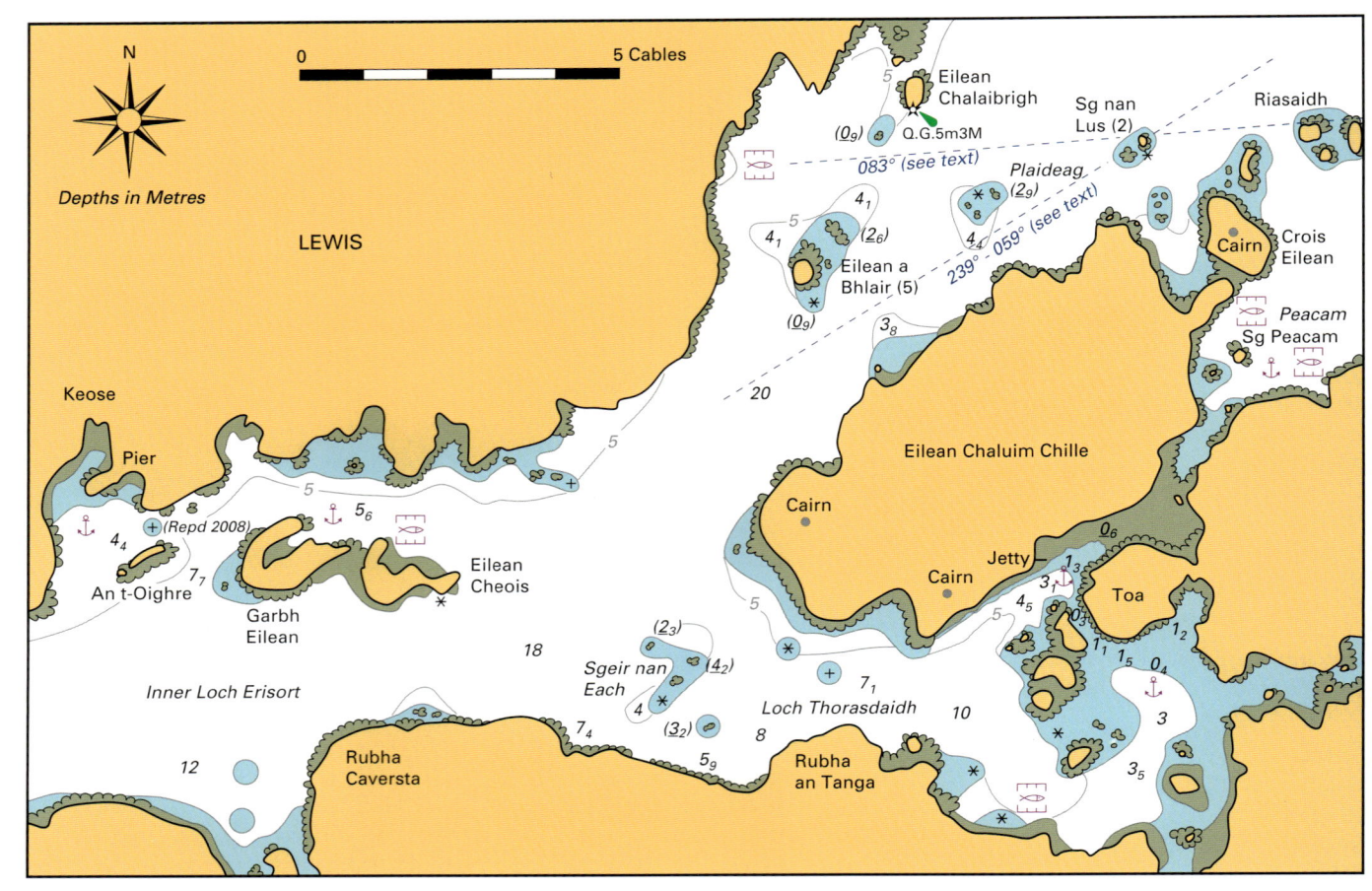

INNER LOCH ERISORT AND LOCH THORASDAIDH

Admiralty Chart
2529, 1794, 1757
Imray Chart
C67
Ordnance Survey
14
Cruising Scotland
p.196

Inner Loch Erisort

Directions

The entrance to the inner loch requires special care as a large reef, Plaideag (dries 2·9m), lies in the centre. The principal entrance passage is south of Plaideag and should be approached south of Sgeir nan Lus (2) on a course equidistant from Sgeir nan Lus and the north point of Eilean Chalium Chille. Thereafter a course of approximately 239° will leave Plaideag to starboard. A useful clearance bearing for avoiding Plaideag both when entering and leaving the Inner Loch is to keep Stac (13), off the north entrance point of Loch Erisort, in line with Sgeir na Lus on a bearing of 059°.

An alternative route is to follow the north shore, passing close north of Eilean Chalaibrigh and then west of Eilean a'Bhlair. Although the channel north of Eilean Chalaibrigh is narrow it presents no difficulty. In certain conditions this passage may be the preferred route for entering and leaving the Inner Loch.

If deciding to pass south of Eilean Chalabrigh beware of the rock (dries 0·9m) lying ½ cable SW of Eilean Chalaibrigh. A transit of 083° with Sgeir nan Lus in line with the north side of Riasaidh clears this rock and the reefs (dries 2·6m) NE of Eilean a'Bhlair.

Anchorage

Keose Enter to the west of An t-Oighre to avoid the rock (reported 2008) in the channel to the north of the island. Anchor south of the jetty in 3m, soft mud, and use a tripping line as the bottom is foul with old moorings. Alternatively, better anchorage can be found north of Garbh Eilean.

Loch Thorasdaidh (Hurista)

Directions

The most easterly rock of Sgeir nan Each is charted as drying 4·2 metres; if it can be identified without doubt, pass at least a cable west of Eilean Chaluim Chille then steer to pass ½ cable east of the rock which dries 4·2 metres until near the south shore and then turn to head for the anchorage chosen.

Otherwise keep Sgeir nan Lus in sight astern, leaving Sgeir nan Each to port, until close to the south shore and then turn to follow it eastwards keeping ¼ cable off, until past Rubh' an Tanga, its most northerly point.

Anchorage

Between the west side of Toa and the jetty on the east side of Eilean Chaluim Chille. Good holding in mud. Alternatively pass south of the most southerly islet in the middle of the south corner of the loch and anchor 1 cable NE of it in 3m. Some swell sets in with strong W or NW winds.

7. East Lewis

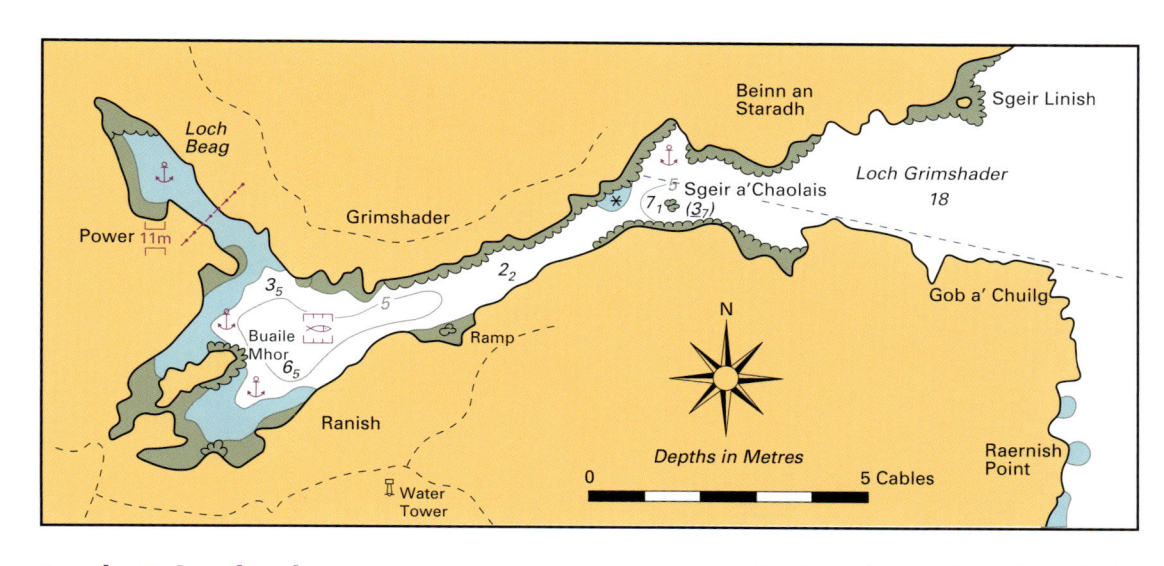

LOCH GRIMSHADER

Loch Grimshader

The head of this loch provides perfect shelter as does Loch Beag, a spur extending 5 cables NW, although the latter is obstructed by a power cable (see text below and plan). At the entrance to Loch Grimshader there is, on the edge of the cliff on the south side of the entrance, a remarkable rock having the appearance of a lion's head.

Tide
Const. –0010 Ullapool (–0430 Dover)

Height in metres

MHWS	MHWN	MTL	MLWN	MLWS
4·8	3·7	2·9	2·0	0·7

Directions
From the north give Sgeir Linish, an above water rock, a wide berth to avoid extending reefs. Sgeir a'Chaolais (dries 3·7m) lies 5 cables within the entrance and when the south point of the entrance is kept in sight this leads north of it. After passing that rock hold to the south shore to avoid rock lying off the north shore. The depth decreases after passing Sgeir a'Chaolais.

Anchorages
Bay north of Sgeir a'Chaolais is reported as quite a good anchorage.

Head of the loch either side of Buaile Mhor. Good anchorage in 7-8m off slip on south side.

Loch Beag can be approached by keeping to the NE side of a very narrow channel, 3m deep, with rocks on SW side. **Caution**: An overhead power cable crosses this channel with a clearance of 11m at HW. The tidal stream in the narrows is 2 to 3 knots. Anchor off the burn on the NW side in 4m, mud. This anchorage is reported to be silting.

Loch Thorasdaidh anchorage between Toa and Eilean Chaluim Chille

CCC Sailing Directions and Anchorages

Outer Hebrides

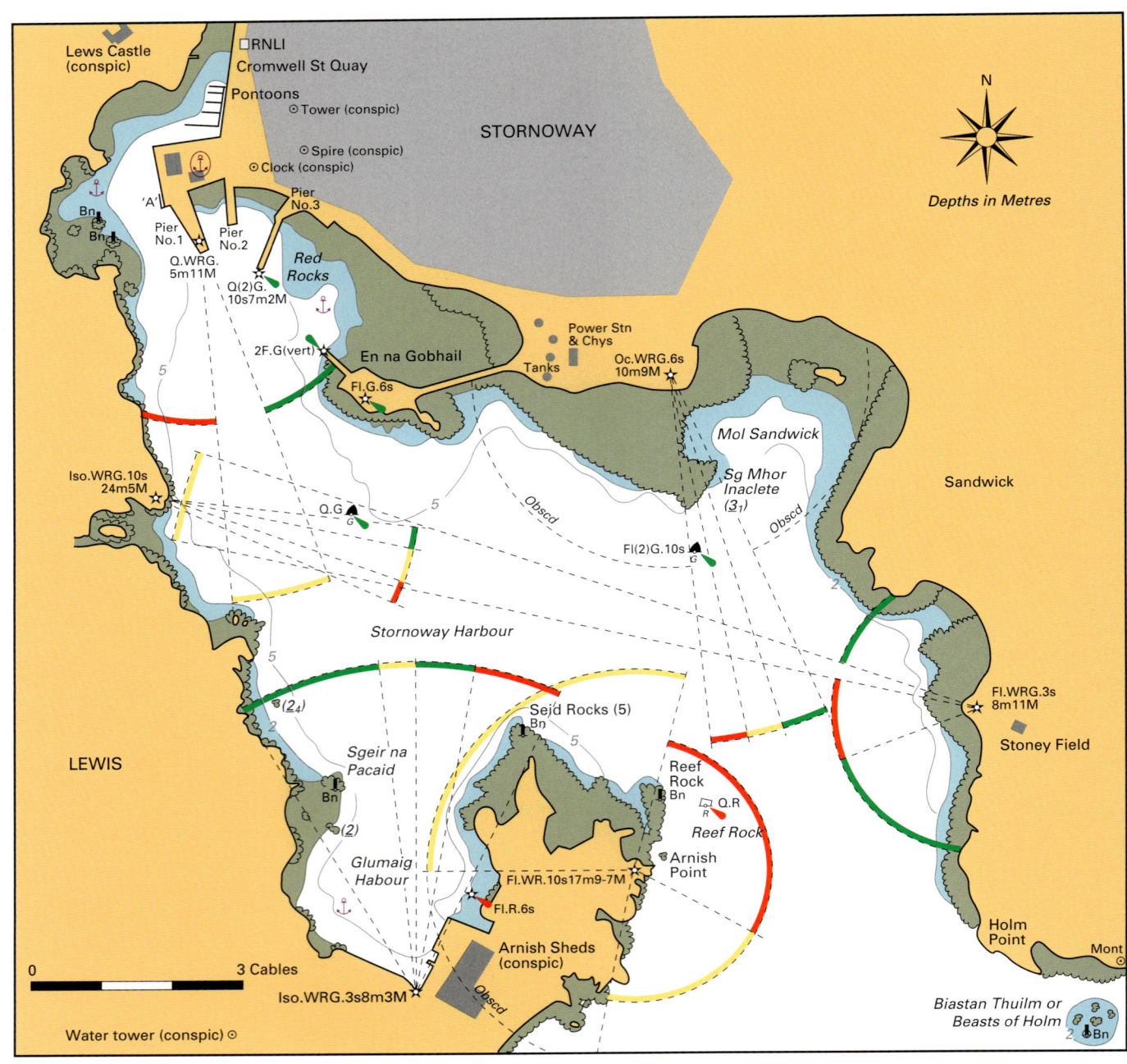

STORNOWAY HARBOUR

Admiralty Chart
2529, 1794, 1757
Imray Chart
C67
Ordnance Survey
8
Cruising Scotland
p.197

Stornoway

Stornoway Harbour is the largest harbour in the Hebrides. It is well sheltered and easy to enter at all states of the tide. With the largest concentration of population in the Western Isles, Stornoway has many facilities in contrast to other parts of the islands. It is 30 miles from the Butt of Lewis to Stornoway Harbour. The Eye Peninsula, east of Stornoway Harbour, is low lying and looks like an island when viewed from some distance off.

Tides

Constant –0010 Ullapool (–0430 Dover)
Height in metres

MHWS	MHWN	MTL	MLWN	MLWS
4·8	3·7	2·9	2·0	0·7

Tidal streams are negligible in the harbour.

Directions

In the approach the 3 grey chimneys of the Power Station on Inaclete Point on the north side of the harbour and the large sheds on Arnish Point, on the west side of the harbour entrance, are very conspicuous. The Memorial Tower on Holm Point can be seen against the skyline on the east side of the harbour entrance.

From the east, 3 miles east of Holm Point, note the Chicken Rock, lying about ¼ mile SW of Chicken Head. It is 5 metres high with a beacon with a spherical topmark, and is marked by a S cardinal light buoy. The Beasts of Holm are rocks a cable SSE of Holm Point at the east side of the entrance which dry up to 2·3 metres and are marked by a green beacon 5 metres high.

Entry to the harbour is straightforward but keep a look out for fishing boats and ferries.

128   CCC Sailing Directions and Anchorages

7. East Lewis

All hazards are marked: those north of Arnish Point by a red can light buoy Q.R and two unlit beacons. Sgeir Mhor Inaclete, off the north shore, has a ruined beacon on it and a green conical buoy, Fl.(2)G.10s. immediately to the south. At night keep in the white sector of each of three sectored lights in turn. Continue past pier No.1 and into the inner harbour. Call the Harbour Office, on Channel 16/12, for berthing instructions.

Berthing

There is a marina at Cromwell quay in the inner harbour which has recently (2014) been extended to provide 80 berths for boats up to 24 metres. There is now more room for visiting yachts but availability should be checked by calling up the Harbour Office on Ch.12 or telephoning (see below). All berths are serviced with water and shorepower and WiFi is available. Showers, toilets and laundrette.

Anchorages

Berthing alongside is usually preferable to anchoring but the following are possibilities.

Port nam Portan on the west side of the harbour opposite the Esplanade Quay (letter 'A' on plan) provides limited anchoring space due to moorings of local boats. Anchor north of the beacons and avoid swinging into the fairway. Holding is reported as poor.

Eilean na Gobhail Anchor in the bay NW of the island. Keep well clear of No 3 Pier. The Ro-Ro terminal is on the west side of this pier. Note shoal water and drying rocks inshore.

Glumaig Harbour Reefs extend 1 cable north of Arnish Point and ¾ cable eastwards from the west side of the entrance. Both are both marked by beacons. Debris has recently been cleared from the sea bed though a strong tripping line is still recommended. Despite the distance from the town and the industrial surroundings it is probably the best place to anchor in the harbour.

Lights

Approach from the east
Chicken Rock (beacon) Q(6)+LFl.15s
Nato Fuel Jetty (Branahuie Bay) 2 FR(vert)11m6M

Harbour Entrance and Approach lights

On or near west shore
Arnish Point Fl.WR.10s17m9-7M
Reef Rock buoy QR
Glumaig Harbour WRG.3s8m3M
 Fl.R.6s
Greeta Light Iso.WRG.10s24m5M

On E shore
Stoney Field Fl.WRG.3s8m11M

On N shore
Sandwick Bay Oc.WRG.6s10m9M
Sg. Mhor Inaclete Light buoy Fl(2)G.10s

Inner Harbour Lights
Eilean na Gobhail Fl.G.6s8m.
Fairway Light buoy Q.G
Slipway (NW of En. na Gobhail) 2F.G (vert)
No 1 Pier Q.WRG.5m11M
No 3 Pier Ro-Ro Terminal Q(2).G.10s 7m 2M

Supplies and services

Diesel can be obtained from the berth at the north end of Esplanade Quay. The facility is operated by the Stornoway Port Authority. The Harbour Office has a full list of the various marine, engineering and repair services which are available.

Shops, supermarket, PO and banks. Chandlery. Hospital. Petrol and Calor gas. Tourist Information Centre. Swimming Pool at Nicolson Sports Centre. Car hire and taxi services. Many hotels and restaurants.

Daily car ferry to Ullapool by Caledonian MacBrayne. Air service to Glasgow, Inverness and Aberdeen and also inter-island air services.

RNLI Lifeboat Station.

Coastguard: MRSC at Battery Point.

Customs: There is no customs office at Stornoway. For clearance contact the office at Aberdeen (see below).

Communications

Harbour Office VHF Ch 12/16 ☎01851 702688
Coastguard ☎01851 702013
Customs (Aberdeen) ☎01224 844610
Western Isles Harbourmaster ☎01851 703773
Hospital ☎01851 704704
Tourist Information Centre ☎01851 703088
Caledonian MacBrayne ☎01851 702361

The coast north of Stornoway is dealt with at the end of Chapter 8 (p.152) as part of the passage round the Butt of Lewis.

Stornoway Harbour from the south. Poll nam Partan on the left opposite Esplanade Quay

8. West of the Outer Hebrides

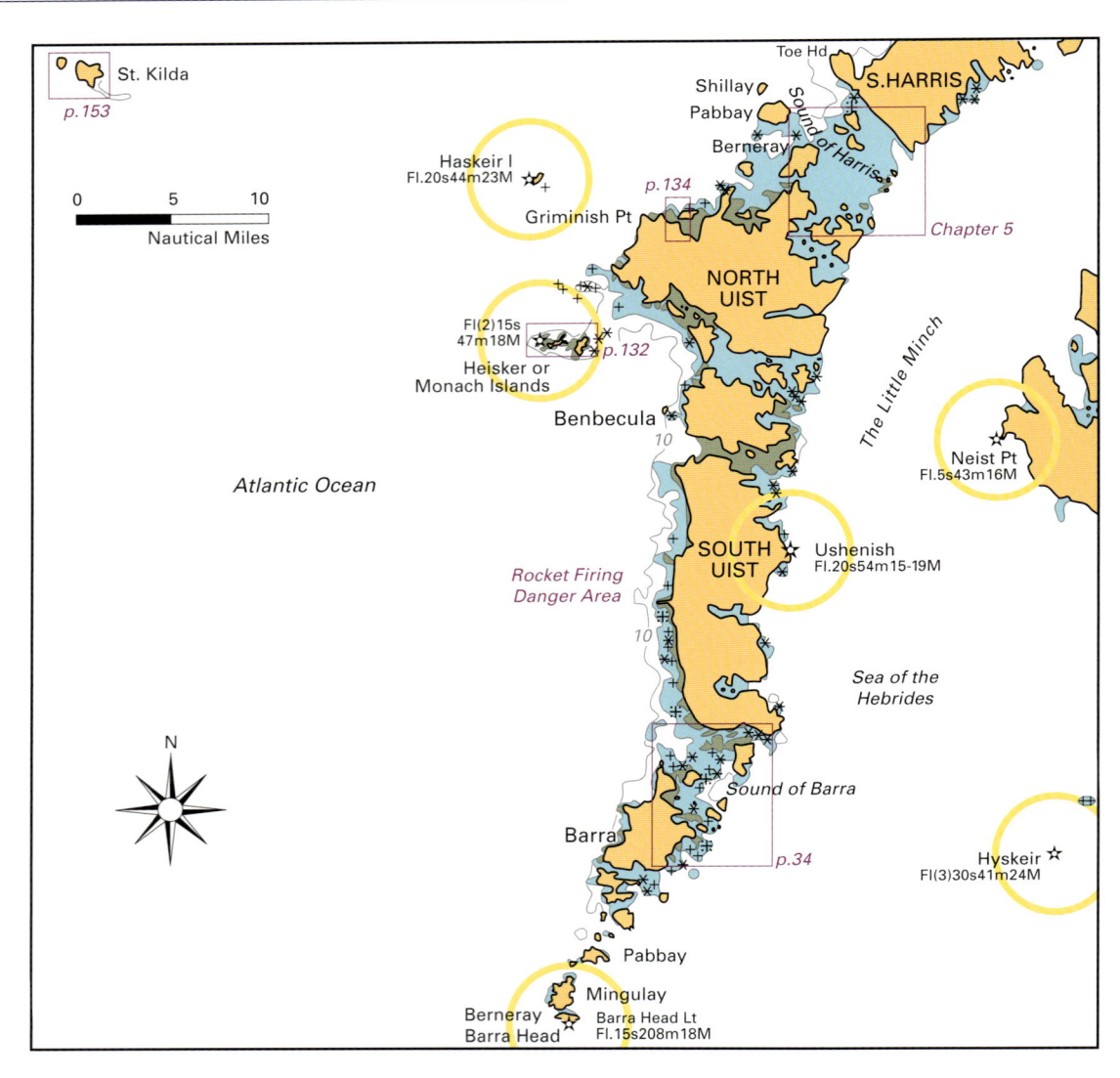

WEST COAST; BARRA HEAD TO SOUND OF HARRIS, KEY PLAN

Admiralty Chart
2722, 2635
Imray Chart
C66
Ordnance Survey
18, 22, 31
Cruising Scotland
p.199

The Atlantic coast of the Outer Hebrides has little shelter and in heavy westerly weather it would be dangerous to run for any of the passages between the islands, especially with a west-going tide when there would be heavy overfalls at the entrance to each sound. In clear visibility some of the lochs on the west side of Lewis provide accessible shelter. Strong tides and heavy seas occur off both Barra Head and Butt of Lewis.

For key plans of passages between islands south of Barra see Chapter I and for waters to the west of Harris and Lewis see p.136.

West coasts of Barra, Benbecula and the Uists

There is no secure shelter between Barra Head and the Sound of Harris. The west coasts of Barra and the islands to the south are generally rock-bound and inhospitable and those of South Uist, Benbecula and North Uist are low lying and lacking in distinctive features. There are many rocks, reefs and shoal patches lying within 3 miles of the shore which cause heavy breaking seas.

130   CCC Sailing Directions and Anchorages

8. West of the Outer Hebrides

These *Directions* have previously included the west entrance to the, now-blocked, Sound of Vatersay as a possible anchorage but because of its exposure to the west, dangerous rocks lying up to ½ mile west of the entrance and the fact that the traditional leading line is now almost impossible to distinguish, it is not recommended. In conditions that would be moderate enough to allow safe entry to Vatersay Sound, it would also be possible to pass safely through any of the other sounds to one of the more secure anchorages on the east side; altogether a much better alternative.

However, in strong easterlies or very light weather, when swell is not a problem, anchoring in Bagh Siar, the bay to the west of Vatersay Bay (p.20) is a useful anchoring option and it can easily be approached using Chart 2769.

In heavy onshore weather the whole coast should be given a good offing of at least 3 to 4 miles.

Tides

South of the Monach Islands
N-going stream begins –0420 Ullapool (+0345 Dover)
S-going stream begins +0205 Ullapool (–0215 Dover)

The tides are under ½ knot at springs and offshore but gain strength as the shallower water round the islands is approached. The tide runs strongly both east and west of the Monach Islands and can reach 2 knots at springs.

Dangers and marks

Off the west side of South Uist drying rocks extend up to a mile from the shore and at the north end of South Uist Ardivachar Rocks, which dry 3·2 metres, are 1½ miles from the shore. The 20-metre contour avoids these dangers by a reasonable margin. Rubha Ardvule, 7 metres high, which lies 8 miles north of the Sound of Barra, is prominent.

Bo Ruag which dries 1·2 metres, lies 3 miles west of the northwest end of Benbecula, close to the 20-metre line, and its position is usually revealed by breakers. There is no clearing mark for this rock on a passage along the coast and the best course when heading north is to steer for the lighthouse at Shillay at the west end of the Monach Isles, or to keep closer inshore.

Firing Range

An inshore danger area extends 20 miles seaward from 2 miles south of Rubha Ardvule to Ardivachar Point and is in frequent use for short range live firing trials throughout the year Monday to Saturday, 1000-1800hrs, this period may be extended to 2359hrs on Tuesdays and Thursdays. Red flashing beacons Iso.R.2s visible by day and flags (red lamps by night) are illuminated and hoisted one hour before live activity commences. The flags are situated at prominent locations throughout the Range. The red flashing beacons are located at North Vedette 57°23'N 07°25'W height 3 metres, Falconet Tower 57°22'N 07°24'W height 15 metres and Range Main Entrance 57°21'N 07°22'W height 9 metres. A Range Safety vessel patrols the actual inshore danger areas when activity is in progress.

An extended range is used for long-range live firing trials. Firing trials will be conducted within discrete areas bounded by the west coast of South Uist out to 11°40'W between 56°25'N and 58°30'N. Stornoway Coast Guard will broadcast a navigational warning whenever this extended range is in use.

A daily Range activity and inshore weather forecast is broadcast on VHF marine Ch 73 after making an alerting call on Ch 12 (local fishing channel). The broadcast is normally made at 1000hrs or 1 hour before Range activity. Information may also be obtained by calling Range Control on ☎ 01870 604535. Alternatively the Guardroom (24hrs) on ☎ 01870 604535 may be contacted. Range Control also monitor VHF Ch 16 during all trial activity.

All timings are UTC. All positions are related to WGS84 datum.

Lights

New lights make some contribution to navigation in this area, as follows:
Monach Islands LtHo Fl(2)15s47m18M
Haskeir Fl.20s44m23M
Whale Rock E card buoy Q(3)10s (57° 54'·9N 8°00'·7W)

St Kilda, 35 miles distant, seen from North Uist

Outer Hebrides

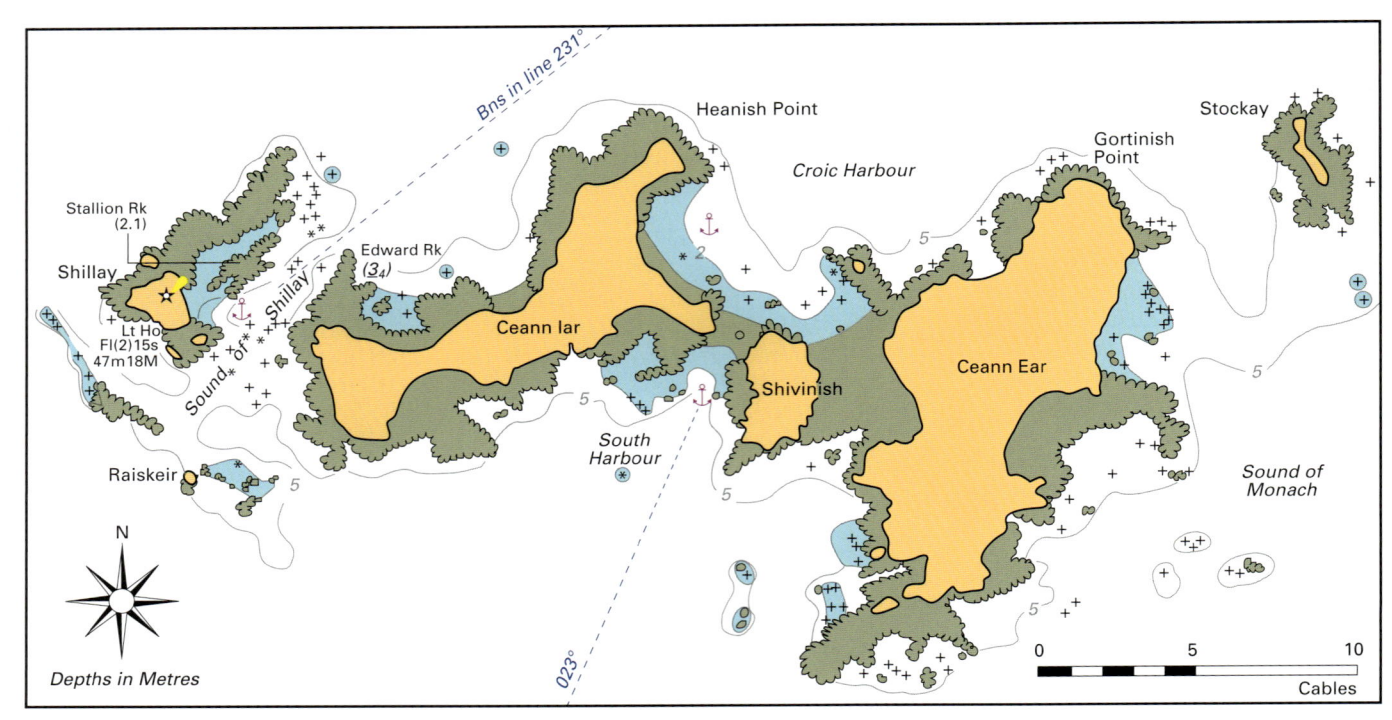

MONACH ISLANDS

Admiralty Chart
2722
Imray Chart
C66
Ordnance Survey
22, 18
Cruising Scotland
p.199

Monach Islands

This group of five low lying islands, also known as the Heisker Islands (not to be confused with Haskeir Island 10 miles to the north), lies about 5 miles offshore in an area of shoals on the west side of North Uist. The lighthouse on Shillay, the most westerly island, is the most conspicuous mark. They offer anchorage and protection from winds from all directions but undoubtedly should only be visited in settled weather.

Great care is needed when in the vicinity of these islands because rocks above water, drying and submerged are scattered over an area between 2½ miles northwest of Shillay and the coast of North Uist northeast of Stockay, to Causamul, which is 8 metres high, 1½ miles west of Aird an Runair, the west point of North Uist. Additionally, the whole area around the Monach Islands and the west end of the Sound of Harris is strewn with creel buoys and floating lines. A good lookout must be kept for them and all buoys given a wide berth.

No large scale chart is available but they are shown at 1:200,000 on Chart 2722 and 1:150,000 on Imray chart C66 and should not be approached without using one of these.

This archipelago is a National Nature Reserve, managed by Scottish Natural Heritage. There is no restriction on access, but visitors are asked not to disturb birds and not to leave litter.

Tides

Constant –0103 Ullapool (–0523 Dover)

Height in metres

MHWS	MHWN	MTL	MLWN	MLWS
4·2	3·0	2·4	1·3	0·4

The north-going stream begins –0420 Ullapool (+0345 Dover)
The south-going stream begins +0205 Ullapool (–0215 Dover)
The spring rate in each direction is 2 knots.

Directions

From the south the approach is straightforward until at least a mile off the Monach Islands. If making for the north anchorage, pass well west of Huskeiran (1·8) but note the 5m patch 2 miles west, then enter John's North Channel passing mid-way between Middle Dureberg (dries 2·7m) on the port hand and West Dureberg (dries 1·2m) to starboard. The SW end of the Middle Dureberg can be approached to within 2 cables as, even if covered, it is normally marked by breakers.

A leading line for John's North channel is the north extremity of Stockay in line with Rueval, the highest hill on Benbecula (view B opposite), bearing 116°. Follow this until the lighthouse bears 204°. Once through John's North Channel the beacons on the eastmost islet adjoining Shillay provide a leading line of 231° into the anchorage. The beacons are sometimes not easily seen, especially when entering against the sun.

In clear weather the channel between Huskeiran and Shillay can be taken as the south end of the former always shows. Keep well off the north and NE end of Shillay as reefs extend for over ½ mile.

From the north leave the Sound of Harris between Pabbay and Shillay through the Sound of Shillay. Head for a position 2 miles west of Griminish Point. As the approaches to the Monach Islands from Griminish Point have many reefs and rocks, maintain a SW'ly course until the lighthouse on Shillay bears 175° then alter course to enter John's North Channel to

132 CCC Sailing Directions and Anchorages

8. West of the Outer Hebrides

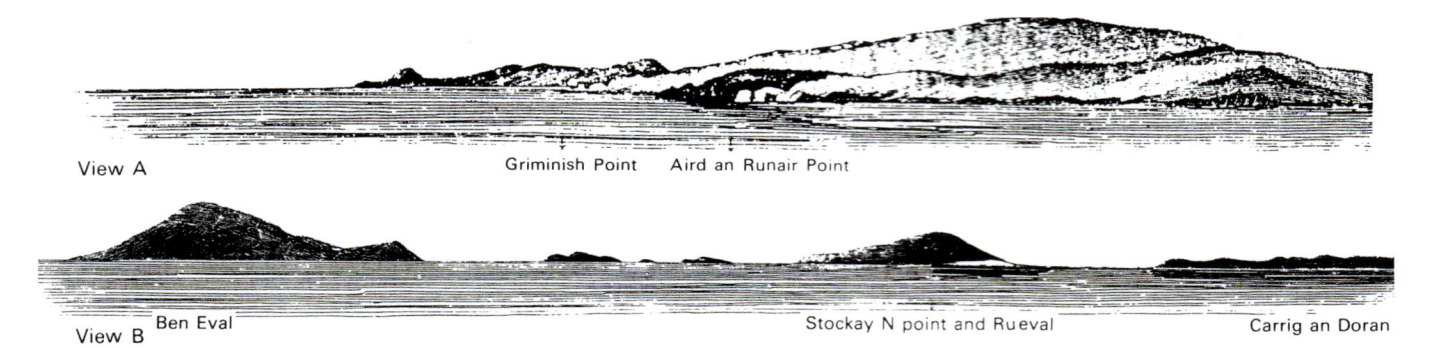

View A — Griminish Point, Aird an Runair Point

View B — Ben Eval, Stockay N point and Rueval, Carrig an Doran

pass mid-way between Middle Dureberg (dries 2·7m) on the port hand and West Dureberg (dries 1·2m) to starboard. Follow the leading line of 116° (view B above) through the fairway and the further directions given above which complete the approach to the Sound of Shillay anchorage.

Alternatively from the north after passing Griminish Point keep 5 cables offshore until Aird an Runair is abeam and then alter to pass through the Sound of Causamul keeping Griminish Point just open of Aird an Runair on a bearing of 029° (view A above) to clear the Charlotte Rocks. Once past these rocks and with Deasker (3) abeam to starboard course can be altered towards the lighthouse on Shillay.

If passing either northwards or southwards through the Sound of Monach note particularly East Rock (dries 1·8m) which lies 7½ cables east of Stockay. Half of Haskeir Island open west of Causamul bearing 333° clears East Rock and Vosgeir (dries 0·6m) which lies 1 mile NNE of East Rock.

Anchorages

Anchorages at Monach Isles are used by lobster fishermen, some of whom have laid moorings there, and creels are left with buoys attached. The islands may be approached by any of the channels described above.

Sound of Shillay The best anchorage at the Monach Isles lies between Shillay and Ceann Iar. It is entered from northeast between Edward Rock which dries 3·4 metres at the end of a reef ¼ mile north of the west point of Ceann Iar, and Stallion Rock which dries 2·1 metres 4 cables northeast of Shillay; other rocks lie up to 3 cables NNW of Stallion Rock.

The stone beacons, on the islet east of Shillay, are 4 metres high and 1½ cables ESE of the lighthouse. When in line 231° they lead in to Sound of Shillay. In westerly winds, anchor in Poll Bane east of the jetty but the bottom shoals abruptly from 7 metres to less than 2 metres about a cable off the jetty. On no account should the anchorage be approached using the south channel.

Croic Harbour The bay on the north side of the main islands provides shelter from east to northwest with a bottom of sand, but with clay in places, and isolated rocks in depths of less than 2 metres. In the approach give Heanish Point a berth of 2 cables.

South Harbour lies between the south side of Ceann Iar and the west side of Shivinish. Several drying rocks lie up to ½ mile from the shores of each island; approach with middle of the isthmus between Ceann Iar and Shivinish bearing 023°.

Shillay, Monach Islands, from the WSW. The beacons are on the islet at the extreme right and the drying rocks in the northwest entrance to the Sound of Shillay are above and left of the lighthouse

Martin Lawrence

CCC Sailing Directions and Anchorages 133

Outer Hebrides

Admiralty Chart
2841, 2722
Imray Chart
C66
Ordnance Survey
18

Northwest coast of North Uist

Between Causamul, 1½ miles west of Aird an Runair, the westernmost point of North Uist, and Griminish Point the coast is clear of off-lying rocks but should not be approached closer than 5 cables.

North of Griminish the coastline shoals badly and there is an increasing number of dangers inshore of a line between Griminish Point and Shillay. If intending to pass through the Sound of Harris the straightforward route is to keep west of the above line and pass through the Sound of Shillay, which is clean, before heading for Colasgeir buoy and the Outer Stromay channel.

Sound of Pabbay

If heading for the Cope Passage or Berneray Harbour, it will save a few miles if the Sound of Pabbay is used. However, this route should only be attempted in fair weather and with sufficient rise of tide. In poor visibility, or if there is any doubt about identifying the various hazards, the Sound of Shillay should be used.

Dangers and marks

Bo Lea which is awash, lies 1½ miles offshore 3 miles northeast of Griminish Point. Causamul in line with Griminish Point 221° and Spuir in line with the southeast side of Pabbay 058° lead northwest of Bo Lea.

Spuir, 2 miles southwest of Pabbay, is 12 metres high. Reefs and detached drying rocks extend ¼ mile south of Spuir and McIver Rocks, which dry 3 metres, lie nearly a mile east.

Spuir Reef, halfway between Spuir and Pabbay, is shown on older charts as drying, but, in fact, it rarely uncovers.

Shoal sand spits and drying rocks extend at least ½ mile from Pabbay and Berneray, and a rock which dries ½ metre, Bo Leac Caolas, lies in the middle of the Sound of Pabbay.

Directions

To pass south of Pabbay, use the above transits to clear Bo Lea then pass close north of Spuir, and head for the north side of Berneray.

When within ½–1 mile of Berneray steer for the north tip of Ensay bearing about 60° to leave Bo Leac Caolas to port and to avoid a shoal spit which extends NNW from Berneray. Once on this course you should aim to pass close to Waypoints 5 and 4 (see *Cope Passage* p.83) and from then on follow *Cope Passage* or *Berneray Harbour* directions (see pp.83, 78).

Caolas a' Mhorain

This channel is the approach to Sound of Berneray (now blocked) between Boreray and Aird a' Mhorain, a mile to the southwest.

Gairgrada, a mile west of Aird a' Mhorain dries 1·8 metres. To clear Gairgrada and reefs off Aird a' Mhorain steer with Boreray touching the north end of the Berneray causeway 090°, then the summit of Lingay under Beinn Mhor 123°.

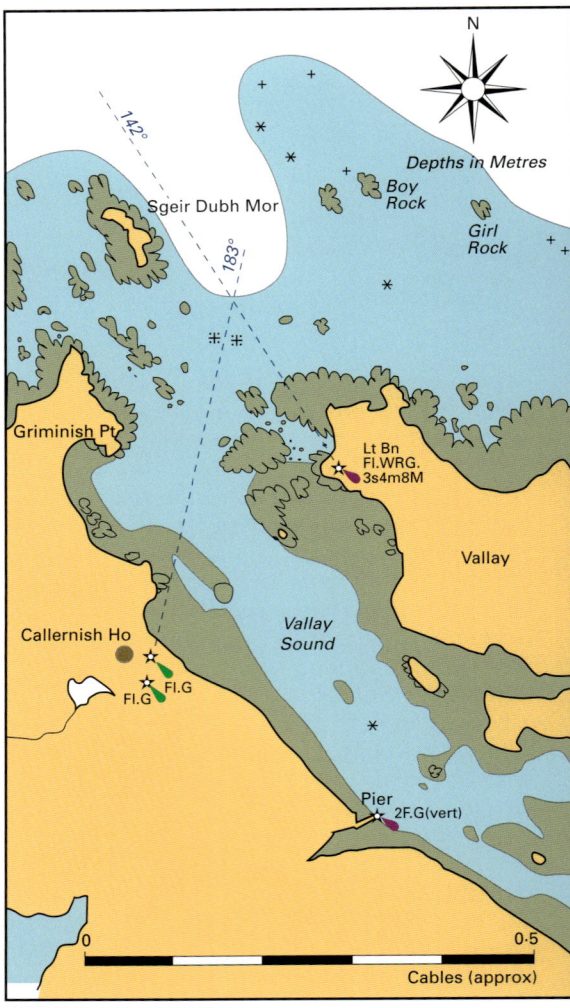

GRIMINISH HARBOUR

The area south and east of Boreray is shoal but that island does provide some shelter from the swell. Boreray makes an interesting excursion in quiet weather, anchoring on sand in the bay on the east side of the island.

Griminish Harbour

Vallay Sound, the shallow inlet west of Vallay, a tidal island, is used as a base for lobster fishing boats during the summer, but the sound is obstructed by drying rocks. The entrance can be difficult to discern, and if it is necessary to attempt it, approach at half tide or above. It would be dangerous to enter this harbour in bad weather, heavy swell, poor visibility or, if entering for the first time, in anything other than benign conditions.

Dangers and marks

When bearing about 200° Callernish House, a conspicuous single-storey house, circular in plan, stands in line with a hollow of the hills in the background, with a conspicuous mast to the right of the hollow.

Sgeir Dubh Mor, a rock above water, stands on a drying reef 2 cables offshore north of Callernish House.

134 CCC Sailing Directions and Anchorages

8. West of the Outer Hebrides

The entrance to Griminish Harbour from the north. Sgeir Dubh Mor at lower centre. Callernish House upper right

Drying rocks lie up to ½ mile offshore north of the west end of Vallay. Vallay light beacon (inconspicuous) stands on the west side of the northwest end of Vallay. A painted rock on the foreshore in line with the light beacon, leads between Dubh Sgeir Mor and these rocks.

Rocks with a clear channel 20 metres wide between them lie between the end of Vallay and Sgeir Dubh Mor. Beacons, (Fl.G.), east of Callernish House, with diamond topmarks, in line bearing 183° lead between these rocks.

Drying reefs extend 1 cable west of Vallay. Their position can be judged by their south eastern extremity which very rarely covers. The clear water and sandy bottom should enable a lookout in the bow to spot other dangers which lie within the sound. The tide runs strongly.

Directions

Approach north and west of Bo Lea keeping north of 57°40'·5N until Vallay light beacon and the painted rock are identified. Approach with these marks in line about 142°. Bring the leading lights into line 183° to pass between two submerged rocks. Follow this line, taking care not to be carried off it by the tidal stream of up to 3 knots, until Vallay Sound opens up. Then enter the sound, keeping close to the line of reefs and an islet off the southwest foreshore of Vallay Island.

Many floats mark the moorings of the local fishing fleet and good sheltered anchorage can be found in about 1·5m.

Lights
Vallay Fl.WRG.3s4m8M
Ldg Lts 183° Fl.G.6/7m4M
Jetty on southwest shore 2F.G(vert) April to October

Services

Fuel and mains electricity at the pier; 1-ton crane; no water at present.

Griminish leading line; breakers can be seen on the rocks between which it leads

Griminish pier

CCC Sailing Directions and Anchorages 135

Outer Hebrides

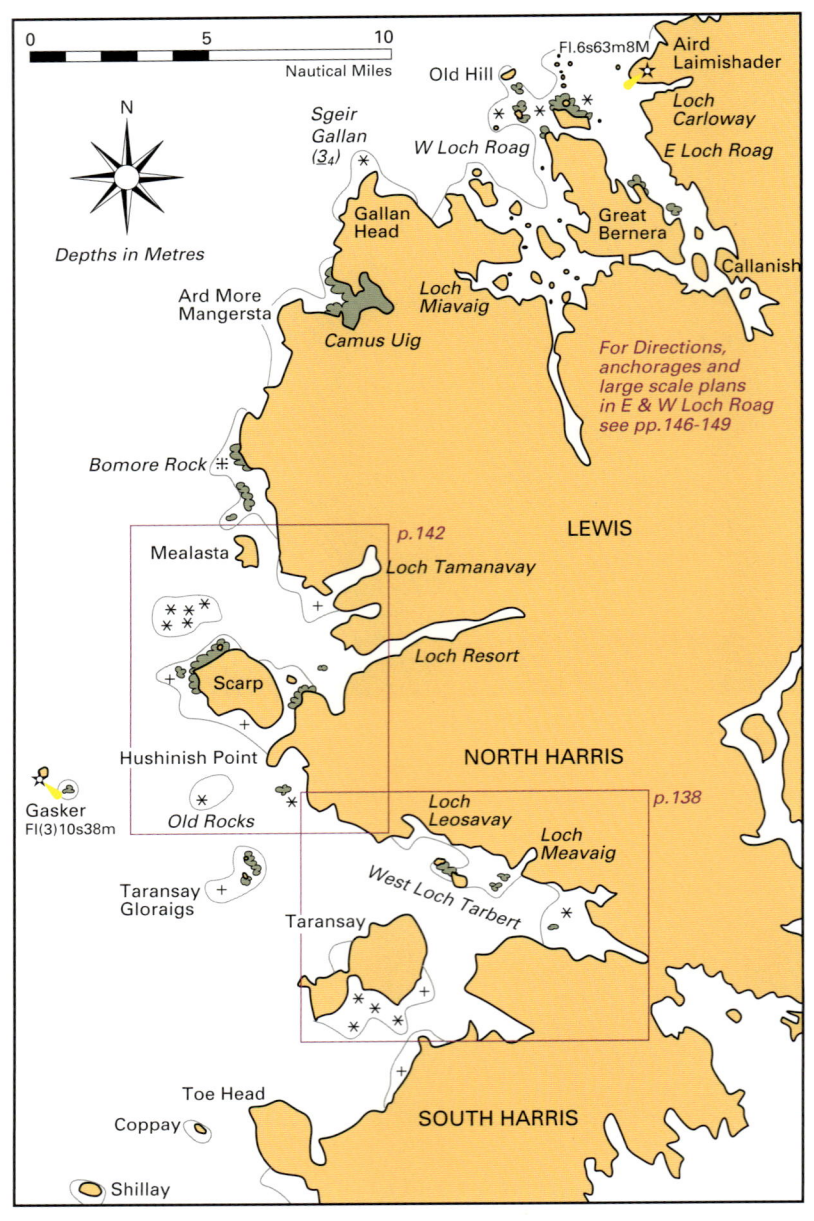

SOUTH HARRIS TO LOCH ROAG, KEY PLAN

Admiralty Chart
2841, 2515, 2721
Imray Chart
C67
Ordnance Survey
18, 13
Cruising Scotland
pp.203-9

Sound of Harris to Loch Roag

Heading north from the Sound of Harris, the first eight miles are fairly free from concealed hazards. Further north there are several areas of submerged and drying rocks with few marks by which to avoid them and a visit to the west coast of Harris and Lewis should only be undertaken in clear settled weather.

Tides

The north-going stream, with the east-going stream towards the Sound of Harris begins +0550 Ullapool (+0130 Dover). The south-going stream, with the west-going stream from the Sound of Harris begins –0020 Ullapool (–0440 Dover).

The streams off Gasker are 2 knots springs in each direction but are weak elsewhere except off salient points.

Dangers and marks

The island of Scarp lies 11 miles north of Toe Head. Taransay Glorigs, an extensive area of rocks above water, drying and submerged, lie 3 miles off the mouth of West Loch Tarbert, and Old Rocks, which dry up to 2·3 metres, lie between Taransay Glorigs and Scarp.

Gasker, 30 metres high, lies 4 miles WSW of Scarp. Obe Rocks, drying and submerged, extend up to 6 cables west of Scarp.

Drying, submerged and above-water rocks lie up to 1½ miles north and northwest of Scarp. Old Rocks and Obe Rocks almost always break in the swell. Bomore Rock, 5½ cables offshore, 1½ miles north of Mealasta, nearly dries. This rock is outwith the coverage of charts 2841 and 2515 and is only shown at 1:200,000 on chart 2721 (see also p.143).

Ard More Mangersta has radio masts and Gallan Head, 4 miles NNE, has a radio mast 177 metres in height. Sgeir Gallan, 3 cables NNW of Gallan Head, dries 3·4 metres.

Directions

Proceeding northwards from Toe Head, steer towards Gasker and pass midway between Gasker Beg and Scarp. Continue on this course until 3 miles north of Scarp (p.143) and then steer towards Ard More Mangersta, though note Bomore Rock (see above) if beating. From Ard More Mangersta, keeping at least a cable offshore clears all dangers until Gallan Head, which must be rounded either close inshore or 5 cables off, to avoid Sgeir Gallan (dries 3·4m) which lies 3 cables NNW of that headland.

From the north head for Gasker; a direct course from Ard More Mangersta to Gasker passes ¾ mile west of Bomore Rock (5 miles north of Scarp) and a mile west of rocks northwest of Scarp, so that position checks have to be kept carefully. When Scarp is abeam a course can be steered direct for the passage between Coppay and Toe Head, but the position relative to Old Rocks and Taransay Glorigs still needs to be watched.

Shelter

From the Sound of Harris and into Loch Roag it is a little over 40 miles. If caught out in bad weather, shelter can be found in Loch Leosavay (p.140) and further north in either Loch Resort or Loch Tamnavay (p.144-145).

Lights

The following lights give some assistance on this passage:
Haskeir (10 miles north of Monach Is.) Fl.20s44m23M
Whale Rock E card buoy Q(3)10s (57° 54'·9N 8°00'·7W)
Gasker Fl(3)10s38m10M
Flannan Isles Fl(2)30s20M
Aird Laimishader, East Loch Roag Fl.6s63m8M

136 CCC Sailing Directions and Anchorages

8. West of the Outer Hebrides

Looking towards Taransay over the NW end of Ensay

Loch na h-Uidhe, the anchorage off Taransay

Outer Hebrides

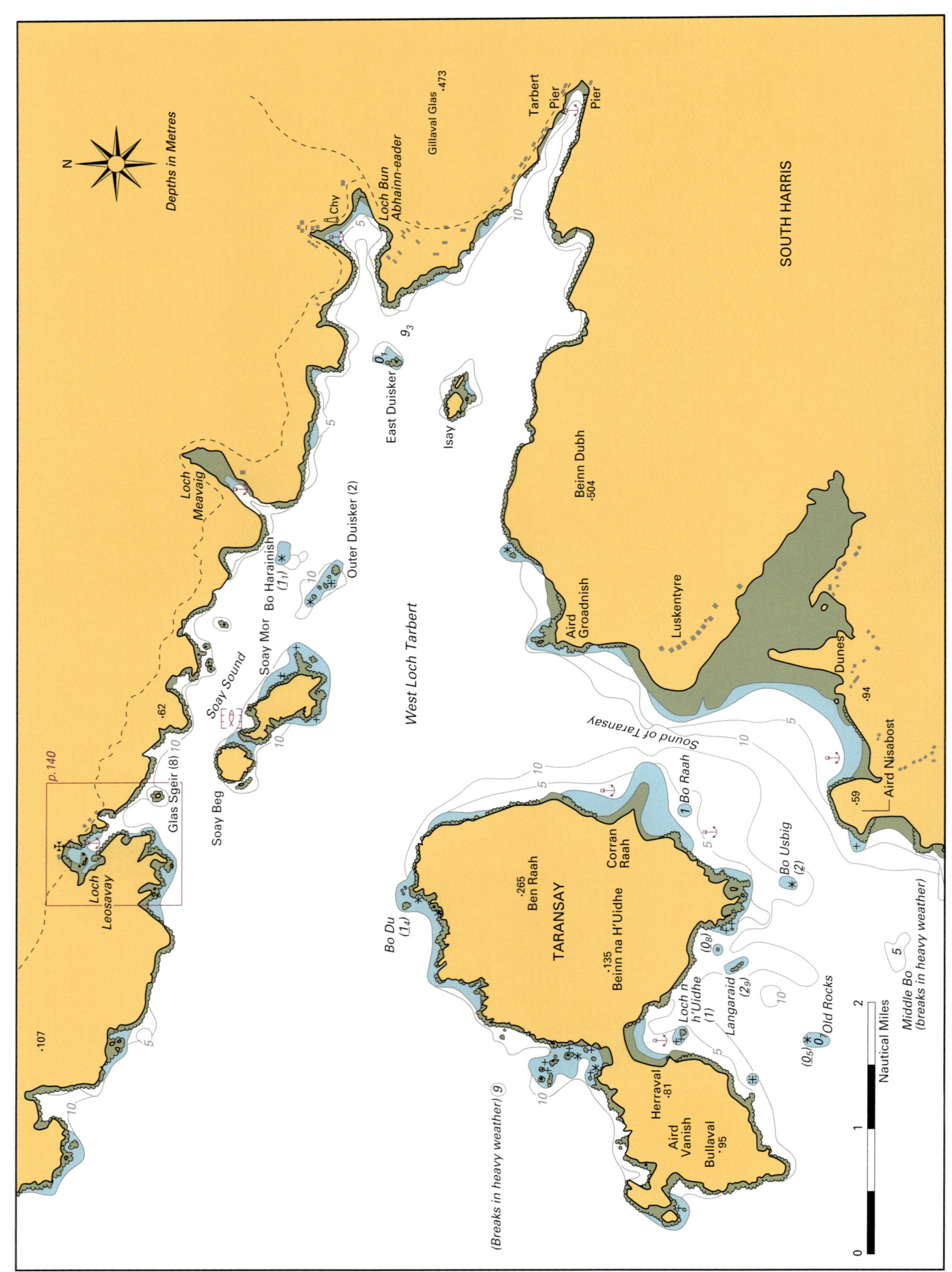

WEST LOCH TARBERT AND TARANSAY

8. West of the Outer Hebrides

Sound of Taransay

Tides
Constant −0053 Ullapool (−0513 Dover)

Height in metres

MHWS	MHWN	MTL	MLWN	MLWS
4·2	3·2	2·3	1·3	0·4

The in-going stream begins +0550 Ullapool (+0130 Dover). The out-going stream begins −0020 Ullapool (−0440 Dover)

Directions
Passing through the Sound of Taransay keep the summit of Coppay in line with Toe Head 244° to pass southeast of Bo Usbig (it is quite easy to confuse Shillay with Coppay). When Aird Nisabost is abeam on the starboard side take a mid-channel course through the narrow part of the sound. Here, Corran Raah and Luskentyre Banks reduce the navigable passage to ½ mile wide. Bo Raah lies 2 cables off Taransay, 4 cables south of Corran Raah, at a depth of 1 metre.

Anchorages
Taransay Anchor in Loch na h-Uidhe, on the south side of the sandy isthmus joining the two parts of the island. Approaching from Toe Head steer for the south side of Aird Vanish, the west part of the island, to avoid Old Rocks (not to be confused with rocks of the same name south of Scarp) which dry 0·5 metre, 7 cables offshore.

Take care to avoid a detached rock awash about two cables offshore, off the end of the reef which extends from Aird Vanish.

Steer towards Ben Raah, the highest point of Taransay until past the middle of the entrance, to clear a rock 1 metre high 2 cables from the west side of the inlet; a reef awash extends northwest from this rock which should be given a wide berth. Langaraid which dries 2·9 metres lies nearly 4 cables off the southwest shore of Taransay and, with Bo Usbig, is in the way when passing between Loch na h-Uidhe and Sound of Taransay.

Camus nam Borgh (Borve Bay) is an occasional anchorage at the west side of the bay 2 miles east of Toe Head. Drying reefs extend 1½ cables off the west point of the bay. Good holding and shelter in strong southerly winds.

Traigh Nisabost is an occasional anchorage off a sandy bay east of Aird Nisabost at the south side of Traigh Luskentyre on Harris.

Sound of Taransay For passage notes see above. Anchor close inshore at the north side of Corran Raah, or in northwest wind, south of the spit, but look out for Bo Raah.

West Loch Tarbert
West Loch Tarbert offers some good anchorages and also the best opportunity for access to shops and public transport that will be found on the west coast.

Tides
As Taransay

Directions
Approaching from the south, either side of Taransay may be taken, the west side being the cleaner. However if proceeding west about, keep 2 cables off the clearly seen offshore rocks on the west side and pass 3 cables off the north end of Taransay to avoid Bo Du (dries 1·4m) and associated reefs.

If entering by the Sound of Taransay see the directions above for passage through.

From the west enter south of the Taransay Glorigs avoiding Bo Molach 5 cables WSW of the Glorigs. Give the north point of Taransay a berth of 3 cables to avoid Bo Du (dries 1·4m). Further into the loch Isay can be passed on either hand to reach the head of the loch.

From the NW (see plan p.142) Pass 1 mile west of Scarp to avoid the Obe Rocks and shallow 3m and 6m rocks further south before altering to pass north of the Old Rocks (dries 0·3m and 2·3m) which lie 1 mile SW of Hushinish Point. Passing 5 cables off Hushinish Point on a course of 145° will leave the Hushinish Glorigs safely to port. The outermost Glorig is 12m high. Thereafter the approach to West Loch Tarbert is straightforward, keeping to the main channel between Taransay and Soay Mor.

Anchorages
Tarbert at the head of the loch. Anchor west of the pier on the south shore; well sheltered though subject to very heavy squalls in strong southerly winds, when Loch Leosavay may be preferable. East Loch Tarbert is a ½ mile walk from the old stone jetty on the south shore. See p.104 for details of the facilities there.

Loch Bun Abhainn-eader provides excellent shelter off the former whaling station, identifiable by a conspicuous brick chimney, although the holding is reported as poor. In the approach, East Duisker, an above water rock with shoal rocks extending 2 cables north of it, can be avoided by keeping to either shore. Anchor SW of the ruined pier in the north arm. Other bays may also be suitable but landing can be difficult. The slip at the fish farm base in the SE corner is convenient for walking to the general store at the filling station on the road at Aird Asaig, from where Calor gas is also obtainable.

Loch Meavaig is NNE of the outer Duisker and should be entered by the southeast side of that rock and east of Bo Harainish which dries 1·1 metres and lies west of a direct line from Duisker to the entrance. Within the entrance there is deep water close inshore. Anchor off the house, about halfway up on the SE shore. The loch dries out 4 cables from the head. This anchorage is subject to southwesterly swell.

Admiralty Chart
2841
Imray Chart
C67
Ordnance Survey
18, 14
Cruising Scotland
p.203

CCC Sailing Directions and Anchorages 139

Outer Hebrides

Glas Sgeir, at the entrance to Loch Leosavay, caught in the evening sunlight makes identification much easier than usual

Admiralty Chart
2841
Imray Chart
C67
Ordnance Survey
18, 13
Cruising Scotland
pp.204-5

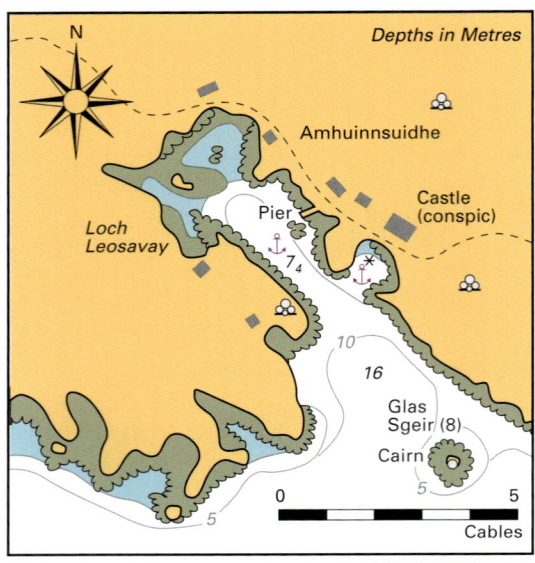

Loch Leosavay anchorage looking south from the head of the inner part of the loch

Loch Leosavay

Loch Leosavay is probably one of the most secure anchorages in the West Loch Tarbert area, being well sheltered and having good holding ground.

Tides

Constant –0053 Ullapool (–0513 Dover)

Height in metres

MHWS	MHWN	MTL	MLWN	MLWS
4·2	3·2	2·3	1·3	0·4

The in-going stream begins +0550 Ullapool (+0130 Dover). The out-going stream begins –0020 Ullapool (–0440 Dover)

Directions

Loch Leosavay is 1 mile northwest of Soay Beag. Glas Sgeir, 8 metres high and surmounted by a stone cairn, stands on a drying reef a cable wide near the northeast side of the entrance to the loch. Entry is straightforward once Glas Sgeir is identified though it merges with the background rocks during the approach. The castle on the north shore is conspicuous when seen from a SE approach.

Anchorage

The inner part of the loch on the west side, opposite the stone quay on the north shore, is sheltered with good holding but beware of reported bottom chains. Use a strong tripping line. Note the drying rock off the stone quay.

Alternatively anchor in the bay off the castle in 4m but the holding here is reported as poor. There is an unmarked drying rock off the steps set into the sea wall at the head of the bay.

Hushinish Bay, 4½ miles west of Leosavay (see plan p.142) and immediately east of Hushinish Point provides an attractive temporary anchorage in offshore winds.

LOCH LEOSAVAY

8. West of the Outer Hebrides

Caolas Scarp from Harris. Sand bar clearly visible

Caolas Scarp looking SE from Scarp

CCC Sailing Directions and Anchorages   141

Outer Hebrides

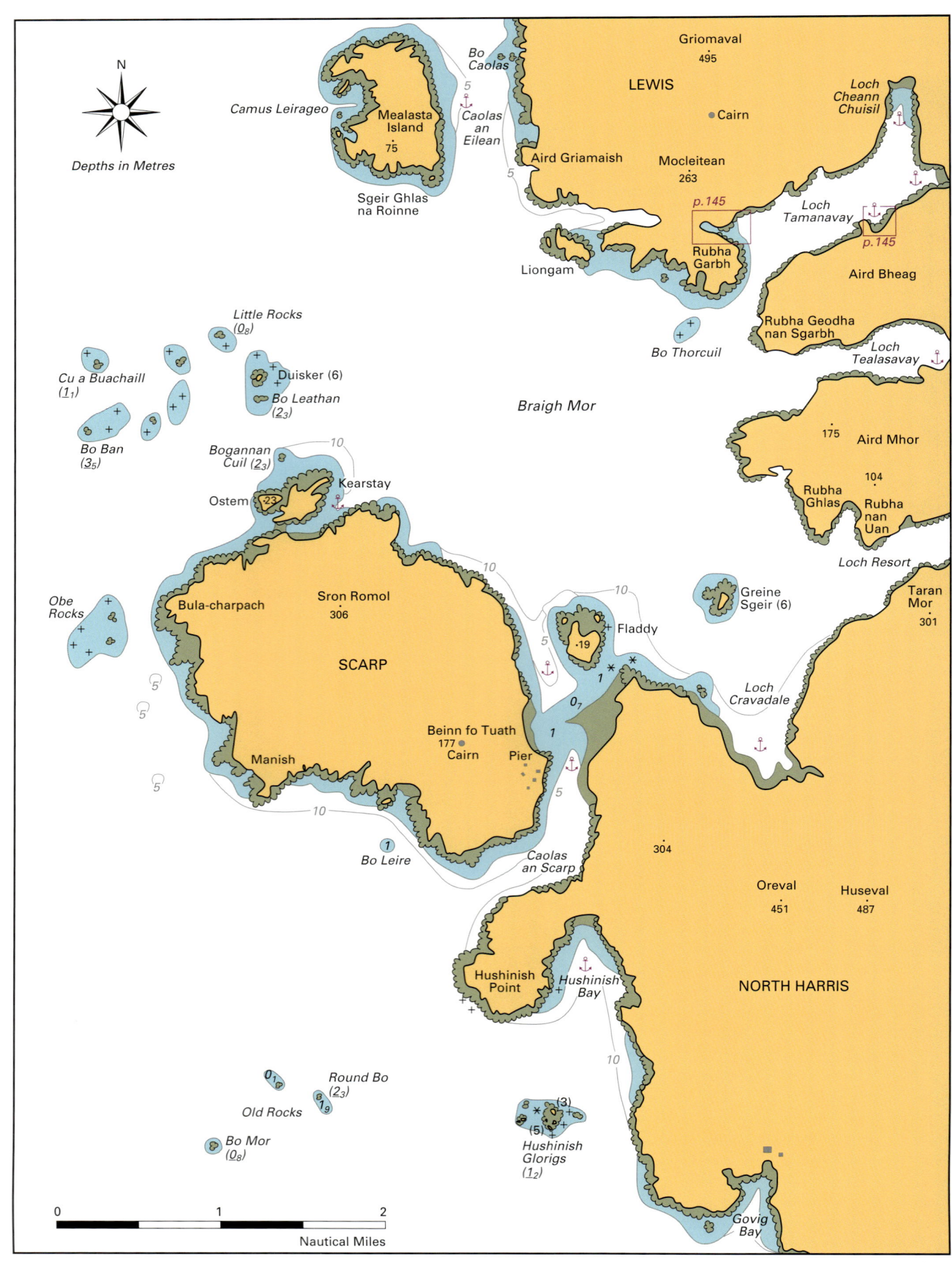

SCARP AND BRAIGH MOR

8. West of the Outer Hebrides

Scarp and Braigh Mor

Lying 11 miles north of Toe Head at the entrance to the Sound of Harris, Scarp is separated from the mainland of North Harris by a shallow sound, Caolas an Scarp, which can be safely navigated under favourable weather and tidal conditions. Braigh Mor is the sound between Lewis and the northeast side of Scarp, leading to several sheltered lochs.

Tide

Tidal streams are slight but 2 knots can be encountered in Caolas Scarp.

Constant –0053 Ullapool (–0513 Dover)

Height in metres

MHWS	MHWN	MTL	MLWN	MLWS
4·2	3·2	2·3	1·3	0·4

Directions

From West Loch Tarbert a passage north of Taransay Glorigs may be taken with care. The tangent of Hushinish Point under the right fall of the summit of Scarp clears these hazards and the Hushinish Glorigs, although this line is not well defined. Passing 5 cables off Hushinish Point provides a sufficient safety margin to avoid the Old Rocks (dry 0·2m and 2·3m) which lie 1 mile off Hushinish Point, the SW entrance to Caolas an Scarp. If continuing northwestwards keep at least a mile off Scarp and follow the directions for the approach to Scarp from the south in the following paragraph.

From the south aim to pass 1 mile east of Gasker Beg (10m) heading north. When abeam Gasker Beg alteration can be made towards Caolas an Scarp, if this route is preferred. Alternatively, to pass west and northabout Scarp, keep at least a mile off to avoid off-lying rocks until it is possible to identify Bo Ban, the SW rock of the Duisker group of rocks lying NNW of Scarp, which is almost always marked by breakers. Keep Toe Head bearing not more than 167° until all the Duisker group have been passed to the west. When the south end of Mealasta Island bears 083° alter to that bearing until 5 cables from the island. If making for Loch Resort head mid-way between Greine Sgeir (6m) and Rubha Glas on the north side of the entrance.

The passage between Duisker and Kearstay, an islet north of Scarp can be used, but rocks which dry 2·3 metres lie up to 1½ cables from both sides, leaving a clear passage 3 cables wide. There are no leading marks and careful chart work, using Chart 2841, is needed.

From the north the clearest approach is to pass 5 cables west of Mealasta. If making for Loch Resort head mid-way between Greine Sgeir (6m) and Rubha Glas, the north side of the entrance.

It is important to note that the coast between Mealasta and Ard More Mangersta is only charted to a small scale by the Admiralty and because of off-lying islets and rocks an offing of at least one mile should be kept (see p.147 for anchorages).

Caolas an Scarp

Passage through this Sound is straightforward provided it is not attempted before half tide as the depth over the bar can be less than 1 metre at LWS. If there is a northerly swell a passage through Caolas an Scarp could be dangerous. A drying sandy spit extends for 3 cables off the Harris shore where the bar is shallowest north of the houses and pier on Scarp. Accordingly hold close to the Scarp shore when proceeding in either direction.

Anchorages

Kearstay A delightful anchorage, sheltered from the open sea, lies between Kearstay and Scarp. Do not attempt the western entrance.

Caolas Scarp There are suitable anchorage depths both sides of the bar in Caolas an Scarp but both are likely to be affected by the tidal streams.

Loch Cravadale A drying rock lies 2 cables off the west shore of this loch. There is an occasional anchorage at the head of the bay.

Admiralty Chart
2841
Imray Chart
C67
Ordnance Survey
13
Cruising Scotland
pp.206-7

The anchorage between Kearstay and Scarp must be one of the best in the Hebrides

Andrew Thomson

CCC Sailing Directions and Anchorages 143

Outer Hebrides

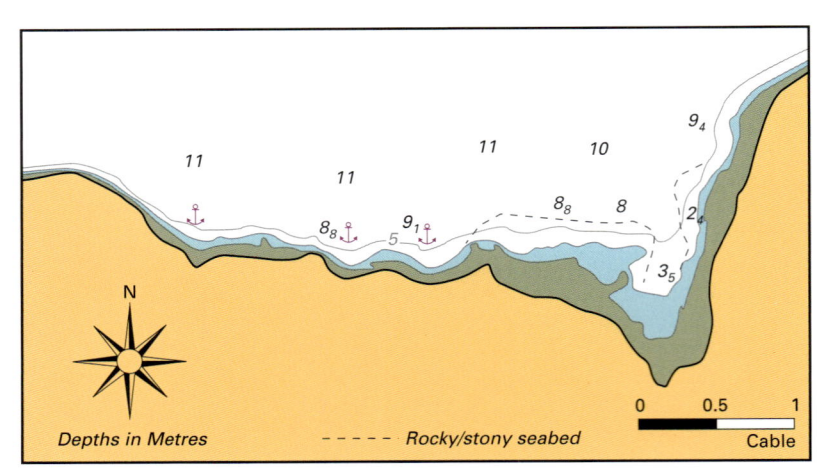

DIRASCAL, LOCH RESORT

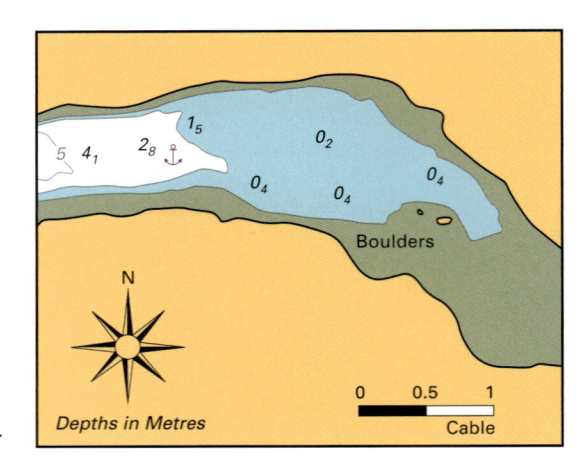

HEAD OF LOCH RESORT

Loch Resort

Loch Resort is 4 miles long and generally no more than ¼ mile wide and for the first mile or so it is flanked by dramatic cliffs, especially on the south side. The loch is entered 2 miles east of Scarp. Greine Sgeir, an islet 6 metres high with reefs drying 1 cable off all sides, lies ½ mile off the entrance.

Anchorage

Dirascal is a small bay 2½ miles up the loch on the south side. Anchor towards the west end of the bay where there is more space and better holding in stiff mud. The Antares chart shows that anchoring in the inlet at the east end is restricted by the rocky bottom on either side.

Head of loch The loch dries out and is shallow for almost ½ mile from the head. Anchor in about 3m, well before the loch bends towards the southeast.

Loch Tealasavay

This loch is exposed to SW and suitable only for occasional anchoring. There is only a small area at the south side of the head with moderate depths in which to anchor.

Loch Tamanavay

This is a well sheltered loch with several anchorages including, for the adventurous, a very small pool recently surveyed by Antares.

Enter by keeping close to the north or preferably the east shore at the mouth of the loch to avoid the Bo Thorcuil Rocks off the middle of the entrance. The NE side of Mealasta Island open of Liongam on a bearing of 330° leads SW of Bo Thorcuil. Do not rely on the sea breaking over these rocks to identify their presence.

Anchorage

Aird Sleitinis This is the bay on the south side of the loch, east of the Aird Sleitinis promontory. For well over forty years this has been reported in these *Directions* as being foul with lost moorings. These may now have either disintegrated or sunk well into the mud, though a tripping line might still be advisable.

Camus na Crotha A white house with dormers overlooks this bay at the eastern end of the loch. Anchor off the house in 8m where the bottom shelves less steeply than off the mouth of the burn on the south side.

The head of Loch Resort is very much more open than the outer part of the loch

Julien Paren - Geograph

144 CCC Sailing Directions and Anchorages

8. West of the Outer Hebrides

The anchorage in Loch Cheann Chuisil at the head of Loch Tamanavay

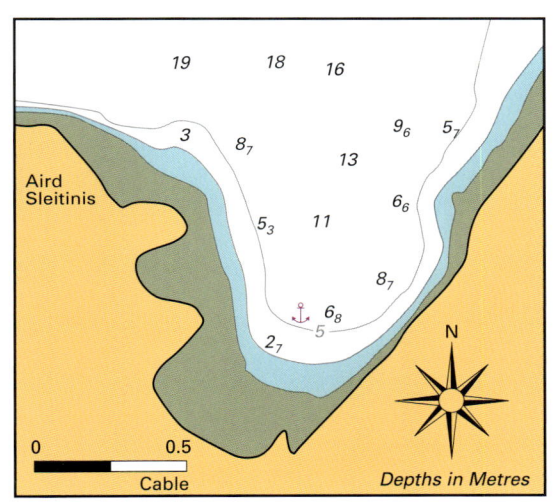

AIRD SLEITINISH, LOCH TAMANAVAY

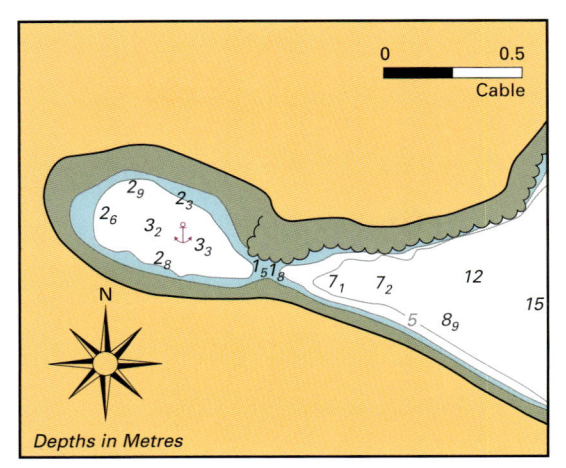

TAMANA SEAR, LOCH TAMANAVAY

Loch Cheann Chuisil This is the northern arm of Loch Tamanavay and gives good shelter. Anchor towards the northeast corner, away from the burn, in about 5m.

Tamana Sear This small pool, approached through a very narrow channel, can only be considered as temporary anchorage in settled weather. With a width of barely 60m at LW a stern line ashore, or a kedge, is advisable.

Anchorages between Braigh Mor and Loch Roag

Mealasta Lies ½ mile from Lewis at the north side of the entrance to Braigh Mor. Caolas an Eilean, between Mealasta and Lewis, provides a tenuous anchorage in settled weather. Bo Caolas, which dries, extends 2 cables from the Lewis shore at the north end of the sound.

If heading north from Mealasta be aware of the charting problems described in the adjacent column and keep a good offing. Bomore Rock (nearly dries) 5½ cables offshore, 2 miles north of Mealasta, is the most dangerous hazard.

Camas Uig 8 miles north of Mealasta, provides an occasional anchorage, particularly in a well sheltered pool behind two small islets in the southeast corner off Carnish. Enter by the southwest side of the more southerly islet. Soundings are less than charted (see chart 2515).

CCC Sailing Directions and Anchorages   145

Outer Hebrides

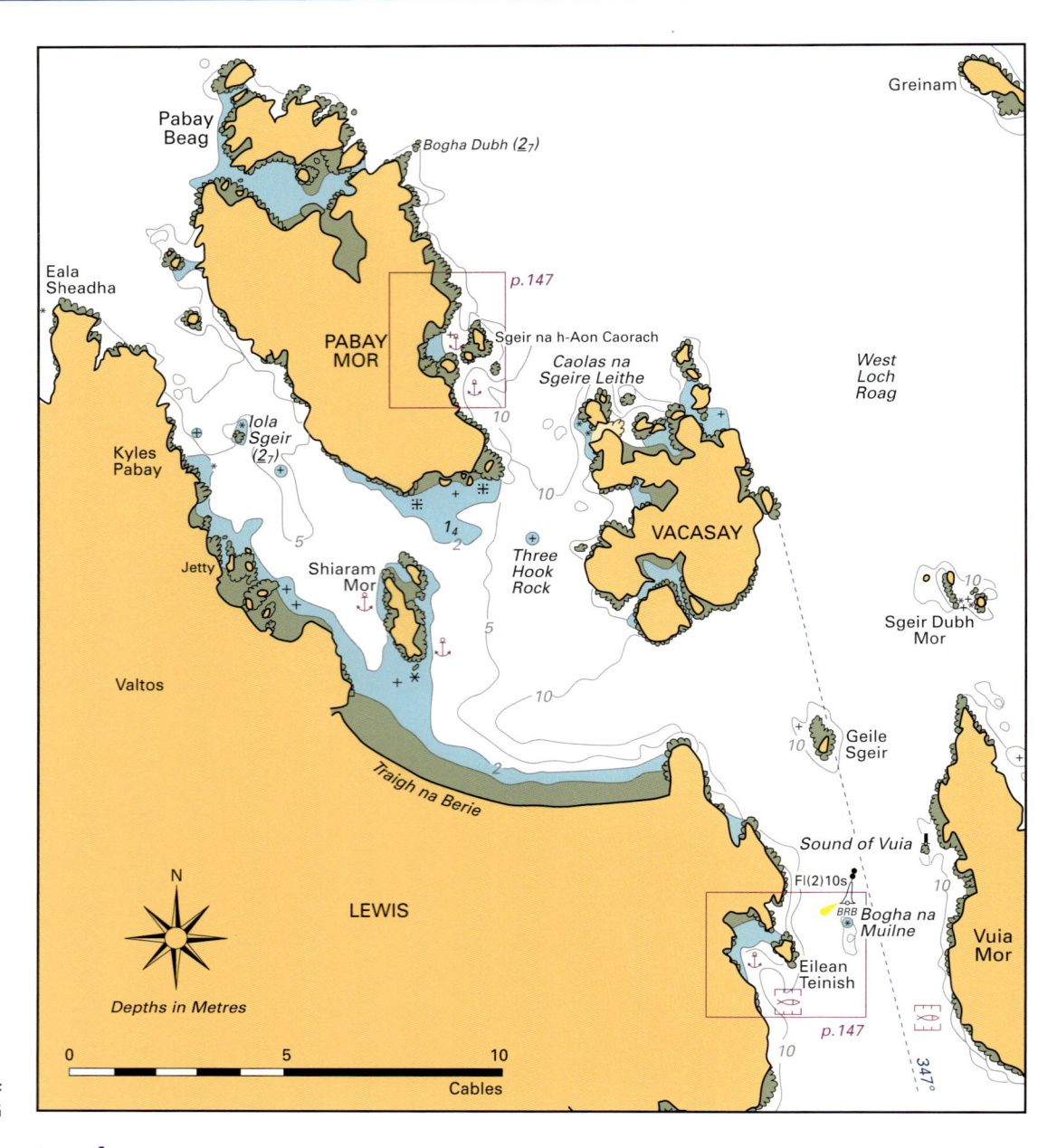

PART OF WEST LOCH ROAG

Loch Roag

Loch Roag, divided into two, East and West, by an almost impenetrable chain of islands, is a remarkable place which could occupy a fortnight of exploring with a small boat if it were not for the difficulty of getting there.

The anchorages described below are only a small selection of many which can be discovered by an enterprising skipper and careful use of Chart 2515; the only drawback being the large number of mussel and fish farms.

With fuel and water available in both lochs and a good bus service from either Miavaig or Bernera to Stornoway it is also a good place to re-provision or change crew.

Tides

Constant –0053 Ullapool (–0513 Dover)

Height in metres

MHWS	MHWN	MTL	MLWN	MLWS
4·2	3·2	2·3	1·3	0·4

Admiralty Chart 2515
Imray Chart C67
Ordnance Survey 13
Cruising Scotland pp.207-9

Off the entrance the northeast-going stream begins –0420 Ullapool (+0345 Dover). The southwest-going stream begins +0205 Ullapool (–0215 Dover). The spring rate is 1 knot
The in-going stream begins +0600 Ullapool (+0140 Dover). The out-going stream begins –0010 Ullapool (–0430 Dover); streams reach 1 knot in the narrower channels

Dangers and marks

The entrance is 7 miles wide between Gallan Head, on which stands a conspicuous radio mast 170 metres high, and Aird Laimishader, on which stands a small light beacon, a white hut 5 metres high at about 60 metres above sea level.

Sgeir Gallan, which dries 3·4 metres, lies ¼ mile NNW of Gallan Head. Between these points are scattered many islets, and the two parts of Loch Roag are separated by Great Bernera.

Old Hill, an islet 92 metres high, shaped like a loaf of bread, and Mas Sgeir, 21 metres high – each lie 1½ miles northwest and north respectively of Little Bernera.

8. West of the Outer Hebrides

West Loch Roag

Directions
The entrance to West Loch Roag is between Gallan Head to the west and Old Hill to the north. Pass Gallan Head, either close inshore or give it berth of 5 cables, to avoid Sgeir Gallan (dries 3·4m) then steer to pass mid-way between Pabay Beag and Harsgeir. If intending to proceed to Miavaig or the upper reaches of the loch pass ½ mile NE of Pabay Mor and Vacsay and bring the east side of Vacsay to bear 193°. Then head to pass mid-way between Geile Sgeir and Rubha Rollinish, passing west of Bogha Bhad Ghlais (dries 2·4m) and east of Bogha na Muilne (dries 0·9m), now marked on its north side by an isolated danger buoy (Fl(2)10s). Note the clearance bearings given on Chart 2515.

Anchorages
Pabay Mor On the east side of Pabay Mor in the bay off Traigh na Cille lying north of Sgeir na Cille (9m). This anchorage is identified by a sandy beach, the only one on the east side of Pabay Mor. Approach the entrance from the NNE holding to the east shore. Anchor in 2 to 4m sand.

Alternatively anchor off the SE side of Sgeir na Cille. When passing through Caolas na Sgeire Leithe, keep at least 1 cable off the outermost islet, Sgeir na Chaorach h-Aon to avoid Bogha Bhealt (dries 2·4m). Anchor off the cave, 5m, in sand.

Valtos In the approach through the sound between Pabay and Vacsay keep in mid-channel but when turning to starboard note the shoal water south of Pabay Mor and Three Hook Rock, a submerged rock 2 cables SE of the SE corner of Pabay Mor. Anchor off the NW or SE sides of Shiaram Mor in 3 to 4m sand. Valtos Pier dries and it should not be approached without local knowledge.

Eilean Teinish Safe anchorage in all summer weather can be found in the Sound of Vuia inside Eilean Teinish. Pass west of the Bogha na Muilne buoy and approach from the south but beware of an extensive mussel farm less than a cable to the SE of the anchorage. Using the Antares chart it should be possible to enter through the channel northwest of Eilean Teinish.

Miavaig Approach through the Sound of Vuia as described above and turn into Miavaig Bay when it opens up. Avoiding the extensive mussel lines, head for the narrow entrance to Loch Miavaig in the SW corner. This leads to a wider area for anchoring. There is a pontoon with water and electricity. Supplies: Diesel (key fob needed), and calor gas. Shop, PO and garage at Timsgarry 2½ miles away by road. Community shop may help with deliveries (☎ 01851 672285).

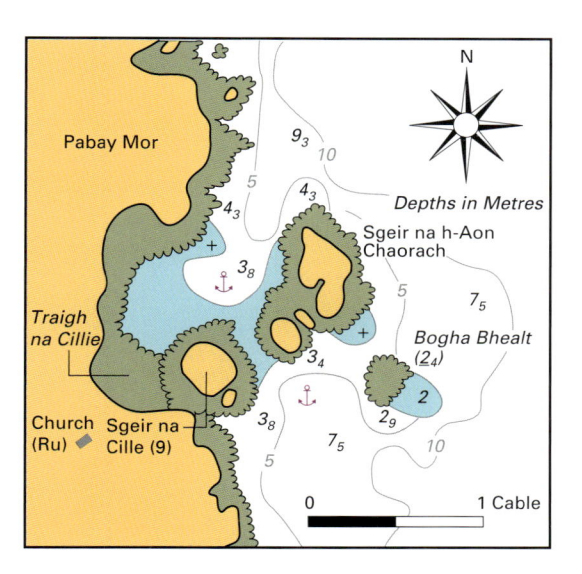

PABAY MOR ANCHORAGES

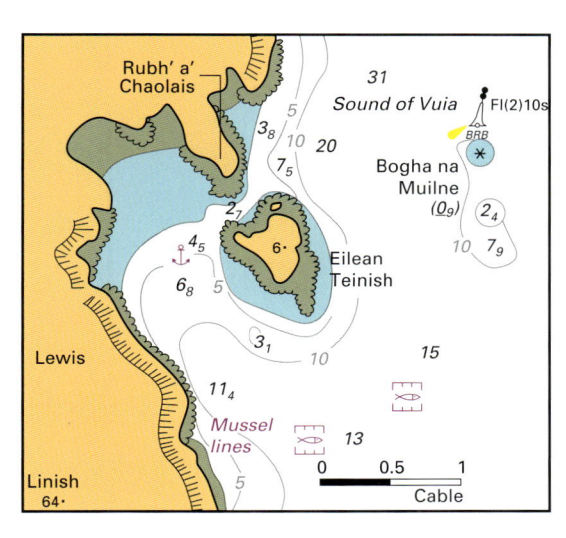

EILEAN TEINISH

The anchorage inside Eilean Teinish. Note the mussel lines off the entrance

CCC Sailing Directions and Anchorages 147

Outer Hebrides

Pabay Mor north anchorage, West Loch Roag

Carloway pier and anchorage

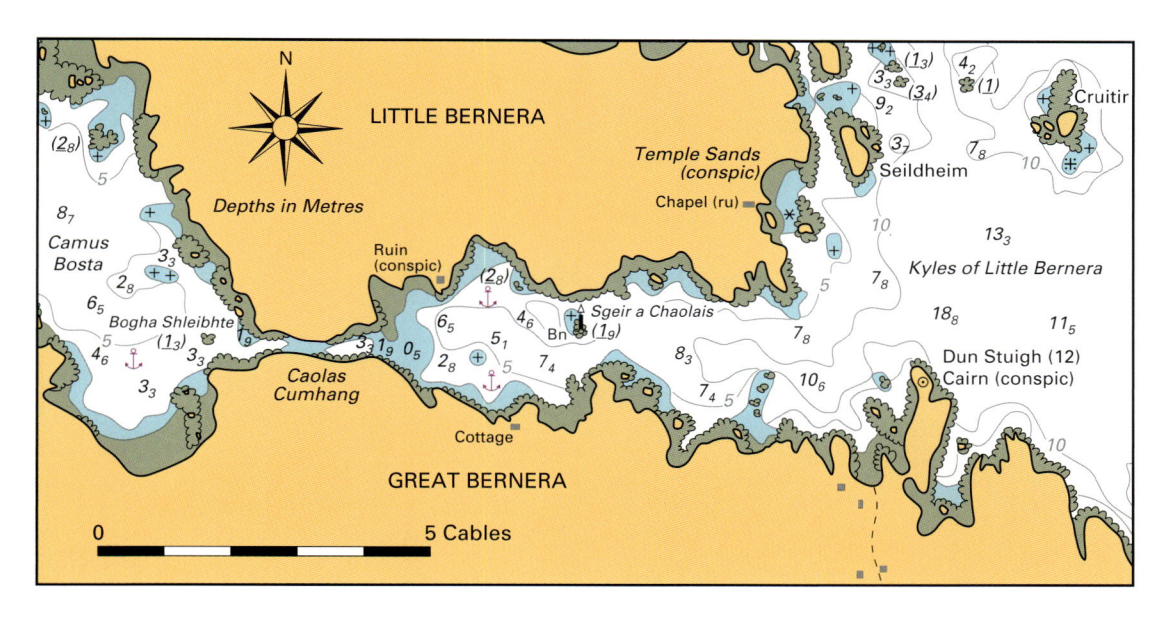

8. West of the Outer Hebrides

BERNERA HARBOUR

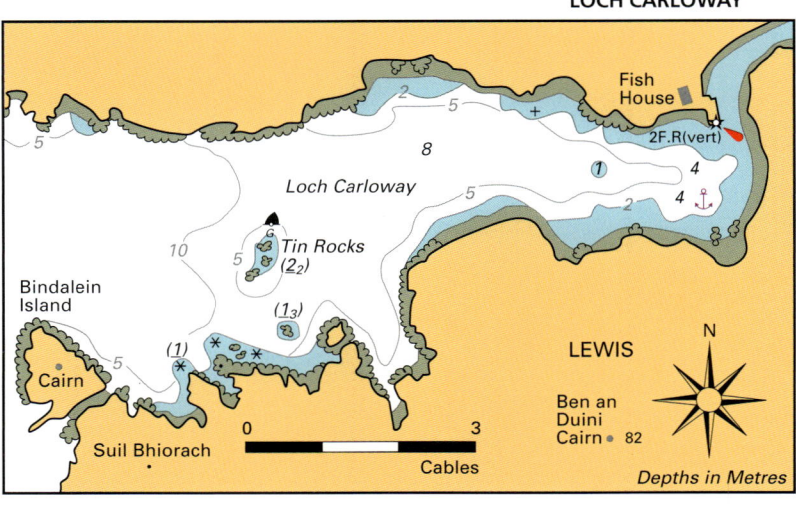

East Loch Roag
Entered between Sgeir Dhearg, 2 metres high 3 cables southeast of Mas Sgeir, and Craigeam off Aird Laimishader. There is also a clear passage 3 cables wide south of Sgeir Dhearg.

Directions
The fairway of East Loch Roag is clean as far as Greinam, an islet 1 cable across about 5 miles within the loch in the middle of the fairway, with a white light beacon 5 metres high at its south end. Rocks over which the depth is less than 2 metres lie up to 2 cables from either shore, but the clear passage is still 4 cables wide.

Directions and anchorages for the inner loch are given on pp.150–151

Tides
See p.146

Lights
Aird Laimishader Fl.6s63m8M
Greinam Fl.WR.6s8m7/8M
East Loch Roag is the only anchorage on the west side of the Outer Hebrides which may be approached at night with the aid of the lights noted above.

Loch Carloway
An easily approached loch on the east side of the entrance of East Loch Roag ½ mile south of Aird Laimishader light beacon. Tin Rocks, in the middle of the loch, are marked on their north side by a green conical buoy.

Carloway Pier, 2F.R(vert) at head, stands at the north side of the head of the loch and a shoal patch with a depth of 1 metre lies in the middle of the loch 1½ cables WSW of the pier. Good holding south of the pier in black mud. The arm of the loch northeast of the pier is shoal, but provides shelter at neaps or for shallow-draught boats.

A slip in the southeast corner of the loch is convenient for landing to visit the broch of Dun Carloway.

Water and diesel at pier (Key fob needed).

Bernera Harbour
A mile south of the entrance to Loch Carloway, this sheltered anchorage lies between Little and Great Bernera on the west side of the loch.

Enter between Cruitir and Dun Stuigh (12), marked by a cairn. To avoid rocks extending from the south shore do not stray south of a line joining Dun Stuigh and Sgeir a' Chaolais (dries 1·9m) marked with a beacon (BW cage on pole) situated well within the harbour. Pass south of Sgeir a' Chaolais.

Anchor north or south of the harbour, noting the rock (dries 2·8) on the north shore and the 2m rock towards the south shore.

The narrow passage to the west through Caolas Cumhang to Camas Bosta has 0·6m at LWS and can be negotiated with great care above half tide when the depth is over 2m. Reconnaissance in a dinghy is advised. The rock (dries 1·3m) at the west entrance to the narrows should be passed on its south side.

Camas Bosta on the west side of the narrows is a fine summer anchorage. Good holding in sand. The approach from West Loch Roag demands special care. There is a restored Iron Age House on shore.

LOCH CARLOWAY

Admiralty Chart
2515
Imray Chart
C67
Ordnance Survey
13
Cruising Scotland
pp.207-9

CCC Sailing Directions and Anchorages 149

Outer Hebrides

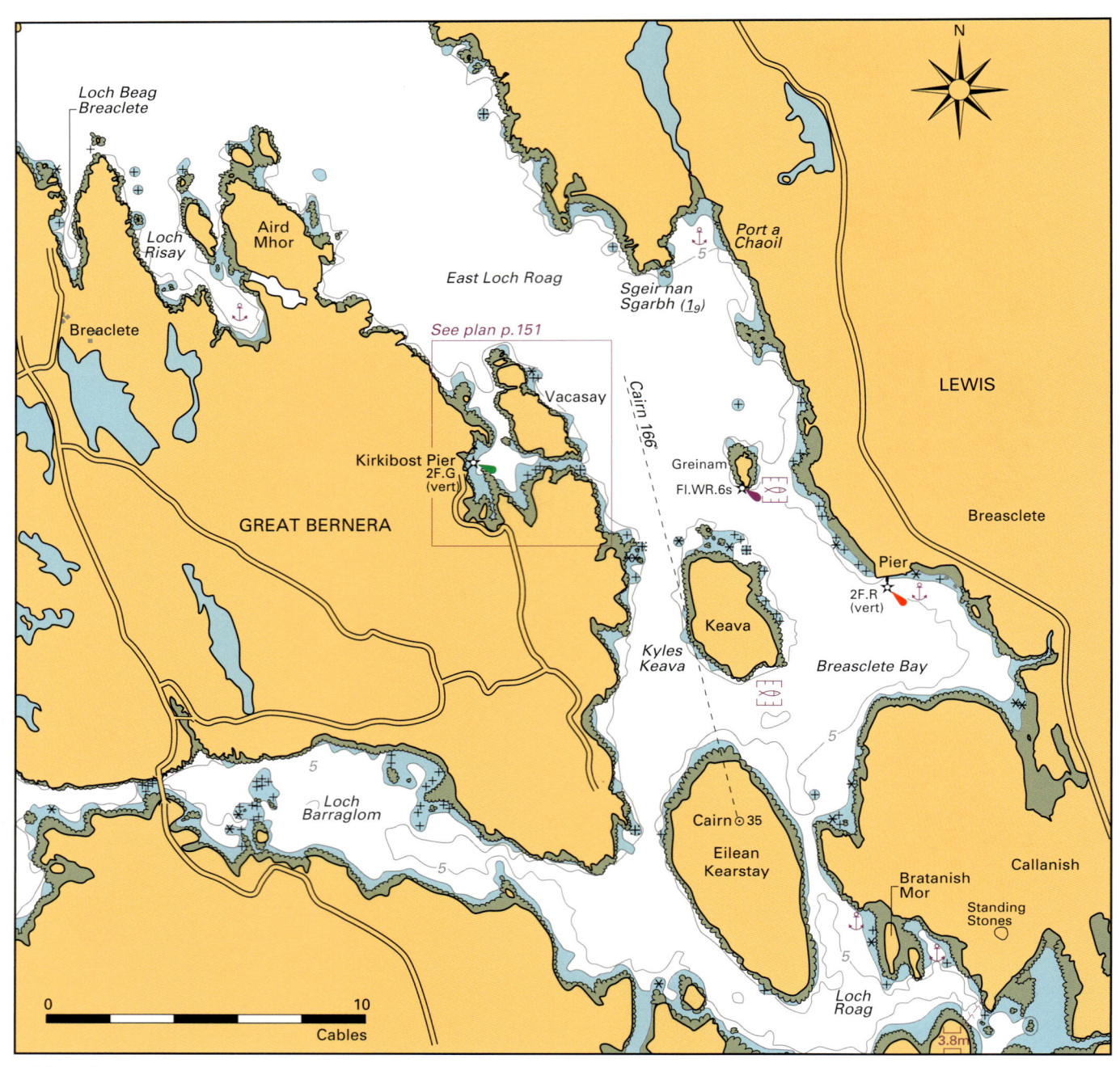

INNER EAST LOCH ROAG

Admiralty Chart
2515
Imray Chart
C67
Ordnance Survey
13
Cruising Scotland
pp.207-9

East Loch Roag (Inner)

As with West Loch Roag, this contains many good anchorages and the additional attraction of the standing stones at Callanish. Both Kirkibost and Breasclete are in regular use by fishing boats and fish farm service vessels and supplies, water and fuel are available.

Dangers and marks

Keava lies ¼ mile south of Greinam light beacon and drying rocks lie up to a cable from its northeast shore. In Kyles Keava between Keava and Great Bernera drying rocks lie on both sides of the north entrance. A conspicuous cairn on Eilean Kearstay in line with the west side of Keava 166° leads between these rocks, but closer to the east rock (dries 1m).

Eilean Kearstay lies ¼ mile south of Keava, with a passage ½ cable wide on its east side and a passage 1 cable wide on its west side. In the east passage a submerged rock lies a cable north of a promontory on the east side of the channel, and a drying rock lies ¼ cable northwest of the same promontory. The west passage has rocks awash and drying up to ¼ cable from its west side.

Anchorages

Loch Risay The pool at the head of the loch is recommended for a remote anchorage. A restored 'norse mill' stands at the outlet from two freshwater lochs on the west shore, and a path from there leads to Breaclete where facilities include a phone, post office and shop, as well as a small museum.

150   CCC Sailing Directions and Anchorages

8. West of the Outer Hebrides

Kirkibost pier, Dubh Thob

Kirkibost (Dubh Thob) is an enclosed basin between Great Bernera and Vacasay Island, which lies ½ mile northwest of Greinam.

A narrow and shallow entrance from the east lies south of Vacasay, and another with rocks marked by light beacons, from the north. In the north entrance a metal column 2 metres high marks a drying rock on the east side of the passage, and another stands on the shore on the west side. Drying reefs extend beyond both perches reducing the channel width to about ⅓ cable. Pass midway between the perches.

Kirkibost pier is on the west side of the basin. A line of drying rocks extends from the south shore to a red beacon half a cable east of the pier head. Anchor in 3m. There is 1·8m alongside the pier. The northern entrance and the basin are lit. See plan for light characteristics.

Supplies: Water and diesel (key fob needed) at pier, public toilets, telephone.

Stores (licensed), post office, community centre with showers and local museum at Breaclete, 3 miles distant. These can also be approached from Loch Risay.

Port a' Chaoil on the east shore of East Loch Roag, a mile north of Greinam, is sheltered from seaward in most weather.

Sgeir nan Sgarbh, which dries 1·9 metres, lies a third of a cable south of the west point of the bay, and a rock which dries 1·3 metres lies about ½ cable off the middle of the head of the bay, with a submerged rock further south. Rocks up to 2 cables offshore, submerged and drying, lie inshore of a line between the east side of the bay and Greinam. Anchor in 3m well offshore. To go further in keep to the east shore to avoid the rocks in the centre of the bay.

Breasclete, east of Keava. Anchor south of old jetty which is east of the conspicuous factory and pier at Rubha Arspaig. Water at the east quay by the white coastguard building.

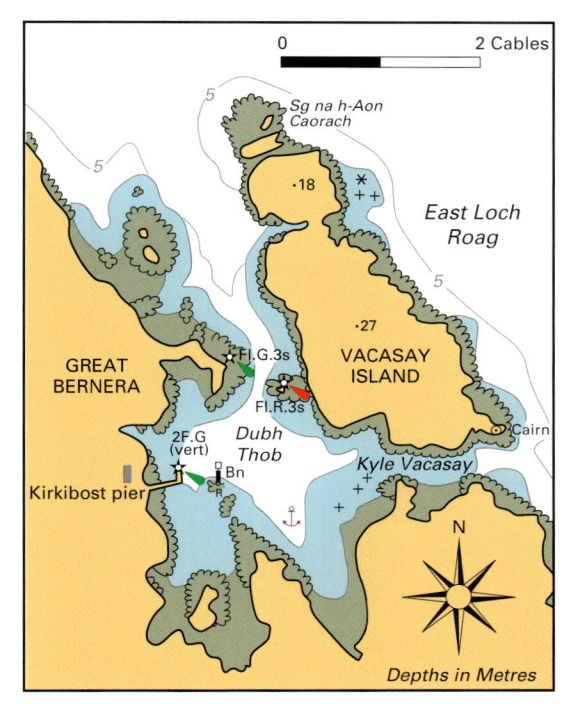

KIRKIBOST

Callanish The best place from which to visit the standing stones is the anchorage east of Bratanish Islands which lies about ¼ mile east of the south end of Kearstay. A submerged rock lies one-third of a cable south of Bratanish Mor, the west island, and another lies one-third of a cable off the east shore of the inlet.

There is also a temporary anchorage NW of Bratanish Mor but note drying rocks up to ½ cable off its west shore.

There is a visitor centre with restaurant at Callanish.

Power cables with headroom of 3·8 metres cross the passage ¼ mile southeast of the islands and bar access further into Loch Roag.

CCC Sailing Directions and Anchorages   151

Outer Hebrides

Jane Routh

Seas off the Butt of Lewis are rarely placid. This photograph was taken in a Force 2-3

Admiralty Chart
2720, 1785, 2721
Imray Chart
C67
Ordnance Survey
8
Cruising Scotland
pp.197-8

The new artificial harbour at Brevig

Martin Lawrence

Gallan Head to Butt of Lewis and Tiumpan Head

The rounding of the Butt of Lewis is considered to be more dangerous than rounding Cape Wrath due to the tidal conditions mentioned below and the ever present swell which is often from different directions. In no circumstances should the Butt of Lewis be approached when white water is seen off it.

The distance from Gallan Head to the Butt of Lewis is about 30 miles, 17 from the Butt of Lewis to Tiumpan Head, and a further 13 to Stornoway. The Butt of Lewis is completely exposed to weather from southwest through north to southeast and there is no shelter between Loch Roag and Stornoway except the new fishing harbour at Brevig in Broad Bay, north of Eye Peninsula, the head of which gives some shelter from southwest. This will involve a detour of about 5 miles.

Note: Tiumpan Head is at the end of the Eye Peninsula, east of Stornoway on the east side of Lewis. To avoid confusion, note that a point about 1½ miles north of Aird Laimishader is also named Tiumpan.

Tides
At the Butt of Lewis:
The northeast, east and south-going stream begins –0435 Ullapool (+0335 Dover)
The north, west and southwest-going stream begins +0150 Ullapool (–0230 Dover)

The spring rate in each direction is 4 to 5 knots close to the point, with eddies on the downstream side of the point

About a mile offshore the streams run at 3 knots; the point should be given a berth of at least 5 miles, which must be allowed for in calculating the length of the passage, unless the wind is both fair in direction and moderate in strength, and the tide is going in the same direction.

Tidal streams on the northwest side of Lewis turn 15 minutes later and run at 1½ knots at springs. Tidal streams on the east side of Lewis turn about an hour earlier and the maximum spring rate is 2 knots.

Dangers and marks

Aird Laimishader lies 7 miles northeast of Gallan Head, and the islets in the mouth of Loch Roag between them are conspicuous.

Hen Shoal, a mile offshore, 7 miles southwest of the Butt of Lewis, at a depth of 9 metres, may cause some disturbance at the surface.

Port of Ness, on the east side of Lewis 2 miles southeast of the lighthouse, provides some shelter from the west in a sandy bay with moderate depths. A drying boat harbour stands on the north side of the bay.

Braga Rock which dries 3·4 metres lies 2 cables offshore 3½ miles southeast of the lighthouse. Tolsta Head open of Cellar Head 180° leads east of the rock.

Tolsta Head is prominent with a vertical cliff 66 metres high at its end.

Brevig Harbour is a modern harbour, opened in November 1995, on the west side of Broad Bay, west of the Eye Peninsula. The entrance, 20m wide, faces approximately south, with a double dog-leg leading to an inner basin 50m x 30m. McIver Rock, awash in the middle of Broad Bay, is clear south of the approach.

Lights
Aird Laimishader Fl.6s63m8M
Flannan Islands Fl(2)30s101m20M
Butt of Lewis Fl.5s52m25M
Tiumpan Head Fl(2)15s55m18M

8. West of the Outer Hebrides

Flannan Islands

A group of rocky islands, with a lighthouse, 17 miles west of Lewis and occasionally visited by yachts although there is no good anchorage.

The main group of islands comprises Eilean Mor with a lighthouse on the summit, and Eilean Tighe. Two islets, Gealtaire Beag (8) and Gealtaire Mor (10) lie about half a mile east of Eilean Tighe. There are two other groups of smaller islands, the Soray group being half a mile south, and the other 2 miles west comprising Roareim and Eilean a' Ghobha. The best island upon which to land is Eilean Mor.

Tide
Const. −0031 Ullapool (−0451 Dover)
Height in metres

MHWS	MHWN	MTL	MLWN	MLWS
3·9	3·0	1·7	1·4	0·5

Light
Eilean Mor Lt Ho. Fl(2)30s101m20M

Anchorage
The bottom is bare rock and the large-scale Admiralty chart shows few soundings. Of the two landing places the concrete steps of the western one have been washed away. None of steps are now maintained and they may be in a dangerous and unusable state. The NLB can accept no responsibility for unauthorised mooring or landing.

The shores of Eilean Mor and Eilean Tighe are steep to without hidden dangers except as shown on the plan. Anchoring in 7m close to Eilean Mor might be possible, or in much deeper water further off. A tripping line should be used as the bottom is rock. A swell is normally present.

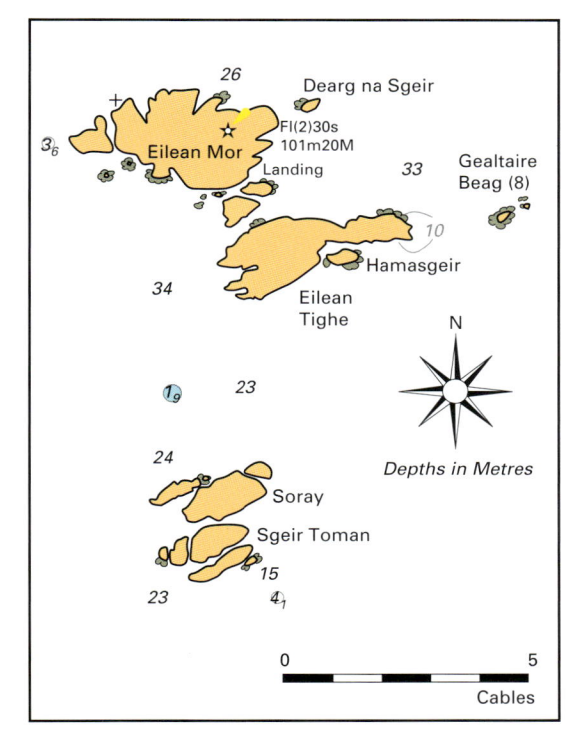

FLANNAN ISLANDS

Admiralty Chart
2524, 2720
Imray Chart
C67
Ordnance Survey
460 (1:25,000)
Cruising Scotland
p.202

Flannan Islands; Eilean Mor seen from Eilean Tighe

Eilean Tighe from Eilean Mor, Flannan Islands

CCC Sailing Directions and Anchorages 153

Outer Hebrides

Village Bay, St Kilda

Admiralty Chart
2524, 2721
Imray Chart
C66
Ordnance Survey
18
Cruising Scotland
p.201

St Kilda

The St Kilda Group consists of four islands: St Kilda (otherwise named Hirta), Dun, Soay and Boreray. There are three significant stacks; Levenish just over a mile east from the extremity of Dun, and Stac Lee and Stac an Armin each about 2 cables west and north of Boreray respectively.

The whole group of islands is designated a World Heritage Site. The main island was inhabited until 1930 and is now owned by the National Trust for Scotland (NTS), leased to Scottish Natural Heritage (SNH). Apart from the area used by the QuinetiQ MoD Hebrides Ranges, the island is managed by a warden on behalf of NTS and SNH, who lives at the `Factor's House', a white house just above the range buildings. The warden's permission must be obtained to go beyond the village.

Visibility and weather suitable for visiting St Kilda do not occur frequently and a yacht must be prepared to clear out at short notice.

Access to the islands is subject to comprehensive bye-laws, displayed on a notice board at the pier. These should be studied, and in particular they prohibit the landing of dogs, introduction of alien plant or animal species, and removal or damage of any plants, bird, or animal from the islands.

Tides

Constant –0055 Ullapool (–0515 Dover)

Height in metres

MHWS	MHWN	MTL	MLWN	MLWS
3·3	2·5	1·8	1·2	0·4

Around St Kilda the northeast-going stream begins +0545 Ullapool (+0125 Dover).
The southwest-going stream begins –0030 Ullapool (–0450 Dover).
Close to the islands, streams run at up to 3 knots, and heavy tide rips extend right across the channel between Dun and Levenish when wind and tide are opposed.

Passage

It is 42 miles from Pabbay on the west side of the Sound of Harris to St Kilda. Other departures for St Kilda might be taken from Berneray (49 miles), Monach Isles (34 miles) or Vaccasay (53 miles). If the visibility is good the group comes into view when about half way across, shaped like a full rigged sailing ship, but, when nearer, the islands and stacks are seen separately. In clear settled weather an overnight passage could be made, but there are no lights to assist such a passage except the leading lights at St Kilda which have a range of 3 miles.

Should the weather deteriorate when either on passage to or from St Kilda and the options of returning to the Sound of Harris or seeking shelter in Loch Resort are decided against, the likelihood is that the best alternative will be to make for East Loch Roag.

154 CCC Sailing Directions and Anchorages

8. West of the Outer Hebrides

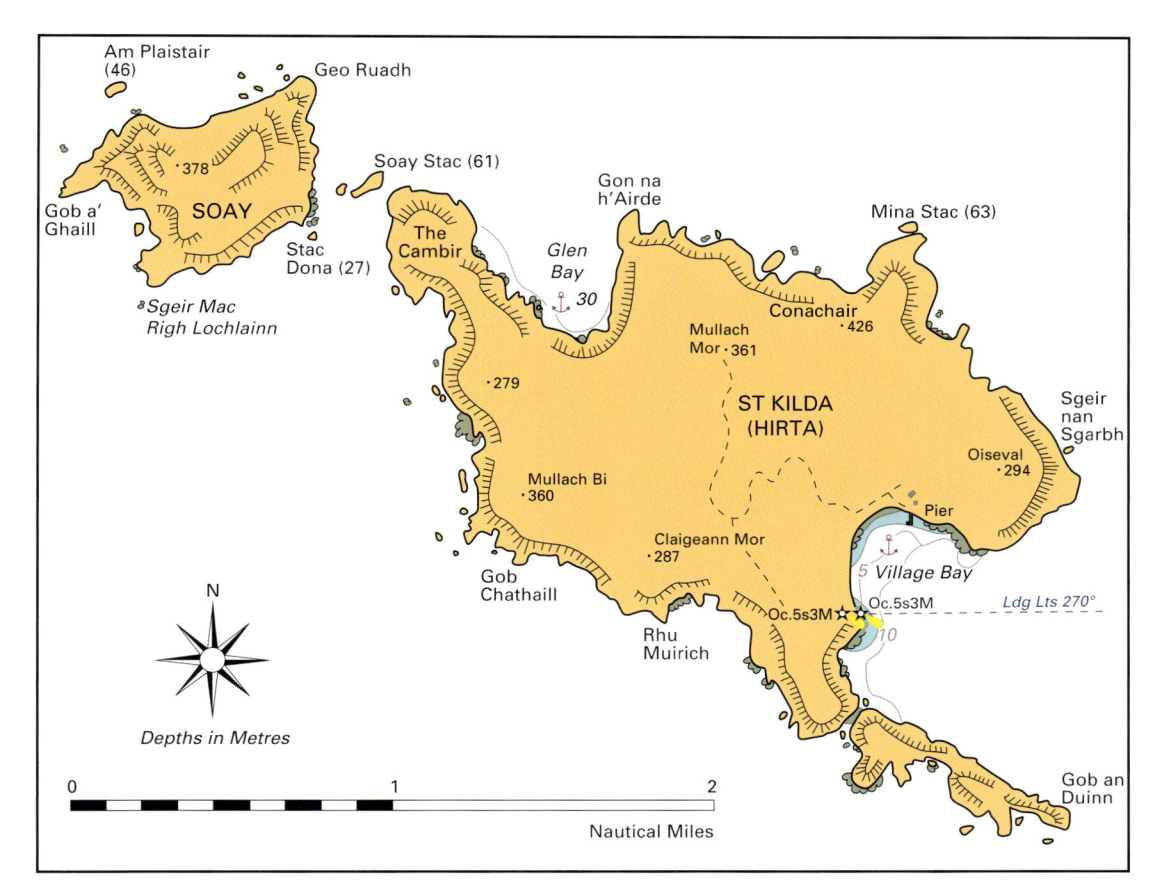

ST KILDA

Directions

In the approach to Village Bay note the position of Levenish (55), the stack lying 1½ miles east of Dun, which has a ridge of rock, Na Bodham drying 1·5m close-in on the east side, and shoal water extending west for 4 cables. Between Levenish and the SE end of Dun there are overfalls with wind against tide (3 knots at springs). These overfalls extend across the channel between Dun and Levenish. Village Bay which faces SE is sheltered on the west side by Dun and is free from hidden dangers although on occasions a strong tide rip sets across the mile wide mouth of the bay. If approaching west-about round the island of Soay beware of the tide race with a north-going tide off the NW side of Soay.

Anchorage

Village Bay Although a full Atlantic swell sets into the bay there is reasonable shelter in 5-6m off the pier below the church. Good holding in hard sand. However it is essential to clear out should the wind come from between east and south. In such conditions a lee can be had anywhere off the shores round the island which are clear outside one cable and, as a last resort, in heavy weather from south or east shelter might be found in Loch a' Ghlinne (Glen Bay) on the north side of Hirta but depths are too great for anchoring except very close to the shore, and winds are accelerated by the cliffs. The bottom is rocky and the anchor must be buoyed. This anchorage must be vacated if there is any tendency for the wind to go north of west.

There is always some swell in Village Bay unless there has been a prolonged period of calm. It is advisable not to delay going ashore to visit the island as it may be necessary to clear out at short notice should a serious swell develop. To land make for the west side of the pier and if necessary move to the root of the pier where there is a small cove with shelving sand.

Lights
Ldg Lts 270° Oc.5s26/38m3M

Communications
Stornoway CG has pointed out that they are unable to receive traffic from yachts in Village Bay, so that yachts reporting arrival should do so before entering the bay.

Stac an Armin, the most northerly of the St Kilda group, with Boreray in the background

CCC Sailing Directions and Anchorages 155

Appendix

Charts and other publications

Although a full set of Admiralty (UKHO) charts remains the ideal, for those who can afford the cost and space, there are now many options for the leisure sailor. For the waters covered by this book, the Imray charts C65, C66 and C67 offer more convenient coverage for passages across the Minch and around the coasts of the Outer Hebrides than their Admiralty counterparts but only the Admiralty charts include St Kilda. Although the Admiralty Leisure Folios have not, at the time of writing, been extended to include all the Outer Hebrides they do provide a very economical selection of larger scale Admiralty charts.

There is, of course, an ever-increasing number of digital charts for use with chart plotters, computers, tablets or smart phones and both Admiralty and Imray charts are available in digital form as a secondary source of information. A further development of the digital chart is the extra-large scale series produced by Antares Charts. This is described in more detail in the Introduction (p.5) and, although there are only a few locations in the Outer Hebrides included in their list, it is planned that by the time this book is published more will be available.

Admiralty charts

The following Admiralty charts relate to the waters covered by this volume. They are grouped according to their scale:

Group (i) charts are at a scale of 1:200,000 or smaller. Complete coverage at this scale should be carried. Several of this group of charts omit any detail within inshore waters.
Group (ii) charts are at a scale of 1:100,000 or greater. These are essential and should be carried as appropriate for the extent of the cruise which is contemplated.
Group (iii) charts are principally large scale plans, many of which are included in sketch form in these Sailing Directions.

Group (i)
2635	Scotland, West Coast	500,000
2720	Flannan Isles to Sule Skerry	200,000
2721	St Kilda to Butt of Lewis	200,000
2722	Skerryvore to St Kilda	200,000

Group (ii)
1757	The Little Minch - Northern Part	100,000
1785	North Minch - Northern Part	100,000
1794	North Minch - Southern Part	100,000
1795	The Little Minch - Southern Part	100,000
1796	Barra Head to Point of Ardnamurchan	100,000
2515	Armore Mangersta to Tiumpan Head	25,000
2529	Approaches to Stornoway	25,000
2769	Barra Head to Greian Head	30,000
2770	Sound of Barra	30,000
2802	Sound of Harris	21,000
2841	Loch Maddy to Loch Resort	50,000
2904	Usinish to Eigneig Mhor	25,000

Group (iii)
2524	Islands of the NW Coast of Scotland *St Kilda, Flannan Islands, Sule Sgeir and Rona*	Various
2825	Lochs on E Coast of Uist *Loch Skipport, Loch Carnan, Loch Maddy, Loch Eynort, Loch Eport*	12,500
2905	East Loch Tarbert	12,500

Admiralty Leisure Folios

Admiralty Leisure Folios consist of up to 30 A2-size sheets, directly reproduced from part of the equivalent full size Admiralty charts, printed on plain paper and sold in an acetate wallet. At the moment only Folio 5616, Ardnamurchan to Shiant Islands, includes charts of the Outer Hebrides. This folio deals principally with the mainland north of Ardnamurchan up to Gairloch, Skye and the Small Isles but the east coast of the Outer Hebrides from Barra Head to South Harris is included together with the Sea of the Hebrides and the Little Minch. The charts also contain many inset plans taken from the larger scale Group (ii) and Group (iii) charts above.

Availability

Admiralty charts are available from Admiralty Chart Agents, which are established in most major ports and yachting centres in the UK. Imrays are Admiralty Chart Agents and can supply Admiralty charts print on demand, publications and products by post as well as, of course, their own publications. www.imray.com

Admiralty Chart agents in Scotland:
Chart Co, Unit 5 St Luke's Place, Glasgow G5 0TS,
☏ 0141 429 6462
Poseidon Navigation Services Ltd, Maritime House, Deskford, Cullen, Buckie, Moray, AB56 5TR
☏ 01542 841245

Some other outlets, mostly larger marinas and yacht centres, will usually supply Admiralty charts, together with most of the Imray publications. They generally stock a good selection of local charts, although others will have to be ordered, sometimes at a premium.

Chart index

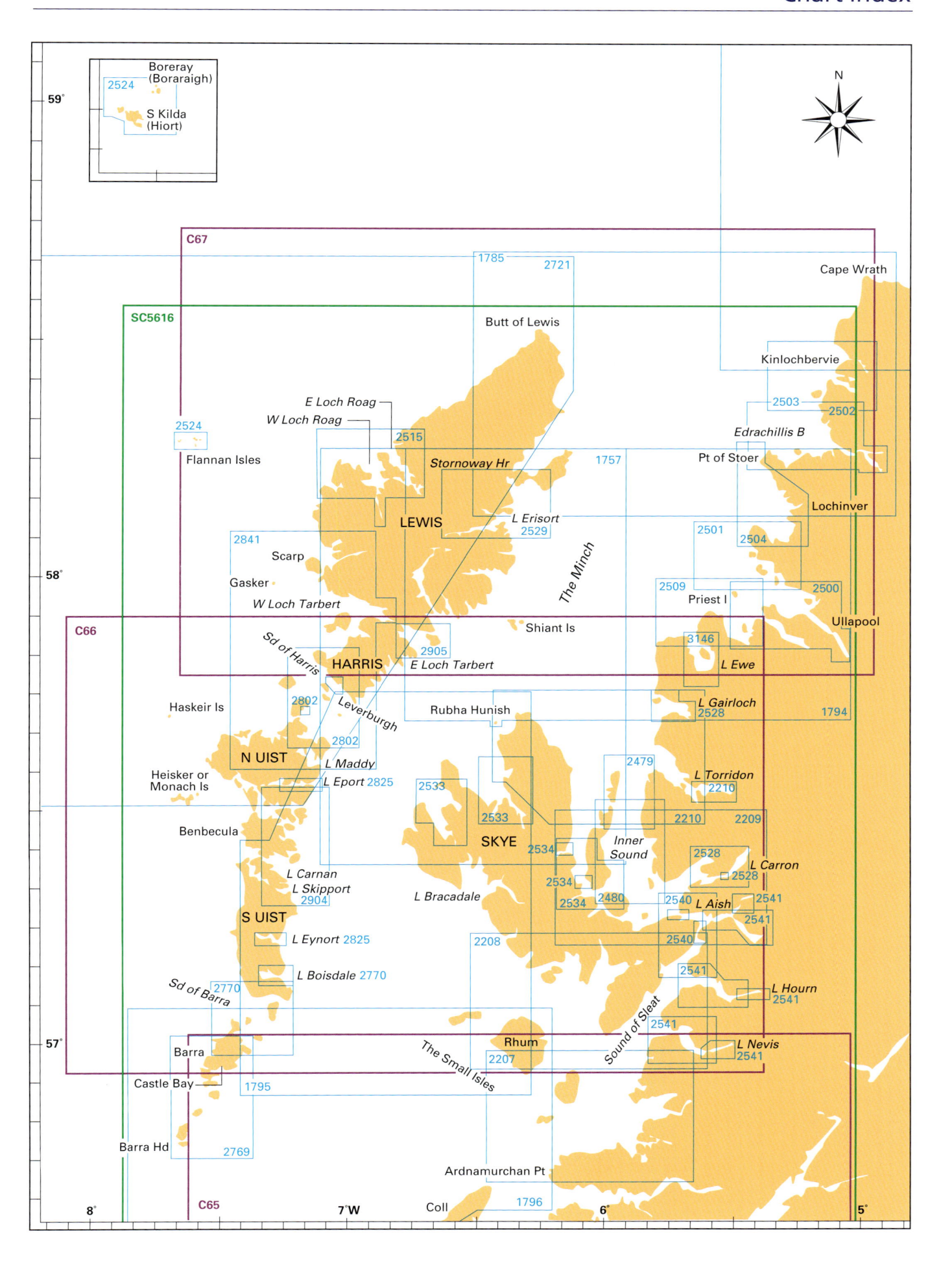

CCC Sailing Directions and Anchorages

Outer Hebrides

ANTARES CHART SELECTOR

0 5 10
Nautical Miles

Butt of Lewis

LEWIS

E Loch Roag
W Loch Roag

Miavaig Bay

Little Loch Roag

Loch Tamanavay *Loch Cheann Chuisil* *Risay* Hurista *Loch Mariveg*
Tamanavay
Dirascal *Head of Loch Resort* *Narrows Anchorage*
Scarp Loch Resort *Seaforth Island* *Loch Seaforth* *Lemreway*
Gasgeir North Minch
Loch Maaruig *Head of Loch Bhrollum*
Eilean Thinngarstaigh *Tob Smuaisibhig*
Tob Bhrollum
Loch Valamus
Plocrapool Bay *North Harbour Scalpay* Shiant Is
Head of Loch Stockinish **HARRIS** *E Loch Tarbert*
Loch Scadabay
Loch Beacraik *Loch Grosebay*
St Kilda Pabbay Leverburgh *Loch Stockinish Entrance*
Loch Finsbay
Sd of Harris *Lingarabay*
Rodel

Grey Horse Channel *Duntulum Bay*
Opsay Basin
Calm Bay Ascrib Islands
North Uist *Loch Maddy Harbour* Uig
Bagh Aird *Loch Snizort*
Monach Islands *Loch Langais* *Acairseid Lee*
Sound of Shillay *Croic Harbour* *Bagh a Bhiorain* *Eilean Iosaigh*
Ronay Sound Inner *Haunaray Sound* Loch Dunvegan
Flodday Sound
Ronay Outer *Castle Bay*
Wiay Beag
BENBECULA
Wiay & Peter's Port *Loch Bharcasaig* Loch Bracadale
Bagh a Mhanaich *Gesto Bay*
SOUTH UIST *Wizard Pool & Caolas Mor* *Oronsay*
Carbost and Talisker Distillery
Eastern Anchorages
Loch Eynort *Struthan Beag* **ISLE OF SKYE**
Loch Scavaig
Lochboisdale
Marina *Soay Harbour*
South Boisdale *Loch Hartavagh*
Eriskay *Haun Bay* Canna Harbour *Kilmory Bay*
Acairseid Mhor *Loch Scresort*
BARRA *Stack Islands* Canna Boat Harbour **RUM**
Loch Obe *Gighay & Hellisay*
Bagh Beag *Sgeirislum* Sea of the Hebrides Hyskeir Lighthouse
Cornaig Bay *Castlebay*
EIGG
Fisherman's Passage *Gallanach Bay* *South Bay*
MUCK *Port Mor*

158 CCC Sailing Directions and Anchorages

Publications

Antares Charts

Throughout this book mention has been made of *Antares Charts*, a portfolio of extra large scale plans produced from recent surveys and intended for use with GPS in conjunction with a variety of plotting software applications on PCs and tablets. They are more fully described in the Introduction on p.5.

The portfolio now contains so many plans that a simple list of them does not adequately illustrate their location, especially when a number of them have unfamiliar names. So, with the kind permission of Bob Bradfield of *Antares Charts*, we have reproduced here his chart selector which shows at a glance all the plans for the area covered by this book.

These are up to date as far as and including the 2017 issue. New charts are constantly being added and a full list of all the current and possible future charts can be seen on the *Antares* website: *www.antarescharts.co.uk*

Imray charts

The area included in this book is covered by the following Imray C series of charts which are all drawn at around 1:150,000 scale (except where noted), with inset plans, on waterproof material, in folded format and sold in an acetate wallet at approximately A4 size. They can also be obtained flat by special request.

C65   Crinan to Mallaig and Barra   1:150,000
      Plans Sound of Luing, Lynn of Lorn, Tobermory, Castle Bay, Mallaig, Entrance to Caledonian Canal, Oban

C66   Mallaig to Rudha Reidh and Outer Hebrides   1:150,000
      Plans St Kilda, East Loch Tarbert, Loch Maddy, Loch Carnan, Loch Boisdale, Dunvegan, Portree, Loch Gairloch, Kyleakin, Uig

C67   North Minch and Isle of Lewis   1:146,000
      Plans Loch Inver, Stornoway Ullapool, Loch Inchard (Kinlochbervie), Loch Carloway

2800   The West Coast of Scotland
2800.1 Crinan to Tobermory and Fort William 1:160,000
2800.2 Loch Crinan to Garbh Eileach 1:50,000
       Plans Craobh Haven, Crinan Basin.
       Inset Continuation of Loch Melfort
2800.3 Cuan Sound to Loch Spelve and Kerrera Sound 1:50,000
       Plans Oban, Loch Feochan Entrance, Cuan Sound
       Inset Continuation of Loch Spelve
2800.4 Oban to Loch Aline and Port Appin 1:50,000
       Plans Dunstaffnage Bay, Oban
2800.5 Loch Aline to Tobermory and Loch Sunart 1:50,000
       Plan Tobermory
       Inset Continuation of Loch Sunart
2800.6 Loch Linnhe South and Loch Creran 1:50,000
       Inset Continuation of Loch Etive
2800.7 Loch Linnhe and Loch Leven 1:50,000
       Plans Corpach Sea Loch, Corran Narrows, Loch Leven Narrows
       Inset Continuation of Loch Leven

Ordnance Survey Maps

1:50 Landranger Maps cover the Outer Hebrides as follows:

OSL 8   Stornoway and North Lewis
OSL 13 West Lewis and North Harris
OSL 14 Tarbert and Loch Seaforth
OSL 18 Sound of Harris
OSL 22 Benbecula and South Uist
OSL 31 Barra and South Uist

Admiralty publications

West Coast of Scotland Pilot, 2014 1st Edition (NP 66B), with supplements to date.
Tidal Atlas N Coast of Ireland and W Coast of Scotland (NP 218).
Admiralty Tide Tables Vol 1 (NP 201).
Admiralty List of Lights Vol A (NP 74).

Other publications

Almanacs

The Cruising Almanac, Cruising Association, Imray
Reeds Western Almanac, Adlard Coles Nautical
Reeds PBO Small Craft Almanac, Adlard Coles Nautical.

General books

Cruising Scotland, Mike Balmforth & Edward Mason, Imray, 2015 2nd Edition
The Scottish Islands, Hamish Haswell-Smith, Canongate 2014 3rd Edition
An Island Odyssey, Hamish Haswell-Smith, Canongate 2014 2nd Edition
Hebrides, Peter May, Riverrun 2013
The Hebrides, An Aerial View of a Cultural Landscape, Angus and Patricia Macdonald, Birlinn, 2010

Contact telephone numbers and websites

Imrays – Charts, sailing directions ☏ 01480 462114 www.imray.com
Clyde Cruising Club ☏ 0141221 2774 www.clyde.org
Citylink bus travel enquiries ☏ 0990 505050 www.citylink.co.uk
Rail travel enquiries ☏ 0345 484950 www.railtrack.co.uk
CalMac (MacBraynes) ferry enquiries ☏ 0800 066 5000 www.calmac.co.uk/timetables
Sail Scotland www.sailscotland.co.uk
Stornoway Coastguard ☏ 01851 702013
RYA Scotland ☏ 0131 317 7388 www.ryascotland.org.uk
Western Isles Harbourmaster ☏ 01870 604991
Stornoway Port Authority ☏ 01851 702688

Slips suitable for launching trailed boats

(WIC indicates a slip owned by Western Isles Council; there may be a charge for its use)

Vatersay causeway 56°56′N 07°34′W *WIC*
Castlebay 56°56′N 07°31′W MacBraynes; behind linkspan
Eoligarry, north end of Barra 57°01′N 07°26′W *WIC*
Ardveenish 57°00′N 07°25′W *WIC*
Lochboisdale fishery pier 57°08′N 07°19′W *WIC*
Loch Skipport fish farm 57°20′N 07°16′W *private*
Peter's Port 57°23′N 07°15′W *WIC*
Kallin 57°24′N 07°15′W *WIC*
Cheesebay 57°39′N 07°06′W *WIC*
Newton ferry 57°41′N 07°13′W *WIC*
Leverburgh 57°46′N 07°01′W
Ceann Dibig, East Loch Tarbert 57°53′N 07°49′W *WIC*
Kyles Scalpay ferry 57°53′N 07°41′W *WIC*
East Tarbert fishery pier/slip 57°54′N 07°49′W *WIC*
Stornoway 58°12′N 06°23′W
Kirkibost, Loch Roag 58°13′N 06°48′W *WIC*

CCC Sailing Directions and Anchorages

Outer Hebrides

Quick reference table of provisions, services and supplies

Water	A	Alongside, by hose
	T	Tap on jetty or quay
	N	Nearby tap
Shop	S	Several, or supermarket
	L	Local, well stocked village store
	B	Basic
Diesel	A	Alongside, by hose (key fob usually needed, see p.11)
		* indicates no fob needed but large quantities only
		** indicates available without key fob through local agents
	G	Garage (usually needs to be carried some distance)
Petrol	P	(usually needs to be carried some distance)
Calor Gas	C	
Repairs	H	Hull
	M	Marine engine
	E	Electronics (engineer may need to come from a distance)
Chandlery	Y	Yacht
	F	Fishermen's chandlery
	I	Ironmonger, hardware store, which may be better than nothing
Visitors' moorings	V	(including those provided by hotel for customers)
	P	Pontoon
Catering	R	Restaurant
	B	Bar
	S	Showers
Bank	£	
Rubbish disposal	D	
Crane	1	Capacity in tons

Note: Figures following reference letter indicate the distance in miles from the landing place.

Page	Place	Water	Shop	Diesel	Petrol	Calor Gas	Repairs	Chandlery	Visitors' moorings	Catering	Bank	Rubbish disposal	Crane
22	Castlebay	A	S	G	P	C		FI	VP	RBS	£	D	
24	Vatersay (Causeway)	A		A									
28	Northbay	A		A*						RB			1
36	Eriskay	A	L 1½	A		C 1½		I 1½	VP	RB 1½	£		
40	Loch Boisdale	A	S 3 L	G	P			I	P	RBS	£	D	
58	Kallin	A		A			H	F				D	1
71	Loch Maddy	A	L	G	P	C			VP	RBS	£	D	
78	Berneray	A		A					V	RS		D	1
86	Leverburgh	A	L	A	P	C			P			D	
95	Stockinish, Pol Scrot	A		A					P			D	
102	Scalpay	A	L	A**					P	RS		D	
104	Tarbert	T	S	G1½	P1½	C1½			VP	RBS	£	D	
128	Stornoway	A	S	A**	P	C	HME	F	P	RBS	£	D	
152	Brevig	A		A									
139	Loch Bunaveneadar		L	G	P	C							
149	Miavaig	A	S 2½	A					P			D	
149	Kirkibost	A	L2	A								D	1
150	Breasclete	T											
149	Carloway	A		A						RBS 1½			1

160 CCC Sailing Directions and Anchorages

Distance tables

Gairloch to Cape Wrath and the Hebrides

Distances given in miles

	Gairloch	Rubha Reidh	Ullapool	Summer Isles	Loch Inver	Stoer Head	Kinlochbervie	Cape Wrath	Loch Eriboll	Stornoway	Loch Shell	Eilean Glas Light Scalpay
Gairloch		12	36	28	38	40	58	68	82	37	28	31
Rubha Reidh	12		23	15	26	26	43	53	68	26	19	26
Ullapool	36	23		12	25	27	45	53	68	42	40	48
Summer Isles	28	15	12		12	14	32	42	56	31	31	40
Loch Inver	38	26	25	12		10	27	35	49	35	37	46
Stoer Head	40	26	27	14	10		17	27	41	30	35	45
Kinlochbervie	58	43	45	32	27	17		14	29	44	50	60
Cape Wrath	68	53	53	42	35	27	14		14	52	57	70
Loch Eriboll	82	68	68	56	49	41	29	14		64	73	84
Stornoway	37	26	42	31	35	30	44	52	64		14	41
Loch Shell	28	19	40	31	37	35	50	57	73	14		11
Eilean Glas Light Scalpay	31	26	48	40	46	45	60	70	84	41	11	

The Outer Hebrides

Distances given in miles

	Canna Harbour	Dunvegan Pier	Castle Bay Barra	Big Harbour Eriskay	Calva Is. Lt Loch Boisdale	Wizard Pool Loch Skipport	Loch Eport Entrance	Weaver's Point Loch Maddy	Loch Rodel	Scalpay Is. Lt, Harris	Loch Mariveg Loch Erisort	Stornoway
Canna Harbour		39	36	28	26	31	37	40	46	51	74	79
Dunvegan Pier	39		52	40	34	27	19	20	21	24	43	48
Castle Bay Barra	36	52		12	20	32	44	47	56	65	87	92
Big Harbour Eriskay	28	40	12		8	20	33	36	45	54	76	81
Calva Is. Lt Loch Boisdale	26	34	20	8		13	27	30	39	48	70	75
Wizard Pool Loch Skipport	31	27	32	20	13		15	18	27	36	58	63
Loch Eport Entrance	37	19	44	33	27	15		4	13	22	44	49
Weaver's Point Loch Maddy	40	20	47	36	30	18	4		10	19	41	46
Loch Rodel	46	21	56	45	39	27	13	10		12	34	39
Scalpay Is. Lt, Harris	51	24	65	54	48	36	22	19	12		22	27
Loch Mariveg Loch Erisort	74	43	87	76	70	58	44	41	34	22		7
Stornoway	79	48	92	81	75	63	49	46	39	27	7	

CCC Sailing Directions and Anchorages

Outer Hebrides

West of the Outer Hebrides Distances given in miles	Barra Head	Castle Bay Barra	Weaver's Point Loch Maddy	Bays Loch Berneray	Loch Rodel	Stornoway	Monach Islands	Village Bay St Kilda	Loch Leosavay	Flannan Islands	Carloway East Loch Roag	Butt of Lewis
Barra Head		16	56	68	64	99	55	70	84	93	109	124
Castle Bay Barra	16		47	60	56	90	54	75	75	96	102	118
Weaver's Point Loch Maddy	56	47		13	9	47	42	62	27	48	54	70
Bays Loch Berneray	68	60	13		12	51	27	51	19	39	45	67
Loch Rodel	64	56	9	12		38	35	55	20	42	47	61
Stornoway	99	90	47	51	38		73	93	60	76	58	32
Monach Islands	55	54	42	27	35	73		34	35	46	58	80
Village Bay St Kilda	70	75	62	51	55	93	34		52	42	65	86
Loch Leosavay	84	75	27	19	20	60	35	52		30	33	54
Flannan Islands	93	96	48	39	42	76	46	42	30		26	45
Carloway East Loch Roag	109	102	54	45	47	58	58	65	33	26		28
Butt of Lewis	124	118	70	67	61	32	80	86	54	45	28	

Crossing to the Outer Hebrides

The Sea of the Hebrides (p.17)

Sound of Mull to Castlebay	50 miles
Sound of Mull to Canna	25 miles
Canna to Castlebay	35 miles
Canna to Eriskay	26 miles
Canna to Loch Boisdale	25 miles
Canna to Loch Skipport	30 miles
Canna to Loch Maddy	40 miles
Gunna Sound to Castle Bay	36 miles

The Little Minch (p.106)

North Skye to Tarbert, Harris	20 miles
North Skye to Loch Maddy	29 miles
North Skye to Stornoway	30 miles
Dunvegan to Tarbert, Harris	29 miles
Dunvegan to Loch Maddy	21 miles

The North Minch (p.120)

South Rona to Loch Shell	33 miles
South Rona to Stornoway	47 miles
North Skye to Loch Shell	20 miles
Badachro to Loch Shell	30 miles
Badachro to Stornoway	38 miles
Loch Ewe to Loch Shell	29 miles
Loch Ewe to Stornoway	33 miles
Loch Inver to Loch Shell	40 miles
Loch Inver to Stornoway	37 miles
Kinlochbervie to Loch Shell	51 miles
Kinlochbervie to Stornoway	47 miles

Submarine exercise areas

Scottish Exercise Areas including SUBFACTS

Warnings of areas allocated for exercises are given by Liverpool, Belfast and Stornoway Coastguards along with the weather forecasts at the times given in the Introduction

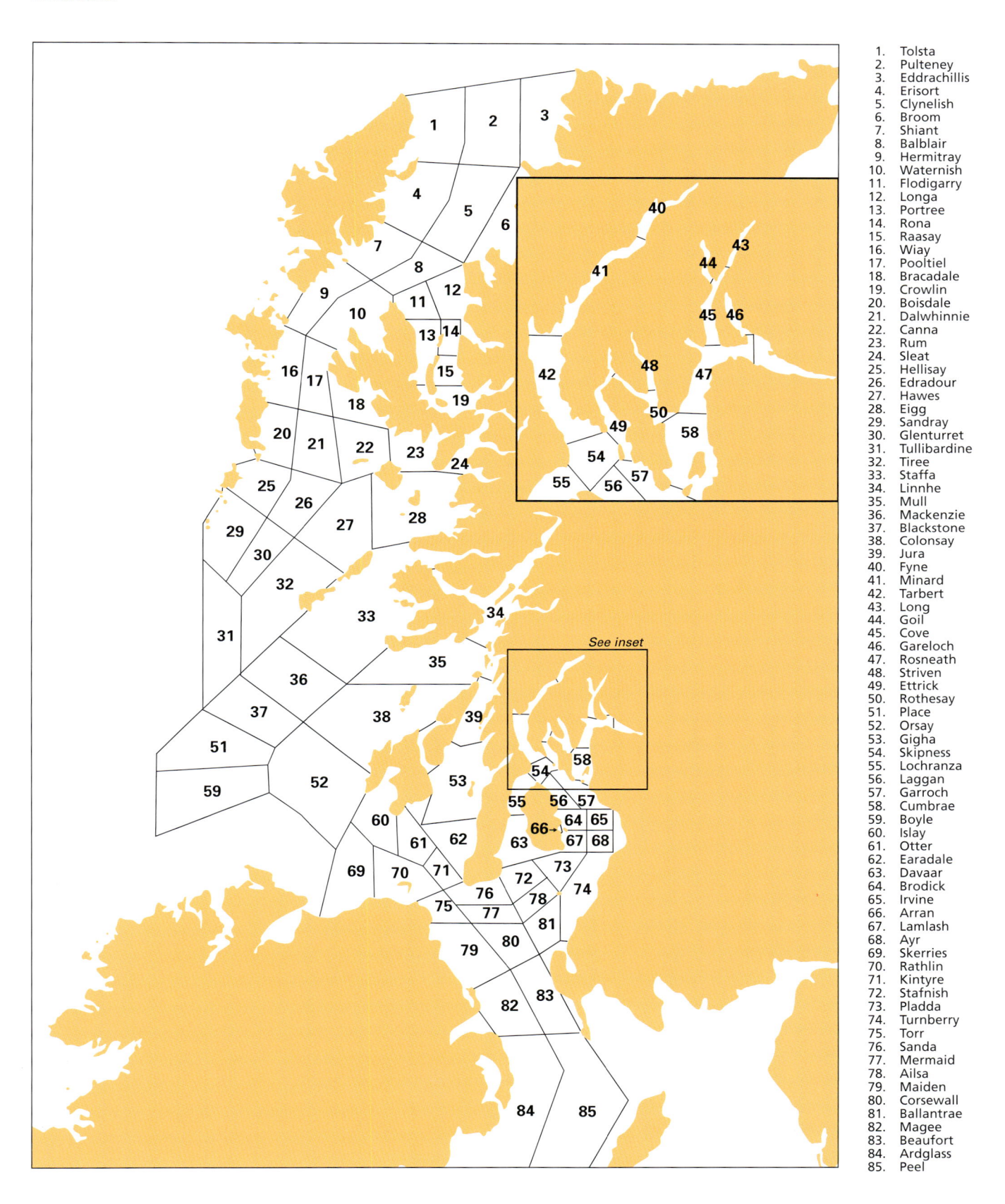

1. Tolsta
2. Pulteney
3. Eddrachillis
4. Erisort
5. Clynelish
6. Broom
7. Shiant
8. Balblair
9. Hermitray
10. Waternish
11. Flodigarry
12. Longa
13. Portree
14. Rona
15. Raasay
16. Wiay
17. Pooltiel
18. Bracadale
19. Crowlin
20. Boisdale
21. Dalwhinnie
22. Canna
23. Rum
24. Sleat
25. Hellisay
26. Edradour
27. Hawes
28. Eigg
29. Sandray
30. Glenturret
31. Tullibardine
32. Tiree
33. Staffa
34. Linnhe
35. Mull
36. Mackenzie
37. Blackstone
38. Colonsay
39. Jura
40. Fyne
41. Minard
42. Tarbert
43. Long
44. Goil
45. Cove
46. Gareloch
47. Rosneath
48. Striven
49. Ettrick
50. Rothesay
51. Place
52. Orsay
53. Gigha
54. Skipness
55. Lochranza
56. Laggan
57. Garroch
58. Cumbrae
59. Boyle
60. Islay
61. Otter
62. Earadale
63. Davaar
64. Brodick
65. Irvine
66. Arran
67. Lamlash
68. Ayr
69. Skerries
70. Rathlin
71. Kintyre
72. Stafnish
73. Pladda
74. Turnberry
75. Torr
76. Sanda
77. Mermaid
78. Ailsa
79. Maiden
80. Corsewall
81. Ballantrae
82. Magee
83. Beaufort
84. Ardglass
85. Peel

CCC Sailing Directions and Anchorages 163

Outer Hebrides

Gaelic for yachtsmen

In order to find the word you want it is helpful to know a little bit about Gaelic grammar. Gaelic words change in a number of ways to form the plural, feminine, possessive, the dative and vocative case of nouns, the past tense of verbs etc. Changes will be found at the beginning, at the end and also in the middle of a word, for example:

cinn see *ceann*
eich genitive and plural of *each* horse
mara genitive of *muir* sea

The change most likely to cause difficulty in looking up a word is the insertion of *h* after a consonant at the beginning. This alters the sound of the preceding letter *(bh* and *mh* and pronounced like English *v*, *ph* is pronounced *f)*. Thus if you are looking for a word beginning with *bh, ch, dh, fh, gh, mh, ph, sh, th*, look it up in the list without the *h*, for example:

bhàn see *bàn*
ghlas see *glas*
mhòr see *mòr*

Some names, particularly those of islands ending in 'a' or 'ay', are of Norse origin. Anyone at all familiar with French and Latin will see correspondences there, for example Caisteil – also Eaglais and Teampuill.

Many words are compounds made up of several often quite common parts, frequently linked by na - nam - nan. The following are the most usual forms of words which commonly occur in Gaelic place names. They often set out to describe the physical features and so give some clues to identification. Some of them occur almost everywhere; most lochs have a Sgeir More and an Eilean Dubh, or vice versa.

Meanings of common Gaelic words

In the entries which follow: Gaelic words are in bold; English equivalents follow in bold within square brackets; information about case, plurals etc. are italicised and the meanings in English are in regular text.

àird, àrd height, (high) promontory
abhainn [avon] river
acarsaid anchorage
achadh [ach] field
àilean [aline] green field
aiseag ferry
allt [ault] burn, stream
aonach hill, moor
aoineadh steep rocky brae
aonach (steep) hill, moor
àrd see **àird**
àros house
àth ford
ault see **allt**
avon see **abhainn**
bà see **bò**
bac (sand)bank
bàgh bay
baile town, village, farm
bàn white, pale, fair
bàrr top, summit, height
beag [beg] little

bealach (mountain) pass, gorge
beàrn gap, crevice
beinn [ben] mountain, hill
beithe birch-tree
binnean pointed hill, peak
bò, *possessive and plural* **bà** cow
bogha, bodha [bo(w)] submerged rock, rock on which waves break
bodach old man
breac [breck] *adjective* speckled, spotted; *noun* trout
bruach bank, hillside
buachaille herdsman, shepherd
buidhe yellow
caileag girl
cailleach old woman
caisteal castle
caladh harbour
calltainn hazel
camas, camus bay, creek
caol, caolas, [kyle] narrow(s), strait
carraig rock
ceann, *possessive and plural* **cinn** [ken] head, point
cill [kil] church, monk's cell
clach stone
clachan village (with a church)
cladach shore, beach
cnap [knap] (small) hill, lump
cnoc [cnok, knock] hillock
còig five
coille wood, forest
coire [corry] kettle, cauldron, whirlpool, steep round hollow in hillside
coll hazel
craobh tree
creag rock, crag, cliff
crois cross
cruach stack, rick-shaped hill
dà two
darach [darroch] oak
dearg red
deas south
dòbhran otter
doirlinn isthmus, (connection to) an island which is accessible at low tide
domhain deep
donn brown
drochaid bridge
druim back, ridge
dubh black, dark
dùn fort, mound
each, *possessive and plural* **eich** horse
ear east
eas waterfall
eilach mill-race; mound
eilean island
fada long
faich meadow

Gaelic glossary

faing sheep-pen, fank
asgadh shelter
feàrna alder-tree
fèith bog
fiacal tooth
fear, *possessive and plural* **fir** man
fireach moor, hill
fliuch wet
fraoch heather
garbh rough, harsh
geal white, bright
geòdha, geò deep cleft in cliffs, chasm
gil glen, water course
glas, grey, green
gleann glen, narrow valley
gobhar goat
gorm blue, green
gualainn shoulder; slope of hill
iar west
iasg fish
inbhir [inver] river mouth, confluence
innis [inch] island, river meadow
iolaire eagle
ken see **ceann**
kil see **cill**
kyle see **caol**
lag hollow, pit
leac slab, flat stone
learg hillside, plain
leathan broad, wide
leth half
liath grey
linne pool, channel
loch lake, arm of the sea
lochan small loch, lake
long, *possessive* **luinge** ship
machair sandy grassed area behind a beach, low-lying plain
maol [mull] headland, bare rounded hill
mòinteach moorland, mossy place
mol, mal shingle (beach)
mòr [more] big, tall, great
muir, *possessive* **mara** sea
mullach summit
òb (sheltered) bay, harbour
odhar dun-coloured
oitir sandbank
òrd, ùird hammer
òs river mouth
plod, pool, pond
poll, puill pool
port port
rath fortress
rathad road
rhu see **rudha**
rìgh king
rinn promontory
ròn seal

ruadh red, reddish-brown
rudha, rubha [rhu] point of land
seachd seven
seann old, ancient
sga(i)t skate
sgarbh cormorant
sgeir skerry, rock
sgùrr rocky peak
sròn nose, (nose shaped) promontory; jutting ridge
srath strath, low-lying valley
sruth current
taigh, tigh house
tarbh bull
tioram dry
tobar well
tràigh beach, strand
trì three
tuath north
tulach hillock
uamh cave
uaine green
ùird see **òrd**

Outer Hebrides

COMHAIRLE NAN ELEAN SIAR

VISITOR YACHTS QUESTIONNAIRE
01 APRIL 2017 – 31 MARCH 2018

OWNER'S NAME: HOME TEL:

ADDRESS:

MOBILE:

POST CODE: E-MAIL:

VESSEL NAME	LENGTH (METRES)

MOORINGS USED	PLEASE TICK APPROPRIATE BOX	DATE
Rodel, Isle of Harris		
Berneray, Isle of North Uist		
Acarsaid, Isle of South Uist		

Please indicate payment choice as per Visiting Leisure Craft Dues 2017 – 2018

SEASONAL COMPOSITION RATE **PLEASE TICK APPROPRIATE BOX**

Visiting Leisure Craft

	£
Single Port Visit where composition rate for private leisure craft has not been paid. All prices exclude VAT	Per visit
Not exceeding 10m	15
Not exceeding 15m	21
Not exceeding 20m	28
Over 20m –per metre	3.17

1 month cruising pass (only available to visiting vessels)

Not exceeding 10m	85
Not exceeding 15m	171
Not exceeding 20m	228
Over 20m –per metre	21.15
Any vessel anchoring in a CnES Harbour not using a pier or other shore based facility shall be liable to 75% of standard harbour dues.	

Please post the completed form to - Comhairle nan Eilean Siar, Harboumaster, Balivanich, Benbecula HS7 5LA or e-mail – harbourmaster@cne-siar.gov.uk

Western Isles Council forms

Comhairle nan Eilean Siar

Application for Contactless Fuel Key

Name……………………………………….... Vessel Name………………………………………...

Address…………………………………….… Registration No……………………………………...

…………………………………………. Home Tel……………………………………………

…………………………………………. Mobile No…………………………………………...

…………………………………………. E-Mail Address……………………………………

Postcode……………………………………….

Are you VAT Registered   Yes/No *

* delete as appropriate

VAT Registration No ………………………….

Please indicate whether fuel is for fishing vessel, fish farm vessel, private leisure craft or commerical purposes

Fishing Vessel	
Fish Farm Vessel	
Private Leisure Craft	
Commercial	

All new applicants to Comhairle Marine Fuel Sales must enter into a Direct Debit agreement for settlement of accounts.

Complete and post to the Comhairle Harbour Office or e-mail to: harbourmaster@cne-siar.gov.uk

For office use -

Debtor Ref	
Key No.	

The rocks don't move...

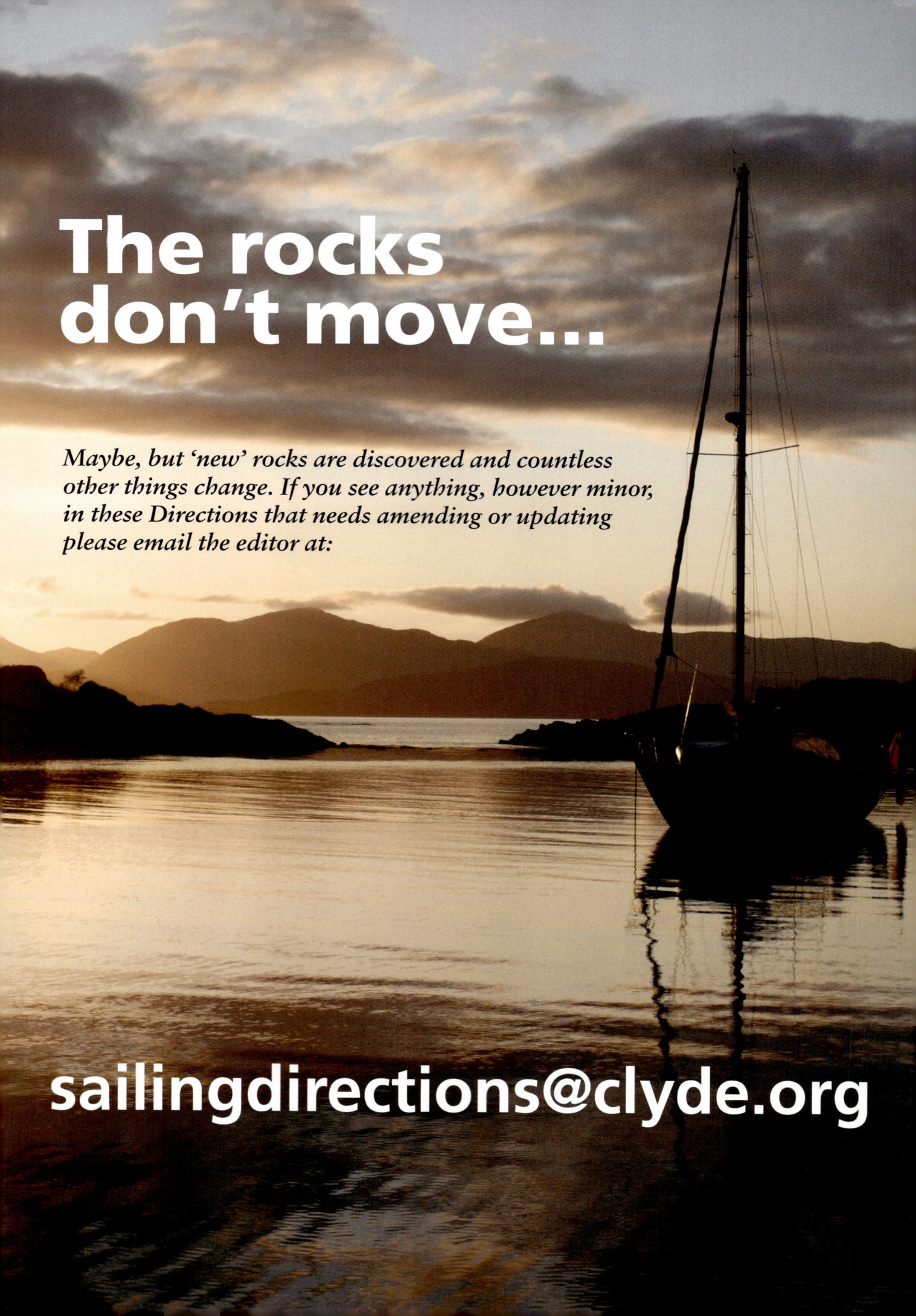

Maybe, but 'new' rocks are discovered and countless other things change. If you see anything, however minor, in these Directions that needs amending or updating please email the editor at:

sailingdirections@clyde.org

Index

Acarsaid Fhalach (Flodday Sound), 60, 61
Acarsaid Fhalach (Hidden Harbour, South Uist), 2, 45
Acarsaid Fhalach (North Uist), 65
Acarsaid Lee (North Uist), 65
Acarsaid nam Madadh (Loch Maddy), 71
Acarsaid Mhor (Eriskay), 36-7
Acarsaid Mor (Hermetray), 75
Acarsaid Nighean Thearlaich (Charles Harbour, Loch Maddy), 71
Admiralty charts & publications, 5, 15, 154, 156
aerial surveying, 5
air travel, 13
Aird Fhalasgair, 123
Aird Sleitinis, 144
Aline Lodge (Loch Seaforth), 109, 111
almanacs, 156
anchorages, 4, 8-9
anchors, 10
Antares Charts, 3, 5, 154
Ardmaddy Bay (Bagh Aird nam Madadh), 68, 69
Ardmaree, 79
Ardveenish, 28, 29

Bagh Aird nam Madadh (Ardmaddy Bay), 68, 69
Bagh Ban (Pabbay, S of Barra), 19
Bagh Ban (Sandray), 20
Bagh Beag (Castle Bay, Barra), 23
Bagh a' Bhiorain (North Uist), 65
Bagh na Caiplich (Ronay), 60
Bagh a' Chaise (Calm Bay, South Uist), 75
Bagh Charmaig (McCormack Bay), 47
Bagh Chlann Neill (Cable Bay), 71
Bagh na Creige (Loch a'Laip), 55
Bagh Diraclett (Loch Ceann Dibig), 104
Bagh Dubh (Loch Boisdale), 41
Bagh Hartavagh (South Uist), 39
Bagh Lathach (Loch Eynort), 43
Bagh Moraig (Moraig Harbour, North Uist), 63
Bagh Siar (Vatersay), 131
Barkin Isles, 125
Barra, 11, 17, 22-35, 130-31
Barra Head, 19

Bay Hirivagh (Barra), 28, 29
Bays Loch (Berneray), 76, 79, 80, 82
BBC Radio Forecasts, 7
bearings, 14
Benbecula, 52-61, 130-31
Bernera Harbour (East Loch Roag), 147
Berneray (S of Barra), 18, 19
Berneray (Sound of Harris), 76, 77, 78-80, 83, 134, 157
berthing, 8, 9-10
Black Island (Barra), 29
Bo Greanamul, 52, 55, 57
books & guides, 156
Boreray (Sound of Harris), 134
Borve Bay (Camas nam Borgh), 139
Bosta, Camas (Bernera), 147
Bradfield, Bob, 3
Braigh Mor (East Loch Tarbert), 101, 107
Braigh Mor (Scarp), 142, 143
Bratanish Islands, 149
Breaclete (Great Bernera), 150, 151
Breasclete (Lewis), 150, 151, 160
Brevig (Broad Bay, Lewis), 152, 160
Brevig Bay (Barra), 26
Broad Bay (Lewis), 152, 160
Bruernish Bay, 28, 29
bus travel, 13, 159
Butt of Lewis, 152

Cable Bay (Bagh Chlann Neill), 71
Caercdal Bay, 43
Cairns of Coll, 17
Callanish, 150, 151
Calm Bay (Bagh a' Chaise, South Uist), 75
CalMac (MacBraynes), 156
Calvay Island (Sound of Eriskay), 38
Camas nam Borgh (Borve Bay), 139
Camas Bosta (Bernera), 147
Camas Orasaidh (Loch Erisort), 125
Camas Thormaid (Witches' Pool), 123
Camas Uig (Caolas an Scarp), 145
Camus na Crotha, 144
Canmore Island (En a' Chinnbhaoraigh), 49
Canna, 17
Caolas Beag (Loch Stockinish), 95, 96
Caolas Luirsay, 48, 49
Caolas a' Mhorain, 134

Caolas Mor (Little Kettle Pool, Loch Skipport), 47
Caolas Mor (Loch Stockinish), 95
Caolas an Scarp, 141, 143
Caolas Skaari, 73
Caolas Wiay Beag, 57
Carloway, 146, 147, 157
Carminish Bay (South Harris), 86
Castle Bay/Castlebay (Barra), 14, 17, 22-3, 26, 157
Causamul (Monach Islands), 132, 133
Ceann Ear & Iar (Monach Islands), 132, 133
Charish (Hellisay), 30, 31
Charles Harbour (Acarsaid Nighean Thearlaich), 71
chart datum, 5, 14
chart symbols, 15
chartering & instruction, 11
charts, 5, 14, 15, 154-6
Cheesebay, 75
Chicken Rock (Stornoway), 120
Citylink, 156
Clachan (North Uist), 65
Cleit Charmaig, 53
Clyde Coastguard, 7, 14
Clyde Cruising Club, 2, 15, 156
coastguard, 7, 13, 14
Comhairle nan Eilean Siar (Western Isles Council), 9, 10, 11, 156, 161
communications, 12-13
contacts, 156
Cope Passage (Sound of Harris), 73, 80, 81, 82-3, 134
Coppay, 73
Cordale Beag (Fuday), 33
Cornaig Bay (Vatersay), 22, 24
Cowper, Frank, 2
Croic Harbour (Monach Islands), 133
Cromore Bay (Peacam), 125
Crosbost (Loch Leurbost), 125
Crown Estates, 9
Cruising Scotland, 15
Curachan (Barra), 3, 26, 28

Daliburgh, 41
Danger Area (South Uist), 131
Deer Island (North Uist), 65
depths, 14
diesel, 11

Outer Hebrides

Dirascal, 144
Direy (Loch Carnan), 50
distances, 14
Drover Channel (Sound of Barra), 35
Dubh Thob (Kirkibost), 150, 151, 160
Dunan Pier (Loch Carloway), 147
Duntulm Bay (Skye), 107

East Loch Roag, 147-9
East Loch Tarbert, 99, 100, 101-5, 107, 139
Eilean a'Cairidh (North Uist), 65
En a' Chinnbhaoraigh (Canmore Island), 49
Eilean Fear Vallay (Loch Maddy), 71
Eilean an Fheidh (Ronay), 52
Eilean Fuam (Sound of Harris), 75, 79
Eilean na Gobhail (Stornoway), 129
Eilean Hingerstay (Thinngarstaigh), 108, 112
Eilean Kearstay (East Loch Roag), 150
Eilean Liubhaird (Loch Shell), 118
Eilean Mhic Shealtair (McCalter Island), 65
Eilean Mhuire (Shiant Islands), 116
Eilean Mor (Flannan Islands), 153
Eilean Orasaidh (Loch Leurbost), 125
Eilean Orasaidh (Loch Mariveg), 122, 123
Eilean Teinish (West Loch Roag), 147
Eilean Thinngarstaigh (Hingerstay), 108, 112
Eilean Thoraidh (Loch Mariveg), 122, 123, 125
Eilean Tighe (Flannan Islands), 153
Eilean an Tighe (Shiant Islands), 116, 117
emergencies, 14
En a' Chinnbhaoraigh (Canmore Island), 49
Ensay, 73, 80, 85, 134, 137
equipment, 10-11
Eriskay, 17, 35, 36-8, 157
Eye Peninsula, 128, 152

Ferramas, 71
Ferry Route (Sound of Harris), 73, 76, 78-9, 81
ferry services, 13, 156
ferry terminals, 10, 11
Fiaray (Sound of Barra), 35
Firing Range (South Uist), 131
Fisherman's Forecast, 7
Fisherman's Passage (Vatersay), 21
fishing & fish farms, 2-3, 9, 10
Flannan Islands, 153
Flodday (North Uist), 68, 71
Flodday (S of Barra), 20
Flodday Sound, 60-61
Floddaybeg (Benbecula), 52, 60
Floddaymore (Benbecula), 52, 60
Fuday, 33, 35
fuel, 11
Fuiay (Barra), 28, 29

Gaelic language, 15, 158-9
gales, 6, 7
Gallan Head, 152
Garbh Eilean (Shiant Islands), 116
Gasay (Loch Carnan), 50
Gighay, 5, 30-32, 33, 35
Gilsay, 81
glossary, 15, 158-9
Glumaig Harbour (Stornoway), 129
Goban Rainich, 112
Gousman, 83
GPS, 3, 5, 6
Greanamul (Barra), 33
Greanamul (Benbecula), 52, 57
Greanamul Deas (Benbecula), 52, 55
Greanem (Sound of Harris), 74, 76, 83
Great Bernera (Lewis), 147, 149
Greinam (East Loch Roag), 147, 149
Grey Horse Channel, 75, 76-7
Griminish Harbour (North Uist), 134-5
Groatay, 74
Groay Group, 73, 81, 85
Grosebay, 97
Gunna Sound, 17
Gunwale (Rangas) Channel, 2

Hamersay, 71
harbour dues, 10
Harris *see* North Harris; South Harris
Hartamul, 36, 38
Haskeir Island, 132
Haun (Eriskay), 37, 38
Haunaray, 60
heights, 14
Heisker Islands (Monach Islands), 35, 131, 132-3
Hellisay, 5, 30-32, 33
Hermetray Group, 73, 74-5
Hidden Harbour (Acarsaid Fhalach, South Uist), 2, 45
Hirta (St Kilda), 154-5
HM Coastguard (HMCG), 7, 13, 14
Hulmetray, 75
Humla, 17
Hushinish Bay, 140
Hushinish Point, 139, 143
Hyskeir (Oigh Sgeir), 17

Imray charts, 5, 156
Inner Oitir Mhor (Sound of Barra), 33, 34, 35
Inshore Waters Forecast & Outlook, 7

jetties, 10

Kallin, 12, 52, 58-9, 157
Kearstay (Scarp), 143
Keava (East Loch Roag), 150
Keiravagh Islands, 54, 55
Kendibig (Loch Ceann Dibig), 104
Keose (Inner Loch Erisort), 126
key card (diesel), 11
Killegray, 73, 80, 83
Kilmaluag Bay (Skye), 107
Kirkibost (Dubh Thob), 150, 151, 160

Lamalum, 33
Lawrence, Martin, 2, 3
Leverburgh, 14, 73, 86, 87, 157
Leverburgh Channel, 73, 81, 83, 86
Lewis, 107, 108-129, 143-50
LIDAR, 5
lifeboats, 14
Lighthouse Beach (Loch Maddy), 71
Lingara Bay, 88, 92
Lingay (Benbecula), 53
Lingay (Sound of Barra), 35
Lingay (Sound of Harris), 81
linkspans, 10
Linne Arm (Loch Skipport), 47
Little Bernera (Lewis), 147
Little Kettle Pool (Caolas Mor, Loch Skipport), 47
Little Minch, 16, 101, 106-7
Loch nam Ban (North Uist), 77, 79
Loch Beacravik, 88, 93, 94, 95
Loch Beag (Loch Grimshader), 127
Loch Bhalamuis (Valamus), 108, 113
Loch Bhrollum, 108, 114
Loch Boisdale, 17, 39, 40-41, 157
Loch Bun Abhainn-eader (Bunaveneader), 139, 157
Loch Carloway, 146, 147
Loch Carnan, 49, 50, 51
Loch Ceann Dibig (East Loch Tarbert), 104
Loch Cheann Chuisil, 145
Loch Claidh, 107, 108, 112
Loch Cravadale, 143
Loch Dunvegan (Skye), 107
Loch Eport, 62, 64-6
Loch Erisort, 107, 108, 124, 125-6
Loch Eynort, 39, 42, 43, 44
Loch Finsbay, 88, 92, 93
Loch Flodabay, 92, 93
Loch Gheocrab, 88, 94, 95
Loch Grimshader, 108, 127
Loch Grosebay, 88, 97
Loch Hurista (Thorasdaidh), 126
Loch Keiravagh, 52, 54, 55
Loch a'Laip, 52, 54, 55
Loch Leosavay, 140
Loch Leurbost, 124, 125
Loch Maaruig, 109, 110
Loch Maddy, 17, 62, 67-71, 107, 157
Loch Mariveg (Mharabhig), 108, 122-3
Loch Meanervagh, 52, 54, 55
Loch Meavaig, 139
Loch Mharabhig (Mariveg), 108, 122-3
Loch Miavaig, 147
Loch Odhairn, 120, 121
Loch Portain, 68
Loch Resort, 144
Loch Risay, 150, 151
Loch Roag, 136, 146-50
Loch Rodel, 88, 89-91
Loch Scaaper, 71
Loch Scadabay, 88, 98, 99
Loch Seaforth, 108, 109, 110, 111
Loch Sheilavaig, 49
Loch Shell, 107, 108, 118-19, 120

170 CCC Sailing Directions and Anchorages

Index

Loch Skipport, 17, 39, 45, 46, 47-8
Loch Snizort (Skye), 107
Loch Stockinish, 88, 94, 95, 96, 157
Loch Tamanavay, 144
Loch Tealasavay, 144
Loch Thorasdaidh (Hurista), 126
Loch Trollamarig, 111
Loch na h-Uidhe (Taransay), 137, 139
Loch Uiskevagh, 52, 56, 57
Loch Valamus (Bhalamuis), 108, 113
Lochboisdale, 40, 41, 157
Lochmaddy, 67, 68, 70, 71, 157
Luirsay Glas, 49, 52

McCalter Island (Eilean Mhic Shealtair), 65
McCormack Bay (Bagh Charmaig), 47
Mackenzie, Murdoch, 5
maps, 6, 156
Maragay Islands, 58
marinas, 4
Maritime & Coastguard Agency (MCA), 7, 13, 14
Maritime Rescue Subcentres (MRSC), 14
Mealasta, 143
Meanish (Sandray), 20
Miavaig (West Loch Roag), 147, 160
Mill Rocks (SW of Hyskeir), 17
Minch, 7, 14, *see also* Little Minch; North Minch
Mingulay, 18, 19
mobile phones, 12-13
Mol Mor (Shiant Islands), 116
Mol a' Tuadh (Shepherds' Bight), 39
Monach Islands (Heisker Islands), 35, 131, 132-3
moorings, 8, 9-10
Moraig Harbour (Bagh Moraig, North Uist), 63
Morrison's Rock (Benbecula), 52
MSI (Maritime Safety Information), 7, 13, 14

navigation warnings, 7
Navtex, 7
Neavag Bay (Benbecula), 57
Nisabost, Traigh, 139
North Bay/Northbay (Barra), 11, 12, 27, 28, 157
North Harris, 111, 136-43
North Minch, 14, 118, 120
North Uist, 62-71, 130-31, 132, 134-5

Ob Lickisto (Loch Ceann Dibig), 104
Ob Meavag (Loch Ceann Dibig), 104
Oigh Sgeir (Hyskeir), 17
Oitir Mhor, Inner & Outer, 33, 34, 35
Opsay Basin, 75, 76
Orasaidh, Camas (Loch Erisort), 125
Orasay (Sound of Harris), 75
Orasay Uiskevagh (Benbecula), 57
Ordnance Survey maps, 6, 156
Ornish Island (Loch Skipport), 45, 47
Oronsay (Loch Maddy), 71

Outer Oitir Mhor (Sound of Barra), 33, 34, 35
Outer Stromay Channel (Sound of Harris), 84, 85, 86

Pabay Mor (West Loch Roag), 147, 148
Pabbay (S of Barra), 18, 19, 73
Pabbay (Sound of Harris), 73, 83, 85
passages, 4, 6, 14, 17
  Little Minch, 14, 101, 106-7
  North Minch, 14, 118, 120
  Sea of the Hebrides, 14, 17
  Sound of Barra, 26, 35
  Sound of Harris, 81-7
Peacam (Cromore Bay), 125
Peter's Port, 53
piers, 10
place names, 15, 158-9
plans, notes on, 14, 15
Plocrapool, 105
Poll Bane (Sound of Shillay), 133
Poll na Cairidh (Loch Skipport), 47, 48
Poll Craigavaig (Loch Eynort), 43
Poll nan Gall (Flodday sound, North Uist), 60
Poll nam Partan (Stornoway), 129
Poll Scrot (Loch Stockinish), 94, 95, 96, 157
Poll an Tighmhail (Rodel), 90, 91
pontoons, 4, 10
Port a' Chaoil (East Loch Roag), 149
Port of Ness, 152
provisioning, 11, 12, 157
public transport, 13

quays, 10

radio weather forecasts, 7
radiotelephones, 13
rail travel enquiries, 156
rainfall, 6
Rangas (Gunwale) Channel, 2
Reef Channel (Sound of Harris), 78-9, 80
Renish Point, 88, 90
repairs, 12
rescue services, 14
restaurants, 12
Risay (Loch Leurbost), 125
Ritchie Rock (Benbecula), 52, 57, 58, 60
road travel, 13
Rocket Firing Danger Area (South Uist), 131
Rodel, 89, 90, 91
Ronay (Benbecula), 52, 57, 58, 59, 60
Rosinish (Pabbay, S of Barra), 19
Rossay (East Loch Tarbert), 105
Ru na Monach (Benbecula), 58
Rubha Arspaig (East Loch Roag), 149
Rubha Bhuailt (Loch Boisdale), 41
Rubha Melvick (South Uist), 39
Rum, 17
RYA Scotland, 9, 156

safety information (MSI), 7, 13, 14
Saghay More, 85, 86, 87
Sail Scotland, 11, 156
sailing directions, notes on, 14, 15
sailing instruction, 11
St Kilda, 131, 154-5
St Michael's Point (Benbecula), 58-9
Sandray, 18, 20
Sarstay, 76
Scalpay, 11, 100, 101, 102-3, 157
Scaravay, 75
Scarilode Bay, 57
Scarp, 136, 139, 141, 142, 143
Scoravik, 102
Scotasay, 105
sea areas, 7
Sea of the Hebrides, 16, 17, 35
sea travel, 13
Seaforth Island, 111
search & rescue, 14
services, 11-12, 157
Sgeir a'Chaolais (Loch Grimshader), 127
Sgeir Ghlas (Loch Shell), 118
Sgeir Hal (Loch Seaforth), 111
Sgeirislum (Barra), 27, 28, 29
shelter, 4
Shepherds' Bight (Mol a' Tuadh), 39
Shiant Islands, 6, 107, 114, 115, 116-17
Shillay (Monach Islands), 131, 132, 133
Shillay (Sound of Harris), 73, 85
Shipping Forecast, 7
Shivinish (Monach Islands), 133
shopping, 11, 12
Skipisdale (Mingulay), 19
Skye, *crossing from*, 4, 101, 106-7
slips, 10, 156
small boat sailing, 4, 156
Small Isles, 4, 17
Snuasimul, 21
Sollas (North Uist), 71
Sound of Barra, 26, 33, 34, 35
Sound of Berneray (S of Barra), 19
Sound of Berneray (Sound of Harris), 134
Sound of Causamul (Monach Islands), 133
Sound of Eriskay, 38
Sound of Fuday, 33
Sound of Harris, 72-87, 88, 132, 134, 143
  passages, 81-7, 136
Sound of Hellisay, 28, 29, 30-31, 33
Sound of Mingulay, 19
Sound of Mull, 17
Sound of Pabbay (S of Barra), 19
Sound of Pabbay (Sound of Harris), 83, 134
Sound of Sandray, 20
Sound of Scalpay, 101, 102, 107
Sound of Shiant, 107
Sound of Shillay (Monach Islands), 133
Sound of Shillay (Sound of Harris), 85, 134
Sound of Taransay, 139
Sound of Vallay (North Uist), 134-5

CCC Sailing Directions and Anchorages 171

Outer Hebrides

Sound of Vatersay, 23, 24, 131
Sound of Vuia, 147
South Harris, 72, 73, 81, 84-7, 88-107
South Uist, 17, 39-51, 130-31
South Uist Rocket Firing Danger Area, 131
Sponish Harbour, 71
Sruthan Beag Channel (Loch Eynort), 43
Stack Islands (Sound of Barra), 35, 36
Staffin Skerry, 74-5
Stanton Channel (Sound of Harris), 73, 81, 82, 83, 84-5
Steisay (Loch Eport), 65
Stockay (Monach Islands), 132, 133
Stornoway, 11, 120, 128-9, 157
Stornoway Coastguard, 7, 13, 14, 156
Stornoway Port Authority, 156
Stromay, 84, 85, 86
SUBFACTS, 160
supplies, 11-12, 157

Tahay (Sound of Harris), 74
Tamana Sear, 145
Tannaraidh (Loch Leurbost), 125
Taransay, 137, 139
Tarbert (Harris), 104, 107, 139, 157
telecommunications, 12-13
telephone contacts, 156
Temple Channel (Sound of Barra), 35
Thormaid, Camas (Witches' Pool), 123
tides, 6, 14
time, 7
Timsgarry, 147
Tiumpan Head, 152
Tob Bhrollum, 114, 115
Tob Cromore, 125
Tob Eishken, 118, 119
Tob Lemreway, 118, 119, 120
Tob Limervay, 108
Tob Shuardail, 125
Tob Smuaisibhig, 112
Toe Head, 73, 136, 143
Tolsta Head, 152
Traigh Nisabost, 139
trailer-sailing, 4, 156
travel & transport, 13, 156

Uig (Skye), 107
Uinessan, 21
UK Hydrographic Office, 3, 5, 15
Urgha Bay (East Loch Tarbert), 105
Urghabeag Bay (East Loch Tarbert), 105

Vacasay Island (East Loch Roag), 149
Vaccasay (Sound of Harris), 74-5
Vallaquie, 71
Vallastrome, 58, 59
Vallay Sound (North Uist), 134-5
Valtos, 147
Vatersay, 18, 20-21, 131, 157
Vatersay Sound, 23, 24, 25, 131
VHF radiotelephones, 13
visibility, 6
visitors' moorings, 9
visitors' yachts questionnaire, 9, 161

warnings, 7
Washington Reef (Sound of Barra), 35
water supplies, 12
weather & forecasts, 6-7
Weaver's Point (Loch Maddy), 68, 71
websites, 15, 156
Welcome Anchorages, 12
West Highlands Anchorage & Mooring Association (WHAM), 9
West Loch Roag, 147-8
West Loch Tarbert, 139-40
Westbound Adventures, 11
Western Isles Council see *Comhairle nan Eilean Siar*
Western Isles Harbourmaster, 156
Wiay, 52, 53, 55
Wiay Beag, 57
winds, 6, 7
Witches' Pool (Camas Thormaid), 123
Wizard Pool (Loch Skipport), 47